STATE OF MADNESS

STATE OF MADNESS

PSYCHIATRY, LITERATURE, AND DISSENT AFTER STALIN

REBECCA REICH

Northern Illinois University Press, DeKalb 60115
© 2018 by Northern Illinois University Press
All rights reserved

27 26 25 24 23 22 21 20 19 18   2 3 4 5
978-0-87580-775-1 (case)
978-1-60909-233-7 (e-book)
Book and cover design by Yuni Dorr

Every effort has been made to contact the copyright holders of the poems and images reproduced in this study. In case of any oversight, adjustments may be made to future printings.

Library of Congress Cataloging-in-Publication Data
is available online at http://catalog.loc.gov

FOR MY PARENTS

Contents

Acknowledgments ix
Author's Note xi

INTRODUCTION 3

CHAPTER 1
SOVIET PSYCHIATRY AND THE ART OF DIAGNOSIS 23

CHAPTER 2
THINKING DIFFERENTLY: THE CASE OF THE DISSIDENTS 60

CHAPTER 3
DIALOGUE OF SELVES: THE CASE OF JOSEPH BRODSKY 101

CHAPTER 4
CREATIVE MADNESS: THE CASE OF ANDREI SINIAVSKII 148

CHAPTER 5
MADNESS AS MASK: THE CASE OF VENEDIKT EROFEEV 185

CONCLUSION 217

Abbreviations 225
Notes 227
Bibliography 261
Index 277

Acknowledgments

A book that stands at the crossroads of disciplines must look in many directions for guidance and inspiration. While conducting research in Russia, Ukraine, the United Kingdom, and the United States, I enjoyed the support of the Andrew W. Mellon Foundation/American Council of Learned Societies Early Career Fellowship Program; the Foreign Language and Area Studies Fellowships Program; the Davis Center for Russian and Eurasian Studies and the Graduate School of Arts and Sciences at Harvard University; and Jesus College at the University of Cambridge. I also benefited from the archival expertise of Tat'iana Khromova of the Memorial Society Archive; Stanley J. Rabinowitz of the Amherst Center for Russian Culture; and the staff of the Beinecke Rare Book and Manuscript Library at Yale University, the Hoover Institution Archives at Stanford University, and the State Archive of the Russian Federation.

Portions of chapters 2 and 3 first appeared in article form as "Inside the Psychiatric Word: Diagnosis and Self-Definition in the Late Soviet Period," *Slavic Review* 73, no. 3 (Fall 2014): 563–84, published by the Association for Slavic, East European, and Eurasian Studies, and "Madness as Balancing Act in Joseph Brodsky's 'Gorbunov and Gorchakov,'" *Russian Review* 72, no. 1 (January 2013): 45–65. I thank those journals for granting me permission to rework the articles here, and their editors and anonymous readers for providing such valuable feedback. I am also grateful for the interest, questions, and critiques I received from the organizers, discussants, fellow presenters, and audience members of the conference "From the New Socialist Person to Global Mental Health: The Psy-ences and Mental Health in East Central Europe and Eurasia" at the University of Chicago; several annual conferences of the Association for Slavic, East European, and Eurasian Studies and the American Association of Teachers of Slavic and East European Languages; the workshop "Interrogations: Psy Sciences, Coercion and Confession in a Time of Cold War" convened by the Hidden Persuaders project at Birkbeck, University of London; and Cambridge's public lecture series "Resistance in Russia and Eastern Europe."

This book has benefited from countless acts of personal generosity and assistance, in particular by the staff and faculty members of Harvard's Department of Slavic Languages and Literatures and of Cambridge's Department of Slavonic Studies. Conversations with teachers, students, and colleagues at Harvard, Cambridge, and beyond stimulated my thinking while allowing me to work in an atmosphere of intellectual exploration and critical rigor. This atmosphere followed me to Northern Illinois University Press, where Amy Farranto and Nathan Holmes deftly facilitated the book's transition from manuscript to print. For their helpful suggestions at various stages, or for their comments on presentations or on drafts of articles or chapters, I thank Alexander Etkind, Rory Finnin, Michael Flier, Simon Franklin, Emily Greble, Susan Larsen, Daniel Pick, Rachel Polonsky, Eugene Raikhel, Kylie Richardson, Sasha Senderovich, Dennis Tenen, Yuri Vedenyapin, Chris Ward, Emma Widdis, and Benjamin Zajicek. I am profoundly grateful to Angela Brintlinger and Benjamin Nathans for their detailed and constructive critiques of the entire manuscript. The late Svetlana Boym was a life force and a formative influence on my work; at Harvard, she and Jonathan Bolton did much to lay the groundwork for this study. William Mills Todd III also sharpened my arguments while setting a lasting example of collegiality and mentorship. Above all, I am indebted to Stephanie Sandler, who, in addition to supervising the project's early stages, has graciously continued to share her erudition and counsel over the succeeding years.

While my brothers Daniel Reich and David Reich pursued careers in medicine and science, I specialized in literature and cultural history. Yet as I deepened my investigation of psychiatry, literature, and dissent in the post-Stalin period, I discovered points of contact among our disciplines that have enabled me to draw upon their knowledge. Vulf Slobodkin and Natalia Tomilina made Moscow feel like home while personifying for me an ideal union of lives devoted to poetry and medicine. My gratitude to Daniel Beer goes beyond words, not only for his clear-eyed readings of my final drafts but most of all for his encouragement, companionship, and love. Our daughter Naomi was born as the manuscript neared publication, enriching us immeasurably. This book is for my father, Walter Reich, whose materials and own work on Soviet psychiatry inspired the project, and for my mother, Tova Reich, who read it again and again and who remains my first teacher in writing and life.

Author's Note

Transliteration from the Russian follows the Library of Congress system. Exceptions in the main text include place names and names of people who broadly published in the English language (Joseph Brodsky, Yuri Glazov) or whose names are Russian renderings of foreign names with English-language analogues (Roy, Natalie). Names of certain well-known figures appear in their most familiar English-language form (Fyodor Dostoevsky, Leo Tolstoy).

Poetry that constitutes the main subject of analysis is quoted in the Russian original followed by English translation, while works that consist entirely or primarily of prose are quoted in the English alone. The sections of Venedikt Erofeev's play *Walpurgis Night, or The Steps of the Commander* in which the characters speak in iambic pentameter are thus treated as parts of a work of prose and presented only in English. Excerpts from Brodsky's poem "Gorbunov and Gorchakov" use quotation marks within square brackets to indicate speech that begins earlier or ends later than the given section. All translations into English are the author's own unless otherwise indicated.

STATE OF MADNESS

Introduction

In 1970, the biologist and writer Zhores Medvedev was forcibly confined to the Kaluga Psychiatric Hospital. In addition to his scientific research, Zhores had rankled the authorities by writing several studies of censorship and science in the Soviet Union that had circulated from hand to hand through the clandestine channels of *samizdat*. Aware of reports that Soviet citizens who expressed unorthodox views were being declared mentally ill and hospitalized, his twin brother, the historian Roy Medvedev, chronicled his efforts to free Zhores in a *samizdat* bulletin of his own.[1] His efforts were evidently successful: prominent scientists and writers voiced their opposition to Zhores's treatment and the biologist was released. In a memoir he then coauthored with Roy, Zhores recalled telling a psychiatrist that he would not write about the experience on one condition: that the psychiatric system continued to leave him alone. "All the more so," he informed the doctor, "since Anton Pavlovich Chekhov already long ago described the case of a healthy person being forcibly hospitalized and so now that plot is lacking in originality."[2] By positioning any account that he might write as a successor to Chekhov's 1892 story "Ward No. 6," Zhores challenged his psychiatric diagnosis through the prism of literature.

Nonconformist writers like Zhores and Roy Medvedev invoked a literary tradition of psychiatric narratives through which to imagine and interpret their own era's experience of pathologization and treatment. Chekhov's "Ward No. 6," which features heavily in that tradition, follows the fate of Andrei Ragin, a physician who once tended zealously to his patients but has since lost faith in his profession. Ragin runs a provincial hospital with a psychiatric unit in its sixth ward; there he makes the acquaintance of the university-educated patient Ivan Gromov. Concluding that Gromov is in fact far clearer-headed than those whom society considers sane, Ragin begins to visit Gromov regularly. The authorities respond by confining Ragin to the sixth ward, and the story concludes with the physician being beaten to death by Nikita, the orderly whose brutality he had overlooked in his former role as head of the hospital. Ragin's intellectual and moral reawakening thus progresses side by side with a descent into what the physician calls the "vicious circle"—or, in Russian, the "enchanted circle" (*zakoldovannyi krug*)—of psychiatric diagnosis:

> When you are told you have something like weak kidneys or an enlarged heart, and you begin treatment for it, or when you are told that you are a madman or a criminal—that is, in a word, when you suddenly become an object of people's attention—you may be sure you have fallen into a vicious circle from which there is no way out. You will try to get out and only mire yourself further. Just give in, because it's too late to be saved by any human efforts.[3]

Ragin describes psychiatric diagnosis as a discursive trap that is impossible to escape once it is entered. Patients may continue to believe themselves sane, but as long as their understanding of mental health overlaps with accepted categories of mental illness, anything they say in their own defense will merely affirm the finding of insanity. By citing Chekhov's story in conversation with his psychiatrist and, later, on the written page, Zhores Medvedev situated Ragin's vicious circle of diagnosis as a literary template for lived experience.

Recent debates have demonstrated the idiosyncratic nature of any effort to impose an overarching definition on the nonconformist and oppositional stances that proliferated in the decades between Joseph Stalin's death in 1953 and the Soviet Union's collapse in 1991.[4] And indeed, citizens who wrote about madness and psychiatric hospitalization in the post-Stalin period expressed differing views through differing genres and with differing degrees of political engagement. What unites them is their presentation of the vicious circle of diagnosis as an attack on what this study collectively terms "dissent." Deriving from the Latin *dissentīre*, or "to differ in sentiment," the verb "to dissent" means not only "to disagree" but also "to think differently."[5] It thus conveys the psychological connotations of the Russian noun *inakomyslie*, which similarly suggests the idea of "thinking differently" by combining the word *inako*, or "different," with the word *mysl'*, or "thought." Dissenters covered a spectrum ranging from those who silenced their *inakomyslie* by keeping it to themselves, to dissenting writers who voiced their thoughts in literary form but did not engage in active protest, to dissidents, or *dissidenty*, who challenged the political status quo in word and deed. When this study deploys the term "dissident," it thus refers to that subset of dissenters who, in keeping with the Latin *dissidēre*, "disagreed" by actively "sitting apart."[6] During the post-Stalin period, both dissidents and dissenting writers found themselves in discursive conflict with a state-sanctioned psychiatric system that defined expressions of *inakomyslie* as evidence of insanity. One of their responses was to produce psychiatric narratives that embraced *inakomyslie* as evidence of their critical awareness and mental health. By questioning the state's authority to declare them mad, dissenters presented thinking differently as the psychological norm.

The interpretive overlap of *inakomyslie* and insanity came to the fore in the late 1960s as word began spreading in *samizdat* that dissidents were being punitively hospitalized. In 1973, an open letter by the dissident members of the Initiative Group for the Defense of Human Rights in the USSR demonstrated with reference to the mathematician and dissident Leonid Pliushch's recent hospitalization how discursive ambiguity could lead to politicized diagnoses: "In our state only a crazy person dares stand against its shortcomings, only a madman speaks openly about the violation of his rights, only a schizophrenic acts against his own wellbeing but in accordance with his conscience and thought."[7] The letter's acerbic tone captures the sense of inevitability that many dissenters ascribed to psychiatric diagnosis in the narratives they released to circulate in *samizdat*, sent abroad to be printed by foreign presses in *tamizdat*, or published from the security of emigration. "However you twist it, any normal, sincere answer you might give merely confirms that you are ill," the dissident Vladimir Bukovskii recalled in his 1978 memoir. "And if you start talking about the KGB persecuting you, then that's already persecution mania. Because even when they asked at the very end whether I thought that I was ill, my negative reply proved nothing, either, for what madman considers himself mad?"[8] For dissenters, punitive diagnosis was indeed a vicious circle that continuously revolved yet another notch with each expression of *inakomyslie*.

Seeking to disarm that discursive trap, dissenters developed a variety of strategies for resisting the pathologization of *inakomyslie*. This study examines one of those strategies: their attempts to challenge psychiatry itself through literary discourse and its own tradition of writing about madness.[9] As long as dissenters could draw on literary tropes and techniques to present *inakomyslie* as the norm, the stigma of diagnosis could conceivably be tempered or dispelled. If psychiatric categories such as schizophrenia and psychopathy structured madness within codified labels that nonphysicians lacked the authority to question, then literary discourse embraced the ambiguities of metaphor and other artistic devices to relocate authority to those who deployed them. Defining madness in abstract literary terms thus enabled dissidents and dissenting writers to both expose and reshape a longstanding cultural association between creativity and insanity. Even as many dissenters accused the state of abusing this association to pathologize *inakomyslie*, it was precisely by portraying the Soviet Union as a madhouse replete with deluded artists of reality that many dissenters depathologized themselves. "And who was to deny that our Soviet reality was nothing more than an imaginary schizophrenic world populated by made-up Soviet people building a mythical communism?" Bukovskii asked in his memoir.[10] Bukovskii's loaded observation that society was suffering from schizophrenia—the very illness with which he and other dissidents were sometimes said to be afflicted—suggests that diagnosis conveyed a fully reversible claim to power during the post-Stalin period.

Allusions to "Ward No. 6" reappear throughout the works that are analyzed in this study, situating the tale as a literary model for dissenters' understanding of their own era's experience.[11] Unlike Chekhov's hero, however, the dissenters who produced those works sought to alter their circumstances by resisting and contesting them through words and actions. While still working as a physician, Ragin sustains the vicious circle of diagnosis by consigning his patients to medical categories and forgoing any effort at treatment. "One should not interfere with people who are going out of their minds," he declares.[12] Even when Ragin himself becomes a victim of the vicious circle that he perpetuated, he decides that it is better to passively "give in" than to halt the circle's inexorable progression. To dissenters who wrote about madness and psychiatric hospitalization in the post-Stalin period, Chekhov's story may well have highlighted their moral responsibility to express their *inakomyslie*. And indeed, unlike the English term "vicious circle," Chekhov's *zakoldovannyi krug* carries supernatural connotations. Ragin does not specify which if any magical forces might break the spell that binds patients to their diagnostic labels, but he does note that mere "human efforts" will not suffice. Written narratives by dissidents and dissenting writers suggest that posing a challenge to psychiatric discourse demanded another way of confronting ideas of madness—a source of diagnostic authority that literary discourse alone could provide.

Creativity, Insanity, and the Literary Tradition

Dissenters referenced a rich tradition of Russian texts about madness and psychiatric treatment that established itself in the premodern period through hagiographic accounts of the "holy fool," who tested society's virtue by pretending to be mad, and folktales about the holy fool's secular counterpart, the simple-minded yet lucky Ivan the Fool.[13] Versions of these paradigmatic cultural figures surfaced in later works of literature as the rise of psychiatry in the nineteenth century reconfigured understandings of madness. In 1833, the poet Aleksandr Pushkin produced several works on the subject of insanity: the narrative poem "The Bronze Horseman," the story "The Queen of Spades," and the lyric poem beginning "God grant that I not lose my mind . . ." The latter work explores the cultural association between creativity and madness from the dual perspective of both the artistic possibilities that insanity presents and the poet's fear of actual pathologization and confinement. By its end, the poet has imagined himself transferred to an asylum that echoes with "The cries of my confederates, / The curses of the guards at night, / The screams, the clanging of the chains."[14] Creativity can indeed give way to insanity—or, at the very least, be conflated with it—when the link between the two categories is taken literally.

And indeed, as Gary Rosenshield has shown in his study of Pushkin's 1833 works, "God grant that I not lose my mind . . ." both captured and informed a literary tradition of writing about madness. Rosenshield accordingly identifies four interpretations of insanity that Russian writers would later draw upon. First, there is the stigmatization of unreason that originated in eighteenth-century France. Second, there is the medicalization of madness as a clinical disease that can be scientifically studied. Third, there is the romanticization of insanity that harks back to Plato's views on the divine madness of inspiration. Fourth and finally, this romanticization of madness is countered by an antiromantic parody— an attitude that went on to shape Nikolai Gogol's story "Notes of a Madman" (1834) and Fyodor Dostoevsky's novella *The Double* (1846).[15] In Gogol's story, the titular madman is the protagonist Poprishchin, a civil servant near the bottom of St. Petersburg's social hierarchy. Poprishchin imagines that his superior's daughter is interested in him, he hallucinates a correspondence between two dogs that satirizes the mores of high society, and he eventually becomes convinced that he is the long-lost heir to the Spanish throne. With Poprishchin's removal to an asylum that he believes to be his rightful kingdom, "Notes of a Madman" establishes itself as a successor to Pushkin's poem and a predecessor to those post-Stalinist psychiatric narratives that would likewise use madness to satirize Soviet society.[16] Related themes emerge in Dostoevsky's novella when the hero, Iakov Goliadkin, comes face to face with his own double. Testifying to the intertextuality of narratives of madness, Goliadkin holds the same rank as Poprishchin, he similarly develops an obsession with a superior's daughter, his insanity leads him to challenge social hierarchies, and by the work's end, he has been locked away, as well.[17] The antiromantic tenor of Dostoevsky's reinterpretation of Gogol's story and thus, indirectly, of Pushkin's poem set the stage for dissenters to subversively investigate creativity and insanity during the post-Stalin period.

The rapid development of the psychiatric profession in the second half of the nineteenth century intensified Russian literature's focus on psychiatry and the psychiatric hospital itself. In this way, Vsevolod Garshin's story "The Red Flower" (1883) follows the fate of a patient who believes that all the world's evil stems from three red poppies growing on the hospital grounds. The imprint of Garshin's story may be seen in Chekhov's slightly later tale "Ward No. 6," but if Chekhov presents the *zakoldovannyi krug* of diagnosis as a vicious circle, then in Garshin's story it remains a space of creative possibility:

> It was as if he were in some sort of magic, enchanted circle that encompassed the entire earth, and in his haughty frenzy he imagined that this circle centered on himself. All of the others, his hospital mates, had gathered here in order to carry out an act that he hazily imagined to be a great endeavor aimed at destroying all evil on earth. He did not know what it would consist of, but he sensed in himself sufficient strength for carrying it out.[18]

The "enchanted circle" of Garshin's hospital is a self-enclosed sphere that licenses the madman to remake reality. Though the sphere may be surrounded by the hospital's walls and thus by entrapment in what Chekhov describes as the vicious circle of diagnosis, in Garshin's work the patient experiences it most immediately as a space of creative freedom. Garshin's tale carries forward the literary tradition of psychiatric narratives by highlighting the sense of artistic possibility that Pushkin explored in his 1833 poem and that many of the dissenters profiled in this study would paradoxically find within the diagnostic labels that they or their works could not escape.

The modernist experiments of the early twentieth century provided the literary tradition with new techniques for depicting madness and other marginal states of mind. At the same time, they stressed the salutary benefits of cultivating artistic awareness—benefits that dissenters would also highlight in the post-Stalin period. Andrei Belyi's novel *Petersburg* (first published in 1913–14), for instance, invokes the delusional extremes of Russian radicalism through the self-conscious use of the hallucinatory devices of sound-play, fragmented discourse, and intertextual references.[19] The *zaum'* or "transrational" poetry of Velimir Khlebnikov and Aleksei Kruchenykh likewise rejects standard modes of speech to examine the creative possibility inherent within basic elements of language itself. In his 1919 article "On Madness in Art," Kruchenykh defended the rationality that emerges through the apparently irrational:

> It is impossible to write nonsense. There is more sense in nonsense than in anything else. If each letter has meaning, then any combination of letters has meaning. If somebody, in an attack of jealousy, spite, or love, starts to write words in an arbitrary assortment (as happens when people are aroused), then what he is really doing is to give a flow of words immediately (without his reason controlling them), words which reflect this feeling and which even outgrow it. Therefore, there are no completely irrational works.[20]

Kruchenykh's modernist insistence on the underlying sanity of what might otherwise seem to be senseless expression contests the pathological implications of creativity in ways that dissenters would mirror in the post-Stalin period.[21] But the idea that artistic awareness could dispel insanity also harks back to those West European novelists of the nineteenth century who, as the critic Shoshana Felman has argued, embraced the madman's voice while negating its madness through the deliberate and cogent representation of insanity. It was in part by developing a self-negating "rhetoric of madness," to use Felman's term, that dissenters affirmed their artistic awareness and thus the sanity of *inakomyslie*.[22]

Yet dissenters were not alone in investigating the psychological consequences of artistic production that conformed to or deviated from sanctioned standards. At the height of Stalinism, the state also claimed that reinventing reality, and depicting that reinvented reality through works of art, would improve society's health. Speaking to the First Congress of the Union of Soviet Writers in 1934, the writer and architect of Socialist Realism Maksim Gor'kii said:

> It is the position of Socialist Realism that existence is an act, a creative act whose aim is the unending development of mankind's most valuable individual abilities for the sake of his triumph over the forces of nature, for the sake of his health and longevity, for the sake of the great happiness that it is to live on an earth that he seeks to remake in keeping with his ever-evolving needs as a marvelous dwelling place for a new, united humanity that functions as a single family.[23]

Gor'kii's comment suggests that, by transforming life into a "creative act" and representing that life in Socialist Realist texts, the state would heal society's ills. These therapeutic benefits were reiterated by social reformers and medical practitioners who linked individual and public health with the state's achievement of its ideological aims. In the wake of Stalin's death, however, the aestheticized nature of Soviet reality came under scrutiny. In his "secret speech" to the Twentieth Party Congress in 1956, Nikita Khrushchev described Stalinist art as delusory and Stalin as its primary dupe. "Everything he knew about the country and agriculture he learned from films," Khrushchev said. "Evidently Stalin thought that was how things really were."[24] Khrushchev's comment implies that, far from illuminating reality, Stalin-era words and images aestheticized it so completely that even Stalin became incapable of separating art from life.

Khrushchev's argument was not dissimilar to the arguments by dissenters that this study examines. Even as dissenters disputed the pathological implications of creativity with regard to themselves, they regularly invoked them to pathologize society. For many, the creative impulse at the heart of the Bolshevik project had fostered an irrationally artistic approach to life. Echoing Khrushchev's logic in his 1957 essay "What Is Socialist Realism," for instance, the writer and critic Andrei Siniavskii highlighted the delusion that had issued from the clash between Socialist Realism's claim to objectivity and the actual subjectivity of its aestheticized vision of reality.[25] That this conflict was the result of a creative impulse gone awry likewise informed Siniavskii's 1987 essay "Stalin: Hero and Artist of the Stalin Era," which places Mikhail Bulgakov's novel *The Master and Margarita* (1928–40) squarely within a literary tradition of psychiatric narratives for its "atmosphere of mass hypnosis, of the psychosis that gripped society through denunciations and the unmaskings of enemies, where the security service, prisons, and interrogations become a kind of theater that mirrors Stalin's theater of unmasking and repression. It's no accident that the events in Bulgakov's novel center on a madhouse that, in the final analysis, encompasses all of Moscow."[26] Contextualizing his own literary investigations of the irrationally aestheticized nature of Soviet reality, Siniavskii positions Bulgakov's psychiatric narrative as their Stalin-era model. For Siniavskii and many other dissenters, the creative nature of Soviet society's madness offered a diagnostic foil for defining and calibrating creative health. If words were capable of generating illusory realities, their narratives suggested, then words could also work to affirm the crucial divide between art and life.

Invoking a literary tradition of psychiatric narratives, dissenters deployed the rhetoric of madness to demonstrate their artistic awareness and shift the diagnostic gaze from themselves to society. They cultivated this rhetoric not only in their real-life interactions with the psychiatric system but also through the creation and circulation of both documentary texts—memoirs, transcripts of psychiatric examinations, letters, essays, manuals on hospitalization, and unofficial psychiatric reports—and imaginative writings such as novels, stories, poems, and plays. Together, these psychiatric narratives gave generically diverse expression to an alternate norm of thinking differently. Felman crystallizes the paradox that they thereby embodied: if the self-proclaimed literary madman's claim to insanity is to be believed, then his madness only exists in name. "*To talk about madness* is always, in fact, *to deny it*," Felman writes.[27] It was thus by talking about their diagnoses in life and on the page that dissenters denied their authority. Marshalling literary discourse, they depathologized *inakomyslie* and defined themselves.

Modernity, Rationality, and Diagnostic Authority

Yet what gave psychiatric narratives their most far-reaching edge was less their attack on psychiatry itself than their broader implication that the Soviet Union was still far from the law-bound, modern, and humanitarian society that the state portrayed it to be. In his speech to the Twentieth Party Congress, Khrushchev had described the Stalin period as a correctable deviation from Vladimir Lenin's original vision. Whereas Lenin had balanced ideological aims with the rule of law and respect for people, Khrushchev said, Stalin turned his predecessor's vision into a vessel for authoritarianism:

> Had this [revolutionary] struggle been carried out according to Leninist ideas, with an eye to skillfully combining Party principledness with a sensitive and attentive relation to people, and in keeping with the wish to draw people toward us rather than push them away or lose them entirely, then we likely would not have seen such a crude violation of revolutionary legality and the terrorization of thousands of citizens.[28]

Khrushchev's speech announced the Communist Party's renewed commitment to building an enlightened socialist society. Just a decade later, however, many believed that commitment to be fraying at the seams. Though the state might no longer have been disappearing citizens into prisons, camps, and firing lines, *samizdat* was exposing new forms of sanction and punishment that indicated that the regime's agenda was still deeply repressive. In 1968, the dissidents Aleksei

Kosterin and Petro Grigorenko (the latter had already been hospitalized and would soon be hospitalized again) made use of psychiatric discourse to write in *samizdat* that the state had succumbed to "that severe—and, for communism, one might say mortal—disease that goes by the name of STALINISM."[29] By asserting their authority to both reveal psychiatric abuses and diagnose the state that perpetrated them, dissenters suggested that society's illness stemmed from the pathologies of its Stalinist past.

Psychiatric narratives by dissenters bear deceptive similarities to the writings of the philosopher and historian Michel Foucault on how the modern sciences have validated subjective norms by casting them as objective truths. And, indeed, many dissenters who spoke out against the abuse of psychiatry mirrored Foucault's ideas in ways that highlight the discrepancies. In his 1961 study *Madness and Civilization: A History of Insanity in the Age of Reason*, Foucault portrays psychiatry as a normative discipline that isolates those who violate social norms and silences patients through medical monologues that prevent both dialogue and communication:

> In the serene world of mental illness, modern man no longer communicates with the madman: on one hand, the man of reason delegates the physician to madness, thereby authorizing a relation only through the abstract universality of disease; on the other, the man of madness communicates with society only by the intermediary of an equally abstract reason which is order, physical and moral constraint, the anonymous pressure of the group, the requirements of conformity.[30]

Illustrating his argument with reference to France, Foucault suggests that modern societies have redefined madness by separating the "sane" from the "insane" and erecting a discursive as well as physical barrier between the two categories. They freed the patient of his physical shackles by both making him "feel morally responsible for everything within him that may disturb morality and society" and ensuring that he "hold no one but himself responsible for the punishment he receives."[31] If the premodern madhouse once defined a space within which madmen could act freely, Foucault argues, then the modern psychiatric hospital promotes a regime of responsibility from which there can be no escape.

When dissenters critiqued both Soviet psychiatry and society as a whole, they regularly pointed to evidence of repression similar to what Foucault cites in his critique of modernity. For what, at first glance, could be more Foucauldian than a society that buttressed its norms with political ideology, a psychiatry that was overtly state-controlled, and physicians who actively hospitalized those who held politically unorthodox views? The difference in degree is to the point, however, as Foucault's focus on the disciplinary nature of bourgeois French modernity does not address the authoritarianism of its Soviet counterpart. According to the historian Laura Engelstein, Foucault's critique relies on two elements that existed in name only in the imperial and Soviet Russian contexts: the state-protected rule of law and the delegation of authority to the scientific professions. The Soviet regime cultivated a patina of legality and independent knowledge while implementing the law arbitrarily and turning psychiatrists and other experts into guardians of its norms. Engelstein argues that the "illusory modernity" of the Soviet state creates a deceptive parallel with Foucault that ignores the authoritarianism that in fact prevailed.[32] Applied to the post-Stalin period, her argument suggests that Soviet psychiatry's punitive excesses belied the liberal understanding of modernity that Foucault analyzes and Khrushchev projected in his secret speech.

Yet it is precisely in this sense that Engelstein's analysis shows how dissenters departed from Foucault's critique. Like Foucault, dissenters criticized Soviet psychiatry for isolating and silencing those individuals who contested the state's authority. Yet in doing so, they attributed punitive psychiatry not to a bourgeois sensibility but to an authoritarian lawlessness and lack of independent expertise. "In almost all the world's countries, the nature of societal relations and of the interrelations of various segments of the population is such that two professions—*the medical profession and the legal profession*—do not fall under the category of state service and do not merge with the state system," Zhores Medvedev wrote in the wake of his confinement. He continued: "While the totalitarian centralization of the medical services has made it possible to introduce the progressive principle of free healthcare for all, it also made it possible to turn medicine into one of its methods of management, control, and political regulation."[33] Soviet psychiatry was different from its Western counterparts in its willingness to act on behalf of the state, Medvedev maintained. Given psychiatry's status as a standard-bearer of Soviet modernity, psychiatric narratives by dissenters thus conveyed the alarming message that the regime had not, in fact, delivered on its promise to build an enlightened and law-abiding society. Moreover, those narratives suggested, only dissenters themselves were capable of critiquing the legality and the commitment to independent expertise that the regime had long been violating. Dissident activists tended to assert their diagnostic and legal authority more explicitly than dissenting writers, who often veered away from active protest. Yet both found ways of reversing the diagnostic gaze to cast themselves as law-abiding psychiatrists to a deranged state.

Implicit in dissenters' assertion of diagnostic authority was the suggestion that psychiatry was not an objective science but rather a subjective art whose claim to truth was best resisted by artistic means. There was real-life precedent to this suggestion, as the psychiatric discipline was just then being tested by rising numbers of citizens who drew on their own creative resources to simulate mental illnesses as a way of avoiding conscription, prosecution, and other duties and sanctions. Aside from wreaking havoc with the psychiatric system, simulation disrupted the diagnostic process in what dissenters repeatedly stressed to be theatrical and thus artistic ways. "The Russian may not be very bright, but he has a flair for practicality, a certain quick-wittedness when it comes to getting into paradise," the dissident poet Viktor Nekipelov observed of the many simulators who were evaluated alongside him in 1974 at Moscow's V. P. Serbskii Institute for Forensic Psychiatry.[34] "The inventive mind will find many opportunities here. As always, the born actors are the first to come and—since a bad example is contagious—their followers and imitators are quick to follow."[35] Depictions of simulation by dissenters suggest that the deliberate feigning of mental illnesses highlighted psychiatry's own inability to distinguish between artistic and actual displays of madness. If even common criminals could use psychiatric discourse to simulate mental illness, after all, then who was to say that psychiatrists were not themselves engaged in constructing their diagnoses and simulating their expertise?

Literary depictions of madness confronted psychiatry in consonant if less tangible ways. When dissenters invoked the self-negating rhetoric of madness or redefined the vicious circle of diagnosis from within, their awareness that the state might pathologize their words and actions effectively put them in the position of choosing to simulate its definition of madness. In tracing the exchange between the aesthetic underpinnings of diagnosis and dissenters' artistic exposure of them, this study in no way seeks to elide the devastating effects of punitive psychiatry. Rather, it highlights the creative and often literary nature of dissenters' strategies for coping with their circumstances. At the same time, it draws attention to the therapeutic purpose that psychiatric narratives could serve. By contrast with what dissenters tended to present as society's lack of artistic awareness, accounts of madness and psychiatric hospitalization provided readers with literary litmus tests for self-evaluation. Readers who concluded that those accounts indicated actual insanity would be revealed as being inclined to irrationally blur the line between art and life. However, readers who recognized the simulative quality of those narratives' rhetoric of madness would affirm their ability to distinguish life from art and in doing so secure their sanity. Intent upon exposing the creative nature of society's mental illness without pathologizing creativity as a whole, dissenters who pursued this approach furnished both themselves and their readers with tools for preserving their own health.

Shifting the terms of evaluation from the psychiatric to the literary, dissenters used their narratives to depathologize themselves and pathologize both society and the state. Yet even Bukovskii, whose memoir evinces no ambivalence about the injustice of his treatment, recalls giving way from time to time to doubts with regard to his own sanity. "Who would warn me when *that* had begun?" he writes, continuing: "Maybe I am the one howling hoarsely, and it only seems to me that the sound is coming from the cell across the way? I—sitting on the bed, rocking back and forth and howling, clutching at my head ... Our actions always strike us as logical, justified. But how could I be sure? Whom could I ask?"[36] Bukovskii's recollection draws attention to several questions that reverberate throughout dissenters' works: Who is sane and who is insane? And who is authorized to tell the difference? If physicians could not be trusted to impartially assess their patients, then patients would need to assess themselves. But how were they to calibrate their health in a society where, as they so frequently portrayed it, madness was the psychological norm? Dissenters of the post-Stalin period produced psychiatric narratives that affirmed their sanity not only to others but also, most importantly, to themselves.

Methodology and Scope

Interdisciplinary by virtue of its thematic investigation of the literary interplay of dissent and psychiatry, this study is also interdisciplinary in its methodology and scope. When dissenters deployed psychiatric discourse in literary ways to depathologize themselves and pathologize the state and society, and when psychiatrists accessed literary discourse to evaluate creative and mental health, both were sketching out the borders of a common forum for exchange. Moreover, they were tapping into the political sensitivities that had come to surround the discussion of madness not only historically but also, more recently, with *samizdat* and foreign revelations of psychiatry's punitive uses. This study suggests that what madness meant became a contested question during the post-Stalin period. Harnessing the literary tradition to confront psychiatrists' right to call them insane, dissenters chronicled the regime's authoritarianism while exposing as a self-serving fiction the leadership's claim to have renewed its commitment to rationality and an enlightened modernity in the wake of Stalin's death.

Works of art have long shed light on medicine and its discontents. Moreover, as scholars of the Medical Humanities argue, critical attention to the narrative mechanisms of diagnosis and to the grayer areas of morality and subjectivity has much to contribute to medical practice.[37] Recent scholarship on the cultural history of Russian psychiatry has thus illuminated both the literary properties of psychiatric texts and psychiatry's engagement with literature itself. As Irina Sirotkina has demonstrated, the wealth of case histories of literary heroes and writers by early Russian psychiatrists reflects the nascent discipline's eagerness to leave its own mark on literary discussions of madness and genius.[38] By the same token, it might be argued that when dissenters produced texts that challenged the authority of psychiatrists, they themselves were conducting a humanitarian critique of medical practices. The trenchant nature of their critique demands that psychiatric narratives be approached from two angles at once. For the most part, this book treats them as primary sources that invite close reading and literary analysis. But it also consults them as secondary sources when the analytical commentary they provide points the way toward new arguments. That the psychiatric narratives under examination themselves offer productive frameworks for inquiry testifies to their cultural and historical significance.

In exploring the interplay of psychiatry and dissent after Stalin, this book investigates a controversial period in Russian and Soviet psychiatric history that to date has been discussed primarily from social, political, and medical points of view. When, in the 1970s and 1980s, Western activists traced the origins of punitive psychiatry, their objective was most immediately the cessation or explanation of an ongoing violation of human rights. Similarly pressing aims drove Soviet dissenters who disseminated information about punitive psychiatry or continued writing on the topic from the safety of emigration. Retrospective analyses of this era in psychiatric history and of allegations of abuse since the collapse of Soviet power in 1991 have further illuminated punitive psychiatry while largely retaining the social and political orientation of earlier years.[39] This study seeks to broaden that orientation by treating the writings of both psychiatrists and dissenters as heirs to a common literary preoccupation with madness and by using techniques of literary analysis to contextualize them and examine their devices.⁴⁰ Situating those writings within the long literary tradition, moreover, it complements existing and emerging studies of other periods in the history of Russian and Soviet psychiatry.⁴¹

Dissenters' literary engagement with psychiatry from the 1950s to the 1980s also opens a revealing window on de-Stalinization and its discontents. Recent years have seen a surge of scholarly interest in the post-Stalin period as researchers have exposed the many ambiguities of those binary oppositions ("conformist vs. nonconformist," "official vs. unofficial," "public vs. private") so persistently applied to Soviet society. Scholars of dissidence have followed this trajectory to shed new light on the ideology and discourse of political activism while reexamining the various protest movements' social impacts and legacies.⁴² Other scholars have turned their attention to the social, political, and cultural realities of de-Stalinization by exploring everyday life under the leadership of Khrushchev and Leonid Brezhnev.⁴³ Adding to this wealth of research, the present study challenges the opposition of "sanity" and "insanity" while also historicizing its development. The categories in question were indeed ambiguous, yet their ambiguity served a purpose: it provided the state and its internal critics with a shared cultural lexicon through which each could assert its own authority by pathologizing the other and depathologizing itself. What madness meant may ultimately have been in the eye of the beholder, but it was in part by defining and redefining the vicious circle of diagnosis that the state and dissenters elaborated their competing views of reality.

Chapter Overview

The literary nature of the interaction of psychiatrists and dissenters opens the way toward literary analysis. Building upon the writings of the philosopher and critic Mikhail Bakhtin, then, psychiatric theories and practices echoed the "monologic" tendency of state discourse to project unity, authority, and completedness and to thereby discourage subversion and debate. A similar monologism typified the aesthetic doctrine of Socialist Realism, rendering psychiatry and state-sanctioned literature mutually intelligible. If the state's own superimposition of psychiatric and literary discourses serves as the focus of chapter 1 of this study, dissenters' efforts to resist its power guide the progression of the succeeding chapters. Both the dissidents analyzed in chapter 2 and the dissenting writers examined in chapters 3, 4, and 5 accordingly promoted a norm of *inakomyslie* in part through "dialogic" discourse. On a thematic level, their written narratives and lived behavior facilitated debate, subversion, and open-endedness. And on a formal level, they questioned authority through "double-voiced" devices such as irony, parody, satire, and humor. "Double-voiced discourse is always internally dialogized," Bakhtin writes. "Examples of this would be comic, ironic, or parodic discourse […] all these discourses are double-voiced and internally dialogized. A potential dialogue is embedded in them, one as yet unfolded, a concentrated dialogue of two voices, two world views, two languages."[44] Bakhtin is referring here to novelic form, but dissenters' responses to diagnosis similarly dialogized psychiatric discourse. This study addresses the diversity of those responses both generically, by analyzing the "literary" nature of documentary as well as imaginative writings, and interpersonally, by extending its analysis to a range of dissenters. It is no accident that so many of the figures in this study made their Jewish origins central to their output or invented Jewish authorial personae who challenged state norms. Jewishness, with its connotations of otherness, became one semiotic marker of the dialogism that dissenters took for the sanity of *inakomyslie* and that the state took for the insanity of dissent.

Chapter 1 thus provides the chapters that follow with a historical and cultural reference point by highlighting the literary preoccupations of psychiatrists and of psychiatric discourse. It suggests that, in the post-Stalin period, psychiatrists celebrated the subjective resourcefulness and skills of the individual physician while continuing to place an overriding emphasis on the objectivity of their conclusions. The result was a self-proclaimed science that tended, as dissenters themselves often noted, to rewrite politically and culturally nonconformist patients' lives in line with standard progressions of disease. Psychiatrists deployed narrative techniques when writing reports, and further pursued what the chapter describes as their "art of diagnosis" by employing the lens of Socialist Realism to analyze the artworks that their patients produced. Yet they also staked a claim to scientific truth—a claim that often demanded that they elide the subjective aspects of their work. Confronted in the post-Stalin years with a sharp increase in the number of simulators and dissimulators whose dramatic displays of mental illness and health suggested that diagnosis might also be a dramatic display, psychiatrists developed methods for rooting out fakers. These real-life performances of alternative psychological states shed light on literary deployments of the rhetoric of madness in that both drew attention to the subjective and therefore manipulable nature of psychiatric practices.

Shifting the study's focus to that subset of dissenters who most frequently became objects of punitive diagnosis, chapter 2 explores the literary qualities of dissident texts about psychiatric hospitalization. In particular, it explores the words and actions of the patients Vladimir Bukovskii and Aleksandr Vol'pin, the psychiatrist Semen Gluzman, and a range of other individuals who openly agitated against abuse. Vol'pin responded to diagnosis by disengaging from psychiatric discourse and confining himself to a purist legal discourse in conversation with psychiatrists and on the page. His influence is palpable in the work of Bukovskii and Gluzman, yet when it came to avoiding hospitalization, these younger activists advocated engaging with psychiatric discourse to preserve a line of communication between patients and physicians. All three criticized the psychiatric establishment for what they described as its manipulation of ambiguous psychiatric terms and for the irrationality and authoritarianism to which they suggested this led. Yet within their narratives they themselves creatively harnessed the ambiguities of psychiatric discourse. Together with other dissidents, they produced an extensive body of texts that used literary tropes, techniques, and traditions to invoke a community for which *inakomyslie* was the psychological norm. By behaving as if they lived in the modern, enlightened society that Foucault describes—and, in doing so, effectively provoking diagnosis—they assumed the role of psychiatrists to an authoritarian state that had lost its mind.

One of the defining moments in the crystallization of dissent came in 1964 with the poet Joseph Brodsky's trial for social parasitism, the diagnostic tenor of which is analyzed in chapter 3. In the buildup to his trial, Brodsky sought to avert investigation by checking himself into a psychiatric hospital, and his resulting diagnosis prompted a court-ordered evaluation that detained him again once his trial began. Together, these experiences evidently convinced the poet that psychiatric hospitalization enforced the Marxist dictum that "existence determines consciousness" when other, less invasive mechanisms of conditioning had failed. Brodsky answered that dictum with his own creative credo that "consciousness determines existence." Yet he also came to fear the insanity that might result should the creative impulse be excessively indulged. He therefore proposed a balance between consciousness and existence in his narrative poem "Gorbunov and Gorchakov" by splitting his poetic voice into a dialogue between two psychiatric patients who respectively embody these codependent forces. And he reiterated the importance of that same balance in his cycle "A Part of Speech" by exploring the émigré poet's loss of contact with his past reality and reluctance to engage with his present one. Only the scaffolding of language itself, Brodsky now indicated, could compensate for the maddening freedom of exile.

What Brodsky called his "art of estrangement" thus broadly recalls the Formalist critic Viktor Shklovskii's theory of "defamiliarization," or *ostranenie*. Art, Shklovskii wrote in 1917, preserves awareness of the material world by depicting that world from an alienated perspective, and it was precisely this awareness that Brodsky sought to achieve by striking a balance between consciousness and existence.[45] As chapter 4 demonstrates, Andrei Siniavskii also suggested that defamiliarization was key to tempering the creative consciousness. But whereas Brodsky mapped the pathological endpoint of creativity with respect to himself, Siniavskii turned his diagnostic gaze on what the chapter terms the "creative madness" of Soviet society. For Siniavskii, the state had driven society mad by coupling Marx's dictum with the inverted claim that the sufficiently enlightened consciousness could still determine existence. The result, Siniavskii suggested in his essays and in the early fiction he produced under the pseudonym Abram Terts, was a creative yet highly irrational conflation of art and life that could only be checked through defamiliarization. By drawing a line between himself and Terts's fiction, Siniavskii stressed his own awareness of the line dividing art and life. During his 1966 trial for anti-Soviet agitation and propaganda, however, the combination of his diagnostically provocative aesthetic and his claim on the stand that art should not be prosecuted led representatives of the state to suggest that he was simulating "nonimputability," or the inability to evaluate and control one's actions as a result of mental illness or impairment. The authorities, like the defendant himself, deemed Siniavskii sane. But by presenting Terts's literary words and the defendant's biographical actions as coordinated efforts to feign nonimputability, they blurred the boundary between art and life in precisely the ways that Siniavskii had pathologized.

Siniavskii's distinction between himself and Terts's fiction was just one way of preserving and signaling artistic awareness, however. Chapter 5 shows how the maverick author Venedikt Erofeev created an "implied authorial persona" who clarified the difference between art and life by self-consciously straddling those two spheres. Erofeev was not an overtly political figure, and it was for treatment of the consequences of heavy drinking that, in the 1970s and 1980s, he underwent his own stays in psychiatric hospitals. But by deploying the rhetoric of madness along with the contemporary imagery of both simulation and punitive psychiatry in his play *Walpurgis Night, or the Steps of the Commander*,

Erofeev turned his hospital experiences into frameworks for expressing dissent. *Walpurgis Night* depicts madness as such a powerful norm across Soviet society that even people who are not insane must feign insanity to fit in. The psychiatric hospital that appears within the play accordingly expands to pathologize society as a whole. The ubiquity of simulation suggests that what seems like insanity is often little more than a theatrical display. Yet since simulated madness can give way to actual madness, those who choose to feign insanity must keep their dramatizations in check. It was precisely by forging a "mask of madness" that blurred the division between art and life that Erofeev modeled a more critical awareness of the boundary between theatricality and reality.

Artistic Awareness and Biographical Experience

Dissenters' defense of artistic awareness harks back to the legacy of literary modernism and, especially, to the ideas expounded by the Russian Formalist critics of the 1910s and 1920s. Seeking to impose more rational limits on the creative excesses of the Soviet project, dissenters explicitly and implicitly mined the Formalist tradition for ways of separating art from life. The Formalist literary critic Roman Jakobson had called for precisely such a separation in an article published in 1921, for instance: "To incriminate the poet with ideas and emotions is as absurd as the behavior of the medieval audience that beats the actor who played Judas."[46] Yet Jakobson's insistence on separating art from life could not account for a post-Stalinist reality wherein written expressions of dissent were liable to be attributed to actual mental illness. Even as dissenters sought to reinstate the line between art and life, many proved ready to dissolve it if and when the need arose. Dissidents, for instance, articulated their critique of diagnosis through literary as well as lived expression. Brodsky's poems affirmed the material imprint of reality even as the poet himself dismissed biographical readings of literature. Siniavskii and Erofeev modeled their own artistic awareness by fictionalizing their personae in different ways. This readiness to straddle the very line that the state had blurred might appear to violate Formalist theory. Yet according to Svetlana Boym, even the original Formalists had been split between those such as Jakobson, who called for separating art from life, and those such as Boris Tomashevskii, who, in 1923, published an article describing authors' biographies as creative extensions of their work.[47] Moreover, she argues, it was precisely to the latter trajectory that critics who revisited Formalism in the post-Stalin period showed a greater tendency to turn.[48] This renewed attention to the interplay of biography and literature was not confined to critics, however: dissidents and dissenting writers also straddled life and art when accessing the rhetoric of madness. Their biographies, like their writings, became creative spheres for self-expression and self-definition.

In the decades following Stalin's death, dissenters challenged the state's pathologization of *inakomyslie* by depathologizing themselves in word and deed. They did so in part by invoking a literary tradition of writing about madness—from its thematic tropes to its formal techniques. Yet psychiatrists who equated thinking differently with insanity also engaged with literature by cultivating an art of diagnosis and incorporating a culturally determined association between creativity and insanity into their clinical narratives of disease. The confluence of psychiatric and literary discourses in the post-Stalin era thus forged a space for debating fundamental questions of normality and reality. In diagnosing what they presented as the delusory nature of the Soviet project, dissenters asserted their own authority to reinstate the awareness that society had lost.

CHAPTER 1

SOVIET PSYCHIATRY AND THE ART OF DIAGNOSIS

When the Soviet Union's most prominent psychiatrist, Andrei Snezhnevskii, died in 1987, the *S. S. Korsakov Journal of Neuropathology and Psychiatry*—a publication that Snezhnevskii had edited for thirty-six years—opened its October issue with a full-page photograph and a lengthy obituary. According to the obituary, Snezhnevskii had been a "true doctor and healer" who began each day meeting with patients and their relatives while producing groundbreaking research that was celebrated worldwide.[1] Having helmed many of the country's top centers for psychiatric research and practice, he had passed on his teachings to generations of students. The state had rewarded him handsomely for his work, the obituary continued, decorating him at different times with one Order of the October Revolution, two Orders of Lenin, and four Orders of the Red Banner of Labor; in 1974, it had named him a Hero of Socialist Labor. Snezhnevskii was decisive when defending his views, the article claimed, and he "always commanded great respect for the precision and clarity of his thought." Yet he never abandoned his "simple" air or his readiness to help those around him.[2] Born just thirteen years before the Revolution and thus "shaped together with our country," Snezhnevskii had defined what it meant to be a Soviet psychiatrist.[3]

Despite these accolades, Snezhnevskii's passing and the onset of perestroika prompted the Soviet psychiatric establishment to turn a new page. In January 1988, the *Korsakov Journal* took the unusual step of opening the month's issue with a letter to its readers. "The atmosphere of creative exploration under the conditions of perestroika in all areas of life demands that each of us fulfill his duty conscientiously, selflessly and without holding back," the editors wrote.[4] In keeping with the Communist Party's new policy of glasnost, or openness, they continued, the journal would now publish lectures on neurology and psychiatry, personal narratives of clinical experience and educational practice, and regular updates on the activities of the All-Union Society of Neuropathologists and Psychiatrists. Also in the spirit of reform and transparency, the editorial board would host a series of reader conferences aimed at critiquing the journal itself.[5]

One major impetus for such reform was the blowback from the human-rights campaign against the punitive hospitalization of dissidents—a campaign that had dogged Snezhnevskii and his colleagues since the late 1960s and that now, with the onset of glasnost, was riveting the public. Whereas in 1987 the *Korsakov Journal* obituary had called Snezhnevskii a "model of selfless service to science and patients," by 1989 the journalist Leonid Zagal'skii was writing in the influential cultural weekly *Literaturnaia gazeta* that it was Snezhnevskii who had facilitated the pathologization of *inakomyslie*, or "thinking differently."[6] For Zagal'skii, Snezhnevskii's theory of forms of "sluggish schizophrenia" (*vialotekushchaia shizofreniia*) that developed slowly and often imperceptibly had provided the state with a flexible and politically congenial tool for discrediting dissenters. "Snezhnevskii's theory made it possible to draw convenient conclusions about any kind of human behavior," Zagal'skii alleged. "What, you think the war in Afghanistan doesn't make sense? Welcome to the psychiatric dispensary. So you're saying the economy is sick to the core? You're the one who's sick in the head."[7] Emphasizing that Snezhnevskii and his colleagues had risen to power in the final years of Joseph Stalin's rule, Zagal'skii portrayed the psychiatrist as a relic of the excesses of that authoritarian regime. If at the time of his death in 1987 Snezhnevskii had been memorialized as a consummate clinician and researcher, just two years later he was being remembered as the architect of a diagnostic system that facilitated the pathologization of *inakomyslie*.

The appearance in *Literaturnaia gazeta* of Zagal'skii's article was just one of many signs that the critique of punitive psychiatry was now mainstream. No longer would talk of psychiatric abuse be confined to the essays, letters, manuals, poems, and works of fiction that dissenters had circulated through *samizdat* and *tamizdat*, a flood of similarly themed articles now indicated; from now on, the problem would be openly discussed.[8] Yet Zagal'skii's depiction of a psychiatric establishment that manipulated psychiatric categories for political purposes was one that dissenters—both dissidents and dissenting writers—had been highlighting for several decades. The forensic psychiatrist Daniil Lunts, of the V. P. Serbskii Institute for Forensic Psychiatry, was, the dissident Vladimir Bukovskii wrote in 1978, a "clean-case master" who "slowly, like a spider, spins a web around his victim. He weaves such a foolproof symptom from every quirk of character and twist of fate that not a single commission would later be able to fault it."[9] At the heart of punitive psychiatry, Bukovskii's commentary suggests, is the physician's capacity for transforming subjective judgments into seemingly objective facts by building diagnostic narratives and massaging psychiatric terms. A similar characterization of punitive diagnosis is evident in the dissident military officer Petro Grigorenko's 1969 *samizdat* account of one of his own evaluations at the Serbskii Institute: "My general impression was that everything had been decided, and that the only reason for holding the evaluation was that the prepared diagnosis needed to be officially 'rubber-stamped.'"[10] For Grigorenko, as for Bukovskii and Zagal'skii later on, punitive diagnosis revealed psychiatry's subjectivity and hence its potential for manipulation.

The state's use of psychiatric hospitalization to suppress dissent has long raised questions of intentionality. Were psychiatrists following explicit or implicit orders when they pronounced dissidents mentally ill? And, by extension, did they and the state indeed believe that resisting the status quo was a mark of insanity? Dissidents in particular tended to argue that psychiatrists like Lunts were well aware of their ethical breaches, and, in their *samizdat* memoirs and reports, they often insisted that such physicians be prosecuted.[11] Following the collapse of the Soviet regime, moreover, Bukovskii gained access to the archives of the Central Committee and came to the conclusion that the Politburo itself had sanctioned the punitive use of psychiatry. "This was no coincidence, no whim of some local agent, but the policy of the Politburo, without whose say-so not one hair on our heads could have been touched," he wrote in 1996.[12] Yet even as he charged the Politburo with planning to create a "psychiatric GULAG," Bukovskii followed the logic of many of the figures profiled in this study by connecting the pathologization of dissent to what he presented as the state's own delusional frame of mind: "Did they actually believe that we were distorting reality, consciously or at least unconsciously? Of course not. But in their language the very concepts of 'reality' and 'actuality' carried a completely different meaning."[13] For him, the pathologization of dissent revealed the delusory nature of the state's own vision of reality:

> Despite all their pragmatism, after all, in actuality they lived in that fantastic world of Socialist Realism wherein it was impossible to distinguish fact from fiction,

information from disinformation. All the more so since they were the sort of people for whom truth is by definition instrumental ("class-based"), subject to their ideology. After all, they also, like the rule of law and order, were governed by the principle of "practicability."[14]

What the state considered to be a "normal" understanding of life was catastrophically divorced from reality, Bukovskii indicated. Yet there was precedent for its irrational vision, he continued: Socialist Realism's own propensity for rampantly conflating fact and fiction. As dissidents and dissenting writers repeatedly emphasized in ways that inform this chapter's analysis, the state-sanctioned aesthetic doctrine was instrumental in shaping social and political norms.

From the late 1960s to the present day, explanations of punitive psychiatry have primarily focused on institutional and political factors such as entrenched professional hierarchies and the subordination of the rule of law to state policy.[15] Soviet dissidents and Western observers have likewise stressed the effect of diagnostic categories such as sluggish schizophrenia and "delusions of reformism," the markers of which appeared to outwardly overlap with dissident behavior. Also a contributing factor, some critics have argued, were the broad definitions of disease that resulted at least in part from the psychiatric establishment's arrangement of mental illnesses along a spectrum or continuum.[16] Still other critics have attributed punitive psychiatry to the generally "under-developed nature of psychiatric science" while faulting Soviet psychiatry, in particular, for failing to sufficiently acknowledge "the evaluative element in the meaning of disease" and thus for allowing subjective judgments to acquire the clout of objective fact.[17] Yet the subjective element of psychiatric diagnosis also contained a significant aesthetic dimension. For the dissident poet Viktor Nekipelov, who was evaluated at the Serbskii Institute in 1974 and wrote a memoir of the experience, psychiatric theory provided certain practitioners with flexible categories for reconfiguring *inakomyslie* as evidence of insanity:

> And indeed, this broad and diffuse mold (which, in another sense, is precise and streamlined, as suits our well-trained dogmatism of thought) can easily accommodate any expression of our "thinking differently," "love of freedom," "love of truth," and so on. "Originality of thought," "heightened interest in social and political problems," "tendency toward conflict situations"—just listen to how they label their symptoms![18]

Taking such critiques of punitive psychiatry's subjective and narrative-building impulse as a launchpad for its own analysis, this chapter suggests that the pathologization of *inakomyslie* stemmed not only from the institutional, political, and theoretical factors described above, but also from the discipline's broad adherence to an established aesthetic framework.

And indeed, dissenters who portrayed psychiatry as a subjective discipline were not inventing an epistemological platform for analyzing psychiatric diagnosis; they were pointing to a subjective stance that certain physicians conceded with pride. As Snezhnevskii himself wrote in 1968, the business of a psychiatrist was making accurate diagnoses based on objective facts and methods. Yet within that context was room for a subjective skill that ultimately amounted to an "art":

> The recognition of a disease and of all the particularities of the patient under examination constitutes a creative act [*tvorcheskii akt*], the success of which depends not only on a sufficient knowledge of the subject and acquired experience, but also on the personal qualities of the physician. According to K. A. Timiriazev, "Science and theory cannot and should not provide ready recipes; the ability to match the technique to the circumstance always remains a matter of personal resourcefulness, of personal art [*iskusstvo*]. This art is what forms the sphere of that which is meant by practice in the best sense of the word."[19]

Citing the pre-Revolutionary scientist Kliment Timiriazev, Snezhnevskii compares a well-wrought diagnosis to a "creative act" not only in its penetration and articulation of the truth of the patient's condition, but also in its revelation of the physician's "art." The success of the diagnosis depends on how well the psychiatrist speaks to and listens to the patient, weighing individual symptoms against general patterns of disease progression. It also depends on how precisely the psychiatrist penetrates to the "essence" of the disease and articulates it in the clinical or forensic report that then emerges. "If, during the examination, the doctor has not managed to grasp the most important thing—the essence—then the report fills up with unnecessary details; it becomes a picture of everyday life and not a medical document," Snezhnevskii concludes.[20] Snezhnevskii's emphasis on the physician's subjective powers of intuition and expression likens diagnosis to an art in both the medical sense of the skill of examining patients and the aesthetic sense of grasping and narrating the disease's essence. However objective psychiatric diagnoses might claim to be, Snezhnevskii's comments would seem to suggest, their success ultimately depends on the subjective capacities of the individual psychiatrist.

Snezhnevskii's description of psychiatric diagnosis as a "creative act" or "art" sheds light on dissenters' own critiques of the subjective excesses of punitive diagnosis. What Snezhnevskii seems to have meant by these terms was the psychiatrist's ability to marshal his or her individual insight, knowledge, and resources to reveal an empirical reality—the patient's psychological state. By contrast, dissenters who criticized punitive psychiatry implied that the subjective component of diagnosis was potentially so extreme as to rule out scientific objectivity. For them, the "art" of the Soviet psychiatrist was art in a far more literal sense: rather than reveal the patient's hidden condition, dissenters suggested, it created or imagined mental disorders where, quite possibly, none existed. What this chapter terms the "art of diagnosis" thus contains an inherent ambiguity. On the one hand, it captures what psychiatrists acknowledged and celebrated as the skillful manifestation of their professional expertise. On the other hand, it highlights the subjective and thus politically manipulable nature of psychiatric diagnosis. And indeed, attention to the aesthetics of both punitive psychiatry and psychiatric practices in general demonstrates that dissenters did in fact have grounds to pinpoint Soviet psychiatry's subjective dimension.

In much the same way as dissenters combined psychiatric and literary discourses when pathologizing the state and depathologizing themselves, physicians accessed literary modes of expression and analysis in their own theoretical and clinical writings. Snezhnevskii and other prominent psychiatrists thus taught students of psychiatry to generate narratives of disease that proved able to flexibly accommodate dissenters' life stories. These reports turned the doctor-patient dialogue into a medical monologue that constructed new diagnostic realities through words. As will be discussed in the following chapter, dissenters were not alone in emphasizing the manipulability of psychiatric diagnosis; even as dissenters produced their own narratives criticizing Soviet psychiatric practices, "antipsychiatrists" in the West were drawing attention to the subjectivity of the discipline as a whole. What heightened that subjectivity in the Soviet case was the particularly authoritative role of the state psychiatrist, whom the government entrusted with the protection of politically and ideologically determined norms. The art of diagnosis—and, in particular, the art of punitive diagnosis—amplified Soviet psychiatry's subjectivity and so its potential for abuse.

Though psychiatrists of the post-Stalin period saw themselves as scientists and defined their "art" as the diagnostician's skill, critical attention to their theories and practices uncovers their adherence to an aesthetic framework. Claims to objectivity collided with claims to subjectivity in such a way as to elide the latter, allowing for the psychiatrist's personal input and facilitating the pathologization of dissent. While the art of diagnosis was certainly not art in the sense of the poems, essays, novels, and plays analyzed in later chapters, it shared with those dissenting texts a readiness to move between psychiatric and literary discourses. In the case of the art of diagnosis, however, that combination acquired the recognizable stamp of the literary doctrine of Socialist Realism. Snezhnevskii was thus echoing the didactic aesthetic of Socialist Realism when, in 1967, he told a *Literaturnaia gazeta* reporter: "The field of psychiatry is intimately tied up with aesthetic and ethical education. And literature, after all, is an education—an ethical as well as aesthetic one." Snezhnevskii concluded with a rhetorical question: "What does this have to do with mental illnesses, with psychiatry? The answer is everything. One must fill a person's life with bright feelings, impressions, reflections. It's a pledge of moral health."[21] Testifying to the aesthetic underpinnings of the diagnostic skill that he himself described as an "art," Snezhnevskii believed that actual art could perform prophylactic and therapeutic functions. Yet only a certain kind of art could serve this purpose, and for Snezhnevskii that evidently meant works that adhered to Socialist Realist standards. By equating those standards with sanity and pathologizing works that deviated from them, Snezhnevskii and his colleagues made Stalinist aesthetics central to their art of diagnosis.

Punitive Psychiatry in Historical Perspective

Cultural manifestations of madness doubled as modes of resistance well before Russian and Soviet psychiatrists girded their art of diagnosis with the claim to scientific truth. When the "holy fools," or *iurodivye*, of the premodern period provoked society into exposing its sinfulness, it was often by feigning madness in dramatic ways. The suspicion with which rulers viewed holy fools was matched only by the authority that some holy fools accrued to question the actions of those in power.[22] Shriekers, or *klikushi*—most often women—similarly asserted their authority by falling into fits that sometimes involved screaming out the names of people who they claimed had bewitched them. That their demonstrations could result in the prosecution of those whom they accused heightened the authorities' suspicion of the validity of their displays of madness.[23] As Julie V. Brown has observed, "At minimum it can be asserted that even the earliest attempts to 'diagnose' insanity were based upon the implicit assumption that the condition of madness could be accompanied by special prerogatives. The result was that a primary concern was the elimination of undeserving pretenders to madness."[24] The cultural phenomena of holy fools and shriekers imbued the authorities with an awareness that dramatic demonstrations of madness were capable of conferring power. At the same time, they paved the way for psychiatrists of the nineteenth and twentieth centuries to cultivate their own methods—artistic as well as scientific—for calibrating the link between creativity and insanity.

The modernization of the Russian state brought a new level of care as the Stoglavyi Sobor council of 1551 decreed that the insane be confined to churches and monasteries. In the 1720s, Peter I secularized supervision of the insane, though in practice it remained in the hands of the church; at the same time, he established civil procedures for determining the health of members of the gentry who simulated mental deficiency in order to be exempted from governmental service. The assumption that being in power meant possessing the authority to declare people mad was confirmed in the 1770s, when Catherine II oversaw the establishment of psychiatric hospitals in Moscow and St. Petersburg and enacted the reforms that led to the founding of the first provincial madhouses, which Brown has likened to prisons, as opposed to hospitals, in their emphasis on confinement over treatment.[25] These dueling emphases persisted under the rule of Nicholas I, who, in the 1830s, both granted permission for the construction of Russia's first private asylum and dismissed the philosopher Petr Chaadaev's critique of Russian society as the product of a diseased imagination.[26] In the 1850s and 1860s, Alexander II laid the groundwork for modern psychiatry by delegating care for the insane to the newly created organ of local self-government, the *zemstvo*, and establishing the first university department of psychiatry. This expansion of facilities led to an increase in the number of regional doctors with psychiatric training and to the founding of the empire's first psychiatric journal.[27] Russian prisons constructed psychiatric wings from 1864, paving the way for the first "special" (that is, penal) psychiatric hospitals to be established in the 1930s.[28]

Yet even as psychiatrists consolidated their scientific authority, as Irina Sirotkina has demonstrated, they made a point of arguing "that the aim of psychiatry was not dissimilar to the literary project of exploring the human soul and reflecting on the psychological ailments of the age."[29] Eager to leave their mark on the artistic discussions of madness that were then occupying society's attention, Sirotkina writes, such psychiatrists published a wealth of "pathographies," or case studies, of deviant literary authors and characters. Moreover, they developed a sense of themselves as writers who possessed their own literary identity and access to signature aesthetic techniques. For Angela Brintlinger, the literary orientation of psychiatry resulted in turn-of-the-century physicians presenting themselves as "heroes of their own psychiatric history."[30] Cathy Popkin has similarly demonstrated how psychiatrists of the late nineteenth century wrote the story of the development of their profession into their patients' stories: the psychiatric report lent narrative shape not only to the patient's disordered self but also to that of the psychiatrist, she argues.[31]

By the twentieth century, then, the psychiatric profession had embedded itself in Russian society's cultural mentality and in its drive toward modernity.[32] World War I brought further modernization as physicians responded to the needs of soldiers returning from the front. Shortly thereafter, the trauma and social upheaval of the Revolution and Civil War highlighted the need for psychiatric care among the general population and for the articulation of new norms and new categories of deviance.[33] Following the consolidation of Soviet power in the early 1920s, physicians turned their attention to developing a psychiatry that would share the philosophical premises and claim to scientific objectivity of Marxist-Leninist ideology itself. Suppressing Freudian psychoanalysis for its excessive "individualism," they embarked upon a decades-long debate about the implications for psychiatric practice of Karl Marx's and Vladimir Lenin's views on consciousness and existence.[34] Marx had famously argued that "it is not the consciousness of men that determines their existence, but, on the contrary, their social existence that determines their consciousness."[35] Lenin, however, had adapted this idea for revolutionary practice by arguing that, if consciousness learned the laws of existence, it could still do much to shape not only existence but also those consciousnesses that formed in its reflection.[36] Early Bolshevik practitioners of "mental hygiene" applied this idea by arguing that the process by which existence and consciousness influenced each other was primarily social and that improvements in workplace and living conditions would therefore improve society's health. For them, society's pathologies were evidence less of "illness" than of normal "reactions" to societal triggers that could be prophylactically disarmed.[37]

Yet already in the late 1920s, a biological countercurrent to the mental hygienists' interpretation of Marxist-Leninist thought was attributing failures of adaptation to defects within the nervous system itself.[38] The biologization of mental illness took place partly in response to the regime's suppression of other psychiatric theories that staked their own claim to organizing life.[39] Against that backdrop, the Swiss psychiatrist Eugen Bleuler's theory of "schizophrenia" initially provided Soviet physicians with a way of accounting for both the biological underpinnings of mental disorder and the patient's social interaction with the world.[40] Following the Second All-Union Congress of Neuropathologists and Psychiatrists in 1936, however, Soviet psychiatry turned toward the fin de siècle German psychiatrist Emil Kraepelin's view of mental illnesses as discrete entities that could be classified according to their progression over time.[41] It was in the context of this Kraepelinian turn that Snezhnevskii began his rise to prominence. In 1951, he and his colleagues cemented their authority at the Joint Meeting of the Presidium of the Academy of Medical Sciences and Directorate of the All-Union Society of Neuropathologists and Psychiatrists, or the Pavlov Session for psychiatry.[42] They also reassessed the relationship between the social and biological mechanisms by which consciousness and existence were said to interact. "The assumption about the uniquely social predetermination of psychosis was incorrect," Snezhnevskii explained in 1967. "The biosocial nature of psychiatric disorders is now an uncontested fact. Moreover, the significance of biological factors may in fact be even greater than that of social ones. I have in mind, above all, inheritance."[43] By subordinating social theories of mental illness to biological ones, Snezhnevskii and his colleagues heightened their discipline's claim to objective description and analysis. At the same time, they developed a new classification of disorders that left considerable room for subjective input. The aesthetic underpinnings of this classification would facilitate the pathologization of *inakomyslie*.

The Narrative Art of Diagnosing Dissent

One of Snezhnevskii's greatest legacies, according to his obituary, was his creation of a psychiatric school—often termed the "Moscow school" of psychiatry by contrast with the schools associated with other urban centers— that specialized in nosology, or the scientific classification of disease.[44] Not only was this approach more objective, Snezhnevskii and his colleagues argued in a joint speech at the Pavlov Session for psychiatry in 1951, but it also had the advantage of being both theoretically and methodologically unified:

> The struggle for a Pavlovian theory of psychiatry will unite Soviet psychiatrists; it will destroy factionalism, those "little schools" of thought. Solitary and few in number, stubbornly still clinging to the old world and trying to reconcile their idealistic concepts with the teachings of I. P. Pavlov, these little groups of idealistically minded psychiatrists isolate themselves from the great mass of psychiatrists who are building Soviet psychiatry on new, genuinely scientific grounds."[45]

Bringing the Stalin-era centralization of the mind sciences to belated fruition, the Moscow school strengthened both psychiatry's claim to objectivity and its theoretical and methodological unity. As David Joravsky has emphasized, Snezhnevskii's editorship of the *Korsakov Journal* and control of major centers of teaching and research helped to secure institutional power in the hands of a small number of physicians.[46] Moreover, the Moscow school's classification of mental illnesses along nosological spectra was itself marked by a unifying impulse, as is made evident by two related diagrams that Snezhnevskii developed and reworked from the 1960s to the 1980s.[47] The first depicted "positive" syndromes, or groups of symptoms typical of mental illness. The second depicted "negative" syndromes, referring to normal behaviors whose absence indicated disease. Both diagrams used concentric circles to superimpose the syndromes on the disorders in which they were found: the wider the circle, the greater the number of circles within it and thus the greater the number of syndromes that theoretically could appear within the corresponding disorder. Schizophrenia, which fell among the mid-sized circles, was accordingly capable of presenting all of the syndromes relating to all of the disorders that corresponded to the smaller circles contained within it. As Joravsky observes, the self-enclosing visual iconography of the diagrams was indicative of the unifying impulse of Soviet psychiatry itself.[48]

In addition to emphasizing theoretical and methodological unity, however, the diagrams testify to the narrative orientation of Snezhnevskii's art of diagnosis: By studying patients over lengthy periods of time, the psychiatrist arranges the facts of their lives into stories of disease that only he or she is authorized to write. As Snezhnevskii commented in 1974, "A syndrome taken in isolation (the patient's 'status' at the moment of examination) testifies to the particularities of just one stage of a disease that in essence constitutes a process—an unending

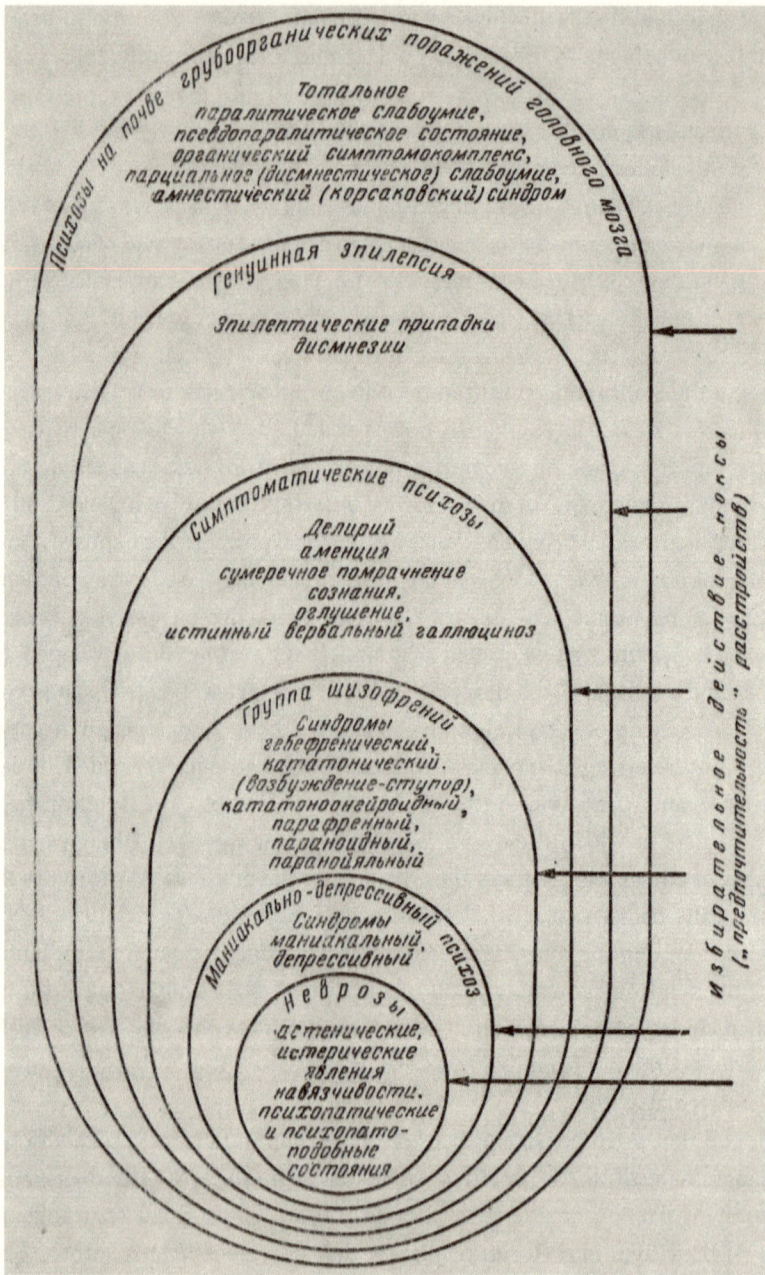

Figure 1. Andrei Snezhnevskii's diagram of positive syndromes, 1960.
Source: A. V. Snezhnevskii, "O nozologicheskoi spetsifichnosti psikhopatologicheskikh sindromov," *Zhurnal nevropatologii i psikhiatrii imeni S. S. Korsakova*, no. 1 (1960): 98.

alternation of stages of development."⁴⁹ Snezhnevskii's emphasis on stages of development reflects his allegiance to Kraepelinian nosology. Whereas throughout the nineteenth century psychiatrists had tended to classify mental disorders according to the symptoms they presented at a single point in time, Kraepelin had proposed a new classification that emphasized a disease's long-term progression—age of onset, course of disease, and likely outcome. His approach had revolutionized psychiatry by addressing what had hitherto posed an intractable diagnostic challenge: patients displayed a dizzyingly wide range of behaviors not only in comparison to each other but also over time, in comparison to themselves. By shifting attention to progression, Kraepelin had both accounted for this variety and established as a discrete entity the disease that became known as schizophrenia.⁵⁰ The Moscow school's allegiance to Kraepelinian nosology was not unique: in 1980, for instance, the American Psychiatric Association embraced neo-Kraepelinian ideas in the third edition of its *Diagnostic and Statistical Manual of Mental Disorders*.⁵¹ Yet the Soviet application of Kraepelinian thought stands out for both the symptomatic breadth of its diagnostic categories and its scope for subjective evaluation.⁵² Armed with the Moscow school's classification system, Soviet psychiatrists proved quicker to diagnose schizophrenia in individuals whose symptoms were reportedly so mild that they could only be discerned after prolonged observation.⁵³ The result was a discipline that broadened the scope for diagnosis while emphasizing the unique nature of the physician's skill at intuiting and articulating the "essence" of diseases.

Girding the narrative orientation of Kraepelinian theory with their own emphasis on unity, Snezhnevskii and his colleagues divided schizophrenia into three course forms. Patients with "recurrent" schizophrenia suffered intermittent attacks punctuated by recovery-like remissions. Patients with "shift-like" schizophrenia endured attacks without ever fully recovering their functioning. Deterioration was most evident in patients with "continuous" schizophrenia, which worsened over time and offered no hope of remission. The Moscow school also divided shift-like and continuous schizophrenia into sub-courses indicating the speed and intensity of the disease's progression. Continuous forms of schizophrenia, for instance, could range from "malignant" to "progressive" to "sluggish," the last of which was diagnosed so frequently that by 1983 it was said to account for nearly half of schizophrenia findings.⁵⁴ Lunts would be criticized for testifying at Natal'ia Gorbanevskaia's 1970 trial that the dissident poet suffered from a sluggish schizophrenia that "has no clear symptoms" and only manifests itself over time. Yet his words in fact accorded with the established trajectory of Gorbanevskaia's diagnosed disorder.[55] Political agendas aside, Lunts's emphasis on long-term progression subscribed to Snezhnevskii's art of diagnosis.

Snezhnevskii and his colleagues also shaped diagnoses by issuing explicit instructions on how to fashion clinical and forensic reports. In 1968, Snezhnevskii described the ideal clinical report as a balance between the individual life narrative of the patient in question and the general narrative of the disease itself:

> There is not and cannot be a set structure for describing the patient's status. A psychological status that is written according to a set structure inevitably turns into a questionnaire and not a description of a patient. One must always begin the description with the main thing, with the most essential manifestations of the disease that show the greatest tendency toward development. After the description of the essence, everything else naturally falls into place.[56]

For Snezhnevskii, the exemplary clinical report was one wherein the individual details appeared to arrange themselves around that narrative "essence" of disease that the psychiatrist intuited and articulated. In 1967, the prominent psychiatrist Iakov Kalashnik presented the exemplary forensic report in similarly prescriptive terms. According to Kalashnik, the first of the report's five sections should identify the authors and list both the details of the criminal charge and any questions asked. The second section should build on previous reports to describe the patient's personal and medical history. The third section should detail the team's own observations and be divided into three parts: physical status, neurological status, and psychological status, the last of which should constitute the heart of the report. "The psychological condition should be set out in a particular order," Kalashnik elaborated. "First one presents evidence concerning the subject's state of consciousness and orientation, followed by a description of the emotional-volitional and intellectual sphere and behavior; then one notes the presence or absence of such symptoms of mental disorder as delusions, hallucinations, and so on."[57] The fourth section, Kalashnik continued, should list objective data such as the results of any psychological or physical tests, while the fifth section should summarize the diagnosis itself and offer a recommendation as to whether the court should hold the individual responsible for his or her crimes. "The conclusions should flow from the data obtained during the examination and analysis of the criminal file, and should concur with the other facts of the case," Kalashnik wrote.[58] Such instructions for writing reports offered forensic psychiatrists a template for lending any subjectively drawn conclusions the authority and force of objective fact.

Illustrating how form could influence content, Kalashnik's narrative structure guides the forensic report that Lunts and his colleagues at the Serbskii Institute prepared on Gorbanevskaia in April 1970. After identifying the examining psychiatrists, the report describes the poet's personal and medical history and details her physical, neurological, and psychological status before presenting a diagnosis of sluggish schizophrenia. According to the report, Gorbanevskaia began showing signs of her condition as early as the eighth grade through frequent displays of "excessive behavior" in school and conflicts with her mother at home.[59] But the slow progression of her alleged disorder meant that it was only later that her symptoms became marked. In 1955, at the age of nineteen, Gorbanevskaia reportedly developed a fear of heights and a depressive mood that led to a suicide attempt. "She became rude to her mother, easily lost her temper, often left home, would go to other cities; she developed, in her own words, a tendency toward 'reflection, impulsiveness,'" the psychiatrists write.[60] Her symptoms affected her capacity for work: she was twice dismissed from university and had difficulty holding down a job.[61] In October 1959, the report continues, the twenty-three-year-old Gorbanevskaia developed a range of nervous symptoms including exhaustion, insomnia, and an unpleasant sensation in the tips of her fingers that prevented her from touching paper. She turned for help to a psychiatrist, who suggested a diagnosis of either schizophrenia or psychopathy with obsessive traits, pointing as evidence to her tendency toward philosophizing and to her allegedly hostile attitude toward her mother.[62]

Gorbanevskaia then spent two weeks at Moscow's Psychiatric Hospital No. 1, or the Kashchenko Hospital, at the end of which she reportedly asked to be released upon becoming convinced that the other patients were healthy people who had made themselves ill by power of suggestion. Her "obsessive thoughts and fears did not pass" following her release, resulting in insomnia and a reduced capacity for work.[63] In 1968, the report continues, Gorbanevskaia's refusal to eat during a pregnancy-related hospitalization necessitated that she be detained in the Kashchenko Hospital.[64] Psychiatrists noted her "emotional coldness, flatness, tendency toward philosophizing" and diagnosed her with sluggish schizophrenia.[65] Following her release just over one week later, Gorbanevskaia was arrested for staging a protest in Red Square and was rediagnosed at the Serbskii Institute with "severe psychopathy, though the presence of a sluggish schizophrenic process cannot be ruled out."[66] Arrested once again in late 1969, she was sent back to the Serbskii Institute, eventually resulting in the evaluation at hand. Gorbanevskaia, the report concludes, suffers from a schizophrenia marked by a "sluggishly progressive course without pronounced aggravation but with a gradual growth of personality changes."[67] The psychiatrists declare her not responsible for her criminal actions and recommend that she be confined to a "special" psychiatric hospital.[68] The poet would be released from her detention only in February 1972.

The arc of Gorbanevskaia's 1970 evaluation illustrates the confluence of Kalashnik's recommendations for writing reports and the structuring framework of the diagnosed disease. Gorbanevskaia's life accordingly falls within the progression of sluggish schizophrenia with obsessive disorders as outlined by the psychiatrist Ruben Nadzharov under Snezhnevskii's editorship in 1972. Sluggish schizophrenia, according to Nadzharov, is "distinguished by a slow course with a gradual development of personality changes that never reach the level of profound emotional devastation typical of severe terminal conditions."[69] It usually presents during puberty through exaggerated transitional-age behaviors, a combination of "neurosis-like symptoms, over-valued ideas, and paranoiac disorders," and disorders of mood and reasoning.[70] In the early stages of the disease, symptoms remain mostly undifferentiated: weakness and fatigue are often coupled with "affective fluctuations, irritability, a certain cutting off of the self, reflection," Nadzharov writes.[71] Over time, however, various disorders begin to dominate either singly or in conjunction with each other.[72] When it comes to sluggish schizophrenia with obsessive disorders, specifically, the obsessions in question accrue alongside an emotional flattening and decline in psychic activity.[73] "Suffering from their disease, patients simultaneously relate with extreme hostility to efforts by those close to them and by the hospital staff to interfere with their carrying out the system of rituals," Nadzharov writes.[74] At the same time, patients in the early stages of this form of schizophrenia may experience incomplete remissions that facilitate "social adaptation and even creative growth. In cases of less pronounced obsessive symptoms, such adaptation remains a possibility over the course of the entire period of the disease."[75]

Interestingly, Gorbanevskaia's political activities feature only peripherally in her Serbskii Institute report; the psychiatrists neither mention her production of *samizdat* nor investigate her views at any length. But other activists saw their politics very much pathologized through such diagnostic prisms as "paranoiac" (*paranoiial'nyi*) syndrome, referring to a delusional mindset that generally leaves reasoning intact, and "paranoid" (*paranoidnyi*) syndrome, indicating a more complex and debilitating system of delusions and hallucinations.[76] The delusional ideas with which dissidents tended to be diagnosed included "reformism," whereby, as Snezhnevskii described it in 1968, patients often proposed plans to save mankind; "persecution," which led patients to detect enemies everywhere; and "litigiousness," which described patients who wrote "endless petitions and complaints, and are constantly found in the waiting rooms of the most diverse institutions, fighting for the restoration of their supposedly violated rights."[77] As was the case with sluggish schizophrenia with obsessive disorders, paranoiac schizophrenia was said to present in adolescence before developing into a system of delusional and overvalued ideas. "In such cases, the question is usually about the everyday content (plot) of the delusion," Nadzharov wrote in 1972 about one form of paranoiac schizophrenia, listing in particular the delusion of reformism with which dissidents were sometimes diagnosed. "These ideas stand out for their limitedness, their monothematic nature. At the same time, when they are carried out, it is as if the person is 'possessed.'" As the disease progresses, the primary delusion usually gives way to a delusion of persecution—another label often affixed to dissidents.[78]

And indeed, a 1966 Serbskii Institute forensic report on Bukovskii follows this trajectory by selecting and organizing details of its subject's life into a diagnostic narrative of "sluggish paranoiac schizophrenia." Following a lengthy hospitalization that came in the wake of an arrest for anti-Soviet activities, Bukovskii had been re-hospitalized in 1965 for helping to organize a public meeting to demand a fair and open trial for the dissenting writers Andrei Siniavskii and Iulii Daniel'.[79] According to his examiners' report the following April, Bukovskii's conflicts with those around him had begun at the age of twelve, but it was only at fourteen that the subject started to fall behind in his studies and to show signs of "philosophical intoxication," declaring his intention to root out a "gang of bandits."[80] At seventeen, Bukovskii reportedly began to demonstrate "a converged system of paranoiac symptoms."[81] After two years of university, the report continues, the subject gave up his studies. A 1962 examination by Snezhnevskii himself produced a diagnosis of "paranoiac schizophrenia, marked by an early onset and a decline in energetic potency."[82] Bukovskii was later arrested and sent to the Serbskii Institute, where psychiatrists revised Snezhnevskii's conclusion to declare that he was suffering from severe paranoiac psychopathy and confined him to the Leningrad Special Psychiatric Hospital.

But following his release in 1965, the report goes on to stipulate, Bukovskii continued to display paranoiac tendencies. These developments necessitated that the patient be reevaluated, leading to the determination that he was indeed suffering from the paranoiac schizophrenia that Snezhnevskii had diagnosed. "Despite outwardly correct behavior," the report concludes, "he demonstrates aloofness, limited accessibility, a philosophizing cast of mind, emotional flatness. He relates to his previous delusional ideas with an insufficiently critical attitude and to his surrounding reality in delusional ways."[83] As would be the case with Gorbanevskaia four years later, the arc of sluggish schizophrenia—here, with paranoiac features—pathologized Bukovskii's efforts to reform Soviet society by filtering them through the art of diagnosis.

In addition to paranoiac schizophrenia, dissidents who underwent evaluation were often diagnosed with paranoiac developments of personality, a condition considered typical of people suffering from psychopathy or possessing psychopathic traits. "Gloomy and resentful, often rude and tactless, prepared to uncover ill-wishers everywhere around them, they frighten off even those closest to them," the psychiatrist Oleg Kerbikov wrote of the disorder in 1968. "Only rarely does one succeed in establishing good relations with them for very long; wherever they go, there are unending conflicts, harassment, struggles with imaginary enemies."[84] What the Soviet psychiatric establishment called psychopathy was said to be both biologically predetermined and socially triggered or aggravated; significantly with regard to the pathologization of dissidents, however, people diagnosed with psychopathic developments of personality tended to be placed in the latter category.[85] Theoretically, such patients might behave normally until a negative influence or traumatic experience triggered their disorder. "This is the signature 'psychopathic cycle,'" Kerbikov wrote. "Psychopathic traits of character lead to conflict and the conflict evokes a psychogenic reaction, in the course of which the psychopathic traits of personality deepen."[86]

This spiraling narrative of psychopathic reasoning propels a 1969 Serbskii Institute report diagnosing Petro Grigorenko with a "mental disorder in the form of a pathological (paranoiac) development of personality with ideas of reformism formed in a personality with psychopathic traits of character and early signs of cerebral arteriosclerosis."[87] The report begins by noting such traumatic experiences as Grigorenko's difficult upbringing and loss of his mother. During World War II, it continues, the subject was reprimanded for criticizing the Soviet army's readiness for battle. He again raised hackles at a

Communist Party meeting in 1961. Transferred to the Far East, Grigorenko reportedly nursed a sense of disappointment, which the psychiatrists link to his development of revolutionary ideas:

> He notes that he was offended by his transfer from Moscow, he believed that he had been deliberately "expelled from Moscow." At that point he came to the conclusion that the government was "rotting," that it had lost touch with Lenin's norms and principles, that it was necessary to raise awareness among the people in order to "destroy" the status quo. [...] He was consumed by these thoughts and considered it to be a "matter of conscience and honor."[88]

Arrested for putting his views in writing and distributing them in Moscow, the report continues, Grigorenko was confined to the Leningrad Special Psychiatric Hospital. Upon his release the following year, he was further traumatized to discover that he had been stripped of his military rank and pension. "In his words," the report notes, "he found himself 'in isolation,' he had been 'run off the rails,' and that was when he decided 'to struggle with the injustice and unlawfulness' that, in his opinion, could be found in the government."[89] In 1969, the subject was detained in Tashkent, reexamined by local psychiatrists and pronounced sane. But investigators requested another evaluation at the Serbskii Institute, resulting in its updated determination of his paranoiac development of personality. The report concludes:

> [The diagnosis] is demonstrated by the psychotic state that he developed during a period of unfavorable conditions in 1964 and that manifested itself in ideas of reformism, reference, and persecution with a high degree of affective intensity. Later, as is evident in the case file and in the results of the current clinical examination, the paranoiac state did not entirely pass, while the ideas of reformism took on a stable character and now determine the subject's behavior; moreover, his preoccupation with these ideas periodically increases in connection with various external situations that do not directly relate to him.[90]

Mirroring what Kerbikov called the "psychopathic cycle," the report presents Grigorenko's state of mind as a spiraling series of causes and effects. Personal loss prompts political protest, which deepens the condition by once again leading to personal loss. Subjecting what it describes as Grigorenko's paranoiac syndrome to the art of diagnosis, the report transforms it into evidence of the subject's paranoiac development of personality.

The narrative orientation of psychiatric discourse facilitated the rewriting of dissidents' lives by explaining not only the present moment, but the past and future ones, as well. "More often than not," Lunts and several coauthors observed in 1976 with regard to uncovering their patients' histories, "dangerous acts spurred by pathological motives come as a surprise to the patient's acquaintances, who only then begin to suspect a mental illness. Retrospectively, however, the disease's continuity can be discerned."[91] But the "continuity" of the disease could also be established prospectively, as Snezhnevskii noted in 1974:

> Diagnosis and prognosis are inseparable concepts. The detection of a disease, of the regularities of its progression, and of all its individual static and dynamic particularities makes it possible to predict its further progression. The condition of a patient at any given moment is the product of the previous—and among other things the initial and hidden—development of the disease. At the same time it contains within itself the potential possibility of predicting the nature of its subsequent development. To make a prognosis is to identify these potential possibilities.[92]

The art of diagnosis resulted in the production of written narratives that caught the "essence" of a patient's condition by situating syndromes within a progression that stretched both backward and forward in time. Such narratives were particularly predictive in the case of schizophrenia, which, according to the Moscow school, allowed for a wide variety of symptoms as the disease progressed but essentially ruled out the possibility of ever returning to the story's start. "Any recovery, intermission, or deep remission following a schizophrenic episode is characterized by changes to the entire makeup of the personality," Snezhnevskii emphasized in 1972.[93] A patient diagnosed with schizophrenia embarked upon a narrative of disease that progressed inexorably forward in time.

The ability to make retrospective diagnoses was important for forensic psychiatrists who were tasked with determining their subjects' responsibility for prior criminal acts. But some psychiatrists also used narratives of disease to predict the likelihood of future crimes. In 1969, for instance, a specialist named V. M. Shumakov published an article in the *Korsakov Journal* comparing schizophrenic individuals who had committed crimes with schizophrenic individuals from the general population and concluding that the former had displayed predictive traits.[94] In a 1976 article, he and several coauthors suggested screening for such traits in order to ward off future crimes.[95] Four years later, he and yet another group of coauthors were stressing a predictive link between criminal behavior and paranoia, specifically:

> Such patients often present themselves as "fighters for justice," uncovering the perpetrators of petty crimes, demanding that they be punished. Their obstinacy and perseverance in making litigious claims frequently lead to chronic situations of conflict and are accompanied by the violation of established rules and order, quarrels, violation of labor discipline, acts of aggression (in family situations the latter are often linked to delusions of jealousy).[96]

Patients with paranoia were especially likely to commit socially dangerous acts, Shumakov and his colleagues claimed. Yet as three Serbskii Institute physicians wrote in 1978, establishing the likelihood of criminal acts remained contingent on the physician's "art": "An accurate prognosis of dangerous behavior only becomes possible based on verbal expressions of the experience of the disease that directly or indirectly testify to the patient's 'criminal' intentions. The physician's art lies in his ability to uncover these dissimulated experiences."[97] It was precisely this subjective art of diagnosis that enabled psychiatrists to reveal the ostensibly objective truth of the patient's condition and thereby the threat that the patient posed. Diagnostic categories thus provided physicians with predictive templates for narrating Soviet lawbreakers' lives.

Performativity and the Medical Monologue

At the heart of the Moscow school's diagnostic process was the spoken dialogue between the psychiatrist and the patient. It was by asking questions, listening to answers, and observing physical behavior, Snezhnevskii argued, that the psychiatrist uncovered the patient's symptoms and determined the disorders to which they belonged. Viewed from the perspective of Mikhail Bakhtin's distinction between the diversity and open-endedness of "dialogic" discourse and the unity and completedness of "monologic" discourse, however, the art of diagnosis leaned toward the latter by giving pride of place to the psychiatrist's own voice.[98] In 1968, Snezhnevskii concurred with the eminent psychiatrist Petr Gannushkin by quoting him as follows: "Our best psychiatrists—Kraepelin, a German, [Valentin] Magnan, a Frenchman, [Sergei] Korsakov, a Russian—were great masters ... even artists when it came to conversing with patients, to getting what they needed from the patient; each approached the patient in his own way, each had his merits and flaws, each reflected himself in the conversation together with all his spiritual qualities."[99] Translated into Bakhtin's terms, Snezhnevskii's art of diagnosis effectively entailed a movement from dialogue to monologue—from the interactive elucidation of the patient's life story to the psychiatrist's authoritative drawing out of its narrative "essence" within the clinical or forensic report. "One must always remember," Snezhnevskii emphasized in 1974, "that in attempting to reveal the personality of the patient, the psychiatrist simultaneously reveals his own personality before him."[100] The more clearly physicians reveal themselves, Snezhnevskii's comments seem to suggest, the more successful their art of diagnosis.

Crucial to the process of moving from dialogue to monologue was how the psychiatrist conversed with the patient. "When examining a patient," Snezhnevskii emphasized in 1968, "the physician first strives to penetrate from the individual to the general regularities and, having discovered them, to return once again to their individual manifestation, their concrete expression in the given patient. This means of investigation is ultimately realized in the diagnosis of the disease and the patient's diagnosis."[101] Even as the psychiatrist gathers information on a single patient, he or she must situate it within a general narrative of disease. According to Snezhnevskii, the psychiatrist should therefore begin with basic observations and open questions (How does the patient spend his or her time? What are the patient's attitudes toward life?) before moving on to more targeted queries (Who are the patient's friends and relatives? Does the patient have any plans for the future?). In asking these questions, the psychiatrist should pay attention not only to what the patient says but also to how he or she says it, taking note of any diagnostically indicative movements or expressions. But the psychiatrist should also steer the patient's responses: "Having given the patient the opportunity to freely talk about his illness, it is important to simultaneously provide direction through the line of questioning."[102] The same principle, Snezhnevskii indicates, applies to the testimony of friends and family: "It is necessary to steer the story that the relatives and acquaintances tell about the development of the disease."[103] The art of diagnosis is contingent upon the doctor's personal skill at directing the dialogue: "The success of a question-based examination depends not only on the knowledge of the investigator, but also on his ability to ask questions. This is determined by the physician's personal qualities and experience. Each psychiatrist speaks with the patient 'in his own way.'"[104] By adopting the monologic aesthetic of psychiatric discourse, the psychiatrist who commanded the art of diagnosis engaged in a form of self-expression.

Yet grasping a disease's narrative "essence" was just one stage of the art of diagnosis; the physician also had to convey that "essence" through the written medium of the clinical report. And to do so, as Ia. I. Khurgin and P. G. Nikiforova wrote in the *Korsakov Journal* in 1966, was similar to producing a work of art:

> The psychiatric diagnosis of many forms of mental illness approaches that class of artistic phenomena wherein the physician's analytical capacities and level of qualification are frequently the deciding factors. In this sense, what becomes significant is the doctor's skill at winning over the patient and "opening him up," his capacity for subsequently presenting his observations and for analyzing the status. It is no accident that we define a good clinical report as a system of descriptions that has reached a high level of clarity and visualization, and that takes up 15 to 20 pages of typewritten text.[105]

What asking questions and writing clinical reports have in common, Khurgin and Nikiforova's comments indicate, is their mutual commitment to coupling analytical rigor with an aesthetic of verbal and visual clarity. As Kalashnik confirmed in 1967 with specific respect to forensic reports, "conclusions that are formulated in a contradictory, confused, ambiguous, and incorrect manner, that do not flow from the case file and from the evidence acquired during investigation of the accused, do not help the court but rather complicate its work and can serve as a source of juridical error."[106] Ultimately, Kalashnik continued, the psychiatrist's reasoning should come across "in such a way that the reader can follow the evidence to the same conclusion."[107] Just as the masterfully conducted conversation between psychiatrist and patient moved from dialogue to monologue, the ideal interaction between author and reader was ultimately monologic in nature. Snezhnevskii thus encouraged his students to express their conclusions in as impersonal a style as possible: "A well-written [psychological] evaluation always contains an objective, universally convincing presentation of scientific facts without the addition of personal interpretation."[108] However subjective the psychiatrist's art of diagnosis, it staked a claim to scientific objectivity.

Yet nowhere did the psychiatrist's voice emerge more authoritatively than in the forensic report, where the monologic discourse of Soviet psychiatry combined forces with the similarly monologic discourse of Soviet law. The

Russian Criminal and Civil Codes had two designations for citizens found to be unable to evaluate and control their actions as a result of mental illness or deficiency: "nonimputability" (*nevmeniaemost'*) and "incompetency" (*nedeesposobnost'*). Article 11 of the Criminal Code defined nonimputability as the inability of such individuals to answer for their crimes.[109] Articles 11, 12, and 15 of the Civil Code, by contrast, defined incompetency as such individuals' inability to independently assert or fulfill their rights and duties.[110] When courts declared citizens nonimputable or incompetent, they generally did so based on psychiatrists' recommendations. Although those recommendations were theoretically not binding, in practice their influence was considerable, due not least to the perceived harmony between a psychiatric system and a legal system that jointly subscribed to Marxist-Leninist ideology. As the psychiatrist Elizaveta Kholodkovskaia wrote of incompetency in 1967: "Normal psychological activity ensures the subject's ability to correctly interact with his social environment and, in particular, to understand the civil and legal norms set forth in the law. A mental illness can deprive a person of this ability, destroying any possibility of a conscious relationship with prevailing objective phenomena and the actions he commits."[111] Kholodkovskaia's comments indicate that psychiatrists equated sanity with a "correct" attitude toward Soviet law during the post-Stalin period. At the same time, they position the forensic psychiatrist as the binding link between psychiatric and legal discourses.

Lunts similarly stressed the discursive bilingualism of the forensic psychiatrist in his 1966 book on nonimputability: "A forensic psychiatric evaluation may be said to constitute a translation of clinical psychiatric concepts into the language of law."[112] Given that court officials lacked the expertise to judge psychiatric evidence for themselves, Lunts emphasized, forensic psychiatrists should supplement their descriptions of the patient's status with clearly articulated legal recommendations.[113] If Snezhnevskii encouraged clinical psychiatrists to cultivate an impersonal style, then, Lunts urged forensic psychiatrists to bring their input to the fore; the forensic report thus offered an ideal environment for showcasing the psychiatrist's art of diagnosis. In 1967, Kalashnik used the words of the renowned psychiatrist Sergei Korsakov to describe the aims of the forensic report: "'The physician must present his conclusions in a clear and simple literary language, using inaccessible terms only if necessary and in that case explaining their meaning. This is necessary in view of the fact that his opinion must be grasped by the judges, the litigators, and the jurors.'"[114] The need to communicate with legal professionals forced forensic psychiatrists to develop an aesthetic that physicians and courts could both understand.

Yet within that monologic aesthetic's claim to objectivity was room for the psychiatrist's subjective input. To use the philosopher J. L. Austin's terms, psychiatrists of the post-Stalin period positioned their clinical and forensic reports as "constative utterances" that described reality in factually absolute ways: the presence or absence of a psychiatric disorder, for instance, or the subject's state of imputability or nonimputability. However, punitive diagnoses also operated as "performative utterances" by appending diagnostic labels that put into practice the medical realities that they claimed to disinterestedly describe.[115] Indeed, Austin writes that one of the primary distinctions between constative and performative utterances is that the former can be proven true or false while the latter cannot be verified.[116] The Moscow school thus bolstered its constative claims by emphasizing that it was possible to definitively determine whether patients could evaluate and control their actions. Lunts, for instance, repeatedly asserted that those who advocated a category of "diminished imputability" were simply licensing forensic psychiatrists to stop short of completing their task.[117] It was in part by presenting their own declarations of nonimputability as constative rather than performative utterances that Lunts and his colleagues in the Moscow school elided the subjective—and thus potentially aestheticized—nature of punitive diagnosis.

According to Austin, performative utterances demand that "either the speaker himself or other persons should *also* perform certain *other* actions, be they "physical" or "mental" actions or even acts of uttering further words."[118] Forensic reports accordingly launched a string of events that cemented the truth value of their initial claims. If forensic psychiatrists reached a finding of nonimputability, for example, they typically ended their reports by not only advising hospitalization but also specifying the type of hospital—an "ordinary" psychiatric hospital run by the Ministry of Health or a "special" prison hospital run by the Ministry of Internal Affairs—to which the patient should be sent. The accused's removal to the recommended type of hospital thus materialized the report's conclusions, graphically affirming their performative power. So, too, did the 1961 and 1971 Instructions on the Urgent Hospitalization of the Socially Dangerous Mentally Ill, which licensed psychiatrists to independently institutionalize people who had been judged to be dangerous to themselves or others.[119] In 1969, the physician Eduard Babaian wrote in praise of this system that, while other countries' policy of requiring a court order hampered therapeutic work, Soviet psychiatrists' ability to bypass the courts meant that they could expedite treatment. Any possibility of diagnostic error would ultimately be addressed by the expert eye of more than one psychiatrist, Babaian argued, and should it be determined that the patient did not require hospitalization, he or she could be released with minimal red tape. That physicians had the power to act quickly and independently was, for him, one of the Soviet system's strengths. "'Our trust in the physician is much greater, and there is not one case in which this trust has proved unfounded,'" Babaian quoted Korsakov as saying.[120] By monologically projecting the physician's authority to single-handedly hospitalize dangerous individuals, the art of diagnosis facilitated the performative transformation of dissidents into psychiatric patients.

The self-affirming aesthetic of punitive diagnosis put such dissidents into a bind: the more firmly they insisted on their sanity, the more divorced from reality they appeared to be. In 1978, the Serbskii Institute psychiatrists Iakov Landau and Margarita Tal'tse stipulated that the patient's release should be made contingent upon his or her admission of the diagnosed illness: "The question of changing a patient's medical condition may be raised at the following signs: the deactualization of delusional ideas that usually comes with the growth of a 'discriminating' critique of one's delusional experiences (of various content) and a critical attitude toward one's past actions."[121] The punitive implications of this approach are evident in the reports that Landau and Tal'tse produced on the dissident Viktor Fainberg in 1968 and 1972, respectively. In 1968, Landau noted together with Lunts and Serbskii Institute director Georgii Morozov that Fainberg demonstrated his illness by attempting "to present himself as a mentally healthy person, thereby revealing a clear lack of critical awareness of his past experience of psychotic episodes."[122] And when, in 1972, Fainberg told psychiatrists at the Serbskii Institute that the Leningrad Special Psychiatric Hospital was confining healthy people for political reasons, another report by Tal'tse, Nadzharov and several other colleagues similarly responded by pathologizing him: "At attempts to convince him of the mistakenness of his judgments, the subject immediately began to argue back and with still greater fervency insisted upon his 'rightness,' pointing to himself personally and to other, as he believes, mentally healthy people who were in the hospital with him."[123] Within the context of an art of diagnosis that performatively materialized its own conclusions, the patient's accusations of abuse merely affirmed his or her need for further treatment.

Recovery, for Landau, Tal'tse, and other psychiatrists, meant acknowledging one's illness in such a way as to affirm the psychiatrist's authority. Yet affirming that authority was precisely what dissidents refused to do. Grigorenko's 1969 Serbskii Institute report thus notes a degree of progress insofar as its subject's recognition of the psychiatrist is concerned: although initially the patient "protested against being subjected to forensic psychiatric evaluation, was agitated, spoke in a raised voice, announced that his transfer to the Institute for evaluation was an 'act of tyranny,'" later he "grew calmer, willingly entered into contact with the physician."[124] Yet the report also pathologizes Grigorenko by noting that he continues to justify his past actions: "He considers his struggle entirely legitimate and the path he has taken to be the only right one."[125] Gorbanevskaia's 1970 Serbskii Institute report likewise notes that, despite her own willingness to engage with her physicians, the patient continues to insist on her sanity: "Considers herself to be a mentally healthy person. Convinced she has been sent for evaluation so as to 'let it all quiet down,' because 'it was better for the prosecutor that way.'"[126] Gorbanevskaia, the psychiatrists conclude in support of their diagnosis, remains "unwaveringly convinced of the rightness of her actions" and continues to lack a "critical understanding of her condition and of the situation that has arisen."[127] The performative power of diagnosis was such that questioning the psychiatrist's authority to impose psychiatric labels could itself confirm the finding of insanity.

SOCIALIST REALISM AS DIAGNOSTIC NORM

Under the leadership of Snezhnevskii, psychiatrists cultivated an art of diagnosis that facilitated the pathologization of dissent. They expressed this art not only through the monologic structure of their clinical and forensic reports but also through their authoritative orchestration of the psychiatrist-patient dialogue. By emphasizing their objectivity and presenting their diagnoses as constative utterances, they elided both the performative artistry of their own practices and the subjective nature of the conclusions thus reached. Yet their continued attentiveness to aesthetic matters came to the fore through their efforts to demonstrate that the artistic output of the insane—from their poems and paintings to the real-life dramatics of psychiatric patients—could be analyzed and classified. "Quite a number of investigations have been devoted to the study of the creative activity of mental patients in the Soviet Union," Babaian, Morozov, and their colleagues Anatolii Smulevich and Valentin Morkovkin emphasized in 1982.[128] Psychiatrists played down the subjectivity of their art of diagnosis in part by asserting their own authority to evaluate the art of their patients. And they drew this authority not only from the monologic psychiatric discourse of the Moscow school but also from the similarly monologic literary discourse of Socialist Realist art.

While the post-1953 process of de-Stalinization brought measured reform across the arts, the Moscow school largely maintained the disciplinary hold that it had consolidated at the Pavlov Session of 1951. The result was a psychiatric culture that preserved the hallmarks of the Stalinist period for decades after the leader's death, and one of those hallmarks was its attentiveness to the Socialist Realist aesthetic doctrine that the Union of Soviet Writers had adopted in 1934. Though initially codified with reference to literature, specifically, Socialist Realism crossed both medium and genre and developed over time.[129] Yet a binding characteristic of Socialist Realist works was their tendency to monologically project authority through positive heroes whose psychologies were marked by wholeness, not division, and whose ideological leanings tended to univocally coincide with those of the author and narrator. This monologism invested Socialist Realist works with a unity of selfhood and expression, on the one hand, and a completed worldview that discouraged dissent, on the other. But Socialist Realism was as much a political phenomenon as it was an artistic one, since the state went about constructing socialism by applying its creative principles to reality itself.[130] Elements of Socialist Realist aesthetics may thus be discerned in the psychiatrist's art of diagnosis. When physicians of the Moscow school measured dissidents' lives against standardized narratives of normality and abnormality, Socialist Realist doctrine provided them with a point of departure.

The Moscow school's approach to diagnosis and treatment mirrored aspects of Socialist Realist narrative. According to the official definition of Socialist Realism, artists were to infuse their depictions of everyday reality with a sense of that reality's "revolutionary development."[131] Both this teleological superimposition of present and future and its monologically authoritative delivery carried over to the art of diagnosis. If Socialist Realist art sought to locate the present within its historical march toward the communist future, for instance, then diagnostic labels such as sluggish schizophrenia similarly claimed to discern the future progression of a disease within present symptoms that were often so mild that laymen were considered incapable of detecting them. It required a trained psychiatrist to elucidate these hidden symptoms in much the same way as works of Socialist Realism cumulatively trained Soviet readers to intuit reality's revolutionary development toward communism from the plot of any given text. According to Katerina Clark, Socialist Realist novels tended to follow a "master plot" wherein the hero underwent an internal revolution that converted him or her from a still-unenlightened state of "spontaneity" to a more knowledgeable and purposeful state of "consciousness."[132] If the clinical or forensic report may be said to have imposed a narrative drive toward illness, then, the patient's acknowledgment of that illness arguably functioned as that revolutionary moment when he or she began returning to health. That dissidents tended to insist on their sanity excluded them from this therapeutic master plot, condemning them instead to a narrative of illness and reifying the performative power of psychiatric diagnosis.

The Moscow school appropriated Socialist Realism as more than an analytical method, however; it also made patients' deviations from state-sanctioned aesthetics a subject of analysis. In addition to validating the "artistic" elements of their own practices, then, Soviet psychiatrists turned the diagnostic gaze on the creative output of their patients. Characterizing the art of the mentally ill as a valuable tool for diagnosis, Snezhnevskii and his contemporaries studied it through a critical vocabulary that reflected Socialist Realist norms. In particular, they echoed the Stalin-era doctrine's preference for thematic clarity over the obfuscation of irony and experimental form. "When it comes to such documents or sketches," Snezhnevskii wrote in 1974 about the artistic output of psychiatric patients, "everything is of interest: the content, the manner of execution, the stylistic character, its finished or chaotic nature; its carelessness or precision, its schematization or saturation with detail; its realism or fancifulness, its tendency toward symbolism or abstraction; its color palette and so on."[133] Some psychiatrists argued that the artwork of the mentally ill was qualitatively unlike the art of healthy people. Others maintained that the art of the sane and the insane demonstrated differences as well as similarities. Still others argued that the creative output of the insane was indistinguishable from the experimentalism of modernist art. In 1982, 1985, and 1986, Babaian, Morozov, Smulevich, and Morkovkin published three studies of the "visual language" of individuals who had been diagnosed with forms of schizophrenia. "Despite the different capacities and professional training of patients, as well as differences in genre and the objects depicted, the type of pictorial languages used in drawings and other graphic representations by schizophrenic patients is largely determined by the course of the disease and the negative changes it has brought about," Snezhnevskii explained in his introduction to the first study.[134] Written in consultation with Soviet art experts and printed bilingually in Russian and

Figure 2. B. G. S., untitled, undated.
Source: E. A. Babaian, G. V. Morozov, V. M. Morkovkin, and A. B. Smulevich, *Izobraziteľnyi iazyk bol'nogo paranoiei* (Basel: Sandoz, 1986), 52 from first page of full text.

English, the books made a case for the Moscow school's emphasis on analyzing the artwork of the mentally ill.

And indeed, all three studies of artworks by patients diagnosed with schizophrenia echo Socialist Realist doctrine by portraying representational art as evidence of greater mental clarity than art that tends toward formal experimentation. The less debilitating the disease's progression, the first study concludes, the more likely the patient is to produce "harmonious" and "joyful" still lifes and landscapes. "The landscape created by patient R. stands out for its particular aesthetic perfection," the authors write of a patient whose disease reportedly presented in adulthood and was not accompanied by major personality changes. "It consists of a broad panorama of a river with a thick forest growing on its banks. The transparent light-green bushes and trees in the foreground and the special treatment of the distant river form a harmonious unity expressed in a composition which utilizes equally both space and colour. The landscape is very light and joyful."[135] By contrast, the artwork of patients who experienced an early onset of schizophrenia with major personality changes and "symptoms of metaphysical intoxication" is described as tending toward "disintegration"—qualities that violated both the representational emphasis and the unity of selfhood and expression that Socialist Realist artworks tended to promote.[136] Literary discourse accordingly informed a psychiatric discourse that was ready to medicalize aesthetic norms. This is further illustrated by the third study's use of the literary term "graphomaniac" to describe a seventy-five-year-old amateur painter whose identity is concealed behind the initials "B.G.S." The painter's "condition resembles in many respects the picture of paranoiac psychopathy," the authors write before concluding: "To use for [B.G.S.'s ideas'] characterization an analogy from the field of literature, this is a kind of 'pictorial graphomania.'"[137] The presence of literary terms such as "graphomania" signals psychiatric discourse's attention to and assimilation of aesthetic categories during the post-Stalin period.

Despite their engagement with state-sanctioned aesthetics, however, all three studies are quick to deny that the artwork of the mentally ill is actual art. In the second study, for example, the authors assert that "even if some of [these artworks] reveal an outward semblance to the works of modernist artists, they constitute a different phenomenon; here, we have an expression of the psychic disorders of the mentally ill in pictorial form."[138] The primary message of the paintings produced by the "graphomaniac" B.G.S. is accordingly reduced to that of the "latent or residual schizophrenia" that it reflects.[139] "The professional standards and techniques demonstrated, in particular, in the works presented in this publication, are extremely low," the authors emphasize. "Nevertheless, the patient regards himself as a great artist at the peak of his fame."[140] By explaining B.G.S.'s belief in his own genius as a manifestation of what they describe as his paranoiac tendency to overvalue a delusional idea, the psychiatrists bend it to their diagnostic gaze. At the same time, they invest that belief with an alternate, psychiatric meaning that reflects the content-driven aesthetic of Socialist Realism. "The self-assertion of the author as a 'great painter' turns out to be the main content of the work," they write.[141] To the extent that the psychiatrists do identify subsidiary "messages" in individual paintings, they present them as part of the assertion of genius that, for them, characterizes B.G.S.'s illness as a whole: "The purpose of B.G.S. is to carry to the spectator his idea, his 'message,' as completely as possible. This is why the idea contained in a picture or sculpture must be explained in the greatest detail."[142] It is by presenting the art of the mentally ill primarily as a carrier of medical data that the psychiatrists cement the scientific core of their own art of diagnosis.

The authors point by way of example to B.G.S.'s deceptively Socialist Realist painting of a bricklayer standing between two brick walls while the slogan "Builder: Labor Breeds Thirst" [*Stroitel': Zhazhda rozhdaetsia v trude*] stretches out behind her. "The incompetent depiction of the hands, resembling the infantilism of children's drawings, where the hands are always painted "worse" than the face, can be seen in many works by B.G.S. It is clear that he regards them as an unimportant detail, especially compared to the overall design," the authors write. "There is also a contradiction in the disparity between the visual image of the woman builder and the content stressed by the explanatory text."[143] Viewing the painting through a diagnostic lens that is in turn informed by Socialist Realist aesthetics, the authors describe it as an image that may have aimed to be both realistic and "optimistic" but failed for reasons of technical incompetence and the irrational inclusion of an ill-fitting caption. At the same time, they pathologize B.G.S. for making "no distinction between museum models and kitsch products, they are all equally important for him as means for expressing his concepts."[144] Both the incommensurability of image and text and the mixing of high and low artistic registers invite psychiatric diagnosis.

Yet all of the traits that the psychiatrists highlight are commensurate with the ironic and deeply citational discourse of the unsanctioned art movements of the period. In the caption, the morpheme *rozh*—derived from *rod*, with its connotations of birth, gender, sex, kin—falls directly over the subject's head in a brick of its own, highlighting it in such a way as to offer a subversively sexualized commentary on the image. Other hints of sexuality abound: a trowel in one of the bricklayer's hands widens into breast-like bulges, while the angle of the bottle of white milk in her other hand draws attention to an identically angled phallus-shaped section of her blouse disappearing between the folds of a red kerchief knotted at her neck. The image does stand at odds with the text, but the message that the resulting disjuncture conveys is far from "optimistic": in spite of the puritanical rhetoric of Soviet propaganda, the painting would imply, Soviet citizens think about nothing but sex.[145] Nor is the painting unique in this regard, as many of B.G.S.'s other works dwell far more overtly on sexual themes. Like contemporary practitioners of Moscow Conceptualism and Sots-Art, B.G.S. quotes the iconography of Soviet power in such a way as to ironically dismantle it from within. And indeed, the psychiatrists respond by pathologizing B.G.S. for giving "pride of place to the idea—the conception. The forms of its realization may vary, depending on reliance on one or another model, whereas the idea itself remains immutable, lapidary, and is, therefore, easily singled out in every concrete case."[146] If the idea-based aesthetic of Conceptualism and Sots-Art violated Socialist Realist norms (in part by exposing the state-sanctioned doctrine's own prioritization of ideology), it also challenged Socialist Realism's discomfort with the ironic mode. Regardless of B.G.S.'s actual psychiatric condition, the Conceptualist character of the artwork that the authors cite in support of their diagnosis highlights the pathologizability of unsanctioned art and psychiatry's medicalization of state-sanctioned aesthetics.

The Moscow school's assimilation of Socialist Realist aesthetics was not confined to the analysis of images and texts produced by individuals believed to be mentally ill, however. As the cynical manipulation of psychiatric categories became more frequent in the post-Stalin period, the art of diagnosis itself became increasingly performative. At the same time, the growth of two other phenomena began to draw psychiatrists' attention: "simulation," or the performance of mental illness by ostensibly healthy people, and "dissimulation," or the performance of mental health by people believed to be mentally ill. In addition to wreaking havoc with psychiatric practice, the feigning of mental illness and health disrupted the unity of selfhood and expression that underlay psychiatry's Socialist Realist aesthetic. Unlike the typical positive hero who spoke in accord with his or her beliefs and whose beliefs tended to echo those of both the author and the narrator, the words of simulators and dissimulators actively concealed the thoughts behind them. In much the same way as the ironic imagery of the painter B.G.S. violated aesthetic norms of transparent expression, then, simulation and dissimulation challenged psychiatrists' "art" of revealing their patients' hidden psychological conditions.

Psychiatrists' concerns about simulation and dissimulation were evidently well-founded. According to a 1983 pamphlet by the psychiatrist V. E. Pelipas, cases of simulation had become ten times more frequent over the 1960s and 1970s.[147] Moreover, Pelipas emphasized, they had become more difficult to detect as simulators rapidly improved their knowledge of psychological and psychiatric categories. "These days lawbreakers under psychiatric examination often manipulate psychiatric terms and concepts with considerable ease; they show an understanding of reactive conditions and schizophrenia, delusional ideas and hallucinations," Pelipas wrote.[148] The most common motives for simulation were the desire to be exempted from employment, conscription, or imprisonment; sick individuals who deliberately aggravated or prolonged their symptoms were also considered to be simulating mental illness. Dissimulation, by contrast, was usually detected in sick people who wished to be released from hospitalization or to be declared responsible for some other reason. Psychiatrists stressed that the dramatization of mental illness or health had to be intentional in order to be classified as simulation or dissimulation; involuntary feigning did not qualify. It therefore followed that the patients best able to fake illness or health would be those whose mental deterioration was still quite mild. Indeed, Lunts specifically noted, dissimulation was most difficult to detect among patients whose disease was progressing at a sluggish pace. Thanks to their ability to blend into society, he explained, such patients all too often succeeded at fooling their physicians and at securing an early release.[149]

Lunts's emphasis on the dissimulative tendencies of patients with sluggish schizophrenia illuminates the obstacles faced by dissidents who sought to prove their sanity: psychiatric theory explicitly anticipated dissimulation by patients diagnosed with that condition. Indeed, Morozov warned physicians that certain patients might turn to dissimulation purely on principle: "These patients seek to prove their mental health; they would rather be held responsible for the act they have committed than be declared sick."[150] Morozov's reasoning sheds light on the conclusions reached by Lunts, Tal'tse, and two other physicians during their 1970 evaluation of the Latvian dissident Ivan Iakhimovich. Arrested for producing and distributing *samizdat*, Iakhimovich was twice diagnosed with paranoiac development of personality: first by forensic psychiatrists in Riga and then again in Moscow at the Serbskii Institute.[151] Upon his arrival in Moscow, the Serbskii Institute's report declares, Iakhimovich willingly detailed his delusions of reformism. Over time, however, he began to systematically conceal his symptoms:

> During discussions with physicians he became more guarded, more strained, he began approaching discussions with a certain agitation, tried to avoid conversations about his prior activities, and, when questioned concretely on the topic, began to make formal declarations that he supposedly views his past behavior as frivolous but that he overcame this by applying scientific methods of reasoning. [...] He drew the physician's attention to the fact that his actions should not be viewed as those of sick person, while at the same time openly stating that he was apprehensive about being declared mentally ill.[152]

Harnessing their art of diagnosis, the authors methodically deconstruct Iakhimovich's apparent return to sane behavior. They foreshadow the concluding charge of dissimulation by countering Iakhimovich's claim to mental health with evidence of his persistently delusional thinking. They provide a motive for dissimulation by highlighting his worry that he will be diagnosed. They explain his capacity for dissimulation by suggesting that prior conversations with psychiatrists might have taught him how to conceal his symptoms. However, it is only in the concluding paragraph that the authors pull together their evidence by giving these behaviors a name: Iakhimovich, they write, displays "an effort to dissimulate his psychological abnormalities and a lack of criticism when evaluating his condition and situation."[153] Moving in standard forensic fashion from disinterested description to firm pronouncement, the report exposes what it portrays as Iakhimovich's dramatization of sanity by subjecting it to the art of diagnosis.

Psychiatrists emphasized the theatrical properties of simulation throughout their writings on the topic. "Certain authors have argued that simulation is nothing more than an ordinary lie," Pelipas wrote in his pamphlet, "yet they immediately contradict themselves by noting that the simulator is not just the 'author' of his lie, but also the 'actor and director.'"[154] Pelipas divides feigners of mental illness into "visual" and "verbal" categories. Both types display a flair for "dramatic" mimicry, he writes, with the difference being that, while visual simulators tend to act out their symptoms, verbal simulators describe them in words.[155] Pelipas further emphasizes the theatricality of simulators by drawing attention to the historical contingency of their dramatized "symptoms." In the

1920s, he writes, citizens simulated insanity by playing the alcoholic or the "wild man." Delusions and depression predominated in the 1930s, while during and after World War II, simulators pretended to suffer from brain injuries or the psychological effects of battle. By the 1960s, he continues, they had started exchanging tips and studying psychiatric texts, with the result being that they became capable of mimicking distinct symptoms such as dementia and hysteria. By the 1970s, those who planned to commit a crime were laying the groundwork in advance by preemptively checking themselves into hospitals in order to obtain "nonimputability passports."[156] Many simulators claimed to be "prominent 'political officials,' 'founders of new parties,' relatives of famous historical figures, 'secret agents' for foreign spy agencies," Pelipas writes. "Frequently, to prove their point, the subjects write 'proclamations,' 'pamphlets,' 'coded letters,' or present drawings of fantastical subjects and images with which they claim to be connected."[157] In addition to presenting the theatricality of simulation as an identifying marker, Pelipas thus draws his readers' attention to the simulator's traffic in politicized words and images.

Seeking to distinguish not only between simulators and genuinely symptomatic people, but also between art produced in service of simulation and art that sprang from actual mental illness, physicians flagged a range of behaviors as typical of fakers. According to Pelipas, for instance, simulators often declared that they were writing poems or symphonies. Others accompanied their theatrical displays with "charts, drawings, notes, entire 'treatises' in which abstract, empty discourses alternate with banalities and excerpts from popular science journals."[158] Noting that such creative efforts might seem convincing, physicians advised their students to keep an eye on the bigger picture. After all, the physician Nina Felinskaia wrote in 1967, even simulators followed certain predictable rules: "When examining the psychological state of a possible simulator, one must keep in mind that even though simulation constitutes a highly individualized creative act and in each particular case one must work out specific ways of uncovering it, there nevertheless exist general laws that characterize different forms of simulation."[159] Having identified the disease that a particular patient was suspected of simulating, psychiatrists were advised to check for incompleteness and contradiction in the nosological picture. Their approach to uncovering simulation—and, indeed, to examining the artworks that suspected simulators produced—was thus to reaffirm the authority of psychiatric diagnosis and its standardized narratives of disease. The subjective art of diagnosis could trump the art produced by patients, but only for as long as physicians could maintain its standing as an objective science.

A Discursive Exchange

Soviet psychiatrists straddled two identities in the decades following Stalin's death. On the one hand, they emphasized the scientific nature of psychiatric diagnosis and presented their own subjective input as a grounded dimension of that objective practice. On the other hand, they imbued what they described as the diagnostician's "art" with literary assumptions and techniques that left room for personalized and even politicized interpretation. The resulting combination of psychiatric and literary discourses facilitated the pathologization of dissent. But it also provided dissenters with a foil for challenging the psychiatrist's diagnostic authority, while affirming their own authority to make diagnostic pronouncements about the mental and creative health of Soviet society. The following case studies chronicle how dissidents and dissenting writers mirrored the artistry and thus subjectivity of diagnosis by making use of the literary tradition to redefine the categories analyzed in this chapter. Whether it was by subversively manipulating psychiatric discourse, depicting insanity in words or images, or consciously deploying aesthetically deviant devices such as irony, humor, and parody, dissenters turned their supposed madness into a means of preserving or demonstrating health. Their clash with psychiatrists unfolded as a discursive exchange between dueling arts of diagnosis, each of which asserted its own authority over what it meant to be mad.

CHAPTER 2

THINKING DIFFERENTLY: THE CASE OF THE DISSIDENTS

Toward the end of the 1960s, reports began to spread through the domestic channels of *samizdat* and the foreign publication outlets of *tamizdat* that nonconformist citizens were being diagnosed with mental illnesses and confined to psychiatric hospitals. Such reports included transcripts of encounters with psychiatrists, official psychiatric records, independent evaluations of those records, personal accounts of hospitalization, letters to Soviet and Western authorities, manuals on aspects of compulsory treatment, poems, works of fiction, and more. Their authors ranged from former patients to concerned psychiatrists to compilers of unsanctioned journals that exposed violations of human rights. All were *inakomysliashchie*, that is, "differently thinking people" who shared the dissenting frame of mind of the writers profiled in subsequent chapters. Yet whereas those dissenting writers tended to adopt imaginative modes of expression, these figures stand out as dissidents for their political and social activism and their general (though not exclusive) preference for expressing their views in documentary form. Together, their psychiatric narratives reveal a shared perception that psychiatric abuse had resulted both from the ambiguity of psychiatric discourse itself and from the state's conflation of *inakomyslie*, or "thinking differently," with insanity. Drawing on literary techniques and traditions to invoke a community of creative individuals for whom *inakomyslie* was the psychological norm, dissidents depathologized themselves and pathologized the state.

However daunting imprisonment might be for citizens accused of political crimes, most dissidents argued that confinement to a *psikhushka* was worse.[1]

Unlike inmates of prisons and labor camps, patients confined to psychiatric hospitals could be detained indefinitely. Classified as "nonimputable"—the legal term for people deemed unable to evaluate and control their criminal actions as a result of mental impairment or illness—they were often prevented from representing themselves in court. Certain psychiatrists were known to subject healthy individuals to physical and psychopharmacological treatments that produced real and alarming signs of mental disorder. Release, moreover, was usually made contingent on the patient's acknowledgment of errors in reasoning. This last condition was particularly problematic for dissidents whose opinions were crucial to their sense of self and who therefore perceived such acknowledgment as "recantation." The dissident Viktor Fainberg wrote in a *samizdat* essay about the Leningrad Special Psychiatric Hospital that "from the moment a political prisoner arrives in a special psychiatric hospital, at the very first meeting the doctors offer the following choice: Renounce your beliefs or be confined indefinitely. As the head of the 11th department informed me in no uncertain terms, 'Your disease is *inakomyslie*.'"[2] Fainberg's report of his psychiatrist's acknowledgment of the term *inakomyslie* stands as an exception to the rule. Again and again in their psychiatric narratives, dissidents point out that what they describe as *inakomyslie*, their psychiatrists insist on labeling insanity. With each expression of dissent only increasing the likelihood of diagnosis, dissidents experienced punitive psychiatry as a discursive trap that tightened as patients struggled with it.

Harnessing their own discursive resources in order to disarm that trap, dissidents began producing psychiatric narratives that redefined their purported insanity as *inakomyslie*. As the dissident and former patient Leonid Pliushch wrote in the late 1970s, for instance, "There is a certain grain of truth in the claims of Soviet psychiatrists and KGB officers that everyone in the USSR who decides to stand up against the existing regime is psychologically abnormal. Indeed, a naked, sensitive conscience, an inability to live 'with lies' and evil, a poor adaptability to such a society—all these are signs that a person has crossed the borders of the conformist and philistine norm."[3] Pliushch depicts the politicization of psychiatry as a perversion of medical ethics. Yet he, like others who wrote on the topic, concedes that dissidents do manifest certain psychological differences that psychiatrists might pathologize. "Who among us has not found himself shouting 'Madman!' when seeing someone do something the motives of which we don't understand?" the dissident Aleksandr Podrabinek similarly asked in *Punitive Medicine*, the book-length report on psychiatric abuse that he completed in 1977.[4] Even as Pliushch, Podrabinek, and other dissidents criticized psychiatrists for pathologizing *inakomyslie*, they joined them in attributing political resistance to a distinctive state of mind. Those who expressed their dissent aloud were often aware that they might be pathologized. But for them, asserting their own authority and dismissing the authority of the state meant behaving as if they really did live in a society where *inakomyslie* was the norm.

Central to the critique of Soviet psychiatry was the charge that psychiatric discourse was itself ambiguous, paving the way toward subjective conclusions. As the dissident and former psychiatric patient Vladimir Bukovskii and the dissident psychiatrist Semen Gluzman stipulated in their "Manual on Psychiatry for Differently Thinking People," which they wrote and released in 1974:

> Mental illnesses can as a whole be split into two groups: 1) pseudo-illnesses that have tentatively been distilled from the chaotic pile of facts that have amassed over the centuries and declared to be independent forms, and 2) true illnesses with a cause known to science and a characteristic dynamic. If the model of the first is purely rhetorical, then the second kind is based on concrete scientific discoveries, and its models are "demonstrable."[5]

Drawing a line between "rhetorical" and "demonstrable" categories, Bukovskii and Gluzman present the former as ripe for misuse by physicians who practice what chapter 1 terms the "art of diagnosis." Yet even as they denounced the creative manipulation of psychiatric discourse, dissidents proved ready to manipulate that discourse in their own creative ways. The dissident mathematician Aleksandr Vol'pin disengaged from both literary and psychiatric discourses in protest at their ambiguity, proposing instead a legal discourse that would, in his view, resist politicization. By presenting his own case as evidence of the state's conflation of insanity and *inakomyslie*, however, he transformed himself into a living embodiment of the very ambiguity that he critiqued. Bukovskii and Gluzman meanwhile engaged with psychiatric discourse while urging their readers to subvert its ambiguities when conversing with psychiatrists. The majority of the narratives that dissidents produced were fact-based accounts and analyses of events. Yet even these documentary texts featured literary tropes and techniques, while the imaginative texts that dissidents also produced were overtly literary in both form and content.[6] Literature offered dissidents an authoritative prism through which to challenge psychiatry's art of diagnosis.

In addition to highlighting the ambiguity of psychiatric discourse, dissidents made use of that ambiguity to reverse the diagnostic gaze. "Thank God there are still some 'abnormal' people in our country—people who are not only psychologically healthy but also morally healthy, who imbue our spiritually sick society with a culture of freedom and democracy, and who as a result are condemned to confinement in psychiatric hospitals," Podrabinek wrote in his *Punitive Medicine*.[7] By embracing the term "abnormal" as a banner of health, Podrabinek not only exposes but also subverts its ambiguity to depict thinking differently as the psychological norm. Bukovskii meanwhile stressed the literary pedigree of inverting psychiatric discourse in this manner: "We weren't at all afraid to be called psychos," he wrote in his memoir. "On the contrary, we were glad of it: Let these fools consider us psychos—or rather the other way around, let these psychos consider us fools. We recalled all those books about madmen: [Anton] Chekhov, [Nikolai] Gogol, [Ryūnosuke] Akutagawa, and of course [Jaroslav Hašek's] *The Good Soldier Švejk*. We laughed our heads off at the doctors and ourselves."[8] Inverting the slur *psikh* to characterize representatives of the state, Bukovskii similarly both exposes and subverts the ambiguity of diagnosis. At the same time, he situates himself and others like him within a genealogy of literary writers who asserted their diagnostic authority in related ways.

But it was not only within psychiatric narratives that Soviet dissidents asserted their own diagnostic authority. Writing more broadly in the 1980s, for instance, the émigré dissident Yuri Glazov invoked the metaphor of madness to critique what he described as society's "behavioral bilingualism":

> A man who manipulates his behavior between what is officially allowed and what he personally and in a close circle reveals as his beliefs is in Soviet society considered a sane man, though actually he is a kind of schizoid. If any person is unable to behave himself on these two watertight levels of official and non-official thinking, speaking and behaviour, and proclaims his real thoughts in an unofficial way, he is considered by the officials to be an abnormal man and suffers from one of several possible forms of persecution, including confinement to a mental hospital."[9]

Glazov argues that what makes dissidents unique is their determination to be "monolingual in a society which allows only a schizophrenic existence."[10] Yet dissidents inhabited the overlap of insanity and *inakomyslie* in what might also be described, to develop Glazov's terminology, as distinctly "bilingual" ways. By demonstratively straddling two interpretations of their behavior, they projected their awareness of society's "schizophrenia" and thereby their own sanity. For them, the ambiguity of psychiatric discourse paradoxically enabled self-definition.

To be sure, the dissident tactic of redefining diagnosis was largely born of necessity. When it came to the reality of hospitalization, after all, dissidents were virtually powerless before psychiatrists. The more insistently they proclaimed their sanity, the more closely they could be said to fit the state's diagnostic categories. It was only in the pages of *samizdat* or *tamizdat* that they could subvert their subordinate position by mirroring the authoritative rhetoric of an idealized state that followed its laws and of an idealized psychiatry that resisted politicization.[11] This chapter explores this mirroring by examining both contemporaneous texts, many of them written for unsanctioned circulation, and retrospective texts printed in emigration or produced decades later. The further in time these psychiatric narratives are separated from the events they describe, the more confident and clearly articulated their redefinition of insanity as *inakomyslie* tends to become. Yet even texts produced in anticipation or immediate recollection of confinement highlight the ambiguities of diagnosis. The writing of psychiatric narratives allowed dissidents to assert their own authority in ways that were not possible in life.

The dissident campaign against Soviet psychiatric abuse unfolded concurrently with a Western critique of psychiatry that began in the early 1960s with the publication of several "antipsychiatric" studies suggesting that psychiatry was not an objective science but a pseudo-scientific guardian of social norms. The psychiatrists Thomas Szasz and R. D. Laing respectively described psychiatry as a form of social labeling and insanity as a stigma applied to those who could not or would not adapt.[12] The sociologist Erving Goffman characterized the psychiatric hospital as a "total institution" for imposing social norms and moral discipline.[13] Perhaps the most lastingly influential theoretical text, however, was the historian and philosopher Michel Foucault's *Madness and Civilization: A History of Insanity in the Age of Reason*, a study of the silencing and isolation of madness in France from the Renaissance through the Enlightenment and into the nineteenth century.[14] The popularization of antipsychiatric ideas across Western countries combined with the hardening of Cold War divisions to bring Soviet abuses to the world's attention. Following criticism of Soviet practices at the World Psychiatric Association's congress in Mexico City in late 1971, the *S. S. Korsakov Journal of Neuropathology and Psychiatry* dedicated the bulk of an issue to articles repudiating antipsychiatry. Among those articles was a review of

Foucault's study that asserted that "reading *Madness and Civilization* confirms that as soon as psychiatry departs from general pathology and the clinical-biological method, the conditions are created for the appearance of extreme views that lead to its repudiation."[15] By ignoring clinical realities in favor of anthropological and philosophical abstractions, the reviewer argued, the antipsychiatry movement had impugned psychiatrists everywhere.[16]

Ironically, however, the negative attention devoted to antipsychiatry helped to spread the movement's ideas among informed individuals within the Soviet Union. Rebuked for a lecture he gave at the Institute of Psychiatry in 1970, the young psychiatrist Iurii Savenko was advised to rehabilitate himself by preparing a second lecture, this time on the problem of antipsychiatry. Researching the material was an eye-opening experience for him, and he was not alone in reacting that way. He later recalled that his acquaintances also felt that the antipsychiatry movement's focus on psychiatry's repressive tendencies had captured something essential about the Soviet experience.[17] Bukovskii and Gluzman declared in their "Manual on Psychiatry" that what the antipsychiatrists had succeeded in showing was that "when categories become amorphous and 'scientific schools of psychiatry' multiply in number, the unjustifiable broadening of psychiatric expertise becomes a real possibility."[18] And indeed, the influence of antipsychiatry would prove long-lasting: twenty-seven years later, Savenko—now president of the Independent Psychiatric Association of Russia, a professional and human rights organization founded in 1989—would proclaim Foucault to be "one of the most pertinent thinkers from our perspective."[19] Trickling down through sanctioned and unsanctioned channels, Western antipsychiatric ideas informed the critical vocabulary through which Soviet dissidents exposed abuse.[20]

Yet even as dissidents applied antipsychiatric ideas to Soviet practices, they routinely rejected the movement's attacks on the science of psychiatry as a whole. "Alas, confinement is inevitable," Gluzman wrote in criticism of antipsychiatry in the 1980s. "'Antipsychiatric' schemes are as untenable as the next. A sick person who poses a danger to society must be confined like any lawbreaker who is conscious of his actions. But there is confinement and then there is confinement."[21] For Gluzman, as for others who protested the abuse of Soviet psychiatry, the repressive mechanisms that antipsychiatry revealed were typical less of the liberal societies that Foucault had described than of those authoritarian societies that violated their own laws and subordinated psychiatry to political agendas. Savenko and the psychologist Liubov' Vinogradova accordingly argued in 2005 that the word "antipsychiatry" was something of a misnomer when it came to Foucault, whose critique of psychiatry could instead be attributed to the discipline's own process of internal evolution. If "antipsychiatry" were taken to refer to arguments that violated or undermined psychiatry's most basic principles, Savenko and Vinogradova suggested, then "the most famous indirect form of antipsychiatry is the use of psychiatry for nonmedical purposes"—that is, political purposes. For Savenko and Vinogradova, being a conscientious psychiatrist meant declaring oneself an "anti-antipsychiatrist," who simultaneously opposed both psychiatric abuse and antipsychiatric calls for abolishing the discipline as a whole.[22] By focusing their critique of psychiatric practices on Soviet abuses in particular, psychiatrists and psychologists like Savenko, Vinogradova, and Gluzman preserved the possibility of an alternate psychiatry that could be trusted.

Whereas Foucault had based his critique of psychiatry on the model of modern France, with its rule of law and delegation of expertise to the scientific professions, dissidents thus attributed psychiatric repression to the lawlessness and political inference that they saw at work in Soviet psychiatry and society. As Podrabinek emphasized in *Punitive Medicine*:

> We believe that a system whereby people are confined to psychiatric hospitals for nonconformist behavior would be impossible in Western countries, and for that reason statements by antipsychiatrists apply to those people whom we believe to be mentally ill. However, those very same words seem to us entirely justified and indisputable when applied to Soviet conditions. The claims of the antipsychiatrists are just as fair when applied to our conditions as they are wrong, in our view, when applied to Western ones.[23]

Citing a 1976 article in the *Korsakov Journal* as his main source on antipsychiatry, Podrabinek reconfigures the quotations it cites from Szasz and Laing as evidence for his critique of Soviet psychiatry.[24] To the extent that they were aware of them, then, dissidents like Podrabinek repurposed antipsychiatric arguments to describe the Soviet state's legacy of authoritarianism. Indeed, they suggested that it was precisely by building a more liberal society that citizens would mitigate and possibly eradicate abuse. Reversing the doctor–patient hierarchy to cast themselves as law-abiding and independent psychiatrists to an irrational state, they behaved as if that liberal society was already in existence. "Like a paranoiac consumed with a fantastical idea," Bukovskii wrote in his memoir, "[the state] cannot and does not want to acknowledge reality; it turns its delirium into reality and forces its reasoning on everyone. We will never free ourselves from terror, we will never achieve freedom and security until we completely refuse to acknowledge these paranoid realities, until we counter them with our own realities, our own values."[25] Turning psychiatric discourse back on the state, Bukovskii suggests that only those who risk diagnosis by behaving as if they live in a healthier reality are capable of curing the Soviet madhouse.

Embodying the Ambiguity of Diagnosis

Aleksandr Vol'pin was born in 1924 to the poet and translator Nadezhda Vol'pin and the popular poet Sergei Esenin, who committed suicide in 1925. Looking back on his teenage years, Vol'pin would describe himself as an "unbalanced, agitated youth" with his own attraction to suicidal thinking.[26] Shortly after the German invasion of 1941, a military physician exempted him from duty by diagnosing him with schizophrenia at an examination so brief that Vol'pin would conclude that someone had likely pulled strings in his favor.[27] In 1949, he was arrested for "systematically conducting counterrevolutionary agitation, writing poems of an anti-Soviet nature and reading them to others."[28] Viewing hospitalization as preferable to imprisonment, he staged a suicide attempt to provoke a psychiatric evaluation and was confined to the Leningrad Special Psychiatric Hospital.[29] He was released to internal exile one year later, but the consequences of his actions proved longer-lasting. In 1957, Vol'pin was rearrested and confined to Moscow's Psychiatric Hospital No. 4, also known as the Gannushkin Hospital. Another arrest two years later prompted a lengthy detention at the Leningrad Special Psychiatric Hospital and several other institutions. Vol'pin was released in 1961, only to be targeted in the Soviet press after a bilingual collection of his poems and essayistic work titled *A Leaf of Spring* was published abroad, in *tamizdat*. The author responded by filing a lawsuit against the magazine *Ogonek* and one of its feuilletonists and by dispatching a letter of complaint to Nikita Khrushchev; as a result, he was once again hospitalized for several months.[30]

In late 1965, Vol'pin helped inaugurate what would become an annual tradition of "glasnost meetings" by circulating a "civic appeal" inviting people to gather on Moscow's Pushkin Square to demand a fair and open trial for the recently arrested writers Andrei Siniavskii and Iulii Daniel'.[31] Following the protest, which took place on December 5, KGB chief Vladimir Semichastnyi informed the Central Committee that a number of its organizers—Vol'pin and Bukovskii among them—were suffering from mental illnesses.[32] A memo by the Moscow City Committee pronounced a similar diagnosis upon Vol'pin, Bukovskii, and other participants before reporting that several had already been confined to psychiatric hospitals. But the underlying problem was broader, the City Committee noted:

> Given that certain literary organizations—for instance, the "Green Light" motorists' club—have seen a rise in the activity of the various questionable people and schizophrenics ([Vladimir] Batshev, [Iuliia] Vishnevskaia, etc.) who participated in this provocation, the Party's City Committee has taken measures to strengthen the leadership of the literary organizations with politically mature people and to purge them of their antisocial elements.[33]

Dissidents would later describe the trial of Siniavskii and Daniel' as a catalyst for social action. But with regard to the pathologization of unsanctioned creativity, it is significant that the City Committee interpreted that social action as evidence of the prevalence of mentally ill individuals within literary organizations, specifically.

Whereas Bukovskii was hospitalized in connection with the Pushkin Square protest, Vol'pin was detained and then released. Over the following years, however, he continued to attract the authorities' attention by appearing as a witness for the defense in Bukovskii's 1967 trial, supporting the dissidents Aleksandr Ginzburg, Iurii Galanskov, Aleksandr Dobrovol'skii, and Vera Lashkova during their Trial of the Four in 1968, and testing his legal right to emigrate by applying for a US visa.[34] According to one of the several transcripts he wrote of the events surrounding his final hospitalization, a policeman entered his apartment on February 14, 1968, along with a psychiatrist who said that Vol'pin was overdue for a checkup. Vol'pin demanded to see the psychiatrist's papers. Discovering that they had expired, he charged the psychiatrist with unlawful detention under Article 178 of the Criminal Code and with unlawful incarceration under Article 126.[35] Next he wrote a note asking his wife to "spread the word about this incident as widely as possible. As I write (hastily, as you see) this letter, I am preparing a little closing scene about my involuntary removal from my home."[36] He then told the psychiatrist, "You have not presented me with any documents proving your right to forcibly remove me. I do not accept that people might consider my hospitalization voluntary. Therefore, I will not voluntarily cross the threshold."[37] Two orderlies moved Vol'pin to the other side of the door, after which Vol'pin accompanied them to the ambulance. Upon arriving at Moscow's Psychiatric Hospital No. 1, also known as the Kashchenko Hospital, Vol'pin again refused to cross the threshold.[38] Vol'pin spent a total of two months at the Kashchenko Hospital and one month at Psychiatric Hospital No. 5, or the Stolbovaia Hospital, before a wave of domestic and international pressure secured his release.

Vol'pin challenged the diagnostic authority of his physicians by arguing that psychiatric discourse was too fraught with ambiguity to facilitate reliable communication. "The word 'schizophrenia' has no precise meaning," he explained in an interview. "If you bring together a group of psychiatrists and ask each one, 'What is schizophrenia?' each will give his own definition, and among those definitions there will be significant differences."[39] For Vol'pin, diagnosis was less a science than an art in its linguistic ambiguity and potential for manipulation. Seeking to bypass such ambiguity and manipulation, Vol'pin distanced himself from his own poetic efforts and confined himself during encounters with psychiatrists to what he portrayed as the rational language of Soviet law. He then produced a string of psychiatric narratives that projected his own legal authority. This two-part strategy, which reached its pinnacle with the 1968 transcripts, reflects Vol'pin's defining role in the formulation of Soviet "civil obedience," or the dissident tactic of demanding that both citizens and the state answer to the law. As Benjamin Nathans has shown, Vol'pin developed this stance as part of a larger project to conceptualize a transcendent means of communication. Vol'pin argued that people who take refuge in ambiguous language regularly fall victim to blind faith and error. The solution, he suggested, was to master modal logic, which analyzes the certainty with which pronouncements are made. Having honed their critical capacities, citizens would be able to read the constitution and legal codes with more precision and, as Vol'pin argued in his widely circulated *samizdat* manual "Juridical Instructions for People Facing Interrogation" (1969), prepare themselves to insist during interrogations that their investigators adhere to the letter of the law.[40]

It was precisely Vol'pin's emphasis on logic that his psychiatrists declared pathological, however. On March 6, 1968, a team of psychiatrists from the V. P. Serbskii Institute for Forensic Psychiatry declared that "over the last 6–7 months the patient's condition has worsened" and diagnosed Vol'pin with a shift-like form of schizophrenia characterized by "persistent paranoiac disorders."[41]

Vol'pin, however, did not soften his stance. Responding to friends' suggestions that he relax his legalism, he wrote in a letter released to *samizdat*, "I always avoided following advice of this sort and did so fairly openly. This is why many people consider me crazy. So let them."[42] Vol'pin knew that his civil obedience provoked diagnosis, yet according to his own psychiatric narratives, he scrupulously maintained it when addressing authorities. As he wrote about his decision to seek *tamizdat* publication of *A Leaf of Spring* in a draft of his letter to Khrushchev: "Was it pathological? Perhaps. I strove to be sincere without worrying about being called crazy. I do not know what constitutes a normal psychological state, and think that it is each person's right to maintain his psyche in whatever condition is compatible with his duties."[43] Highlighting both the ambiguity and manipulability of binary categories such as "normality" and "abnormality," Vol'pin acknowledges the likelihood that psychiatrists might take his *inakomyslie* for insanity. Yet for him, being "sincere" means maintaining his principles despite the diagnostic consequences. By embracing his pathologization to the extent that it overlapped with his own definition of sanity, Vol'pin turned himself into a living embodiment of the ambiguity of psychiatric discourse that legal discourse would theoretically dispel.

Though the danger of ambiguous language is thematically central to *A Leaf of Spring*, it reveals itself only gradually as the collection moves from Vol'pin's poems of the 1940s and early 1950s to the 1959 essay, "A Free Philosophical Treatise, or An Instantaneous Account of My Philosophical Views." In the essay, Vol'pin observes that literary discourse's irrational power renders poetry useful for catalyzing revolt: "Despite everything, I love poetry to this day, if only because fire is best fought with more fire, and the past illusions engendered by poems are best stamped out with the aid of new poems."[44] Yet the collection as a whole counters diagnosis by progressively rejecting both literary and psychiatric discourses in favor of a legal discourse that answers to logic and thus ostensibly lacks their ambiguity. Vol'pin confirms this movement in the collection's opening remarks by dating his most recent poems to those times in his life "when the atmosphere of spiritual oppression upset my balance."[45] Where the poetry of his youth had bred irrational expression, the collection implies, the logical rigor of "A Free Philosophical Treatise" illustrates his rationality.

Having yet to dedicate himself to logic, however, the teenage Vol'pin displaces diagnosis primarily by means of literary devices in the 1941 poem "Schizophrenia." The poem begins by loosely narrating the author's first encounter with psychiatrists:

... Я дождался конца болтовни докторов
И пошел к ней. Смеркалось.
Я вошел и сказал, что не буду здоров ...
—Рассмеялась!
... Я ей все рассказал (был белей мертвеца),
От конца до начала,—
Рассмеялась, как будто иного конца
От меня и не ждала ...
... А на улице тихо светила луна—
И не только поэтам:
В эту лунную ночь разыгралась война
Тьмы со светом,—
И она (если все это было во сне,—
Значит, сон лицемерил)
Говорила так долго, и все о войне ...
Я молчал и не верил,
Что сжигают Варшаву, Париж и Москву
Ради стран или денег:
Просто бьется в припадке, кусая траву,
Великан-шизофреник.

7/IX-1941[46]

... Having heard out the doctors' nonsensical spiel
I set off. It was evening.
I came in and announced I would now be unwell.
She started laughing!
... I reported it all (I was white as a corpse)
From the end to beginning—
And she laughed as if saying she'd always supposed
I would come to that ending ...
... But outside glowed the moon with that same quiet sheen
And not only for poets:
For that night was the start of a great war between
Daylight and darkness—
And then she (if all this was confined to a dream
Then the dream was misleading)
Kept on talking and talking with war as her theme ...

> I kept mum, not believing
> That Warsaw and Paris and Moscow could burn
> Just for borders or profits:
> It was simply the grass-biting seizure of a
> Schizophrenic colossus.
>
> September 7, 1941

The auspicious dateline establishes a poetic analogy between Vol'pin's diagnosis and three ambiguously overlapping historical prisms: the September 7, 1812, Battle of Borodino, at which Russia crippled Napoleon's army on its way to Moscow; the German invasion of Poland and bombardment of Warsaw in September 1939; and Adolf Hitler's invasion of the Soviet Union, which by September 7, 1941, was just reaching Leningrad. As the Moscow fires of 1812 blaze side by side with the Warsaw fires of 1939, and by extension with the Leningrad fires of the present day, time folds in on itself to suggest that little has changed. A similarly ambiguous collapsing of cultural references is generated by the use of the word *velikan*—translated here as "colossus" but also signifying "giant"—as the term harks back to Aleksandr Pushkin's and Mikhail Lermontov's descriptions of Napoleon and the Russian general Mikhail Kutuzov in their poems "Napoleon" (1821) and "Two Giants" (1832).[47] By contrast with Pushkin and Lermontov, Vol'pin does not specify the identity of his giant, a choice which serves to highlight the giant's eternally "schizophrenic" nature. What began as a description of Vol'pin's own encounter with psychiatrists harnesses the ambiguity of psychiatric and literary discourses to pathologize a society that compulsively goes to war.

Vol'pin conflates individual and worldwide madness through a host of sharply contrasting binaries ranging from the poet's own "misleading" dream to society's "great war between / Daylight and darkness." The peaceful indoor conversation between the poet and the woman stands in stark contrast to the war outside, while the calmness of the moon above conflicts with the chaos of the earth below. This schizophrenically ruptured setting is mirrored by a host of narrative models that similarly transform the poet's diagnosis into a metaphor for a world gone mad. The imprecise "nonsensical spiel" (*boltovnia*) of psychiatric discourse gives way to the poet's inverted retelling of it from end to beginning, and then to the woman's rambling speech, which stretches through the night as if lacking all order. The repetition of verbs beginning in *raz-* (*rassmeialas'*, *rasskazal*, *razygralas'*) likewise conveys fragmentation, while the dashes and ellipses lend the poem as a whole a halting and therefore disjointed momentum. The momentum is further impeded by the metrical structure: the tetrameter of the first and third lines of each of the five quatrains alternates with the irregular dimeter and monometer of the second and fourth lines, bringing the poem to abrupt and often unpredictable stops. Yet this fragmented structure only emerges by way of contrast with the regular *AbAb* rhyme and anapestic meter that the poet soberly maintains. The world may be succumbing to mental illness, but the poet's continuing artistic control stands as proof of his own capacity to regulate his actions.

"Schizophrenia" reveals the young Vol'pin's readiness to manipulate the ambiguity of psychiatric discourse by literary means. But this readiness lessened over time as Vol'pin grew suspicious of literary language and began responding to the ambiguity of diagnosis through the prism of logic. That Vol'pin announced this shift through the medium of poetry indicates that he was still divided, however. The decision may be clear in the 1946 verse "Whether I'm indeed my father's son . . . ," but how it will play out remains open to question:

> От отца родного ли рожден,
> Или непосредственно от славы,
> Любопытством тонким наделен,
> Презирал я детские забавы.
> В девять лет я знал, что на Луне
> Солнце днем горит на небе черном.
> Часто думал: вот куда бы мне . . .
> С этой целью стать решил ученым,
> И, презренья к жизни не тая,
> Лет в пятнадцать мыслил только строго . . .
> Для таких неистовых, как я,
> Кантором проложена дорога.
> . . . Переменны ранние мечты:
> Лет в семнадцать (это было летом),
> Полюбив доступность пустоты,
> Я едва не сделался поэтом,
> Но язык мой беден и смешон,
> А движенья вычурно-корявы . . .
> От отца родного ль я рожден
> Или непосредственно от славы?
>
> 23/I-1946[48]

> Whether I'm indeed my father's son,
> Or immediately born of glory,
> Nature made me curious from day one,
> And an ardent foe of children's stories.
> Learning at just nine that on the Moon
> Daytime can be when the sky is darkest,
> Often I would think: I'll go there soon …
> Leading me to choose the path of science,
> And I never hid my scorn for life
> At fifteen, for I sought only rigor,
> Those with raving natures like myself
> All too often go the way of Cantor.
> … Reveries of youth blow hot and cold,
> For at seventeen (one summer morning),
> Drawn by its admittance to the void,
> I almost made poetry my calling.
> But my tongue is feeble and inane,
> And my motion affected and flowery,
> Am I really my own father's son,
> Or immediately born of glory?
>
> January 23, 1946

The poem is, from its opening line, fundamentally concerned with parentage—both identifying it and determining its prognostic significance: "Whether I'm indeed my father's son, / Or immediately born of glory." And indeed, the issue of parentage was acute for the twenty-two-year-old Vol'pin, who not only had been born out of wedlock but also had a father whose psychiatric history was known. Esenin had been the alleged catalyst for an "epidemic" of copycat suicides that early Bolshevik critics had blamed on the decadence, individualism, and isolation that reportedly characterized his poetry and way of life and consequently "infected" Soviet society. Stories of Esenin's drinking and hospitalizations may also have loomed large for Vol'pin through the testimony of firsthand witnesses such as Vol'pin's own mother.[49] Describing Esenin in a 1984 memoir, for instance, Nadezhda Vol'pin raised the possibility of schizophrenia, the illness with which her son had later been diagnosed.[50]

At the heart of "Whether I'm indeed my father's son …" is thus the anxiety that, despite the poet-father's absence, his psychological condition may shape the son's development. Vol'pin responds by switching allegiance to another father figure, the Russian mathematician Georg Cantor, who died just six years before Vol'pin was born: "Those with raving natures like myself / All too often go the way of Cantor." Like Esenin, Cantor had suffered mental breakdowns and had been repeatedly hospitalized. But he also charted a career path for Vol'pin by spurning the arts and devoting himself to logical reasoning; indeed, his work in set theory would lay the foundations for Vol'pin's own research.[51] Though both father figures displayed pathological tendencies, then, they channeled them in different ways. Citing his own "raving" nature, Vol'pin points to the possibility that he too may be predisposed toward madness. Yet by tracing his lineage to Cantor rather than to Esenin, he redefines that predisposition as evidence of the logical mindset that will keep any pathological tendencies in check. And indeed, though the younger Vol'pin was known to introduce himself as "Esenin-Vol'pin," the appearance of the hyphenated surname on the cover of *A Leaf of Spring* prompted his older self to observe in a draft of his letter to Khrushchev that "I've long been tired of this pseudonym and wanted to free myself of it this time. I fear that now I shall never be able to do so."[52] Vol'pin's rejection of the "pseudonym" Esenin indicates that, by the early 1960s, his choice of father figures was set.

The poem begins with Vol'pin's birth and moves forward through chronological markers ("born," "at just nine," "at fifteen," "at seventeen," "one summer morning") that emphasize the poet's precision of memory and thought. Vol'pin describes his youth as a time of not only creative promise but also disorienting indecision between career paths. Both the choice of calling and its diagnostic implications are encapsulated by mention of the "Moon" (*Luna*), which to a literary writer might constitute a poetic metaphor but to a scientist constitutes a precise geographical destination that will one day be reached with the help of mathematical reasoning. Significantly, however, the moon also suggests "lunacy," confirming that the potential for madness dogs both trajectories. The creative individual must choose between literature and logic—and only the latter path will sustain his sanity. That the poet does choose logical order would seem to be reflected in the work's methodical *AbAb* rhyme structure and rigorously observed trochaic pentameter. But a sense of indecision remains in both his reluctance to jettison the poetic medium entirely and his closing reconfiguration of the opening lines: "Am I really my own father's son, / Or immediately born of glory?" Where the beginning of the poem appeared to wave aside the significance of the poet-father's legacy, the final question mark indicates the son's regret at having failed to embrace his poetic potential. The choice of logic over literature is an irreversible choice between potential selves, the final lines indicate by replacing the unstressed particle *li* with the stressed pronoun *ia*, or "I."

Within a few years of completing "Whether I'm indeed my father's son...," Vol'pin was making good on his promise to decisively abandon literature for logic. Written in the wake of Vol'pin's 1949 arrest and hospitalization, the poem "Fronde" lambastes the inaction and insanity that result from ambiguous language:

> Нам было пресно—петь псалмы на воле
> И лить елей, порядку не вредя,—
> И стыдно жить, гнилой урок твердя
> В наш гнусный век о прежнем произволе.
> И мы смеялись, как мальчишки в школе,—
> А славящим всемирного вождя
> Мы вторили, забавным находя:
> —Хвала, хвала великому Лойоле!
> ...И вот мы доигрались: мы в тюрьме...
> Крепки ли мы? Что нам грозит? В уме
> Мелькают безнадежные догадки...
> ...Мы запирались в солнечные дни
> Для самой беспокойной болтовни...
> ...Какая глупость—фронда без рогатки!
>
> Ленинград, тюрьма №2 (психбольница)
> 7/XI-1949[53]

> It bored us all to sing those psalms so sprightly,
> To pour libations and forgo the sword,
> And shamed us, in a time that we deplored,
> To testify to past oppression tritely.
> And just like little schoolboys we laughed lightly,
> And when they praised the universal lord,
> We gleefully repeated, word for word,
> "Bow down before Loyola the almighty!"
> ...So much for child's play: we're in the clink...
> Do we stand strong? What threatens us? We think
> In momentary bursts of hopeless guessing...

...On sunny days we'd lock ourselves inside
And anxiously talk nonsense side by side...
...What foolishness: a *fronde* whose sling is missing!
                              Leningrad, Prison No. 2 (psychiatric hospital)
                              November 7, 1949

Even as it explores the diagnostic consequences of language that embraces literary ambiguity, "Fronde" follows "Schizophrenia" in collapsing time through three historical prisms. In the first, the poet compares Joseph Stalin to Ignatius of Loyola, the sixteenth-century founder of the Jesuits and opponent of the Reformation. He recalls with bitterness how he and his friends took refuge in laughter and empty "psalms" instead of spurning literary language to speak out plainly. The second historical prism revolves around the Fronde (named after *fronde*, or "sling") a series of insurrections against the French crown in the seventeenth century. Like the *frondeurs*, the poet and his friends had talked of freedom. But because they did so from behind closed doors, their words had resulted in "nonsense" (*boltovnia*)—a language comprehensible only to themselves and, significantly, the same "nonsense" language spoken by the psychiatrists in "Schizophrenia." The third prism emerges in reference to the poem's own date of composition: November 7, or the anniversary of the 1917 Revolution. The ironic implication is that the Bolsheviks' once-inspired aim to wipe out tyranny has foundered like the aims of earlier revolutionaries.

    "Fronde" is the only poem in *A Leaf of Spring* that is explicitly linked to Vol'pin's stay in the Leningrad Special Psychiatric Hospital; the other poems composed there refer to a generic "prison," or *tiur'ma*. Rendered above as "in the clink," the words *v tiur'me* (literally "in prison") appear in "Fronde," as well. Yet Vol'pin emphasizes their psychiatric associations through explicit reference to the poem's place of composition and through their end-stressed rhyme with *v ume*—translated here as "think" but literally "in the mind"—in the poem's only couplet. Buried in the center of the sonnet as if to mirror the poet's captive state, the consecutive rhyme affirms a causal relationship between insanity and confinement. Those who think differently but fail to speak differently might as well be locked away, the poet implies, as all they have managed to do is dream up a reality that no one else shares and cultivate a language that no one understands. *Inakomyslie* indeed borders on madness when it embraces the ambiguity of literary discourse over logic-based communication, the poem as a whole suggests. Mounting dashes and ellipses capture the isolated and increasingly inarticulate nature of the poet's calls for reform and, indeed, cast doubt on the intelligibility of poetry itself. Playing on the word *fronde* ("a *fronde* whose sling is missing!"), Vol'pin urges his readers to cultivate a new language and to arm themselves in verbal revolt.

By 1959, Vol'pin's linked discomfort with literary and psychiatric discourses had reached a climax. Poetry, he explains in his essay "A Free Philosophical Treatise," is rife with ambiguity and therefore ripe for creative manipulation: "I will note that this defect in our reasoning is a paradise for poetry, which is right at home with this obscurantism. This is precisely why for the past eight years I have felt contempt for this art form which so drew me earlier."[54] However rousing, Vol'pin argues, literary discourse entrenches the fuzzy reasoning that keeps people enslaved. "We must free ourselves of the influence of people with their stunted language and find a scientific expression for the concept of freedom. Only when we achieve this will we be able to trust our thoughts, while until then they will be held captive by that language through which two-legged males and females ply each other with gifts."[55] Vol'pin accordingly repudiates his own poems; his only reason for including them in *A Leaf of Spring*, he states in the introductory remarks, is as evidence against the legality of his hospitalization. In 1949, he notes, he had been arrested primarily for his verse. Yet instead of imprisoning him, the state had treated his poems as evidence of mental illness and declared him nonimputable. Rather than engage with psychiatric discourse to refute his diagnosis on medical grounds, or with literary discourse to assert his poems' aesthetic merit, Vol'pin adopts a legal discourse that bypasses both psychiatry and literature to prioritize logic: "With regard to the official version of things, which casts me as nonimputable, I recommend that my intellect be judged by my scientific works and my poems."[56] Critiquing the pathologization of his poems from a logically consistent legal perspective, Vol'pin implies that it is the state that is prone to erroneous reasoning. At the same time, he invites the reader to join him as an expert who can judge both him and the state based on a similarly rational appraisal of evidence.

Vol'pin thus accompanied his critique of literary discourse with a logical critique of psychiatric discourse that exposed both the ambiguity of diagnosis and its potential for creative manipulation. What the state defines as a correct understanding of reality is actually rooted in ideologically motivated fictions, he suggests in "A Free Philosophical Treatise":

> [The state's ideological] principle would go something like this: In order to prove the necessary premise A, we will prove the similar premise B, and in this way we will consider A to have been proven.

The second postulate, without which they after all could not function, would go like this: A thinking person would not argue with us about whether B resembles A, as in that case he would not be a thinking person due to not understanding his personal or public usefulness.

And for the practical execution of their theory in life, they must add a third postulate, which—in the case of humane demagogues—consists of two parts:

a) He who does not understand his personal usefulness is sent to a madhouse;

b) He who does not understand his public usefulness is sent to prison or put to death.

In addition, the following principle is necessary for metatheory:

1) "To understand" means to understand as we understand, or sometimes as another person does;

2) He who does not want to understand something will not understand it.

At least this would be an honest system, the conclusiveness of which would be proven to all by postulates *a* and *b*, assisted by *1* and *2*.[57]

Vol'pin challenges the psychiatric distinction between sanity and insanity by encasing it within a logical proof. Whenever the state finds itself unable to prove an ideological concept, he asserts, it irrationally proves other concepts in its place. Anyone who rejects these substitutions is accused of intentionally or unintentionally not "understanding" the truth, and is duly punished by imprisonment or hospitalization. Yet as Vol'pin suggests in one of many admissions of his own non-understanding, befuddlement is the only defensible response to a nonsensical conception of reality: "I have avoided discussing the distinction between the Marxist terms 'metaphysical determinism' or 'fatalism' and 'dialectical determinism' because I do not know what 'dialectical determinism' means."[58] Vol'pin's pathologizable assertions of non-understanding acknowledge the discursive trap of diagnosis in such a way as to redefine *inakomyslie* as sanity. For him, it is the logically minded patient and not the psychiatrist who stands outside this ideological muddle and traces its fallacies back to their source.

Vol'pin's works suggest that, if psychiatric discourse indeed rivals literary discourse in the promotion of faith and commission of error, then punitively diagnosed individuals must find another framework for depathologizing themselves. For Vol'pin, this framework was legal discourse, since in his view the law—however imperfectly written—had the advantage of articulating a behavioral code to which the state and its citizens could be held to account. When Vol'pin disengaged from psychiatric discourse during his 1968 hospitalization, then, he did so by confining himself to the discourse of law. As he explained in a draft of a subsequent lawsuit against several psychiatrists:

> I do not intend, whether in this complaint or during these proceedings, to discuss matters with regard to which the burden of proof does not fall on me and which I am not procedurally required to clarify. Specifically, I am willing to set aside the question of whether I have a mental illness, since from a legal perspective the presence of one would not alone be sufficient justification for the use of compulsory hospitalization.[59]

Vol'pin translates his diagnosis from psychiatric discourse to legal discourse in much the same way as he shifted from literary discourse to legal discourse when discussing his poems in *A Leaf of Spring*. Rather than contest his "symptoms," he suggests that they do not, as described, prove nonimputability. He similarly asserted his legal authority by preparing transcripts of his 1968 conversations with psychiatrists such as the Serbskii Institute's Daniil Lunts. The following transcribed passage is highly indicative:

> Lunts: How do you relate to these hospitalizations? Do you consider them justified?
> Vol'pin: I consider them illegal. I consider the charges made against me—both times—to be juridically incorrect.
> Lunts: If I understood you correctly, you consider both instances of your commitment for compulsory treatment unjustified because you do not agree juridically with the legality of the charges against you?
> Vol'pin: Yes, that's exactly right. Incidentally, we are here to discuss medical questions, not juridical ones.[60]

Here, once again, Vol'pin bypasses psychiatric matters by rephrasing Lunts's question in legal terms. His barbed comment that the purpose of an examination is to "discuss medical questions, not juridical ones" implies to both Lunts and any potential readers that psychiatric discourse is incapable of mediating the unambiguous interaction that legal discourse facilitates. By rejecting psychiatric discourse for legal discourse both in reality and within his own psychiatric narratives, Vol'pin redefined his diagnosis as confirmation of his capacity for rational thought.

Dissidents criticized psychiatrists for equating the *samizdat* expression of *inakomyslie* with biographical insanity. Yet the consonance between Vol'pin's legalistic way of talking with psychiatrists and his legalistic way of writing psychiatric narratives suggests that Vol'pin did in fact treat his written works as an extension of life practice. If in reality Vol'pin invited diagnosis by behaving in pathologizable ways, on the pages of psychiatric narratives such as the following transcript from 1968, those behaviors could demonstrate his own authority:

> She [the psychiatrist], again: "Do you love your mother?" "In all likelihood." "I am asking if you love your mother very much." "Let's analyze this. My mother is a woman. I think that I love a woman if I prefer her presence to her absence, with the exception of those times when I prefer the opposite. I think that I love a woman very much if I prefer this means of preference to any other." "Well, now I have a clear picture: a typical case of autistic reasoning." She immediately prescribed me treatment with Aminazine, noting that if I did not take it voluntarily, I would get injections.[61]

Vol'pin's transcript draws attention to the physician's reliance on norms such as the expectation that a person should unquestioningly love his mother. But for Vol'pin, love is an arbitrary notion, making it impossible for him to answer the physician's question with a "yes" or a "no." The most accurate reply he can give is "in all likelihood." When pressed further, Vol'pin breaks down the question into elements he can address with certainty. The psychiatrist asserts her authority by diagnosing him with autistic reasoning and prescribing the antipsychotic drug Aminazine. By capturing the exchange in written form, however, Vol'pin asserts his authority as a logician to expose the irrationality and authoritarianism of the state.

Vol'pin's strategy for psychiatric examination rested on the twin assumptions that the law could indeed be interpreted in a logically consistent fashion and that psychiatrists who engaged in punitive hospitalization might one day be made to answer for their actions. These assumptions must be regarded as rhetorical gestures, however, in their idealistic positing of a legal discourse that could be unambiguously applied and in their implied prediction of a reversal of power that might bring dissidents justice. In his scientific work, as well, Vol'pin believed it was incumbent on researchers to follow ideas to their logical conclusions without regard to practical constraints:

> Nearly every scientist or engineer says to me, "These ideas got into your head, and perhaps they truly are very important, but you should be the first to try applying them." But what interested me were not the applications, but the very possibility of these ideas—the question of what "possibility" means, and so on. This is the logician's approach, and it would be difficult to expect anything else from me.[62]

Even Vol'pin's friends questioned whether the letter of the law had any relevance for a society in which the law was all too often ignored. "Alik's idea was brilliant and mad at the same time," Bukovskii later wrote of Vol'pin. "The idea essentially boiled down to not acknowledging reality but rather—like schizophrenics—living in our own imagined world, in the world that we would like to see."[63] As Bukovskii's conflation of insanity and *inakomyslie* implies, Vol'pin embodied the ambiguity of psychiatric discourse by turning his diagnosis into a defense of the normality of thinking differently. "I didn't have anything against being crazy as long as I was living there," Vol'pin later recalled of life in the Soviet Union. "So I'm crazy. What difference does it make? I'm freer to act as I like. It's even pleasant."[64] Diagnosis not only validated an alternate norm of dissent; it also ensured a measure of freedom.

Vol'pin's willingness to incur pathologization for behavior that he equated with sanity presages the critique of social adaptation that dissidents such as Aleksandr Solzhenitsyn would advance during the 1970s.[65] In the mid-1960s, however, such measures still struck many as extreme. When Vol'pin began organizing the Pushkin Square protest, "for many friends the first reaction was, 'You've lost your mind!'" his wife Viktoriia Vol'pina recalled. "But naturally they were in no position to change his mind by logical means, nor did he accept any arguments about the danger. He had a slogan: 'Down with the survival instinct and with moderation!' It was on this axiom that Alek based his relations with the government."[66] To the extent that Vol'pin made exceptions to this axiom, he did so in keeping with his commitment to logical consistency. Citizens could lie to investigators, he argued, but only if they first announced that they might not tell the truth.[67] Similarly, citizens on the stand could hedge their words to avoid pathologizable displays of non-understanding. "Unfortunately, it is very risky to answer negatively when asked 'Do you understand the charges?' since that will supply the investigation with the excuse to have you sent for psychiatric evaluation," Vol'pin wrote. "Better to answer more delicately: 'Not entirely, as certain words in the charge have dual meanings.'"[68] When the law was indeed deployed in ambiguous ways, Vol'pin allowed for the possibility that dissidents might take refuge in those ambiguities. Loopholes rather than exceptions, however, such limited acts of self-preservation highlight the overall consistency of Vol'pin's legalistic stance.

Subverting the Ambiguity of Diagnosis

Where Vol'pin disengaged from psychiatric discourse to assert himself as a legal authority, the dissidents Vladimir Bukovskii and Semen Gluzman advocated strategic engagement to convey the message of mental health. Bukovskii, who was born in 1942 and and matured as an activist under Vol'pin's influence after meeting him in 1961, supported the older man's commitment to civil obedience.[69] He reiterated this commitment in his memoir, arguing that "power is submission; it is the willingness to comply. For this reason each person who refuses to comply with violence decreases this violence by precisely one two-hundred-and-fifty-millionth."[70] Such statements aside, however, Bukovskii and Gluzman regarded the punitive uses of psychiatry as dice so loaded by the authorities that some degree of accommodation was justifiable and even advisable. The dissident under evaluation was caught within a discursive trap, they reiterated in their contemporaneous and retrospective writings: what he or she deemed sane behavior would likely be taken for evidence of insanity. Communicating with psychiatrists was no moral failure under such circumstances; it was a matter of self-preservation.

Yet even survival strategies could double as gestures of dissent, Bukovskii and Gluzman indicated by subverting the ambiguity of diagnosis to postulate an alternate psychiatry that would not engage in punitive pathologization. Bukovskii, a one-time biology student who had turned to political activism in his teens, was arrested in 1963 for possessing several copies of the Yugoslav dissident Milovan Djilas's book *The New Class*; in 1965 for helping Vol'pin to organize the December 5 demonstration in Pushkin Square against the trial of Siniavskii and Daniel'; in 1967 for organizing another public meeting to protest the arrests of Aleksandr Ginzburg, Iurii Galanskov, Aleksandr Dobrovol'skii, and Vera Lashkova; and in 1971 for circulating *samizdat*, slandering the Soviet Union to foreign journalists, and accusing Soviet psychiatrists of hospitalizing dissidents.[71] Bukovskii's evidence for psychiatric abuse stemmed partly from his own lengthy hospitalizations in 1963 and 1965; after his 1971 arrest, the Serbskii Institute would reevaluate him and declare him imputable. But his ongoing campaign also reflected his efforts to demonstrate that such abuses were widespread. Following revelations of the hospitalization of other *inakomysliashchie*, Bukovskii obtained forensic reports on six dissidents and, in the winter of 1970–71, dispatched them to foreign psychiatrists for independent examination. The cover letter he included engages with psychiatric discourse by positioning its addressees as guardians of their profession's integrity. Rather than contest their diagnostic authority, it deferentially states that "only psychiatric specialists are qualified to speak authoritatively about the degree to which the [diagnostic] conclusions can be trusted."[72] Moreover, it likens the movement against psychiatric abuse to recent protests by Soviet physicists against the proliferation of nuclear weapons. Acknowledging the limitations of evaluations conducted "in absentia," or without immediate access to the patient, Bukovskii recommends that his addressees confine their judgment to the files themselves: "Therefore I ask for your opinion only on the following question. Do the conclusions presented here contain enough scientifically grounded data to come to not only a finding of mental illnesses, but also a finding of the necessity of strictly isolating these people from society?"[73] Bukovskii counters the art of diagnosis by invoking an alternate psychiatry that retains its "scientific" credibility. At the same time, his person-to-person mode of address disrupts the Soviet psychiatric monologue to launch a dialogue between himself, a former patient, and representatives of that alternate psychiatry.

Following his arrest in 1971 and trial the following January, Bukovskii was sentenced to two years in prison, five years in labor camps, and another five years of internal exile. It was at the Perm-35 camp that he first met Gluzman, a Ukrainian psychiatrist and the author of an unofficial reevaluation of the dissident military officer Petro Grigorenko. Born in 1946, Gluzman embarked on his own path toward dissidence in the late 1960s when, having read a *samizdat* article on punitive psychiatry, he decided that the subject merited professional inquiry. Like Bukovskii, Gluzman conceptualized his intervention as a psychiatric version of the dissident physicist Andrei Sakharov's protest against the proliferation of nuclear arms. He soon focused his attention on the case of Grigorenko, who had been punitively hospitalized first from 1964 to 1965 and then again in 1969. Acquainting himself with forensic psychiatric practices, Gluzman obtained copies of Grigorenko's *samizdat* writings and psychiatric reports. He then spent a year composing his "In Absentia Forensic Psychiatric Report on the Case of Petro Grigor'evich Grigorenko," with help from the psychiatrist Fima Vainman and the typist Liuba Seredniak, before forwarding it to Sakharov in Moscow. Following Gluzman's 1972 trial for anti-Soviet agitation and propaganda and his subsequent imprisonment, Sakharov released the report to *samizdat*.[74]

Gluzman built his investigation on an extensive body of written and oral sources: the psychiatric reports from Grigorenko's KGB file, individual testimony by family and friends, and Grigorenko's own writings on military affairs and human rights. The psychiatrist later described the experience of reading these documents as a personal interaction with Grigorenko himself:

> This utter stranger, who was at that moment being compulsorily treated in a special hospital run by the Ministry of Internal Affairs, became more and more comprehensible to me. And more and more familiar. My understanding of the logic of his actions and thoughts became ever clearer. Intelligent and sincere, he was trying to explain himself to a brick wall. He tried to be clear and honest when talking to doctors, while they described his logic and honesty in rigid psychiatric terms. The more sincere his words, the more pronounced the psychiatric symptoms with which they labeled him.[75]

For Gluzman, as for other dissidents, the pathologization of *inakomyslie* was a discursive trap built from "rigid psychiatric terms" that were ultimately ambiguous in meaning. By increasing awareness of that ambiguity and its potential for manipulation, Gluzman sought to relegitimize his profession. "The discovery that my field was being used to punish *inakomysliashchie* was more than I could physically bear," he would later recall.[76] Where Vol'pin had disengaged from psychiatric discourse, Gluzman, who was a trained psychiatrist, engaged with its terminology. For him, as for Bukovskii, fighting abuse meant challenging punitive diagnosis from within.

Gluzman thus contests Grigorenko's diagnosis through both the prescribed narrative structure of the forensic report and the discursive framework of diagnostic categories. As is demonstrated in chapter 1, contemporary psychiatric practice stipulated that forensic reports begin with an overview of legal questions before moving on to the patient's biography, a summary of the psychiatrists' observations, a statement of their diagnostic conclusions, and an overview of their legal recommendations. Signaling its adherence to psychiatric discourse, Gluzman's report largely stays true to this structure. Following an "Introduction" discussing punitive psychiatry, a section titled "Juridical Foundation" asserts Gluzman's right to evaluate Grigorenko in absentia. A section titled "Biographical Information" then lists the facts of Grigorenko's personal and psychiatric history, after which an "Analytical Section" pits Gluzman's interpretation of those facts against the conclusions drawn by state psychiatrists. Describing Grigorenko's diagnosis as a *postroika*, or "construction," on the part of those physicians, Gluzman draws attention to the art of diagnosis by demonstrating the ease with which a person's life can be made to fit the progression of a disease.[77] Yet rather than reject psychiatric discourse entirely, he models a more critical approach to it by following the forensic practice of saving his diagnostic and legal opinion for the report's "Concluding Section." Grigorenko, Gluzman declares, is both sane and imputable, and if any legal action is to be taken, it should be directed against his psychiatrists.

Even as he challenges Grigorenko's diagnosis, then, Gluzman signals his allegiance to the psychiatric discourse that he and Grigorenko's examiners share. "We have based our work on the theoretical tenets of current Soviet psychiatric science and on the practical experience of forensic psychiatry within this country as a branch of psychiatry generally," he writes before invoking his authority as a psychiatrist to systematically review Grigorenko's reports.[78] The facts as Gluzman presents them are as follows. Grigorenko was first declared nonimputable in 1964, when psychiatrists at the Serbskii Institute diagnosed him with a "paranoid development of personality stemming from early cerebral arteriosclerosis."[79] Asserting that he had made a full recovery, physicians at the Leningrad Special Psychiatric Hospital released him in 1965.[80] In 1969, Grigorenko was arrested in Tashkent, where in August of that year a local team of psychiatrists declared him both sane and imputable.[81] By November, however, he had been reclassified as nonimputable by a team of Serbskii Institute psychiatrists, who diagnosed him with a "pathological (paranoiac) development of personality with ideas of reformism formed in a personality with psychopathic traits of character and early signs of cerebral arteriosclerosis."[82] Highlighting the discrepancies between the Serbskii Institute's 1964 and 1969 reports, Gluzman surmises that the psychiatrists altered their earlier diagnosis largely upon realizing that it would not accommodate ideas of reformism. By describing Grigorenko's diagnosis as a "paranoiac," rather than "paranoid," development of personality with ideas of reformism that were attributable to "psychopathic traits of character" as well as to "early cerebral arteriosclerosis," Gluzman argues, the psychiatrists "constructed" the diagnosis they required.[83]

Gluzman supplements this argument with sub-points that model a more accountable deployment of psychiatric discourse. He revisits Grigorenko's biographical documentation to conclude that the Serbskii Institute psychiatrists had no basis for finding an early progression toward illness; he points to real-life events that establish the real-life basis for Grigorenko's supposed delusions; he charges the psychiatrists with making selective use of primary evidence; and he criticizes the Serbskii Institute reports for tending toward generalizations.[84] Throughout, however, he stresses that his concern is less with psychiatric discourse itself than with its manipulation by practitioners. Stressing the ambiguity of one of Grigorenko's forensic reports, he declares that "a psychological profile written in this manner is professionally illiterate, since 'productive psychopathological symptoms' and 'rigidity and circumstantiality' carry starkly different diagnostic connotations and in no way reinforce each other; the use between them of the word 'however' is therefore unjustified."[85] The "illiterate" deployment of psychiatric discourse engenders ambiguity and facilitates the pathologization of rational political ideas, Gluzman argues:

> As psychiatrists, we do not take it upon ourselves to analyze and judge the sociopolitical problems connected with [Grigorenko's political] organization and its pamphlets; but the unwillingness of the investigative authorities to conduct a competent and scientific textological evaluation of the pamphlets (a violation of the law in its own right) forces us to evaluate their contents as a whole, inasmuch as it is possible.[86]

Though Gluzman does go on to analyze Grigorenko's writings, the reluctance he expresses is indicative. If he is forced to use his psychiatric expertise to depathologize Grigorenko's political views, then it is because state practitioners have been the first to expose psychiatric discourse to political interference.

Gluzman uses psychiatric discourse to do more than negate Grigorenko's diagnoses, however; he also deploys it when making a positive case for Grigorenko's sanity. A provocative speech that Grigorenko gave in 1941 thus becomes a demonstration of mental health in that it stood "in full accord with his convictions, his way of thinking, was logical, flowed directly from his previous life, and was based in reality and hard facts."[87] The subject's activities in the 1940s and 1950s similarly "testify to the complete preservation of Grigorenko's intellectual and adaptive capacities."[88] In short, Gluzman concludes, Grigorenko's reasoning and behavior "constitute a unified progression of mental life, in which each period flows naturally from the one that preceded it and is never interrupted by unexpected and incomprehensible actions, judgments, and statements."[89] Drawing on his own professional training, Gluzman makes use of psychiatric discourse to argue for Grigorenko's sanity. Moreover, he argues for Grigorenko's normality by twice citing the Tashkent psychiatrists' contention that Grigorenko's views are typical of his milieu.[90] Normality, Gluzman concludes, must accommodate the possibility of thinking differently and translating that difference into social action. "But can we really dismiss the criticism of errors, however 'high-ranking,' as pathological reasoning?" Gluzman asks. "No, such acts have occurred over and over again in the development of society, and although they are typical of only a relatively small number of people with a critical turn of reasoning and character, they in no way constitute a mental pathology."[91] For Gluzman, *inakomyslie* is a specific cast of mind that indicates insight and not insanity.

Arrested in 1972 and sentenced to seven years of labor and three years of exile, Gluzman found himself confined alongside Bukovskii in the Perm-35 labor camp. The camp held other political prisoners who were interested in learning more about punitive psychiatry, so not long after making each other's acquaintance, Bukovskii and Gluzman presented them with a lecture on the topic.[92] Bukovskii then suggested to Gluzman that their joint perspective might be of use to a wider audience. "He convinced me by saying, 'Listen, you and I are a very unusual pair. You're a psychiatrist; I'm a former psychiatric victim. So this will be very serious from the point of view of publicity,'" Gluzman recalled in an interview.[93] What emerged was their "Manual on Psychiatry for Differently Thinking People," a *samizdat* handbook for psychiatric examination. Gluzman wrote his sections of the manual while working in the camp hospital. Several months later, his draft disappeared from its hiding place; the sections written by Bukovskii, who had meanwhile been transferred to prison in Vladimir, were preserved. Gluzman found an opportunity to rewrite his own portions when tasked with repairing the roof of a house. Having convinced another prisoner to do the repairs for him, he wrote while every so often hammering on the roof. The pamphlet was bound into a capsule and given to Valerii Rumiantsev, a former KGB officer who had been prosecuted for telling foreigners about his organization's activities and who was just then completing his sentence. Rumiantsev transported the capsule to Moscow and delivered the documents to Iulii Daniel', who released them into *tamizdat* and *samizdat*.[94]

Like Bukovskii's letter to foreign psychiatrists and like Gluzman's "In Absentia Report," the "Manual on Psychiatry" engages with psychiatric discourse. Yet significantly it does so by referencing the literary tradition of psychiatric narratives and subverting psychiatric discourse through the literary device of parody. Bukovskii and Gluzman thus cast their primer as a pragmatic and psychiatry-specific alternative to Vol'pin's "Juridical Instructions." The punitive examination is a uniquely lawless space, they argue, rendering legalistic strategies likely counterproductive. Indeed, it is precisely in order to bypass the law that investigators often turn to psychiatric hospitalization:

> A. Vol'pin's "Instructions" on behavior under investigation, which are widely known to readers of *samizdat*, now appear to have one significant drawback: the "juridical position" that A. Vol'pin recommends for investigation (demanding that the investigator respect the letter of the law, knowing in detail and asserting one's legal rights) prevents the investigator from conducting your case "cleanly," intimidating your witnesses during confrontations, playing around with testimonies in interrogation files, and so on. This exhausts the investigator and forces him to examine you for psychological defects and to petition to have you sent for psychiatric evaluation.[95]

Adhering to legal discourse may provoke pathologization, Bukovskii and Gluzman caution their readers; differently thinking people should therefore temper their legalistic stance with a cynical pragmatism. Gluzman later reiterated the point: "I think our text is more frightening than Vol'pin's precisely because it shows that it was impossible to defend oneself within this system of Soviet legal coordinates."[96] For Bukovskii and Gluzman, the only way to ward off diagnosis, or at least to ease conditions of treatment, was to engage with psychiatric discourse.

Like Vol'pin, both Bukovskii and Gluzman argued that those examined for political reasons were unlikely to alter their fate: "It goes without saying that should a psychiatrist make it his goal to pathologize you, any answer or action on your part may be evaluated accordingly."[97] Yet rather than advise disengaging from psychiatric discourse, Bukovskii and Gluzman urged their readers to subvert it by manipulating its ambiguities for themselves. "I translate into their language the fact that I am sane," Bukovskii explained in an interview. "Language is not a luxury. It's a way of communicating. As long as you can communicate a correct message, the language performs its function."[98] Despite the fact that Vol'pin's literalist legalism constituted an effort to transcend miscommunication, Bukovskii and Gluzman feared that it would backfire in the psychiatric setting. "The twentieth century has brought us face-to-face with the problem of communicability," they write in their manual. "Today representatives of different professions who speak the same language have trouble understanding each other. In the psychiatrist's office too much will depend on your ability to communicate."[99] In order to overcome this barrier, the authors argue, differently thinking people should acquaint themselves with psychiatric discourse. They should remember that their physicians define sanity and insanity differently than they do, and choose their words carefully to convey the right message: "You will have the opportunity to evaluate the psychiatrist's intellectual level and way of leading a conversation. Your task is to speak with him 'in the same language, on the same conceptual level.'"[100] For the differently thinking person who grasps the ambiguity of diagnosis, communicating with psychiatrists means putting that ambiguity to use.

What, then, does conveying the message of sanity involve? According to the manual, the first step is to present oneself in accordance with the social norms on which psychiatrists base their diagnoses. Bukovskii and Gluzman parody these norms in a sample biography that reads like a mock hagiography:

> You were born a healthy child, learned to sit up, walk, and talk on time. [...] You shared the interests of your age-group and circle: You loved movies, books (but not only "science fiction"), games; you felt love for family members, shared your family's interests and concerns. [...] Keeping in mind what you already know about the psychology of the psychiatrist, do not show any interest in contemporary "modern" art or, especially, any understanding of it. You do not confine your free time to autistic pursuits such as reading, gardening, contemplation of nature, and works of art.[101]

The biography acts as both a practical primer on psychiatric discourse and a literary parody of social norms. The "normal" citizen does not think differently; indeed, he barely thinks at all. He prefers material pleasures to spiritual contemplation, and communal activities to isolated pursuits. His aesthetic tastes are for the literal and comprehensible: realism rather than fantasy, representation rather than abstraction. The less he understands of modern art that violates state-sanctioned norms, the saner he is seen to be. (Gluzman's own poetry typifies the language that this normal person might avoid: it is spiritual, impressionistic and often free of meter and rhyme, and when it does deploy the rhetoric of madness, it uses it to convey either numb indifference or creative inspiration.)[102] Moreover, the normal citizen speaks to physicians simply and directly, without resorting to literary language: "Try not to use expressions that could be judged 'symbolic associations' (to take an example from Grigorenko's experience: when he was asked a question about the 'motives' for his 'antisocial activity,' Grigorenko replied: 'I couldn't breathe.')."[103] The art of performing normality is to make the performance as artless as possible.

Even as it engages with psychiatric discourse, then, Bukovskii and Gluzman's manual harnesses literary tropes and techniques to challenge that discourse's unscientific deployment. "All of our recommendations are geared toward an 'aggregate dissident,'" the authors write, parodying the classificatory terminology of contemporary psychiatry.[104] At times the parody goes so far as to turn psychiatry's diagnostic lens back on itself. Bukovskii and Gluzman thus describe the normal Soviet citizen as a "rentier living off his investments." This rentier, they continue, "is a person of average intellect, bourgeois tastes; civilized rather than cultured, averse to risk . . ., content with a modest but stable social position ('it's a long way down'), not easily carried away; lacking any creative ability, a firm supporter of authority; his guiding principle in life is his survival instinct."[105] Who, then, fits this social norm? It later emerges that the state's model for normality is the average psychiatrist himself.[106] Bukovskii and Gluzman structure their text in such a way as to expose psychiatry's reflexive reasoning. If the sample biography belongs to none other than the psychiatrist, then the ideal interaction between the psychiatrist and the patient is not a dialogue but the monologue of a doctor who is talking to himself.

Bukovskii and Gluzman reverse the diagnostic gaze by turning the art of diagnosis into a creative opportunity on the part of differently thinking patients. It is thus the physician and not the patient who undergoes psychiatric evaluation, falling into one of six categories that parody the classificatory emphasis of diagnosis. The Novice Psychiatrist believes in the therapeutic aims of his profession, the authors write.[107] The Researcher is likewise a believer but prefers not to involve himself in forensic evaluations. The patient may recognize the Dissertator for his eagerness to turn the patient into a subject of research. The Voltarian is a lover of art and literature; as a physician, he is disillusioned with his profession, but his "cowardly" disposition prevents him from pursuing reforms.[108] More dangerous is the Philistine, a typical rentier who "does not understand phenomena such as surrealist art ('Can horses really fly?'), contemporary poetry ('But where are the rhymes?'), and so on"; talk of philosophy and art should therefore be avoided. And the patient is virtually powerless before the Professional Executioner, who consciously pathologizes healthy individuals.[109] Bukovskii and Gluzman's six-part classification of physicians—which Gluzman explicitly described as an "artistic representation"—parodies psychiatric discourse in literary ways to assert its own diagnostic authority.[110]

Dissidents attributed the politicization of psychiatry to the ambiguities of psychiatric discourse while channeling those ambiguities in different ways. Vol'pin disengaged from them in conversation with psychiatrists and in his writings, yet in doing so he transformed himself into a living embodiment of the ambiguity of *inakomyslie* and insanity. By contrast, Bukovskii and Gluzman engaged with psychiatric discourse both sincerely, when appealing to the professional integrity of psychiatrists, and parodically, when manipulating diagnostic terms to communicate a message of sanity. "It's like you have a convoluted mirror and it reflects a wrong picture," Bukovskii recalled. "It's a lie. So I would have to change my face in such a way as to get a correct face."[111] For Bukovskii, the need to convince psychiatrists that one was sane superseded the imperative of sincere self-expression. Though Bukovskii and Gluzman did not go so far as to advocate full recantation, Bukovskii's memoir suspends judgment of those who did recant under pressure from psychiatrists.[112] The parodic profile of the normal citizen accordingly ends with a sample explanation for how the patient came to question authority:

> Your *inakomyslie* arose under the influence of books, stories of eyewitnesses and victims of repression, your family and school upbringing (if circumstances allow you to bring up these details painlessly), as a result of a sober, objective appraisal of reality. However unpleasant it may be, the best motivation you can offer for the actions being imputed to you is: "I wanted to be famous, to become well known; I did not understand the seriousness of the consequences, I did not look at myself from an outsider's perspective; I did not realize I had gone too far," and so on.[113]

Far from constituting a serious recommendation that *inakomysliashchie* shrug off responsibility for their actions, this passage illustrates how they might subvert psychiatric discourse in such a way as to convey their suggestibility. If the patient has been corrupted by society, after all, then he or she can theoretically also be influenced for the better. By urging their readers to become conversant with the "outsider's perspective" of psychiatric discourse, Bukovskii and Gluzman provided them with a strategy for controlling the lines of communication with the state.

The Alternate Norm of Thinking Differently

As the discursive trap of diagnosis tightened in the 1960s and 1970s, dissidents redefined insanity as *inakomyslie* by disseminating news of punitive psychiatry. Their unsanctioned accounts invoked a community of differently thinking people who confronted psychiatric discourse in such a way as to assert their own diagnostic authority. Although the assertion of such authority was unlikely to avert psychiatric detention in any immediate sense, its proposition of an alternate norm of thinking differently suggested a law-bound alternative to what dissidents perceived as the continuing authoritarianism of life after Stalin. Moreover, it acted as a therapeutic comfort for dissidents who feared they might indeed go mad under the psychological or pharmaceutical pressures of diagnosis and hospitalization. Several months after Leonid Pliushch's confinement to the Dnepropetrovsk Special Psychiatric Hospital, the dissidents Tat'iana Khodorovich and Iurii Orlov released an article titled "They're Turning Leonid Pliushch into a Madman. To What End?" Attributing Pliushch's decline primarily to the effects of medication, the authors declare that "Pliushch is being deprived of his reason, he is perishing spiritually, he is losing his 'I,' that very 'I' that distinguishes him from other people; in a word, he is ceasing to be a NORMAL PERSON."[114] And indeed, as Pliushch would later confirm, "I became increasingly afraid that I would help my executioners by really losing my mind."[115] For Pliushch and other dissidents who experienced and exposed the punitive uses of psychiatry, "normality" meant both thinking differently and translating those thoughts into words and action.

Dissidents experienced psychiatric diagnosis as an isolation and a silencing akin to what Foucault describes in *Madness and Civilization*. Where reason and unreason had once engaged in dialogue, Foucault argues, the modern period erected in that dialogue's place the "language of psychiatry, which is a monologue of reason *about* madness."[116] And indeed, to revisit chapter 1's application of Mikhail Bakhtin's terms, Soviet psychiatric discourse was distinctly "monologic" in both its projection of authority and unity and its aversion to diversity and exchange. What dissidents were determined to show was that their silencing and isolation had not been "total," in the words of Foucault: "Confinement, prisons, dungeons, even tortures, engaged in a mute dialogue between reason and unreason—the dialogue of struggle."[117] In answer to the monologism of psychiatric discourse, dissidents cultivated a "dialogic" discourse that embraced singularity, irony, and open-endedness. For them, the silencing and isolation of diagnosis could be shattered by the dialogism of thinking differently.[118]

Crucial to validating this alternate norm was the recruitment of psychiatrists who would themselves be ready to engage in dialogue. Vol'pin thus ended one of his 1968 transcripts by declaring that, "in the event of this document's circulation, I invite all the members of the commission to append any objections, additions, and corrections that may arise."[119] Vol'pin's provocative suggestion that punitive psychiatrists join his struggle posits a psychiatrist-patient dialogue that depathologizes rather than pathologizes *inakomyslie*. Bukovskii invoked a similar dialogue by releasing dissidents' reports to foreign psychiatrists, while Gluzman's "In Absentia Report" demonstrated that such psychiatrists could be found within the Soviet Union itself. Gluzman and Bukovskii's "Manual on Psychiatry" in turn modeled the dialogic exchange that might unfold between such psychiatrists and their patients. And in 1974, Khodorovich imagined the reversal of norms that would take place when Pliushch's sanity was established: "For me, L. Pliushch is not only *more normal* than the state psychiatrists who punished him, he is more normal than the entire department by whose bidding that punishment was so slavishly organized. It would be far more fruitful to examine the logic of *their* personalities and actions from the perspective of the psychiatric norm, and I think that sooner or later this investigation will take place."[120] In 1977, Khodorovich's vision materialized with the founding of a dissident group called the Working Commission to Investigate the Use of Psychiatry for Political Purposes, which, for several years, released bulletins on psychiatric detention and used apartments as walk-in clinics where dissidents could be prospectively or retrospectively evaluated. While the reports it produced were not publicly released, the Working Commission regarded the KGB's regular surveillance of their activities as insurance against subsequent hospitalization. "The very fact that an evaluation had taken place became a defense against psychiatric abuse," Podrabinek later recalled.[121] If psychiatric narratives rhetorically invoked a physician-patient dialogue that validated rather than stigmatized dissent, then the Working Commission turned that dialogue into a lived reality.

The *samizdat* literature on psychiatric detention challenged the silencing and isolation of diagnosis by dialogically illustrating the normality of *inakomyslie*. Yet even individual texts embraced dialogue as a literary technique and invoked a community of creative dissenters. In February 1968, for example, the dissident poet Natal'ia Gorbanevskaia sought treatment for complications of pregnancy only to find herself transferred to the Kashchenko Hospital. Following her release, she compiled her letters to friends and family, adding commentary to each, in a *samizdat* sketch titled "Free Medical Assistance." The sketch puts Gorbanevskaia's past and present selves in literary dialogue, illustrating the diagnostically suspect norm of thinking differently. Over the course of the account, the past self gradually becomes aware of what the present self already knows:

Gorbanevskaia has become the latest victim of punitive psychiatry. "Well, why are they holding me here?" the past self asks on February 14, when she has been refused release from the maternity ward.[122] The present self clarifies matters by interjecting that news of Vol'pin's hospitalization arrived the following day. This is followed by the past self's conclusion, in a letter dated February 15: "Now I see that they have most likely decided to put me away in the same place as Alik."[123] Gorbanevskaia's dialogue between past and present selves rhetorically illustrates the increased understanding that dialogue can generate.

As becomes clear by the end of the narrative when the past self likens herself to Iurii Galanskov, another dissident poet who had been hospitalized, the alternate norm of thinking differently is rooted in a sense of literary belonging.[124] The present self thus appends a poem dedicated directly to Galanskov:

В сумасшедшем доме
выломай ладони,
в стенку белый лоб,
как лицо в сугроб.

Там во тьму насилья,
ликом весела,
падает Россия,
словно в зеркала.

Для ее для сына—
дозу стелазина.
Для нее самой—
потемский конвой.[125]

Locked inside the madhouse,
Go and wring your hands out.
White-browed to the wall:
Face-first in the snow.

Into violent shadows,
Icon-face still bright,
Russia plunges downward,
Mirrors to each side.

> For the son she treasured,
> Stelazine is measured.
> For herself it's the
> Convoy to Pot'ma.

Written in response to Galanskov's 1966 hospitalization, Gorbanevskaia's poem validates the norm of thinking differently by challenging psychiatric discourse through literary discourse and its own tradition of psychiatric narratives. Isolated and silenced inside the hospital, the addressee begins to behave in irrational ways: "Go and wring your hands out. / White-browed to the wall". By the second stanza, however, the poet has reversed the diagnostic gaze to position Russia as the cause of the addressee's distress. The country becomes a metaphorical madhouse, an Orthodox icon-like hall of mirrors that collapses into its own reflection: "Russia plunges downward, / Mirrors to each side." Martyred by the antipsychotic drug Stelazine, the addressee becomes a Christ-like "son" who is sacrificed for a motherland that has lost its mind. Even as the poet pathologizes Russia by chronicling its own internal fragmentation, however, she holds it responsible for its actions. The fate of Russia is closely linked with that of "Pot'ma," the transit point for a constellation of camps where dissidents (including, by mid-1968, Galanskov himself) were confined during the post-Stalin period. As if stressing the theme of confinement, the poem adheres to an *aaBBcDcDeeFF* rhyme pattern that walls in the alternating rhyme of the central quatrain with the couplets of the quatrains to either side. Subsuming Russia's irrationality and lawlessness within this organizing structure, the poet affirms her own authority. Literary discourse assimilates psychiatric discourse to depathologize *inakomyslie* and to pathologize both society and the state.

Like Vol'pin, Bukovskii, Gluzman, and Gorbanevskaia, the dissidents Roy and Zhores Medvedev challenged the trap of diagnosis by dialogizing psychiatric discourse in their writings. Following his civil commitment in 1970, Zhores Medvedev, a biologist, was diagnosed with schizophrenia for what physicians described as his "poor adaptation to his social environment" and the "split personality" evident in his wide range of interests.[126] Zhores and Roy responded by embracing the "split personality" label through rhetorical manipulation and literary device. "Having a diverse set of interests is the norm and not a pathology," Zhores reportedly informed one psychiatrist.[127] Roy, in the meantime, told his brother's physicians that since he was Zhores's identical twin they should examine him, as well.[128] After Zhores's release, the brothers translated their "split personality" into literary form by coauthoring a memoir with the playfully obfuscatory title *Who Is Mad?* In the memoir, Zhores and Roy present their story in alternating chapters that highlight the distinctions between their voices while rhetorically implying that the alleged insanity of the one is in fact indistinguishable from the *inakomyslie* of the other. Like Gorbanevskaia's dialogue between past and present selves, and like Bukovskii and Gluzman's coauthorship as patient and physician, the Medvedevs' memoir asserts its diagnostic authority by translating its authors' *inakomyslie* into literary form and thus equating it with sanity.

Grigorenko himself affirmed the norm of thinking differently in both his *samizdat* narratives and the memoir he published in 1981, four years after leaving the Soviet Union. Whereas members of the Tashkent team of psychiatrists examined him for nearly three hours and displayed a willingness to think for themselves, he argues in a *samizdat* comparison of his two 1969 examinations, the Serbskii Institute psychiatrists spent twenty minutes with him and let their chairman do most of the talking. Grigorenko ends his account by offering his own diagnosis of the evaluations: the Tashkent procedure was properly "medical" in its tolerance of dissenting views, while the Serbskii Institute procedure was "investigative."[129] The idea that dissenters might number psychiatrists among their ranks carries over to Grigorenko's memoir through the invocation of a future dialogue between psychiatrists and differently thinking patients:

> I became convinced that one could speak with psychiatrists as well as teachers. This confirms the ideas I developed in confinement: one must speak with everyone and one must speak only the truth. [. . .] It seemed to me, however dimly, that such a way of behaving, inherent to the most normal essence of man, would spontaneously spread and lead to the crowd's spiritual rebirth as a society of PERSONS [*obshchestvo CHELOVEKOV*]—rational, proud, independent in everything and tolerant of each other, voluntarily cooperating in the course of interaction.[130]

Grigorenko's use of the irregular plural *CHELOVEKOV* to envision a diverse "society of PERSONS" suggests both the possibility of dialogue and the distinctiveness of each of the community's members. Just as Grigorenko asserts his sanity by expressing his unorthodox thoughts, a healthy society holds its citizens to a norm of thinking differently. And indeed, according to another transcript of the Serbskii Institute evaluation that Grigorenko released to *samizdat*, the dissident did speak his mind to psychiatrists. "Of course,"

Grigorenko reportedly told Lunts and his colleagues, "if the only Soviet citizen whom you regard as normal is he who obediently bends his neck before every bureaucratic abuse of power, then, of course, I am 'abnormal.' However often and much they might beat me, I'm incapable of such obedience."[131] Highlighting the ambiguity of the term "abnormal," Grigorenko invites his psychiatrists to join him in redefining it as the norm. In doing so, he implies that they, too, might partake in the dialogue that defines the "society of PERSONS."

Looking back in the 1980s, Gluzman described punitive psychiatry as a product of the authoritarian mentality instilled by Stalin not only throughout the general population but also among psychiatrists themselves.[132] By adjusting standards of mental health to fit their own conformist behavior, he argued, psychiatrists had transformed prevailing social norms into pseudo-objective medical facts. The result, Gluzman concluded, was a pathological society that was no longer capable of thinking for itself:

> And yet... the need to invest one's individual life with as much meaning [*smysl*] as possible is fundamental to each of us. The loss of meaning is fatal to life and leads to neurosis ("noogenic neurosis," it is called). And we are not content to trust our "gut instinct" when it comes to understanding the meaning of life; we also think [*myslim*]. [...] Any *inakomysliashchii* is an "enemy of the people" from the point of view of the dictator, for a harshly systematized society is terrified of a plurality of opinions.[133]

As Gluzman emphasizes in literary fashion through his marked repetition of words that derive from the root *mysl*, or "thought," the metaphorical sickness of Soviet society stems from citizens' inability or unwillingness to think independently. Only *inakomysliashchie* who invest their lives with meaning by embracing and acting upon their psychological differences are capable of healing such a society.

The continuity between lived and written responses to psychiatric examination indicates that dissidents responded to diagnosis not only within the confines of the hospital but also by affiliating themselves with a community of writers that stretched across both time and space. In addition to referencing Grigorenko and Vol'pin, then, Bukovskii and Gluzman dedicate their "Manual on Psychiatry" to Pliushch and preface it with an epigraph from a 1950 play by the writer Andrei Platonov that features as a character Petr Chaadaev, the philosopher whom Nicholas I declared mad in 1836.[134] In the epigraph, Chaadaev and a young Pushkin highlight the ambiguity of psychiatric discourse to which dissidents would repeatedly point in the post-Stalin period:

> Aleksandr: You're a madman yourself!
> Chaadaev: Why am I a madman?
> Aleksandr: You understand equality but live in servitude.
> Chaadaev (thoughtfully): Then you are right: I am a madman.[135]

Platonov prefigures dissident approaches by having Chaadaev shift the diagnostic gaze from himself to society through the prism of his own pathologization. That Chaadaev does so at the prompting of Russia's national poet—the same Pushkin who in life would go on to explore the slippery slope between creativity and insanity in his poem "God grant that I don't lose my mind . . ."—testifies to the literary orientation of Bukovskii, Gluzman, and other dissidents.[136] If the state insisted upon using psychiatry's art of diagnosis to pathologize *inakomyslie*, then dissidents would come together to present dissent as the norm.

WRITING AS ACTION

Psychiatric narratives by dissidents envisioned a rational society wherein dialogue and dissent would be protected by both the rule of law and an independent medical establishment. Paradoxically, these were the very liberal structures to which Foucault had attributed psychiatric repression. But for dissidents, the abuses of psychiatry stemmed instead from the authoritarian system inherited from Stalin. If society were ever to regain its health, they argued, its members would have to engage in dialogue, and it was the responsibility of differently thinking people to show them the way. "People value your work," Vol'pin assured the recently rehospitalized Grigorenko in a 1970 letter. "Keep working, and your spirits will stay high and the time will pass quickly." Recalling how another hospital had allowed him to keep writing implements ten years earlier, Vol'pin sent Grigorenko a pen and several cartridges.[137] The following week Grigorenko informed his wife that, though Vol'pin's letter had heartened him, the pen and cartridges had not arrived.[138] Tellingly, Vol'pin responded by publicizing the issue in an open letter to Solzhenitsyn himself: "It seems to me that if a person's tongue were detachable, then it would as a rule be taken away from patients in psychiatric hospitals, and the arguments in favor of this would be purely medical and would sound indisputable."[139] Access to pen and paper is a human "right,"

Vol'pin declared in his letter.[140] "Give Grigorenko a fountain pen, and give it to him not only so he can continue the scientific work I advised him to take up in my letter, but also so he can communicate not only with his descendants, but with all of us, as well!"[141] For Vol'pin, the written word constituted the surest antidote to both punitive diagnosis and authoritarianism.

Yet given that many dissenters felt silenced and isolated even outside the hospital, there were broader benefits to writing. In 1977, Podrabinek and the dissident poet Viktor Nekipelov compiled a *samizdat* collection of personal accounts by dissenters who had been hospitalized. They titled the collection *From the Yellow Silence* (*Iz zheltogo bezmolviia*) in reference to the term "yellow house" (*zheltyi dom*), a colloquialism for "madhouse." In their introduction the editors recall hearing a patient being forced into a straitjacket: "Can words convey the bloodcurdling, inhuman screams that then resounded for several hours in the nighttime silence of the Butyrka prison?"[142] For dissidents, psychiatric detention was a space of "yellow silence" in which patients became so dehumanized that even afterward they lacked the words to describe it. Yet articulating that experience was ultimately necessary for confronting authoritarianism and injustice. The editors accordingly exhort their readers "to respond to this collection not as a series of short stories but as eyewitness evidence for a future (or perhaps in absentia) trial of punitive psychiatrists."[143] Giving expression to the dissenter's silenced words, literature becomes a sphere for taking action.

CHAPTER 3

DIALOGUE OF SELVES:
THE CASE OF JOSEPH BRODSKY

The poet Joseph Brodsky was just ten or eleven, by his own account, when he first grasped the literary essence of dissent. "It occurred to me that [Karl] Marx's dictum that 'existence conditions consciousness' was true only for as long as it takes consciousness to acquire the art of estrangement; thereafter, consciousness is on its own and can both condition and ignore existence," he wrote in his 1976 essay "Less Than One."[1] As Brodsky described it in the essay, existence sculpts consciousness by linguistic means, transforming it into "mental cuneiform," a system of writing whose stone corporeality resembles the cortical folds of the brain.[2] The consciousness that wishes to "condition and ignore" existence must therefore do so linguistically, as well. Brodsky reinforced his "art of estrangement" by "walking out" from those institutional structures (school, the military, various jobs) where the language of everyday reality imprinted itself on citizens' minds.[3] But for him, the most effective means of reversing Marx's dictum was ultimately the literary act. "A writer's biography is in his twists of language," Brodsky noted.[4] The poet who commanded the literary art of estrangement had the power to rewrite reality itself.

The word "estrangement" is tellingly ambiguous in the original English of "Less Than One." One way to understand it is as *otchuzhdenie*, or alienation, in keeping with Viktor Golyshev's 1992 translation of the essay into Russian: by flipping Marx's dictum around, the writer psychologically alienates himself.[5] "A certain advantage of totalitarianism is that it suggests to an individual a kind of vertical hierarchy of his own, with consciousness at the top," Brodsky maintained. "So we oversee what's going on inside ourselves; we almost report to our consciousness on our instincts. And then we punish ourselves."[6] The individual who rejects the regime of existence constructs an alternate regime of consciousness with its own psychiatrists, informants, and courts of law. And for Brodsky, that alternate regime was best supported by the scaffolding of literary discourse. "Well," the poet said in an interview, "I belong to a generation of Russians, maybe 'generation' is too rich here, maybe I should narrow it a little bit, for whom, for a variety of reasons, partly as a reaction against the communal realm, the literature was the main art. We embraced the notion of individualism, of human autonomy, the notion that you are on your own in a big way."[7] As for societal responses to such alienation, Brodsky evidently came to the conclusion that psychiatry was the state's most intrusive mechanism for subordinating the creative consciousness to its regime of existence. Chapter 1 of this study demonstrated that elucidating the relationship between consciousness and existence had long been a priority of the Soviet psychiatric establishment, and that the pathologization of dissent in the post-Stalin period must therefore be viewed within the context of these Marxist-Leninist terms. Following his two stays in psychiatric hospitals in late 1963 and early 1964, Brodsky repurposed the categories of consciousness and existence to push back against the equation of creative dissent with madness. Yet his psychiatric experiences evidently left him with the fear that if consciousness achieved its goal of fully alienating itself from existence, then creativity might indeed give way to insanity and its poetic companion: silence.

Like many of the dissident narratives analyzed in chapter 2, Brodsky's autobiographical essays fold imaginative tropes and techniques into ostensibly documentary texts. Unlike the authors of those narratives, however, Brodsky was not a political or social activist, and to the extent that he channeled his own dissent toward his psychiatric experiences, he did so primarily through the medium of verse. This chapter analyzes the art of estrangement in two of Brodsky's major poetic works, the fourteen-canto narrative poem "Gorbunov and Gorchakov" (1965–68) and the cycle "A Part of Speech" (1975–76). Set in a psychiatric hospital, "Gorbunov and Gorchakov" explicitly presages the reversal of Marx's terms that Brodsky would propose in "Less Than One." But it also suggests that embracing material existence can serve to ground the creative consciousness. "I must say," the poet admitted in 1976 with regard to his alienated stance, "I went quite far in that direction; perhaps too far. Anything that bore a suggestion of repetitiveness became compromised and subject to removal."[8]

Seeking to counteract the pathological consequences of alienation, Brodsky transformed his art of estrangement into a tense yet therapeutic balance between existence and consciousness. The word "estrangement" accordingly transcends alienation to broadly suggest the "defamiliarization" or *ostranenie* that the Formalist critic Viktor Shklovskii identified as the essence of art. As Shklovskii argued in his 1917 essay "Art as Device," the alienated point of view that art provides can restore a person's awareness of reality.[9] By alienating consciousness from existence, then, Brodsky paradoxically reinvigorated their connection. Svetlana Boym notes that "the Marxist slogan shaped several generations of Soviet dissidents of alienation; yet the ghost of that Soviet 'material existence' that Brodsky ritually exorcises from his poetics leaves its traces throughout his oeuvre."[10] And indeed, "Gorbunov and Gorchakov" suggests that sanity and self-expression require continued contact between the forces of consciousness and existence.

The benefits and perils of reversing Marx's dictum take center stage in "Gorbunov and Gorchakov," where the dialogue between the title characters represents a dialogue between consciousness and existence themselves. That these two psychiatric patients have a symbiotic as well as parasitic effect on each other may be deduced from their "speaking" surnames. Gorbunov embodies consciousness, as is shown below, but his name derives from a physical trait—*gorbun*, or "hunchback"—that reveals his subjugation to existence. Gorchakov, by contrast, embodies existence, but the presence in his name of the psychological trait of *gorech'*, or "bitterness," similarly attests to the impact of consciousness. Gorbunov and Gorchakov's inverted names capture the tensions of the dialogue of selves that, for Brodsky, sustains creative expression. It is only by maintaining that highly fraught balance that the characters avoid splitting into the broken monologues that eventually lead to silence. The very dialogue that the psychiatrists pathologize is vital to a healthy frame of mind, Brodsky suggests, and particularly to the health of the dissenting writer whose identity is rooted in language itself. As Brodsky commented in an interview, "The nature of a poem is in a sense a discourse, a dialogue, even with yourself as it were. It's a dialogue with yourself."[11] Though Brodsky abstained from active political protest, his writings thus resemble those dissident texts that dialogically depathologized *inakomyslie*, or "thinking differently."

Brodsky's commitment to dialogic expression coalesced in the wake of his psychiatric hospitalizations and went on to inform his attitude toward emigration. In his 1987 essay "The Condition We Call Exile, or Acorns Aweigh,"

Brodsky returned to the idea that alienation can result in a solipsistic creativity that amounts to the silence and isolation of madness: "One more truth about the condition we call exile is that it accelerates tremendously one's otherwise professional flight—or drift—into isolation, into an absolute perspective: into the condition at which all one is left with is oneself and one's language, with nobody or nothing in between."[12] Brodsky was writing from the personal experience of having been expelled from the Soviet Union fifteen years earlier. Where the language of Soviet existence had previously balanced out the language of consciousness, the creative freedom of exile had opened the way for the latter to isolate itself to the point of incommunicability. Several years after emigrating, then, Brodsky revisited the themes of insanity and silence in his cycle "A Part of Speech." Just as Gorbunov had drifted into a free yet ultimately self-silencing state on the eve of Gorchakov's release from the hospital, the poet of "A Part of Speech" explores the pathological consequences of unfettered creativity. Exile severs the therapeutic dialogue that sustains both sanity and self-expression. It is only by grounding himself in the material reality of language itself that the poet can hope to regain his bearings.

This chapter combines literary and historical analysis to examine the repercussions of Brodsky's psychiatric experiences. It thus departs quite markedly from the poet's own dismissal of biographically informed readings of literary works. "I've been to prison three times, mental institutions twice, but it didn't in any way influence what I write. It has no bearings. It's part of my biography, but biography has absolutely nothing to do with literature, or very little," Brodsky commented in 1991.[13] Despite his considerable body of autobiographical texts, Brodsky winced at the notion "that if we know the circumstances of an author's life in detail we will understand his works."[14] Speaking to the Lithuanian poet Tomas Venclova in 1988, moreover, he linked his dismissal of biographical interpretation directly to his reversal of Marx's dictum: "Literature is a phenomenon that in general is not determined by the political climate. It is that instance when consciousness determines existence, and not the other way around."[15] Brodsky again equated literature with consciousness, on the one hand, and biography with existence, on the other, in a 1991 interview with David M. Bethea:

> You see, the general tenor or raison d'être for biography is the belief that through knowing the facts of this and that life we will understand his work better. Basically that harks back to the [. . .] Marxist dictum that *bytie opredeliaet soznanie*

["existence determines consciousness"]. Which is partly true but only ... Well it's only adolescence related. So to speak, it is true up to the age of fifteen. But after the age of fifteen your *soznanie* is formed and from then on it starts to influence your *bytie* and you begin to make choices that very often are quite impractical.[16]

If consciousness was in fact capable of creatively determining existence, Brodsky continued, then the poet was particularly possessed of this capacity. Art "is at best parallel to one's life," he told Bethea. "And I think the life could be better explained through one's art than the other way around."[17] For Brodsky, biographically focused interpretations merely enforced Marx's dictum; readers should therefore situate literary works within the new realities that their authors generate.

Yet as Bethea himself notes, Brodsky's resistance to biographical analysis is countered not only by a large body of autobiographical essays, poems, and interviews, but also by the poet's careful cultivation of his own authorial persona. Asked during his 1964 trial for social parasitism why he had never enrolled in a writing program, Brodsky responded: "I didn't think you need to educate yourself [to become a poet ...] I think it comes from God."[18] Bethea reads Brodsky's statement as evidence that, despite his aversion to "crude biographism," the poet was in fact quite deeply invested in the biographically freighted rhetoric of literary martyrdom. "How can the poet (or reader) have it both ways, how can he be a rightful heir to the Pushkinian legacy of sacred sacrifice *and* claim that his life really does not matter, or that it matters only to the point that it has enabled him to write in the first place?" Bethea asks.[19] Bethea's rhetorical question is confirmed by Brodsky's repeated presentation of poetry as a dialogue between consciousness and existence. "Though it may be crass to say so," Brodsky acknowledged in 1992, "existence has proved capable of defining the artist's consciousness, and proof of this can be found in the means the artist uses."[20] Far from unilaterally subordinating existence to consciousness, the art of estrangement preserved the balance that sustained both sanity and self-expression.

The Material Imprint of Psychiatric Experience

Born in 1940, Brodsky first came to the attention of psychiatrists in 1962, when a Leningrad military commission recommended that he be evaluated in order to determine his fitness for service. By his own admission, Brodsky was eager to avoid the draft; a well-placed doctor's visit secured him a diagnosis of psychopathy and an exemption from peacetime duty by reason of "neuroses and a heart condition."[21] That diagnosis evidently suggested a practical solution one year later, when a series of public denunciations spearheaded by a militia leader named Iakov Lerner made it clear that Brodsky had attracted the authorities' attention.[22] On December 28, 1963, Brodsky attempted to deflect that attention by checking himself into Moscow's Psychiatric Hospital No. 1, also known as the Kashchenko Hospital. Physicians there noted what they described as the poet's arrogant behavior, ironic tone, and tendency toward philosophizing, and confirmed the diagnosis of psychopathy when Brodsky left the hospital several days later.[23] According to Lev Loseff, the disturbing surroundings of the hospital coupled with the political and emotional pressures to which Brodsky was being exposed led the poet to fear for his mental health and to demand that he be released without delay.[24]

Brodsky's psychiatric history was thus well established by February 13, 1964, when the poet was arrested on charges of social parasitism in compliance with the 1961 decree "On the Intensification of the Struggle Against Persons Who Avoid Socially Useful Labor and Lead an Antisocial, Parasitic Way of Life." On February 18, at the first of two hearings, Brodsky's lawyer attempted to make use of that history by requesting that his client's ability to work be evaluated by psychiatrists.[25] The judge agreed, and Brodsky was sent to the forensic wing of Leningrad's Psychiatric Hospital No. 2, also known as the Priazhka Hospital, for the purposes of determining "1. Whether Brodsky suffers from any mental disorders and whether this disorder rules out the capacity for work. 2. If a disorder and the capacity for work are present, can he be compelled to work in places of compulsory resettlement."[26] Three weeks later, the Priazhka physicians concluded that Brodsky "presents psychopathic traits of character but does not suffer from a mental illness and is capable of evaluating and controlling his actions. His neurological and psychological state of health is such that he is fit for work. Brodsky's lack of evident neurological and psychological disturbances does not rule out the possibility of subjecting him to administrative means of pressure."[27] Brodsky's diagnosis of psychopathic traits of character established his "imputability" for his actions, indicating that he could be prosecuted as charged. On March 13, the poet's second hearing took place, resulting in a sentence of five years of labor.

The Priazhka physicians described Brodsky as a man who reasons purposefully and clearly, is in full possession of his faculties, does not report hallucinations, and has no complaints about his health. At the same time, they highlighted his resistance to evaluation and his rejection of the charges arrayed against him:

> Actively defends himself and maintains his interests. Considers the charges against him to be wrong, not serious, absolutely unfounded. States that he is only being charged because "certain scumbags have nothing better to do"; mentions Lerner in this regard. Sees nothing wrong with his way of life. He did not work because he saw no need. Believes that it is more interesting and useful for him to occupy himself with literary matters. He believes that what he has written and published is quite enough to put him on a par with workers.[28]

Framed as a description of Brodsky's psychological condition, the report pathologizes not only the poet's behavior but his creative efforts, as well. The psychiatrists dwell on Brodsky's "sense of self-importance and superiority" and "independent," "confident," and "defiant" demeanor.[29] They observe that the poet "does not consider himself guilty of anything, as he considers his activities in literature, poetry, translation to be enough to justify not working."[30] Their own view of those activities is decidedly different: Brodsky, they write, is "prone to overrating himself, his literary abilities."[31] By contending within a psychiatric report that Brodsky is exaggerating his literary talent, the physicians recast their subjective opinion of his poetic output as a statement of medically validated and thus objective fact. Chapter 1 chronicled the diagnostic significance that psychiatrists of the post-Stalin period placed upon their patients' art. When it came to evaluating such art, moreover, the psychiatric establishment's view of "healthy" production largely accorded with Socialist Realist aesthetics. The perceived parity of psychiatric and aesthetic norms licensed Brodsky's psychiatrists to read their patient's poetry through a diagnostic lens.

In addition to declaring the poet able to work, Brodsky's psychiatric report notes the presence of "psychopathic traits of character," a variant of Brodsky's earlier diagnosis that may have contributed to the poet's sense that psychiatry aimed to subordinate consciousness to existence. The contemporary Soviet understanding of the term "psychopathic" implied persistent deformations of character resulting from biological and social factors.[32] Psychopathy could theoretically take multiple forms and, although Brodsky's type is not specified in the report, his examiners may have had "hysterical" characteristics in mind. Patients with psychopathy of the hysterical type were said to be emotional, egotistical, attention-seeking, and extreme in their judgments; as the prominent psychiatrist Iakov Kalashnik emphasized in 1961, they might "command a strong intellect and demonstrate an aptitude for some branch of knowledge and art," but they had "no aptitude for systematic and focused work."[33] In the absence of psychosis, they could be prosecuted for their crimes. Yet because they were so susceptible to environmental influences, they could also be reeducated through sustained exposure to a more wholesome way of life. "The primary task with regard to psychopaths, just as with regard to other prisoners, comes down to reeducation by way of involvement in socially useful work and a return to an honest working life," Kalashnik concluded.[34] The five years of labor to which Brodsky was sentenced would not only punish him, in other words; they would also restore him to health.

Though the physician Vladimir Lupandin later reported that Andrei Snezhnevskii, the USSR's most prominent psychiatrist, once told him that he had declared Brodsky schizophrenic, the record does not suggest that Brodsky was ever formally diagnosed with a major mental illness or hospitalized for punitive reasons.[35] Both of Brodsky's evaluations were in a sense voluntary, the first arranged by friends to deflect arrest and the second requested by the poet's lawyer in order to lighten a likely sentence.[36] What makes Brodsky's experience of diagnosis and hospitalization significant is the sense it appears to have given the poet that the primary purpose of the psychiatric profession was to enforce a linguistic regime of existence. During the second hearing, a witness named Smirnov referred ironically to Brodsky's psychiatric history: "What happened was that his fancy friends started kicking up a fuss and demanding. 'Ah! Save this young man!' But he has to be treated (*lechit'*) with forced labor, only forced labor, and no one will help him, no fancy friends of his."[37] Despite affirming both Brodsky's sanity and the need for punishment, Smirnov proved quick to deploy a pseudo-psychiatric vocabulary in laying out his arguments. Even after Brodsky was found responsible for his actions, then, both his trial and his sentence continued to be perceived as a form of psychiatric "treatment."

The idea that Brodsky would benefit from a change of environment encompassed the charge that he himself was creating a negative environment through his poetry and behavior. According to a memo by the Young Writers' Commission of the Leningrad Writers' Union, Brodsky had "defiled" the youth, "poisoning their brains with unbelief, pessimism, exhorting them to inaction."[38] Tracing Brodsky's "parasitism" to a possible source, critics repeatedly cited the deviant behavior of two of Brodsky's friends, Oleg Shakhmatov and Aleksandr

Umanskii, and the poet's 1962 arrest in connection with them.[39] Such narratives of social contagion were in turn given a biological twist by a pensioner named Nikolaev who, appearing as a witness during the trial, blamed Brodsky's parents for bringing up the poet badly and Brodsky himself for transmitting that upbringing to his readers and imitators. "Listening to Brodsky, I recognized my son," Nikolaev said. "My son also said he thinks he's a genius. Like Brodsky, he doesn't want to work. People like Brodsky and Umanskii exert a pestilential influence on their peers."[40] The prosecutor echoed Nikolaev's diagnostically freighted language: Brodsky, he said, was an "ideologically filthy person," and the poet's admirers were "crooks, parasites, lice, and insects" who "splatter saliva" around them.[41] The epidemic implications of parasitism were being taken literally: Brodsky posed a threat to society's health.

Had the trial taken place several years later, when reports of psychiatric abuse were rapidly emerging, Brodsky and his friends might well have avoided drawing attention to his diagnosis. But at the time there evidently appeared to be advantages to having a psychiatric history. "Every day spent in a hospital for the mentally ill poses a serious threat to Brodsky's health. His illness is such that he requires only outpatient treatment and observation and, above all, normal, calm conditions," the journalist Frida Vigdorova wrote to Roman Rudenko, the procurator general of the Soviet Union, following the trial's first session, which she attended and transcribed.[42] Another journalist, Ol'ga Chaikovskaia, echoed Vigdorova's request in her own letter to Rudenko: "It cannot but be a cause for alarm that Brodsky is psychologically a semi-sick person; he is registered in a psychiatric dispensary with a diagnosis of progressive psychopathy (according to the Kashchenko Hospital's diagnosis); these kinds of methods could transform a semi-sick person into a person with a serious sickness."[43] During the trial's second hearing, Brodsky's lawyer similarly attributed the poet's behavior to his "psychopathic traits of character."[44] And, seven months later, when Brodsky was already serving his sentence, the poet's parents revisited his psychiatric history in their own request for clemency: "We fear that because of his poor health he will not withstand such a long stay in the harsh conditions of the North. Our son suffers from a progressive heart defect, is afflicted with psychopathy, and is blind in one eye."[45] The promotion and minimization of Brodsky's psychiatric status captures the dual meaning—the double-edged sword of benefit and peril—that diagnosis carried at the time.

Even Brodsky expressed concern about the fragility of his mental health when requesting to be discharged from the Kashchenko Hospital. "I will really go mad here, get me out of this place immediately," he reportedly told a sympathetic psychiatrist.⁴⁶ During the trial, however, he vacillated between making use of his psychiatric history and attempting to cover it up:

> Defense Counsel: Are you registered at a psychiatric clinic?
> Brodsky: Yes.
> Defense Counsel: Did you undergo inpatient treatment?
> Brodsky: Yes, from the end of December 1963 to January 5 of this year in the Kashchenko Hospital in Moscow.
> Defense Counsel: Do you think that your illness prevented you from working regularly in one place for a long period of time?
> Brodsky: Maybe. Probably. On second thought, I don't know. No, I don't know.⁴⁷

Brodsky's vacillating reaction to his lawyer's citation of his psychiatric history testifies to the poet's ambivalence about his own experience of hospitalization and diagnosis. On the one hand, Brodsky's psychiatric record offered a line of defense should forensic psychiatrists confirm that psychological problems had prevented him from working. On the other hand, a declaration of mental illness might have seemed like a self-fulfilling prophecy given Brodsky's fragile state; after his release from the Kashchenko Hospital, the poet had reportedly attempted suicide.⁴⁸ The same exchange may therefore point to Brodsky's unwillingness to pretend to be something that he was afraid of becoming.

Brodsky's readiness to make use of his diagnosis was tempered by what Lev Loseff has described as the poet's real fear of losing his mind.⁴⁹ "The main thing is you watch yourself," Brodsky later said of psychiatric evaluation. "You think that maybe you are really going insane. When you cross the threshold they tell you that the first sign of good mental health is sound sleep, and you lie in your bed and you can't sleep."⁵⁰ The poet's inability to sleep was made more frightening by what Brodsky later called the hospital's "violation of proportions"—a lack of spatial and temporal logic that could drive a person mad. "The relation between the size of the windows and the size of the room itself was somewhat strange, slightly disproportionate," the poet said. "That is, the windows were, it seems, maybe an eighth smaller than they should have been in relation to the dimensions of the room. And it was precisely this that drove me into a frenzy, that almost drove me crazy."⁵¹ Despite the fact that, as Brodsky declared, psychiatric evaluation was "the most horrendous thing I have been through," the poet internalized diagnostic concepts and drew attention to his neurotic tendencies when conversing with friends.⁵² Diagnosis and the experience of hospitalization exposed Brodsky to psychiatric discourse and transformed that discourse into a vocabulary for describing the fragility of the creative mind.

The threat of psychiatric diagnosis takes on nightmarish shades in "New Year at the Kanatchikova Dacha," a poem Brodsky wrote shortly after his release from the Kashchenko Hospital in January 1964:

> Спать, рождественский гусь,
> отвернувшись к стене,
> с темнотой на спине,
> разжигая, как искорки бус,
> свой хрусталик во сне.
>
> Ни волхвов, ни осла,
> ни звезды, ни пурги,
> что младенца от смерти спасла,
> расходясь, как круги
> от удара весла.
>
> Расходясь будто нимб
> в шумной чаще лесной
> к белым платьицам нимф,
> и зимой, и весной
> разрезать белизной
> ленты вздувшихся лимф
> за больничной стеной.
>
> Спи, рождественский гусь.
> Засыпай поскорей.
> Сновидений не трусь
> между двух батарей,
> между яблок и слив
> два крыла расстелив,
> головой в сельдерей.
>
> Это песня сверчка
> в красном плинтусе тут,
> словно пенье большого смычка,

ибо звуки растут,
как сверканье зрачка
сквозь большой институт.

«Спать, рождественский гусь,
потому что боюсь
клюва—возле стены
в облаках простыни,
рядом с плинтусом тут,
где рулады растут,
где я громко пою
эту песню мою».

Нимб пускает круги
наподобье пурги,
друг за другом вослед
за две тысячи лет,
достигая ума,
как двойная зима:
вроде зимних долин
край, где царь—инсулин.

Здесь, в палате шестой,
встав на страшный постой
в белом царстве спрятанных лиц,
ночь белеет ключом
пополам с главврачом

ужас тел от больниц,
облаков—от глазниц,
насекомых—от птиц.[53]

Time to sleep, Christmas goose,
With your face to the wall,
with your back to the dark,
with your lens set on fire in your sleep
like a necklace of sparks.

Not the Magi, not the ass,
not the star, not the snow,
that delivered the child from death,
spreading out like the rings
from the slap of an oar.

Spreading out nimbus-like
in the dark forest brush
toward the white shifts of nymphs,
and in winter and spring
with their whiteness they slice
through the bands of swelled lymph
past the hospital wall.

Go to sleep, Christmas goose.
Fall asleep in all haste.
Do not fear your own dreams
wedged between the two stoves,
between apples and prunes,
your two wings opened wide,
and your celery head.

There's a cricket in song
in this red baseboard here,
and it sounds like a great singing bow,
for the melodies grow,
like the pupil's own sparks
through the huge institute.

"Go to sleep, Christmas goose,
for I tremble in fear
of your beak—by the wall
in the cloud of the sheets
by this baseboard below,
where glissandos grow loud,
where I noisily sing
out the song that I sing."

> For the nimbus beams rings
> in the manner of snow,
> rippling one at a time
> across two thousand years,
> till they capture the mind
> like a winter times two:
> like the wintertime dales
> of the insulin realm.
>
> Here in Ward No. 6,
> in the barracks of fear,
> in the white dominion of veiled
> faces, night becomes white
> with the doctor and key
>
> in the hospital fear
> fills the body, like clouds
> fear eye sockets, bugs: birds.

The poem—whose title refers colloquially to the Kashchenko Hospital—stands as one of a series of poems that Brodsky wrote about the Nativity. Combining the religious metaphor of Christ's birth with the medical metaphor of mental illness, its haze of destabilized words and images resembles a drug-induced delirium. Verbs such as the repeated "spreading out" (*raskhodias'*) lack clear subjects and morphologically suggest a sense of splitting apart; the identity of the quoted speaker—who may be an outside observer, a cricket, or the poet himself—is in flux; idioms are eviscerated (*noch' beleet kliuchom* evokes both the key to the ward and the phrase *kipet' kliuchom*, harking back to the rippling spring mentioned earlier in the poem). The poet's associative, self-generating language is that of a creative consciousness spinning out of control. The reference in the penultimate verse to Anton Chekhov's "Ward No. 6" gives this behavior a name by placing the poem squarely within the Russian literary tradition of psychiatric narratives. In Chekhov's story, the opposition between sanity and insanity blurs when the physician Andrei Ragin comes to believe that a patient locked in the mental ward is more lucid than those who are considered sane. The price of identifying with madmen is that one may go mad or be so labeled; the difference is immaterial, as Ragin discovers when he too is confined. Brodsky's poem similarly suggests that the creative impulse that psychiatry pathologizes may indeed, if left unchecked, become a harsh reality.[54]

The poem unfolds as a lullaby of sorts as the poet vacillates between the fear of not sleeping ("Time to sleep") and the terror of sleeping ("Do not fear your own dreams"), while transforming himself into a "Christmas goose," an image that suggests both crucifixion and surgery. The Christ child's nimbus (*nimb*) expands outward like ripples from the slap of the oar to evoke the circular plate on which the Christmas goose lies prostrate with its wings splayed. The white-robed nymphs of the poet's religious visions morph into the white-robed doctors of his psychiatric reality; the whiteness of the Nativity, the Christmas feast, and the snow outside are indistinguishable from the whiteness of the hospital walls, bed sheets, and uniforms inside. This merging of whites creates a "winter times two" that bridges both the spatial separation between outside and inside and the temporal separation of the "two thousand years" since the birth of Christ. The dissolution of space and time in this all-white environment frightens the poet, but it also provides him with a creative blank slate on which consciousness can freely determine existence. Framed like an icon between two radiators and ringed by the Byzantine colors of apples and prunes as he is readied for suppertime sacrifice—or perhaps lobotomy—the poet focuses his attention on the chirp of a cricket that is trapped within the ventilation system. The image once again references the literary tradition by recalling the young Aleksandr Pushkin's designation as the "cricket" by the Arzamas literary circle in the early nineteenth century.[55] Issuing from a "red baseboard" that resembles the "red" corner in which icons are set—though also, ironically, the twentieth-century reworking of this practice through the veneration of images of Party leaders—the cricket's chirp symbolizes both creative freedom and the material confines of Soviet life. The resulting dialogue between consciousness and existence maintains the poet's grip on reality, but it is a tenuous one. For as the poet's terror and tongue-tied syntax reveal—"in the hospital fear / fills the body, like clouds / fear eye sockets, bugs: birds"—psychiatry threatens to tip that balance toward a self-silencing insanity.

Brodsky's psychiatric experiences both confirmed the pathological extremes of creativity and provided the poet with a conceptual vocabulary for describing them. The generational dislike for psychiatry that Brodsky described in "Less Than One" was therefore personal, as well:

> I've said somewhere else that Russians—at least my generation—never resort to shrinks. In the first place, there are not so many of them. Besides, psychiatry is the state's property. One knows that to have a psychiatric record isn't such a great thing. It might backfire at any moment. But in any case, we used to handle our problems ourselves, to keep track of what went on inside our heads without help from the outside.[56]

For Brodsky, psychiatry facilitated the imposition of existence on consciousness through the application of diagnostic labels from which there could be no escape. As such, it both repressed the poet and confirmed the pathological extremes of creative freedom. Rejecting diagnostic labels was crucial for Brodsky and other dissenters who insisted on defining themselves. Yet it also meant coping on their own in time of psychological need. Seeking affirmation in the literary tradition of psychiatric narratives such as Chekhov's "Ward No. 6," dissenting writers resisted pathologization. But for Brodsky, such comforts were evidently not enough to avert the threats of madness and silence. Sanity and self-expression both demanded that the poet take responsibility for maintaining and regulating his own dialogue of selves.

Poet as Patient in "Gorbunov and Gorchakov"

In contrast with the considerable interest in Brodsky's shorter works, sustained examinations of "Gorbunov and Gorchakov" have been few to date. An early analysis by Carl R. Proffer emphasizes the characters' respective adherences to nonconformist and conformist paradigms of thought. The physicians, Proffer writes, pathologize Gorbunov's "dangerously introspective and philosophical" reasoning and his tendency to think in "religious" terms. Gorchakov, by contrast, is "passive, practical, and prosaic," in keeping with the state's conception of normality.[57] Gorbunov and Gorchakov may be separate people or they may be "schizoid" voices within one mind, Proffer notes.[58] Lev Loseff's later readings take exception to Proffer's description of Gorbunov and Gorchakov as "hallucinatory" voices and argue for the poem's presentation of madness as "not a particular pathological condition but a generalized existential Adversity," a "dialogue between two selves."[59] If these selves are split along any identifiable line, it is not the "schizoid" line between two inner voices, the political line between conformism and nonconformism, or the Freudian line between the conscious and the unconscious. Rather it is the biological line between the right and left hemispheres of the brain, according to Loseff. Gorchakov, Loseff argues, is the right-brained "emotional imaginative fearing self," while Gorbunov is the left-brained "reasoning logical fearless self."⁶⁰ Loseff proposes that the poem's conversational structure may have been the direct or indirect result of a contemporary surge of interest in the philosopher and critic Mikhail Bakhtin, whose concepts of "monologism" and "dialogism" echo throughout this study's own analysis of the writings of dissenters.⁶¹ And indeed, Proffer and Loseff's interpretive differences—in particular, their ascription of poetic and prosaic attributes to opposite characters—highlights the dialogic interpenetration of Brodsky's two heroes.

Marked by distinct names, speech patterns, thematic concerns, and birthdays (Gorbunov, like Brodsky, was born in May, while Gorchakov was born in March), the heroes nevertheless appear to be separate aspects of a single poet's mind. Their dialogues and monologues, which are supplemented from time to time by the interjections of physicians and fellow patients, together present what Brodsky would describe as a self-contained "universe."⁶² The theme of dialogue is formally confirmed by the absence of attributory notations; utterances are separated only by quotation marks, as if to stress that dialogue is the very material from which the poem springs. Despite their ongoing conflict, moreover, both of the characters repeatedly emphasize their need for dialogue, as Gorbunov does here:

> [«]Ночь. Губы на два голоса поют.
> Ты думаешь, не много ли мне чести?
> Но в этом есть особенный уют:
> пускай противоречие, но вместе[»].⁶³

> ["]It's night. My lips are singing in two voices.
> You say you think it's more than I deserve?
> But I would say the coziness is worth it:
> If we're together, contradiction's fine.["]

Gorbunov's use of the word "contradiction" (*protivorechie*) captures the necessity of dialogic exchange by combining the word *protiv* ("opposite") with the word *rech'* ("speech") while simultaneously suggesting that the balance of consciousness and existence is highly unstable. The psychiatrists urge Gorchakov, the voice of existence, to drown out Gorbunov's voice of consciousness, while Gorbunov alienates himself from Gorchakov and the oppressive reality he represents. The result is mutually assured destruction as Gorbunov and Gorchakov both give way to silence. Self-expression cannot endure once the poet's art of estrangement is lost.

As Valentina Polukhina has observed with reference to "Gorbunov and Gorchakov," the poet's use of language to alienate himself from reality results in an alienation from language itself.[64] Yet Brodsky's insistence on the autonomy of consciousness must also be viewed within the wider context of the poet's efforts to achieve a creative balance. The fifth canto thus distills dialogue to its lexical core by transforming Gorbunov and Gorchakov into He Said (*On Skazal*) and He Said to Him (*On Emu Skazal*), attributory notations that are absent throughout the rest of the poem. These units of reported speech are indeed alienated from their semantic essence, yet together they balance each other out:

«И он сказал». «Вот так булыжник вдруг
швыряют в пруд. Круги—один, четыре...»
«И он сказал». «И это—тот же круг,
но радиус его, бесспорно, шире».
«Сказал—кольцо». «Сказал—еще кольцо».
«И вот его сказал уткнулся в берег».[65]

"And he said." "Suddenly a rock is flung
into a pond. The rings—first one, then four..."
"And he said." "Yet another ring, the same,
although its radius is surely wider."
"He said—a ring." "He said—another ring."
"And then his he-said washed up on the shore."

Brodsky compares the resounding of He Saids to the ripples produced by a rock thrown into a pond, evoking not only the oar-stroke's slap in "New Year at the Kanatchikova Dacha" but also the outward rippling of sound waves from words. The shores of the pond contain the medium through which the ripples travel while also limiting the ripples' radius. In much the same way, the title characters—whether they are personified as Gorbunov and Gorchakov or depersonified as He Said and He Said to Him—support their interaction through "contradiction." The echo that threatens to drown out each of the voices is the same echo that keeps dialogue flowing.

In addition to contradicting each other's words, Gorbunov and Gorchakov subscribe to adversarial understandings of human psychology. Gorbunov's dreams are rife with symbolic language and motifs that link the claim that "consciousness determines existence" to Freudian psychoanalytic theory. Gorchakov's dreams, by contrast, are grounded in the materialist claims of Soviet psychiatric discourse that Brodsky associated with Marx's dictum that "existence determines consciousness." Brodsky was outspoken in his rejection of Freud and Marx, telling an interviewer in 1991 that he—and, in his opinion, all Soviet citizens his age—had an "allergy" to both thinkers. Freud and Marx had broadened man's understanding of himself while leaving man fundamentally unchanged; they were therefore "useless," in Brodsky's view. "I don't argue with them so much as push away from them, and laugh at them a bit, and try to discredit them in the consciousness of my readers, because they take up too much space in the modern consciousness."[66] Though Gorbunov's alienation undoubtedly hews more closely to the credo of "Less Than One," neither character has the poet's full sympathy. Rather, Gorbunov and Gorchakov must remain in dialogue in order to find an equilibrium.[67]

Gorbunov and Gorchakov's allegiances to consciousness and existence dominate the poem's initial stanzas as the title characters interpret their own dreams in keeping with their respective psychological paradigms. The poem begins with Gorchakov addressing Gorbunov:

«Ну, что тебе приснилось, Горбунов?»
«Да, собственно, лисички». «Снова?» «Снова».
«Ха-ха, ты насмешил меня, нет слов».
«А я не вижу ничего смешного.
Врач говорит: основа всех основ—
нормальный сон».[68]

"Well, Gorbunov, what did you dream about?"
"Why, chanterelles, of course." "Again?" "Again."
"Ha ha, you've cracked me up, there are no words."
"And I don't see what you find so amusing.
The doctor says: There's nothing we need more
than normal sleep."

Gorbunov dreams of nothing but chanterelles, Freudian metaphors for creativity not only in their resemblance to sexual organs but also in their rhyme toward the end of the canto with *stranichki*, the genitive singular of a diminutive form of *stranitsa* ("page"), which is a space on which words are inscribed. He defends his recurring dreams of chanterelles by citing what Brodsky described as his own physicians' assertion that the best indicator of health is regular sleep. And indeed, the consonant cluster *s-n* (from *son*: "sleep" or "dream") repeats eight times in the first stanza alone. The theme of dreams gives rise to the theme of language, as "Gorbunov" and *snov*, the genitive plural form of *son*, are linked by way of rhyme to *slov*, the genitive plural for *slovo* ("word"). These themes are in turn connected with the theme of madness in the second verse, as *bol'nitsa* ("hospital") rhymes with *snitsia* ("to dream") and *stranitsa* ("page"). In just two verses, Brodsky has allowed the poem's concerns with dreams, language and madness to seemingly spring from language itself, like the spontaneous generation of chanterelles in Gorbunov's dreams.

Whereas Gorbunov's chanterelles nod to psychoanalytic theory, Gorchakov's dreams embody the regime of existence that Brodsky attributed to psychiatric discourse. Gorchakov's nocturnal visions are devoid of literary symbolism: fragmented, photograph-like images of concerts, avenues, faces, childhood, and the madhouse where Gorchakov now lives.[69] When Gorbunov cites Freud to make the argument that "man's a captive of his dreams," Gorchakov responds with the materialist claim that dreams are shaped by habitual actions:

«Фрейд говорит, что каждый—пленник снов».
«Мне говорили: каждый—раб привычки.
Ты ничего не спутал, Горбунов?»[70]

"But Freud says man's a captive of his dreams."
"And they told me that man's a slave to habit.
Is there a chance you flubbed it, Gorbunov?"

Gorchakov rejects Gorbunov's Freudian credo in such a way as to voice his support for Soviet psychiatry's emphasis on the conditioning influence of biological and social factors. And indeed, by translating the Russian word *opredeliaet* as "conditions" rather than "determines" in his essay "Less Than One," Brodsky suggests that the state resorts to psychiatric manipulation when less invasive means of ensuring conformity fail. Just as Gorbunov links himself with Freud's ideas by prioritizing human consciousness, Gorchakov echoes Marx and psychiatric discourse by giving existence pride of place. One can only dream about what one has experienced, Gorchakov says; dreams are reflections of material reality.

The ideological underpinnings of Soviet psychiatry permeate the fourth canto as Gorchakov informs on Gorbunov through a blend of political and medical terminology:

«Ну, Горчаков, давайте ваш доклад».
«О Горбунове?» «Да, о Горбунове».
«Он выражает беспартийный взгляд
на вещи, на явления,—в основе
своей диалектический; но ряд—
но ряд его высказываний внове
для нас». «Они, бесспорно, говорят
о редкостной насыщенности крови
азотом, разложившим аппарат
самоконтроля».[71]

"Well, Gorchakov, it's time for your report."
"On Gorbunov?" "Of course, on Gorbunov."
"The views he holds on things and happenings
are quite unpartyminded; at their core
there is a dialectic but a few—
a few of his opinions are quite new."
"No doubt this is all due to such a rare
degree of saturated nitrogen
within the blood: The organism loses
self-control."

Throughout the canto, the psychiatrists and Gorchakov translate Gorbunov's creative credo into material, diagnostic terms. The ongoing conversation between Gorbunov and Gorchakov is thus not dialogic but "dialectical," in Gorchakov's telling, while the state of mind that Gorbunov expresses is dismissed as being "unpartyminded." Urged on by the psychiatrists, Gorchakov moves back and forth between clinical observations (Gorbunov's joined eyebrows, asymmetrical features and prominent nose vessels) and flagrantly unmedical political denunciations:

[«]"Преувеличен внутренний наш мир,
а внешний, соответственно, уменьшен"—

    вот характерный для него язык.
    В таких вот выражениях примерных
    свой истинный показывает лик
    сторонник непартийных, эфемерных
    воззрений... »[72]

    ["]'Our inner world exaggerates itself,
    which leads our outer world to narrow in'—

    that is the sort of language that he uses.
    It's more or less in statements of this kind that
    this backer of unpartyminded, fleeting
    opinions shows the world his truest face..."

Noting that it is primarily through language that Gorbunov reveals himself, Gorchakov uses psychiatric discourse to assert his authority over his constant companion. Psychiatry not only advocates conditioning the mind; it also carries out that conditioning by redefining Gorbunov's words.

The destabilization of the poetic mind leads to the loss of dialogue. In the tenth canto, the hospital accordingly becomes a "vacuum"—a place where sound no longer travels:

    «Стоит огромный сумасшедший дом».
    «Как вакуум внутри миропорядка».[73]

    "A monumental madhouse stands ahead."
    "A vacuum in the order of the world."

Underscoring the link with Brodsky's experience of evaluation and with the distortion of space and time in "New Year at the Kanatchikova Dacha," the "violation of proportions" that led the poet to fear for his sanity is here reflected in the image of a sundial with a radius that is gradually narrowing to zero:

    «Вторая половина февраля.
    Смотри-ка, что показывают стрелки».
    «Я думаю, лишь радиус нуля».
    «А цифры?» «Как бордюрчик на тарелке...[»][74]

"The second half of February's here.
Just look at what the dial's hands are showing."
"It seems to me the radius is zero."
"The numbers?" "Just a border on a plate...["]

The smaller the radius gets, the less time it takes for the sundial's hand to circle the perimeter, if it circles at all. Time is cancelled out along with space in the perpetual darkness of wintertime Leningrad. "The hospital, like the prison, is a kingdom of timelessness," Brodsky wrote more generally to Proffer in English after undergoing a medical procedure at a hospital near Leningrad in 1971. "I spend here only 3rd day, but they poured off (together) in solid nothing gulping hour by hour and seeming more endless because this bread (or wine) is Future [sic]." Nearly eight years after undergoing psychiatric evaluation, Brodsky still experienced even nonpsychiatric hospitals as institutions with "more Time than Space."[75] The harsh consequences for dialogue are evident in "Gorbunov and Gorchakov," given that it was through a similar radial metaphor that Brodsky described the back-and-forth rippling of He Saids in the fifth canto. Separated from Gorbunov in the eighth canto, Gorchakov connects his own burgeoning "monologue" with the "radius of the nighttime dial"—a similarly darkened sundial that has lost its bearings. In the vacuum of the artificially lit hospital, the dialogue between consciousness and existence breaks down.

Gorchakov's adherence to the hospital's regime of existence is captured by his limited vision; not only is he unable to read without eyeglasses, but he also cannot see past the building's walls. When Gorbunov points to the constellations, Gorchakov says that he needs a telescope. All that meets his eye when he looks out the window is a mirror image of the lit ward:

[«]Какие звезды?! Пол и потолок.
В окошке—отражается палата[»].[76]

["]What stars?! There's just a ceiling and a floor.
The window looks out on the ward's reflection.["]

Emanating as he does from hospital existence, Gorchakov merely causes the ward to multiply when he looks outside. Unlike Gorbunov, who has a wife and child to return to upon his release, he has no external supports:

[«]О Горбунов! я чувствую при встрече

с тобою, как нормальный идиот,
себя всего лишь радиусом стрелки!
Никто меня, я думаю, не ждет
ни здесь, ни за пределами тарелки,
заполненной цифирью[»].[77]

["]Oh Gorbunov! It may seem idiotic

but every time we meet I feel as if
I'm nothing but the dial's radius.
There is no one expecting me, I think,
not here and not outside the boundary of
that dinner plate with numbers round its edge.["]

Gorchakov is less a full-fledged patient of the hospital than an embodiment of its cure: a Gorbunov in whom existence will prevail in keeping with psychiatry's agenda. When Gorchakov signs his release slip, then, he quite literally assumes the psychiatrists' point of view:

[«]Эй, Горчаков, вы не могли бы
автограф свой?» «Я нынче без очков».
«Мои не подойдут?» «Да подошли бы[»].[78]

["]Hey, Gorchakov, could you sign here?"
"You know I can't without my spectacles."
"Would mine not work?" "Why yes, they'd work quite well.["]

Gorchakov sees best with the psychiatrists' eyeglasses because he emanates from their distorted regime of existence. Should he be capable of living outside the hospital, it would be a testament not to his own mental health, but to his perceptual alignment with the state's similarly distorted view of reality. And if Soviet society is indeed a giant madhouse, as many of the dissenters in this study claimed, then in a sense Gorchakov, like Gorbunov, will never be released. Nevertheless, Gorchakov looks forward to being discharged and sets himself the task of metaphorically opening Gorbunov's eyes: "Where's Gorbunov?! I must enlighten him! .." (*Gde Gorbunov?! Glaza emu raskryt'! . .*).[79] His own eyes acclimated to the hospital's view of reality, Gorchakov thinks that if Gorbunov "sees" things in his way, he will also be cured.

By contrast, Gorbunov rejects material reality by rooting himself outside the hospital:

«Но сам-то я—вне радиуса». «Чушь!
А кто же предо мной?» «Лишь оболочка».
«Ну, о неограниченности душ
слыхал я что-то в молодости. Точка».⁸⁰

"I'm free to step outside the radius."
"Oh please! Then who's right here?" "That's just a shell."
"Well, in my youth I heard a thing or two
about the soul's infinity. Full stop."

The physical Gorbunov—to the extent that he exists—is merely a "shell" for a consciousness that cannot be confined to the hospital's walls. Brodsky deepens the radial metaphor by likening Gorbunov to the moving leg of a drafting compass that is fastened on external supports:

«Я радиус расширил до родни».
«Тем хуже для тебя оно, тем хуже».
«Я только ножка циркуля. Они—
опора неподвижная снаружи».⁸¹

"I've stretched the radius out to my kin."
"Which means that things are getting worse for you."
"We are a compass: I'm one leg, and they
stand firm to root me in the outer world."

Unlike Gorchakov, Gorbunov is rooted outside the hospital radius and thus remains spiritually unconfined. The hospital's negation of space and time does not affect him as long as he reaches out to his family or the stars. Where Gorchakov needs reading glasses to look at nearby objects and a telescope to see the stars, Gorbunov can view the constellations independently:

«Вон Водолей с кувшином наклонился».
«Нам телескоп иметь здесь хорошо б».

«Да, хорошо б». «И ты б угомонился».
«Что?! Телескоп?! На кой мне телескоп!»
«Ну, Горбунов, чего ты взбеленился?»[82]

"Aquarius is bending with the jug."
"If only we could have a telescope."
"If only, yes." "And then you would calm down."
"Say what?! A telescope?! A telescope—
for what?" "Hey, Gorbunov, why blow a fuse?"

Gorbunov rejects Gorchakov's suggestion that they acquire a telescope because, for him, the stars are not material realities but figments of his creative imagination. Pointing a telescope at them would confine them to the hospital just as Gorchakov's wearing of the psychiatrists' eyeglasses imbues him with their diagnostic perspective.

The running image of the telescope is symbolically significant as it captures Gorchakov's adherence to psychiatric discourse and thus to a hospital-bound visual perspective that Gorbunov rejects. As the characters' balance tips, however, the telescope encroaches on Gorbunov. Caught in a nocturnal monologue when, like Brodsky himself, he is unable to sleep, Gorbunov reports a sense of physical contraction:

[«]Из-за угла в еврейский телескоп
глядит медбрат, в жида преображаясь.
Сужается постель моя, как гроб.
Хрусталик с ней сражается, сужаясь.
И кровь шумит, как клюквенный сироп.
И щиколотки стынут, обнажаясь.
И делится мой разум, как микроб,
в молчанье безгранично размножаясь![»][83]

["]Peering through his Jewish telescope,
the orderly seems kike-ish in the corner.
My bed is growing narrow, like a coffin.
My lens is battling with it, narrowing.
And like cranberry syrup my blood pounds.
And my uncovered ankles start to freeze.

And microbe-like, my reason is dividing,
proliferating vastly in the silence!["]

Gorbunov's vision of the orderly's telescope is pointedly Freudian in its phallic innuendos. But it is also notable for the fact that the telescope is "Jewish": it faces backward in much the same way as the Hebrew script runs from right to left. Instead of being magnified by the telescope, Gorbunov experiences a sense of contraction that recalls the contracting radii of the ripples and sound waves in the fifth canto and of the sundial in the tenth. Gorbunov's subordination to a telescope that hitherto captured Gorchakov's adherence to psychiatric discourse illustrates the power of diagnostic labels.

Testifying to the impact of Brodsky's own encounter with psychiatric discourse, though, the feeling of contraction may also point to the poet's experience of one of punitive psychiatry's more notorious practices: patients were sometimes wrapped in wet sheets and placed next to hot radiators, the sheets contracting upon drying and thus painfully constricting.[84] In "Gorbunov and Gorchakov," the poet responds by losing touch with reality and splitting into a plethora of selves:

[«]Но то, что на два делится, то тут
разделится, бесспорно, и на двести.

А все, что увеличилось вдвойне,
приемлемо и больше не ничтожно.
Проблему одиночества вполне
решить за счет раздвоенности можно[»].[85]

["]But surely something that can split in two
could one day also split into two hundred.

And everything that's heightened two times over
is worth its salt; it starts to count for something.
For solitude's a problem that's best solved
by starting up a process of division.["]

The experience is thrilling yet terrifying. On the one hand, internal multiplication brings creative freedom. On the other hand, it dilutes the measured dialogue that sustained the balance between consciousness and existence. Diagnosis becomes a self-fulfilling prophecy when the dialogue of selves breaks down.

In keeping with the theme of sight, the final split between Gorbunov and Gorchakov is precipitated by an argument as to whether vision is determined by consciousness or existence. Gorbunov says that man is chiefly defined by his ability to dream, and illustrates his point by mentally conjuring a seascape that has nothing in common with the hospital scene. Gorchakov immediately takes offense:

«А человек есть выходец из снов».
«И что же в нем решающее?» «Веки.

Закроешь их и видишь темноту».
«Хотя бы и при свете?» «И при свете . . .
И вдруг заметишь первую черту.
Одна, другая . . . третья на примете.
В ушах шумит и холодно во рту.
Потом бегут по набережной дети,
и чайки хлеб хватают на лету . . . »
«А нет ли там меня, на парапете?»
«И все, что вижу я в минуту ту,
реальнее, чем ты на табурете».[86]

"But man descends directly from his dreams."
"And what is it that makes him him?" "His eyelids.

By shutting them you usher in the darkness."
"And when it's light?" "And when it's light as well . . .
And suddenly you notice the first detail
And then another . . . then a third appears.
A rumbling in your ears, your mouth is cold.
And then some children running down the quay,
and seagulls catching bread while flying high . . ."
"But where do I appear on that embankment?"
"Why, everything I see at that one moment
is far more real than you there on that stool."

Gorbunov's reiteration of his Freudian claim that man's existence is shaped by dreams drives Gorchakov into a rage. Material existence is not a matter of choice, Gorchakov insists, pointing to the details of his hospital gown and daring Gorbunov to deny that he sees them. When Gorbunov responds by indeed denying it, Gorchakov lets his physical fists do the convincing; Gorbunov's eyes remain closed and Gorbunov himself remains mute from that point on. On the one hand, Gorbunov's silence may be read as a metaphor for dissent: pounded by the forces of material existence, consciousness retreats into a space of visual and verbal freedom where it can construct a new, dream-like existence that leaves its creative impulse unchecked. On the other hand, the incommunicability of this new existence leads to a madness that brings the poetic dialogue to a halt: the poem ends with Gorchakov addressing an insentient Gorbunov and then trailing off into an ellipsis upon getting no answer. The loss of dialogue leads both existence and consciousness to abandon language, the former by retreating into violence and the latter by retreating into dreams. Creative liberation inevitably comes at the price of self-expression.

The depiction of the psychiatric hospital as an incubator of silence may reflect the poetic silence that Brodsky evidently experienced during his own psychiatric evaluation. Although Brodsky continued to produce new poems in prison after his arrest, he reportedly did no writing at the Priazhka Hospital.[87] As "Gorbunov and Gorchakov" suggests a decade before Brodsky composed the cycle "A Part of Speech," words overcome "things" by materializing themselves as new "parts of speech." But in doing so, they themselves become "things" that can similarly be devoured by language:

> «Вещь, имя получившая, тотчас
> становится немедля частью речи».
> «И части тела?» «Именно они».
> «А место это?» «Названо же домом».
> «А дни?» «Поименованы же дни».
> «О, все это становится Содомом
> слов алчущих! Откуда их права?»
> «Тут имя прозвучало бы зловеще».
> «Как быстро разбухает голова
> словами, пожирающими вещи!»[88]

"A thing that has been named immediately
and right away becomes a part of speech."
"And body parts?" "By all means, those as well."
"And this place, too?" "It has a name: a house."
"And days?" "Of course those have been named as well."
"Oh, all of this transforms into a Sodom
of hungry words! And what gives them the right?"
"A name, of course, would sound more frightening here."
"How rapidly the head is swelling up
from all these words that keep consuming things!"

Consciousness pushes back against existence by generating its own "parts of speech" to counter the "things" that keep it confined. The advantages of "naming" reality are evident in "Gorbunov and Gorchakov": "Names are a defense from things" (*Nazvaniia—zashchita ot veshchei*).[89] But because newly materialized "parts of speech" themselves become "things" that can be renamed, the end result is poetic silence:

«Но ежели взглянуть со стороны,
то можно, в общем, сделать замечанье:
и слово—вещь. Тогда мы спасены!»
«Тогда и начинается молчанье[»].[90]

"But if you take a wider view of things,
you might, in general, still make the point:
a word is one more thing. Then we are saved!"
"Then all that's left is silence setting in.["]

This, then, is the silence that the poet has in mind when he describes the hospital as a vacuum—a place where sound can no longer travel and where space and time have been canceled out. The pronunciation of a word determines existence while also constituting a new existence that can be determined and silenced in its turn.

It is thus by inverting Marxist syntax, as Brodsky would suggest in "Less Than One," that Gorbunov interrupts Gorchakov's recitation of the "existence determines consciousness" dictum and pointedly flips it into reverse:

«Но бытие...» «Чайку тебе?» «Налей...
определяет...» «Греть?» «Без подогрева...
сознание... Ну ладно, подогрей».
«Прочел бы это справа ты налево».
«Да что же я, по-твоему—еврей?»[91]

"Existence..." "Do you want some tea?" "Sure, pour...
determines..." "Should I warm it up?" "Don't warm it...
the consciousness... all right, sure, warm it up."
"You should have read that phrase from right to left."
"And why is that? Am I some sort of Jew?"

Echoing his vision of the reversed "Jewish telescope," Gorbunov reverses Marx's dictum by reading it from right to left, like the Hebrew language: not "existence determines consciousness" (*bytie opredeliaet soznanie*), as Gorchakov argues, but "consciousness determines existence" (*soznanie opredeliaet bytie*). The creative dissenter stands out like a Jew for both his isolation from society and his deviant way of using words. But the potential for reversing Marx's dictum also lies within the Russian language, since the indistinguishability of nominative and accusative declensions of inanimate neuter nouns means that both *bytie* and *soznanie* can be read as subject and object.[92] Whether the capacity for reversing Marx's dictum originates in the Russian or in the Hebrew, it is language that mediates the dialogue of selves.

Gorbunov's dissenting stance does not stop Gorchakov from using his own language to restore the original dictum, however. Several stanzas later, Gorchakov manipulates the common root of the words "existence" (*bytie*) and "true existence" (*bytië*) to produce the negated "true non-existence" (*nebytië*):

[«]Пока у нас совместное житье,
нам лучше, видно, вместе по причине
того, что бытиё...» «Да не на "ё"!
Не бытиё, а бытие». «Да ты не—
не придирайся... да, небытиё,
когда меня не будет уж в помине,
придаст своеобразие равнине».
«Ты, стало быть, молчание мое...»[93]

> ["]As long as we remain in common lodgings,
> it would seem best we stick together since
> the true existence . . ." "You pronounced it wrong!
> Not true existence, but existence." "Don't—
> don't raise a ruckus . . . yes, true non-existence,
> when every trace of me has disappeared,
> will lend some needed contour to the flatland."
> "Then you must be none other than my silence."

If "parts of speech" are also material "things" that can suppress the creative consciousness, then the poet is ultimately defenseless against the language of existence and its negating prefix *ne*. Whether "consciousness determines existence" or "existence determines consciousness" boils down to a "twist of language," as Brodsky would put it in "Less Than One"—a reminder of the power of words to silence as well as liberate the mind.

Despite his cynicism about psychiatry, Brodsky took his psychiatric experiences to heart when it came to evaluating himself. Just as the dissenting writer generates self-consuming "parts of speech," psychiatric discourse imposes diagnostic labels that may lead to insanity and silence. Falling under his psychiatrists' linguistic sway, Gorchakov enacts this process on Gorbunov:

> [«]Эй, Горбунов!.. на кой мне Горбунов?!
> Уменьшим свою речь на Горбунова![»]⁹⁴

> ["]Hey, Gorbunov! . . . but who needs Gorbunov?!
> Let's wipe out Gorbunov by way of language!["]

Gorchakov declares his intention to erase Gorbunov from his vocabulary, demonstrating that if existence does succeed in negating consciousness, it will be by linguistic means. The poet puts himself at risk of silence by creating an alternate reality through words:

> [«]Молчанье—это будущее слов,
> уже пожравших гласными всю вещность,
> страшащуюся собственных углов,
> волна, перекрывающая вечность[»].⁹⁵

["]For silence is the future of those words
whose vowels have consumed the world of things
that quake in terror of their selfsame corners;
a wave that wraps across eternity.["]

The consequences of this linguistic self-consumption are harshest for the poet, who defines himself through language and is therefore prone to being redefined and silenced. If the creative dissenter plays at the border of madness, then diagnosis fixes that madness with a clinical "part of speech" from which the poet cannot escape.

To be sure, the poem's end is a narrative necessity, yet it is perhaps to the silence that follows the end of all poetry that the poet gestures when he highlights language's self-devouring power. Literary production protects the creative consciousness from the ravages of existence. But by the same token it incites that consciousness to consume itself. "One gets done in by one's own conceptual and analytic habits—e.g., using language to dissect experience, and so robbing one's mind of the benefits of intuition. Because, for all its beauty, a distinct concept always means a shrinkage of meaning, cutting off loose ends," Brodsky wrote in 1976.[96] Brodsky's psychiatric narrative suggests that the sundering of inner dialogue inaugurates a state of freedom at the price of sanity and speech. Having first explored the consequences of this dialogic breakdown in the hospital setting of "Gorbunov and Gorchakov," Brodsky revisited them when he left the Soviet Union for a life in emigration.

Poet as Exile in "A Part of Speech"

Insanity and silence might seem antithetical concerns for a poetic work as controlled and expressive as Brodsky's cycle "A Part of Speech." But it is precisely the destabilized dialogue between consciousness and existence and the associated specter of self-consuming words that link the collection with "Gorbunov and Gorchakov." Having first developed the "part of speech" concept in connection with his psychiatric experiences in 1963 and 1964, Brodsky reworked it with reference to exile in the wake of his June 1972 emigration. In "Gorbunov and Gorchakov," consciousness and existence provided each other with the dialogic counterpoint that maintained the poet's art of estrangement. The loss of that counterpoint split them into monologues whose "parts of speech" consumed themselves. The fear that something similar might happen resurfaces in 1975 and 1976 through "A Part of Speech." Exile frees consciousness to determine existence—here, by remaking the present existence in the image of the longed-for past. But because that past is now irretrievable and thus a product of the poet's imagination, the interplay of existence and consciousness is less a two-way dialogue than a pathologically alienated monologue. "This way lies either madness or the degree of coldness associated more with the pale-faced locals than with a hot-blooded exile," Brodsky wrote of life in emigration in his 1987 essay "The Condition We Call Exile, or Acorns Aweigh."[97] Amid the silence and isolation of exile, the only alternative to the creative "madness" of the Gorbunovian monologue is the uncreative "coldness" of the Gorchakovian monologue. Cut off from its past existence and reluctant to productively engage with its present one, consciousness therefore launches a new art of estrangement by grounding itself in the material reality of language itself. "For one in our profession," Brodsky wrote, "the condition we call exile is, first of all, a linguistic event: he is thrust from, he retreats into his mother tongue."[98] The reality of language supports the dialogue of selves that sustains both sanity and self-expression.

Brodsky described language as a material substance: the means by which consciousness both conversed with its surrounding existence and generated new existences of its own design. "Art is a form of resistance to the imperfection of reality, as well as an attempt to create an alternative reality, an alternative that one hopes will possess the hallmarks of a conceivable, if not an achievable, perfection," Brodsky commented in 1992.[99] In the absence of the existential echo that exile strips away, language itself provides an anchor for the creative consciousness. And for Brodsky, that anchor manifested itself most immediately through poetic form. "The poet who wishes to make his statements a reality for his audience must formulate them as a linguistic inevitability, a matter of the law of the language. Rhyme and meter are his weapons in attaining this goal," Brodsky wrote.[100] Responding in 1971 to a draft of Proffer's translation of "Gorbunov and Gorchakov," Brodsky accordingly highlighted the importance of the formal conventionality of his psychiatric narrative. "I can say nothing about G+G," he wrote in English. "Rather, almost nothing. Because I'll never understand completely free verse. All the thing is looking more modernistic than it was in Russian. Necessity of rhymes here is more obvious than anywhere."[101] If rhyme proves more necessary "than anywhere" in "Gorbunov and Gorchakov," it is evidently because it grounds the poet's creative excesses. What Loseff describes as the poem's "very strict formal symmetry," with its unflagging adherence to iambic pentameter and its regular rhyme pattern, thus offered a counterweight to the chaos of the unchecked consciousness.[102] That counterweight is tested in "A Part of Speech," however, as Brodsky offsets his continued use of rhyme with the looser rhythm of a *dol'nik* meter that plays at conventional metrical structures through what Barry Scherr has called "false starts" that are abandoned as the poems move on.[103] The freedom of exile disrupts consciousness' dialogue not only with its past and present existences, but also with the formal buttressing that language might alternatively provide.

It is thus from the destabilized perspective of a Gorbunov who has been severed from his native Gorchakov that Brodsky narrates "A Part of Speech." The passage of time and Brodsky's passage to the West had evidently not erased the imprint of the poet's psychiatric experiences. Just as Gorbunov drifted into a dreamlike realm of creativity, exile becomes a creative state in which the poet overlays his present reality with a now-imaginary past. According to George L. Kline, who knew Brodsky during what he calls the unproductive months of the poet's early exile, "my clear and painful impression was of a poet who feared that he might *never* write again."[104] When Brodsky produced the poem "In the Lake District" in late 1972, then, it was precisely the fear of silence that he set about describing:

Все то, что я писал в те времена,
сводилось неизбежно к многоточью.[105]

It was a time when anything I wrote
unraveled without fail into ellipsis.

The image of the "ellipsis"—the punctuation mark with which "Gorbunov and Gorchakov" fades out at its end—points to the overarching linguistic prism through which Brodsky portrayed both hospitalization and exile. Maximally expressive in its wealth of possible meanings, an ellipsis is also mute in its refusal to articulate them. The later publication of "A Part of Speech" may well have seemed a case in point, eliciting as it did minimal attention both in the Soviet Union, due to censorship, and in the West, where Russian-language readers were few.[106] As in the psychiatric hospital of Brodsky's youth, language becomes the means by which the dialogue of selves is not only sustained but also—and much more frighteningly—snuffed out.

The specter of insanity that haunted "Gorbunov and Gorchakov" accordingly resurfaces in "A Part of Speech" through numerous depictions of mental disintegration and the repetition of psychiatrically themed terms such as "madness" and "to lose one's mind." The first of these sets the cycle's tone beginning with the opening poem:

> Ниоткуда с любовью, надцатого мартобря,
> дорогой уважаемый милая, но не важно
> даже кто, ибо черт лица, говоря
> откровенно, не вспомнить уже, не ваш, но
> и ничей верный друг вас приветствует с одного
> из пяти континентов, держащегося на ковбоях;
> я любил тебя больше, чем ангелов и самого,
> и поэтому дальше теперь от тебя, чем от них обоих;
> поздно ночью, в уснувшей долине, на самом дне,
> в городке, занесенном снегом по ручку двери,
> извиваясь ночью на простыне—
> как не сказано ниже по крайней мере—
> я взбиваю подушку мычащим «ты»
> за морями, которым конца и края,
> в темноте всем телом твои черты,
> как безумное зеркало повторяя.[107]

> From nowhere with love, on Marchober the tenth,
> to my dear respected sweetheart, although it's no use
> guessing who (since the shape of your face, if I may be
> so frank, is now long past remembering) or whose
> faithful friend (your own, someone else's) wishes you health
> from that one of five continents that cowboys bear forth;
> I loved you much more than the angels and himself,
> which is why I'm now farther from you than from both;
> late at night, in a slumbering valley, its nethermost pit,
> in a town that's sunk in snowdrifts doorknob-deep,
> on the bed in the night with the sheets all atwist—
> though below on that subject there's hardly a peep—
> I'm mooing out "you" till the pillow is beat,
> torn asunder by seas that stretch on as if endless . . .
> in the darkness my body condemned to repeat
> your shape like a mirror succumbing to madness.

As was the case with "New Year at the Kanatchikova Dacha" and its allusion to "Ward No. 6," the poem establishes an immediate connection with the Russian literary tradition of psychiatric narratives. "Marchober," after all, is the fantasy month to which Poprishchin, the narrator of Nikolai Gogol's story "Notes of a Madman," dates one of his own diary entries. Reminiscent of Poprishchin's epistolary style and imagined exchange of letters between two lapdogs, the poem presents a one-way conversation between the poet and his native past. The result is less a productive dialogue than the monologue of a consciousness that has lost its moorings. The letter's return address is the unmapped "from nowhere," its date is the timeless "Marchober the tenth," its addressee is the gender-bending "dear respected sweetheart" [*dorogoi uvazhaemyi milaia*], and its author is the evasive "it's no use / guessing [...] whose / faithful friend (your own, someone else's)." Words tumble forth as if compulsively unleashed, with the only full stop falling at the poem's end. In the third-to-last line, which is missing the critical negator *net*, a grammatical structure is left unfinished. Indeed, the one successfully articulated word is the poet's "mooing" of the pronoun "you." The "parts of speech" that consciousness generates in order to resurrect its past existence have materialized themselves to the point where the body itself mimics the lost beloved's body "like a mirror succumbing to madness." The mirror is not only mad, however; it is also self-silencing in its shift from verbal to physical expression. By dispensing with its present reality in favor of an irrational dialogue with the past, consciousness materializes its own "parts of speech" to the point where they consume themselves.

Both the creative opportunities of exile and its pathological repercussions resurface throughout "A Part of Speech" as the poet compulsively reimagines his surroundings. In the poem that begins "The North crumples metal ...," for instance, there is little evidence that reality exists apart from the poet's subjective perception of it:

> То ли по льду каблук скользит, то ли сама земля
> закругляется под каблуком.[108]

> It may be the heel that's slipping on ice, or it may be the earth
> that's turning beneath the heel.

The poet vies with the divine for the spinning of the planet, indicating that exile has satisfied consciousness' desire to determine existence for itself. But the result, as the poem beginning with the words "A series of remarks . . ." indicates, is the silence that comes when the dialogue of selves is brought to a halt:

> Это—ряд наблюдений. В углу—тепло.
> Взгляд оставляет на вещи след.
> Вода представляет собой стекло.
> Человек страшней, чем его скелет.
>
> Зимний вечер с вином в нигде.
> Веранда под натиском ивняка.
> Тело покоится на локте,
> как морена вне ледника.
>
> Через тыщу лет из-за штор моллюск
> извлекут с проступившим сквозь бахрому
> оттиском «доброй ночи» уст,
> не имевших сказать кому.[109]

> A series of remarks. It's warm in the nook.
> Gazing on things leaves a trace of its own.
> Water's like glass if you take a quick look.
> Man frightens more than his own skeleton.
>
> A wintertime evening with wine in nowhere.
> A balcony under a willow's assault.
> Braced on an elbow, the body rests there
> like the particles that an ice floe sloughs off.
>
> A millennium hence from the curtain's fringe
> they'll pull out a mollusk that's poking through
> with "good night" still imprinted on its lips
> but no one remaining to say it to.

The poem begins with a battery of declarations, each of which is confined to a half-line or line and accentuated by an end-stress or full stop. The dispassionately objective tone of the delivery merely throws into relief the subjective nature of the observations, however. Reality is nothing more than what the poet makes of it: it is warm in the nook because it feels that way to him, water is like glass because it looks that way to him, life is more frightening than death because it seems that way to him. As the poet himself notes in a direct reiteration of Gorbunov's reality-shaping gaze, vision is one of the primary means by which reality is reinvented: "Gazing on things leaves a trace of its own." Sound is evidently another means, as observations give rise to each other through the medium of language. *Riad* ("series") leads intralinearly to the rhyme of *vzgliad* ("gazing"). The linguistic components of the words *ostavliaet* ("leaves") and *sled* ("trace") unite to produce the word *predstavliaet* and thus the idea of water having the "look" of glass. Aural elements of *steklo* ("glass") themselves give rise to the poet's comparison between *chelovek* ("man") and his *skelet* ("skeleton"). The creative consciousness is free to reinvent existence through language but also increasingly alienated in that endeavor. By materializing its own "parts of speech," it shields itself from the ravages of reality. Indeed, it even materializes itself as a physical body propped up on an elbow and, eventually, as a mollusk preserved for all time. Yet in the absence of true dialogue with the past or the present, the "parts of speech" that the poet produces cannot be conveyed in words; the fossilized mollusk will isolate itself to the point where one day it will have no one to whom it can bid "good night." By cutting off the echo of existence that confined it but also kept it defined, the creative consciousness silences itself.

During his first years of exile, then, Brodsky responded to what was evidently a renewed concern with silence by reconfiguring the Marxist terms through which he had once interpreted his psychiatric experiences. Just as Gorbunov and Gorchakov sought to remain in dialogue despite their divisive "contradiction," the exiled poet of "You know it's winter ..." compulsively addresses his native past:

> Потому что каблук оставляет следы—зима.
> В деревянных вещах, замерзая в поле,
> по прохожим себя узнают дома.
> Что сказать ввечеру о грядущем, коли
> воспоминанье в ночной тиши
> о тепле твоих—пропуск—когда уснула,
> тело отбрасывает от души
> на стену, точно тень от стула
> на стену ввечеру свеча,
> и под скатертью стянутым к лесу небом

над силосной башней натертый крылом грача
не отбелишь воздух колючим снегом.[110]

You know it's winter when your heel leaves a tread.
In the frozen expanses, it's by those who are passing
that the wood-cluttered houses distinguish themselves.
How can one speak of the future, come evening,
when in quietest night to recall your warm—skip—
while you slept is to sever the body from the soul
and to cast its projection over the wall as if
there's a candle using just such a wall
to project in the evening the shadow of a chair;
and when, between the tower silo and the linen sky
spread out toward the forest, the crow wing–chafed air
cannot be made white by the snow whipping by.

Exile renders consciousness so solipsistically autonomous that a track left by the poet's foot is enough to trigger the passing of seasons: "You know it's winter when your heel leaves a tread." Even the snow-covered homes lack a firm identity in the absence of a perceiving subject: "it's by those who are passing / that the wood-cluttered houses distinguish themselves." This sudden autonomy presents the poet with the creative choice that Brodsky would later describe in "The Condition We Call Exile, or Acorns Aweigh": He can either take refuge in the "coldness" of accepting his present reality or condemn himself to "madness" by continuing to address his now-imaginary past. And indeed, the poet repeatedly glances backward ("How can one speak of the future") by lending his memories material form ("and to cast its projection over the wall as if / there's a candle using just such a wall / to project in the evening the shadow of a chair") like the shadow figures in Plato's Allegory of the Cave. As in the allegory, the imagined reality of the shadow play becomes preferable to the material reality that lies beyond the cave's perimeter.[111] Similarly to the psychiatric setting of "New Year at the Kanatchikova Dacha," then, the page-like whiteness of the wall and the "linen sky" encapsulates the creative freedom that ensues when consciousness rejects existence. Yet it also suggests that, as long as the poet continues to cover that whiteness with his ink-like crow-scratchings about the past, true creative freedom will be impossible to achieve: "the crow wing-chafed air / cannot be made white by the snow whipping by." It therefore comes as no surprise that the poet finds himself unwilling or unable to articulate the proper name of the parts of the lover's body: "to recall your warm—skip—/ while you slept." The dialogue of selves that remains one-sided paves the way not only to insanity but also to silence.

Yet the alternative to the "madness" of the unchecked consciousness is the equally silent "coldness" of everyday existence, as the poet declares in "There is always the option . . .":

> Всегда остается возможность выйти из дому на
> улицу, чья коричневая длина
> успокоит твой взгляд подъездами, худобою
> голых деревьев, бликами луж, ходьбою.
> На пустой голове бриз шевелит ботву,
> и улица вдалеке сужается в букву «у»,
> как лицо к подбородку, и лающая собака
> вылетает из подворотни, как скомканная бумага.
> Улица. Некоторые дома
> лучше других: больше вещей в витринах;
> и хотя бы уж тем, что если сойдешь с ума,
> то, во всяком случае, не внутри них.[112]

> There is always the option of leaving the house
> where the avenue's brownness stretches way out
> and comforts your gaze with doorways, the stalks
> of stripped trees, the glinting of puddles, going on walks.
> The breeze stirs the crown of your empty head
> and the avenue thins to the letter "u" up ahead,
> like a face toward its chin, and some barking pup
> flies out of a side street like paper balled up.
> An avenue is all. Certain houses are inclined
> To be better than others: more things on display;
> and if only because if you do lose your mind,
> then at least it wouldn't be under their sway.

The sight of a long stretch of road is both inspiring and unnerving for the exiled poet, who has presumably gone outside to escape the failed attempt at poetic expression that is suggested by the dog's resemblance to "paper balled up." The infinite space of exile promises creative freedom but brings the poet closer to madness. The poet therefore stabilizes himself in the Gorchakovian coldness of his current reality: doorways, trees, puddles, taking walks, the "brownness" of the material street. He also roots himself in that reality by specifically linguistic means, condensing the word "avenue" (*ulitsa*) to the letter "u" to evoke the road's geometric vanishing point and repeating the *u* sound nearly two dozen times over the course of this short poem. Forced to purse again and again as they form the vowel with which *ulitsa* begins, the lips lose their capacity to generate other "parts of speech" as "things" that might be consumed, as well. Submitting to material reality reins in madness, as the poem's final clause attests with reference to the "better" houses: "if you do lose your mind, / then at least it wouldn't be under their sway." But the security that it brings also silences the poet by limiting his creative freedom.

Taking refuge in one's present reality comes at the price of self-expression. Yet as the poet's memories continue to fade, the insanity of continuing to address an imaginary past also paves the way to silence. In this way, neither present nor past provides a stabilizing echo in the poem beginning "... and at the word 'future'...":

> ... и при слове «грядущее» из русского языка
> выбегают мыши и всей оравой
> отгрызают от лакомого куска
> памяти, что твой сыр дырявой.
> После стольких зим уже безразлично, что
> или кто стоит в углу у окна за шторой,
> и в мозгу раздается не земное «до»,
> но ее шуршание. Жизнь, которой,
> как дареной вещи, не смотрят в пасть,
> обнажает зубы при каждой встрече.
> От всего человека вам остается часть
> речи. Часть речи вообще. Часть речи.[113]

> ... and at the word "future," a horde of mice
> rushes out of the Russian tongue to chew savory
> bits off your hole-filled cheese, that tasty slice
> of what once used to be your own memory.
> So many winters have passed that no one can say what
> or who stands in the corner behind the window shades,

and the brain hears a "do" that's less flesh and blood
than the rustle of what once was. For life imitates
that gift horse that shouldn't be looked at too hard:
Whenever you approach it, it flashes its teeth.
From the whole of a man you're left with a part
of speech. A part of speech is all. A part of speech.

The exiled poet utters the word "future" as a way of invoking a new reality wherein "no one can say what / or who stands in the corner behind the window shades." Yet because the ensuing dialogue of selves remains mediated by the language of the poet's past, there can be no looking ahead without looking backward: the pronunciation of *griadushchee*, an obsolete Russian word for "future," breathes life into the "mice" that inhabit the language and looses them on the poet's memories. The image of the mice-like words chewing holes into the poet's "cheese"-like brain suggests the psychiatric practice of lobotomy. And indeed, as Loseff has observed with reference to "Gorbunov and Gorchakov," Brodsky identified the "brain" as the locus of his poetic persona in a marked devaluation of the "heart" that preoccupied Russian poets of previous generations.[114] The poet's voracious "parts of speech" reduce the past to an inaudible "rustle" and transform the poet himself into a "part of speech" that is also gradually consumed: "From the whole of a man you're left with a part / of speech. A part of speech is all. A part of speech." The past becomes as silencing as the present within the soundless vacuum of exile.

Seeking an echo that transcends past and present, the poet turns to the material support structure of his staunchest companion: the Russian tongue itself. Language, for Brodsky, was the means by which the poet achieved—or else failed to achieve—a sustainable dialogue of selves. As Brodsky would write in "The Condition We Call Exile, or Acorns Aweigh," "to be an exiled writer is like being a dog or a man hurtled into outer space in a capsule (more like a dog, of course, than a man, because they will never retrieve you). And your capsule is your language. To finish the metaphor off, it must be added that before long the capsule's passenger discovers that it gravitates not earthward but outward."[115] Brodsky's cosmic metaphor is significant, since outer space is both a soundless vacuum, like the psychiatric hospital of "Gorbunov and Gorchakov," and a visually infinite space that promises freedom. In the final segment of "A Part of Speech," then, the poet dispenses with both his past and his present to root himself in the reality of language itself:

Я не то что схожу с ума, но устал за лето.
За рубашкой в комод полезешь, и день потерян.
Поскорей бы, что ли, пришла зима и занесла все это
города, человеков, но для начала зелень.
Стану спать не раздевшись или читать с любого
места чужую книгу, покамест остатки года,
как собака, сбежавшая от слепого,
переходят в положенном месте асфальт. Свобода—
это когда забываешь отчество у тирана,
а слюна во рту слаще халвы Шираза,
и хотя твой мозг перекручен, как рог барана,
ничего не каплет из голубого глаза.[116]

It's not that I'm losing my mind, I'm just tired of summer.
You grope for a shirt and it's as if the day hadn't been.
If only winter would come and get rid of this clutter:
The cities, the persons, but first: all that's green.
I will sleep fully clothed or read someone's book,
cracking it open entirely at random,
as the year, like a dog that a blindman just spooked,
crosses the pavement where it's required. Freedom
is when you forget the tyrant's full name,
while your saliva tastes sweeter than Turkish delight,
and though your brain's wound up like the horn of a ram,
nothing drips from your clear blue eye.

The poet uses the metaphor of the passing of seasons to capture the exile's choice between the "coldness" of embracing the tangible present and the "madness" of returning to an imaginary past. Summer is filled with the oppressive clutter and color of so many objects that "You grope for a shirt and it's as if the day hadn't been." Winter, by contrast, promises the absence of "green" and thus the page-like whiteness that signals creative freedom throughout the work analyzed in this chapter. But as the poem goes on to indicate, it also threatens to destabilize the poet who continues to reinvent his present reality in the image of the past.

Appearing to grasp his chance at freedom, the poet longs for winter to "come and get rid of this clutter" so that reality can be reimagined. Here, however, the "parts of speech" that consciousness materializes no longer stem from the irretrievable past. The poet forgets "the tyrant's full name," or in the original Russian, the tyrant's "patronymic"—a likely commentary on the political indifference that comes with freedom, since the patronymic stands as the only difference between Joseph Aleksandrovich Brodsky's and Joseph Vissarionovich Stalin's given names. Nor do the "parts of speech" generated by consciousness concern themselves with the present moment: the poet reorders "someone's book" by "cracking it open entirely at random," much as Gorbunov once reversed Marx's dictum by reading it from right to left. What remains in the absence of both past and present is the reality of language itself. Gravitating outward in his own "capsule" of language, the poet can disregard the material boundaries that separate night and day ("I will sleep fully clothed") and the passing years ("as the year, like a dog that a blindman just spooked, / crosses the pavement where it's required"). The resulting balance is precarious, however: the poet's brain is "wound up like the horn of a ram" and the specter of madness continues to loom. "It's not that I'm losing my mind," the poet notes defensively in the opening line. Viewed from this perspective, it is significant that the poet equates "freedom" with a semisedated state wherein "nothing drips from your clear blue eye" and "your saliva tastes sweeter than Turkish delight" (or "Persian halva," in the original Russian). With nothing to ground them in reality but the scaffolding of language itself, the poet's words, like the poet's stopped-up tears, may yet succumb to insanity and silence.

A Precarious Balance

Brodsky responded to the Soviet state's—and, in particular, psychiatry's—implementation of the Marxist dictum that "existence determines consciousness" by developing what he called an "art of estrangement" that theoretically gave consciousness pride of place. Yet in practice that art entailed striking a balance between consciousness and existence: sanity and self-expression both demanded that the poet engage with material reality. As the next chapter suggests, the writer and critic Andrei Siniavskii similarly maintained that balancing the forces of consciousness and existence was necessary for sanity. Yet if Siniavskii focused on what he presented as Soviet society's creative madness, Brodsky was primarily concerned with what happened to dissenting writers whose own creative impulses spun out of control. What Brodsky perceived as psychiatry's embrace of the Marxist dictum led him to test the opposite thesis—proposed with specific reference to psychiatric treatment in "Gorbunov and

Gorchakov" and revisited against the backdrop of exile in "A Part of Speech"—that consciousness could unilaterally determine existence by materializing its own "parts of speech."

The precariousness of the dialogue of selves and its relevance to Brodsky's psychiatric experiences are perhaps best captured by a passage that appears quite late in "Gorbunov and Gorchakov." For Gorbunov, the eye-level painted stripe that runs through the hallways of the psychiatric hospital looks like the infinite horizon of a sea that is filled to overflowing with the linguistic stuff of consciousness. But for Gorchakov, that seascape becomes an "abyss of pure existence" that ultimately renders people "mute":

> «Да, это море. Именно оно.
> Пучина бытия, откуда все мы,
> как витязи, явились так давно,
> что, не коснись ты снова этой темы,
> забыл бы я, что существует дно
> и горизонт, и прочие системы
> пространства, кроме той, где суждено
> нам видеть только крашеные стены
> с лиловыми их полосами; но
> умеющие слышати, да немы».[117]

> "Oh yes, it is the sea. The very thing.
> That same abyss of pure existence where
> we all, like knights, appeared so long ago
> that, if you never raised this theme again,
> I might forget there ever was a bottom
> and a horizon, or whatever systems
> of space you might imagine, other than
> the one where we must see these painted walls
> with their eternal purple stripes; however
> may those who still have ears to hear be mute."

Whereas Gorbunov focuses on the creative opportunities that alienation may bring, Gorchakov's interpretation serves as a reminder that the sundering of dialogue can lead to silence. And indeed, writing "Less Than One" in 1976, Brodsky would describe the very same stripe as "the line of an infinite common denominator" running through the Soviet Union and would go on to emphasize its "maddening" effect. "This decor was as maddening as it was omnipresent," he would recall, "and how many times in my life would I catch myself peering mindlessly at this blue two-inch-wide stripe, taking it sometimes for a sea horizon, sometimes for an embodiment of nothingness itself."[118] By personifying the linguistic forces of consciousness and existence in "Gorbunov and Gorchakov" and exploring their implications for exile in "A Part of Speech," Brodsky captured two ways of thinking that he sought to balance within himself.

CHAPTER 4

CREATIVE MADNESS:
THE CASE OF ANDREI SINIAVSKII

In his 1974 essay "The Literary Process in Russia," the writer Andrei Siniavskii recalled a prison-cell exchange from the months leading up to his 1966 trial for anti-Soviet agitation and propaganda. Assuming the voice of his alter ego Abram Terts, Siniavskii noted parenthetically: "A cell-mate at the Lubianka—a stool pigeon—once told me frankly, 'All you writers should be put in madhouses.' And in some lofty, metaphysical sense, he was right." The cellmate's comment was proof, the author concluded, that "all writing, regardless of its attitude toward power, is forbidden, objectionable, and it is precisely in that lawlessness that all of the joy and all of the essence of writing lies."[1] The "lawless" or criminal nature of art was crucial to Siniavskii's understanding of the writer's place in society.[2] Yet so was the notion that, in Soviet society specifically, what the writer had conceived as a voluntary "crime" against political or aesthetic norms might well be dismissed as involuntary. By the post-Stalin period, the cultural association between unsanctioned creativity and insanity had become so entrenched that even self-stylized literary "criminals" ran the risk of being declared mad.

Born in 1925, Siniavskii was a literary critic who taught at the Gor'kii Institute of World Literature and other respected institutions while publishing his scholarship in leading Soviet journals. But over the 1950s and early 1960s, he also produced more inflammatory works of fiction and nonfiction that he surreptitiously sent abroad to be published in *tamizdat* under the pseudonym Abram Terts.[3] In September 1965, he was arrested along with the writer Iulii Daniel', whose works had appeared in *tamizdat* under the pseudonym Nikolai

Arzhak. The two authors were tried in February 1966 and sentenced to seven years' hard labor and five years' internal exile, in the case of Siniavskii, and five years' labor and three years' exile, in the case of Daniel'. In the months preceding the trial, physicians at the V. P. Serbskii Institute for Forensic Psychiatry declared both authors "imputable," that is, able to evaluate and control their actions and therefore capable of standing trial. Yet when Siniavskii insisted during the trial itself that artistic expression should not be prosecuted, the court, its experts, and many critics and reporters accused him both implicitly and explicitly of simulating "nonimputability." Siniavskii was perfectly sane, the argument went, but by clouding his hostile political agenda in arcane literary discourse that mimicked pathological states, and by claiming that even such literary discourse was irreducible to the adjudicating language of law, he was seeking to evade punishment like a common criminal who feigned insanity in order to sidestep prosecution.

The trial represented a turning point in Siniavskii's life. Yet it also chimed with a major theme of his pretrial work. Under Joseph Stalin, Siniavskii suggested in his writings, the state had harnessed the Russian people's natural artistry to promote a fantastically idealized vision of reality that accorded with Socialist Realist aesthetic doctrine. The result was what this chapter designates "creative madness": a pathological tendency to perceive and represent life itself as if it were a malleable work of art. Siniavskii and Terts jointly presented society's creative madness as both a welcome source of artistic energy and a threat to the stability of its collective mind. Curbing it, they indicated, required a more refined awareness of the distinction between art and life. Together, they modeled that artistic awareness by self-consciously aestheticizing reality in ways that highlighted the abandon with which Soviet society did the same. Moreover, Siniavskii returned to the argument during the trial with reference to the court's characterization of him as a literary criminal who was using Terts's characters as mouthpieces for his own supposedly anti-Soviet views. By equating him with fictional characters, Siniavskii argued, the court was itself conflating art and life. The charge that the defendant was effectively simulating nonimputability thereby illustrated Siniavskii's own claim that society and the state had lost touch with reality.

Yet Siniavskii's distinction between himself and Terts was not so complete as the author would have had the court believe. In an article published in *Literaturnaia gazeta* not long before the trial, the critic Zoia Kedrina lambasted Siniavskii's "split personality" as a means of evading responsibility.[4] Siniavskii was quick to reject the term's psychiatric implications once the trial began. "As the critic Andrei Siniavskii, who published his works in our press, and as the writer Abram Terts, who published his works abroad, I naturally grasped the difference between these two people," he told the court. "But I never considered these differences to be essential or to constitute a split personality."[5] Writing in emigration in his 1982 essay "Dissidence as a Personal Experience," however, Siniavskii embraced that same "split personality" as proof of his artistic awareness: "From the very beginning of my literary career and quite independently of my will, I began to manifest a sort of 'split personality' that exists to this day." He went on: "It seems to me, though, that this 'split personality' is not a question of my personal psychology, but a problem stemming from Abram Terts's artistic style—an ironic, overdone style rife with fantasies and the grotesque."[6] Siniavskii dismisses the psychiatric connotations of Kedrina's diagnosis by redefining his "split personality" through literary discourse. His differences from Terts are aesthetic in nature, he suggests, and as such they do not indicate madness, be it actual or feigned. On the contrary, they testify to his capacity for rationally and responsibly balancing two authorial selves. This chapter accordingly distinguishes between Siniavskii and Terts as stylistically unique entities that ultimately form a unified whole. Aesthetic differences aside, the author and his alter ego were thematically aligned in both their pathologization of Soviet society and their resistance to dismissing literary dissent as simulated or actual madness.[7]

Catharine Theimer Nepomnyashchy and Harriet Murav's illuminating analyses of the interplay of political, legal, and literary discourses across Siniavskii's life and work establish the need for similar attention to biographical experience when analyzing literary and psychiatric discourses. Nepomnyashchy locates Terts's "criminal" essence in his destabilization of language itself while drawing attention to Siniavskii's presentation of literary language as exempt from political judgment.[8] Murav meanwhile highlights the legal dimensions of Siniavskii's claim that literary discourse is far too fraught with ambiguity and metaphor to be evaluated through the comparatively cut-and-dried language of law.[9] This chapter builds on their work to observe that not only did the court, its experts, and a number of critics and journalists accuse Siniavskii of attempting to deny his responsibility for Terts's writings; they did so by invoking psychiatric discourse. Moreover, it argues that Siniavskii himself foreshadowed this charge by coupling his pathologization of the state's tendency to treat life as art with the suggestion that the state itself pathologized literary dissent. "For all his Tertsian play with boundaries," Murav observes with respect to a theme that this chapter reinvestigates from a psychiatric angle, "Siniavskii insists on one boundary above all: the boundary between literature and life."[10] And indeed, Siniavskii and Terts's pretrial work suggests that viewing reality through a Socialist Realist lens had become the psychological norm across Soviet society. Paradoxically, it was the dissenter who exposed that delusion, and who thereby separated art from life, whom the state accused of succumbing to or simulating madness.

At the heart of the clash between the state's and Siniavskii's understandings of creativity and insanity were differing conceptions of the artistic process. The state tended to evaluate creative health through the lens of Vladimir Lenin's "reflection theory," or *teoriia otrazheniia*, while Siniavskii viewed it in keeping with the Formalist critic Viktor Shklovskii's theory of "defamiliarization," or *ostranenie*, and the sharper awareness of reality that it promoted. Reflection theory proceeded from the Marxist formula that "existence determines consciousness"—that very "dictum" that the poet Joseph Brodsky blamed for what he saw as the state's suppression of creativity, as discussed in chapter 3. In addition to presenting consciousness as a one-way reflection of existence, however, Lenin allowed for a two-way process that Brodsky stopped short of attributing to the state. For Lenin, the enlightened consciousness that accurately reflected existence might in turn reshape existence through the creative nature of social practice.[11] "The mastery over nature that is realized in human practice is the result of an objectively true reflection within the human head of the phenomena and processes of nature," Lenin wrote in his 1908 book *Materialism and Empirio-Criticism*.[12] By making room within Marx's formula for man's creative "mastery over nature," Lenin reconfigured existence and consciousness as mutually determining forces and human cognition as possessed of revolutionary power. In 1934, the argument became aesthetic doctrine with the formation of the Union of Soviet Writers and the official definition of Socialist Realism in its statute:

> Socialist Realism, being the fundamental method of Soviet artistic literature and literary criticism, demands of the artist the truthful, historically concrete depiction of reality in its revolutionary development. At the same time, the truthfulness and historical concreteness of the artistic depiction of reality must coincide with the aim to ideologically remold and reeducate the laborers in the spirit of socialism.[13]

According to the Writers' Union statute, the ideal Soviet artist was to both faithfully reflect a "truthful, historically concrete" reality and creatively further its "revolutionary development." Siniavskii, via Terts, would later cite this formulation to argue that the state had conflated what it presented as an objective view of reality with an idealized representation that was delusorily detached from it.

In addition to its literary applications, reflection theory entered psychiatry through reflex theory, or *reflektornaia teoriia*, which offered a physiological explanation for Lenin's reasoning by locating the reflective process within the nervous system itself.[14] In his remarks at the Pavlov Session for psychiatry in 1951, the psychiatrist Andrei Snezhnevskii denounced a colleague for conducting an "active struggle against I. P. Pavlov's reflex theory and in this way denying Lenin's reflection theory."[15] If to question reflex theory was to challenge reflection theory, then Snezhnevskii's message was clear: sanity and insanity would henceforth be defined in keeping with a codified interpretation of Marxist-Leninist ideology. Under Snezhnevskii's leadership, the psychiatric establishment began describing criminal nonimputability as a reflective malfunction of the brain itself. "In the presence of mental illnesses," Daniil Lunts of the Serbskii Institute wrote in 1967, "the manifested mental disorders damage the reflective activity of the brain and evoke a morbidly distorted reflection of the objective workings of actual reality, the results of which can be seen in the incorrect behavior of the patients."[16] Though Lunts found Siniavskii and Daniel' imputable when he chaired the team of psychiatrists that examined them in 1965, the ideological underpinnings of his definition of nonimputability facilitated the hospitalization of other dissenters.

Yet well before the punitive uses of psychiatry were exposed, Siniavskii was already depathologizing literary dissent by pathologizing society and the state. Terts's pretrial writings thus abound with ocular surfaces—mirrors, windows, eyes, and more—that claim to accurately reflect reality while in fact distorting it beyond recognition. "Although the scientist and the artist are observers," a teenage Siniavskii explained in a composition titled "Reflection Theory," "the observer's highest degree of activity is in the production of the phenomena he hopes to study, the creation of something new on the basis of observations."[17] And indeed, Terts's work suggests that the state situates consciousness and existence within a creative loop that invites the former to spin out of control. Both Siniavskii and Terts pushed back against the resulting insanity by cultivating and illustrating a more defamiliarized perspective rooted in Shklovskii's theory of *ostranenie*, which argues that art refreshes one's awareness of reality by presenting that reality as if new or strange and by highlighting the creative process itself.[18] Brodsky, who ascribed to the state the anticreative claim that "existence determines consciousness," explored the pathological extremes of prioritizing consciousness with respect to dissenting writers who took their creativity too far. For him, such madness could only be contained by a defamiliarizing dialogue between consciousness and existence. From Siniavskii's point of view, however, the state's proposal that the enlightened consciousness could determine existence had itself instituted a reign of creative madness. For Siniavskii, the artistic awareness that came with defamiliarization was therefore critical for all of society.

Siniavskii countered the reflective aesthetic of Socialist Realism with Terts's own aesthetic of Fantastic Realism, central to which was the idea that creative madness could be controlled through a process of defamiliarization. "For me the fantastic is inseparable from reality," Siniavskii later explained with reference to Terts's work. "It is not a far-away world but a path or way toward a deeper awareness of reality. Especially as reality itself became fantastic in the twentieth century, casting off the restrictions of ordinary, everyday life."[19] For Siniavskii, Fantastic Realism restored artistic awareness by foregrounding its own aestheticization of reality. In his essay "Art as Device" (1917), Shklovskii had stressed what he called the nonimputability of a life devoid of such awareness. "And so, held imputable for nothing [*v nichto vmeniaias'*], life slips away," Shklovskii wrote before concluding: "And so, in order to reinvest life with sensation, in order to feel things, in order to make the stone stony, there is this thing that we call art."[20] By developing an aesthetic based on the awareness that came through defamiliarization, Siniavskii positioned Shklovskii's theory as an antidote to creative madness.

During his trial, Siniavskii flatly denied that his work conveyed a political message.[21] Writing in 1982, however, he developed the point: "Abram Terts is a dissident primarily in his *stylistic* character."[22] For Siniavskii, Terts was not only a criminal but also a dissident in the sense that his work posed a challenge to the literary norms that the state invested with political meaning. And as Siniavskii affirmed in an expansion of the 1974 anecdote with which this chapter began, to write in such provocative ways could spur diagnostic reactions:

> Writing itself constitutes "thinking differently" [*inakomyslie*] in relation to life. In Russia one of my jailers for some reason once confessed in an intimate moment: "If I had my way, I'd put all writers, without exception, no matter how great—[William] Shakespeare, [Leo] Tolstoy, [Fyodor] Dostoevsky—into one big madhouse. Because all writers do is disrupt the normal progression of life." And I think this

man was maybe right, in his way. Right in the sense that the writer's very existence is a disturbance to society.[23]

Whereas in 1974 Siniavskii had consigned this anecdote to a parenthetical aside, here he turns it into a stand-alone object of analysis. For him, the pathologization of literary "crimes" confirmed the politicized lens through which the state and society interpreted Terts's writings. Siniavskii's elaboration of the anecdote from 1974 to 1982 suggests that he was paying attention to dissident reports of psychiatric abuse.[24] At the same time, it reiterates his own contention that writers and madmen have something in common: both experience the compulsion to create. Where writers differ from madmen is in their ability to control that compulsion through the artistic awareness that defamiliarization brings.

Reflection and Defamiliarization

Siniavskii's first major challenge to the creative excesses of reflection theory came in the essay "What Is Socialist Realism," written in 1957 in the voice of Terts and subsequently sent abroad for *tamizdat* publication.[25] Quoting the official definition of Socialist Realism cited above, Terts draws attention to what he describes as the titular doctrine's teleological nature:

> At the root of this formula—"the truthful, historically concrete depiction of reality in its revolutionary development"—lies the notion of the aim, that all-encompassing ideal toward which this truthfully depicted reality unswervingly and revolutionarily develops. Capturing the movement toward this aim and facilitating the advance of this aim while remaking the reader's consciousness in keeping with this aim—such is the aim of Socialist Realism, the most aim-driven art of modernity.[26]

Terts criticizes Socialist Realism for harnessing citizens' consciousnesses to a fantastic vision of reality that is ideologically determined and therefore highly aestheticized. Rather than call for a more accurate vision of reality, however, he advocates fostering a defamiliarized stance that will theoretically expose such aestheticization. "I place my faith in a phantasmagoric art that proposes hypotheses instead of aims and the grotesque instead of everyday description," he asserts. "It is the fullest way of capturing the spirit of modernity."[27] Where reflection seeks to deflect attention from the state's imposition of its own consciousness on both existence and the consciousnesses that reflect it in kind, defamiliarization preserves the critical distance on which sanity depends. Fantastic Realism accordingly counters Socialist Realism by heightening artistic awareness.

Yet Siniavskii and Terts were not wholly critical of society's creative madness, as for them the artistic energy behind that madness was something to be positively channeled. Lenin, Siniavskii wrote in his essay "A Point of Departure (An Experiment in Self-Analysis)" (1952–60), was "the gigantic swollen central brain of Bolshevism," a pure scientist who calculated and "set the direction, capacity, speed, and efficiency coefficient of administered blows."[28] Stalin, however, possessed the irrational mentality of an artist, and as such he was able to creatively breathe life into Lenin's hyperrational language. As Terts reiterated in 1974:

> Stalin turned on (possibly unaware that he was doing so) the magical forces contained within language, and Russian society, always susceptible to the figurative reception of words, to the miraculous transformation of life into the plot of a novel (which, by the way, is where the beauty and majesty of Russian literature come from), gave itself over to this nightmarish illusion of life in a world of miracles, sorcery, treachery, art, which take over reality before everyone's eyes, and, sending shudders down the spine, offer a certain exquisite thrill of entertainment.[29]

Stalin, Terts suggests, fostered creative madness by harnessing the Russian people's propensity for conflating art and life and using it to realize Lenin's metaphors.[30] Revolutionary phrases such as "imperialist lackey" accordingly took on flesh and blood as Stalinist newspapers envisioned literal lackeys groveling at their imperial masters' feet. Reality became a theatrical delusion—a "mass hypnosis" to which even the leader could not remain immune. "Clearly Stalin both believed and did not believe in his imagination, as befits a true artist," Siniavskii wrote in his 1987 essay "Stalin: Hero and Artist of the Stalin Era."[31] Testifying to the shared conceptual vocabulary that post-Stalinist dissenters deployed in their psychiatric narratives, Siniavskii's diagnosis of the realized metaphor echoes Brodsky's notion that madness is what happens when "parts of speech" are materialized as "things." If Brodsky used this idea to question the sanity of his own poetic creations, however, Siniavskii deployed it to diagnose the creative madness of society and the state. It was by imposing his consciousness on existence, Siniavskii suggested, that Stalin had passed on his own mad artistry to the myriad consciousnesses that reflected his aestheticized vision.

As an antidote to Stalinist reflection, Siniavskii and Terts proposed a more defamiliarized aesthetic that looked back to the modernist experiments of the revolutionary era. Vilified in the 1930s and 1940s, modernism had been cautiously rehabilitated after Stalin's death to the point where even recent memory of the controversy surrounding Boris Pasternak's 1958 receipt of the Nobel Prize in Literature did not prevent the release, in 1965, of the first academic collection of the poet's works. In his own introduction to that collection, Siniavskii wrote that modernist art displayed "that healthy, regenerating strength without which the development of a truly contemporary art is unimaginable."[32] Pasternak, Siniavskii noted, believed that "the catalyst for the creative process comes when we 'stop recognizing reality' and strive to talk about it with the effortlessness and artlessness of the first poet on earth."[33] Siniavskii's language starkly recalls Shklovskii's theory of defamiliarization, an effect that Siniavskii himself pursued through the literary voice of Terts. And indeed, Terts suggested in 1974, society's irrational tendency to conflate art and life could be productively channeled with a higher dose of artistic awareness:

> But being skeptical of the hope that anything in this world can be changed or corrected through the power of words, we must and should make use of our age-old purely Russian habit of perceiving the word as something real, as if it is already in and of itself the kind of act that gets you lined up against a wall—so that this fertilized and fertile earth can bring forth something marvelous, exotic, if not in the sense of life itself then in the narrower wordy, literary one.[34]

Creativity, for both Siniavskii and Terts, was an inherently irrational phenomenon that should be both embraced and checked by the rationality of defamiliarization. Rather than flatly condemn society's creative madness, then, the author encouraged its more measured deployment.

One of Pasternak's most successful means of defamiliarization, Siniavskii suggested in his introduction to the poet's work, was his transformation of the artist's consciousness into an empty yet ultimately self-contained vessel for absorbing existence and transmitting it as if seen anew. Pasternak, Siniavskii asserted, "says little about himself, and from the self, he carefully removes, he hides his 'I.' When reading his poems one sometimes succumbs to the illusion that there is no author at all, that he is even absent as a narrator, as a witness who has seen everything depicted there."[35] If the creative encounter between consciousness and existence is necessarily irrational, then the artist must learn to access that irrationality while imposing rational limits on it. Siniavskii's Pasternak does so not just by defamiliarizing reality through self-elimination but also by foregrounding that self-elimination in defamiliarizing ways.[36] The salutary benefits are made evident in Terts's collection of aphorisms "Thoughts Unawares." At the beginning of the collection, the narrator enjoys the "unaware" irrationality of eliminating his "I" and becoming a conduit for existence itself: "You live like a complete fool, but sometimes the most marvelous thoughts pop into your head."[37] By the closing line, however, he has restored both rationality and awareness by acknowledging his self-elimination and evaluating its results: "The thoughts dry up and stop coming as soon as you begin collecting them and thinking them through ..."[38] Whereas an aesthetic based on reflection licenses the creative consciousness to overwhelm existence, an aesthetic based on defamiliarization prefers to mindfully eliminate the self as a way of checking its creative excesses.

Evidently learning from Pasternak, Siniavskii eliminated his own "I" in part through the literary device of *skaz*. Celebrated by Formalist critics such as Boris Eikhenbaum, *skaz* refers to a narrative style that defies expectations of the unity of narrator and author by self-consciously suggesting the presence of a storyteller who does not coincide with the creator of the text.[39] By concealing himself behind the many *skaz*-like narrators who populate Terts's stories and, indeed, behind the *skaz*-like presence of Terts himself, Siniavskii modeled the self-elimination that was necessary for artistic awareness. Moreover, both he and Terts reinforced that awareness through the heavy use of another device: irony. Irony, like *skaz*, heightens artistic awareness, in its case by conveying a meaning that double-voicedly conflicts with what is literally said. As Terts notes in "What Is Socialist Realism," irony reached its apex in the nineteenth century with the creation of the "superfluous man," that heroic figure whose self-consciousness was so extreme as to spark suspicions of mental illness. Terts underscores the pathologizable nature of the ironic mode with a revealing quotation from the modernist poet Aleksandr Blok: "'The liveliest and most sensitive children of our century fell victim to a disease unknown to physical and spiritual doctors. This disease resembles the maladies of the soul and could be called "irony." It manifests itself in attacks of debilitating laughter, which begin with a demonically mocking and provocative smile and end in violence and blasphemy.'"[40] In place of the superfluous man, Terts goes on to argue, Socialist Realism proposed a new positive hero who "cures himself of fruitless self-examination and the unnecessary pangs of consciousness" by meaning everything that he says and echoing the views of the author himself.[41] From the state's perspective, the positive hero epitomizes creative health. But from Terts's perspective, he embodies the very conflation of art and life that has driven Soviet society mad.

After sending abroad "What Is Socialist Realism," Siniavskii appended an extra page offering Terts's solution to society's madness: "Let the extreme images of [E.T.A.] Hoffman, Dostoevsky, [Francisco] Goya, [Marc] Chagall, and that most socialist of realists [Vladimir] Maiakovskii, as well as many other realists and nonrealists, teach us how to be truthful with the help of preposterous fantasy."[42] Situating himself within a wider community of writers who also explored the aestheticization of reality, Terts redefines his defamiliarized aesthetic as a marker of artistic awareness. And indeed, his Fantastic Realist writings abound with protagonists whose deviant consciousnesses offer that very defamiliarized perspective that Socialist Realism seeks to negate.[43] Taking stock of the Soviet literary scene in his 1988 essay "The Space of Prose," Siniavskii accordingly praised the defamiliarizing effect of recent works of Fantastic Realism. The imaginary world of Tat'iana Tolstaia is "wonderful not because it reflects the wonder of the real world, as we were taught to do," he wrote. "Art reflects itself in the first instance. Art begins with a riddle. And a riddle is always an act of defamiliarization."[44] Presenting Shklovskii's theory as an antidote to the reflective aesthetic of Socialist Realist texts, Siniavskii suggests once again that defamiliarization facilitates artistic awareness. "Art sees that everything, absolutely everything around it is strange, interesting, unique, artistic," he concludes. "Art sees itself in the mirror of reality and stops short in wonder."[45] Where Socialist Realism irrationally conflates art and life, Fantastic Realism uses the "mirror of reality" to reassess its own limits.

Art and Power in *The Trial Begins*

Supplementing his and Siniavskii's essays, Terts explored the consequences of reflection and defamiliarization through fiction, as well. Art, once again, is an irrational process that demands a measure of rational awareness. Characters who prevent this awareness through an aesthetic of reflection display a tendency to conflate art and life to the point of creative madness. Characters who attain this awareness by means of defamiliarization, by contrast, ultimately promote creative health in themselves and those around them. Yet Terts also ascribes a competing definition of sanity and insanity to the state and society—one which equates reflection with creative health while characterizing in pathological terms the very defamiliarization that he defends. Again and again, as if anticipating those revelations of psychiatric abuse that would populate *samizdat* from the late 1960s, Terts's novellas and short stories expose the tendency to equate creative dissent with simulated or actual insanity.

Terts's 1956 novella *The Trial Begins* thus illustrates the idea that the idealistic cores of history's greatest "aims"—Christianity, the Enlightenment, and communism—all collapsed beneath the crippling weight of the antithetical "means" that were used to achieve them. Set at the end of Stalin's rule and narrated by a fictional author-narrator, it loosely follows the efforts of Globov, Moscow's chief prosecutor, to stage the show trial of Rabinovich, a Jewish physician who is accused of performing abortions. Each of the protagonists pursues a personalized aim by imposing his or her consciousness on existence and thus on the consciousnesses that faithfully reflect his or her vision of reality. Globov's wife Marina aestheticizes the reality of her own appearance by turning her admirers into mirrors of herself. The NKVD agents Vitia and Tolia aestheticize Soviet citizens' perception of reality by inventing instruments of mind control. And Globov aestheticizes reality itself by choreographing a theatrical charade of the rule of law. The delusions that ensue are countered, however, by the author-narrator's gradual shift from a reflective aesthetic to a more defamiliarized one that exposes its own aestheticization of reality. Significantly, the author-narrator's model of awareness is the Jewish physician Rabinovich, a dissenting figure whom he accuses of simulating insanity.

Commanding as each does the capacity to control citizens' minds, art and power become inextricably linked. Globov compares a policeman directing absent traffic at night to a conductor directing an orchestra: "At the signal of the conductor's baton the invisible crowds would freeze as if riveted to the spot or torrentially throw themselves forward."[46] Though an actual orchestra may sound like a flood, to the prosecutor "the music did not flow on its own; the conductor was directing it."[47] At the head of this highly aestheticized reality is the Stalin-like Master, a divine figure whose image is omnipresent at a parade attended by Globov and his son Serezha:

> Variously sized portraits of him, each very similar to the other, sailed through the square like a fleet of ships. Going past, the marchers did not look where they were going, but twisted their entire bodies around to turn once more in his direction.

> But the man himself, it seemed to Serezha, was in a strange way absent. Everything indicated that he was there, but it was as if he were missing.⁴⁸

The Master promotes a reflective aesthetic by imposing his consciousness on existence and the myriad consciousnesses that mirror it. His image is everywhere to be seen, wielding a hypnotic effect on his followers. Serezha's sense that the man himself is missing therefore indicates not self-elimination of the type pursued by Siniavskii and Pasternak, but a hypertrophied form of self-expression. The Master's apparent absence serves to conceal the manipulative nature of his claim to omniscience and aestheticization of reality.

When the Master appoints the author-narrator his literary mouthpiece in the Prologue, he similarly hides his artistic input by confining his physical presence to the image of a giant fist suspended in the air. Turning one wall of the author-narrator's apartment into an ostensibly transparent sheet of glass, he paints a picture of the aestheticized reality that he wishes his new spokesman to convey. "The wall of my room grew brighter and brighter," the author-narrator recalls. "Soon it became entirely transparent. Like glass. And I saw the City."⁴⁹ But the city in question is no ordinary metropolis; rather, it is a product of the Master's artistic imagination: "Decorations that were molded, poured, and carved from real gold covered the colossal stone edifices. Granite clothed in lace, reinforced concrete ornamented with bouquets and monograms, stainless steel beautified by coats of cream—everything spoke of the wealth of the people who lived in the Great City."⁵⁰ The wall becomes a delusory window that displays less an objective view of reality than the Master's subjective vision of it. The author-narrator's designated task is to capture this idealized reflection and disseminate it on the written page.

Terts further investigates the link between art and power by refracting reality through the various characters' own creative consciousnesses. Marina, for instance, controls her admirers by idealizing her mirror image. "She wants to fix herself on the slippery reflective surface. Contrary to all laws of physics, for eternity. So that even in her absence her lovely reflection would remain intact."⁵¹ The mirror serves as Marina's canvas for constructing her own reflection of reality:

> Exacting and businesslike, Marina double-checked her proportions. Was her backside drooping? Had wrinkles appeared on her neck? She unceremoniously kneaded her breasts, turned her head from side to side, massaged her stomach.

The mirror served as her carpenter's bench, her drafting table, her easel—the workplace of the woman who harbors dreams of beauty.⁵²

Marina's mirror image is a work of art, as the author-narrator's series of analogies demonstrates. Her admirers accordingly become animated reflections of that idealized vision of reality: "She gazes right through you so you want to turn around, she gazes as if there were a great mirror behind you and she wasn't speaking to you but looking at herself."⁵³ By transforming the consciousnesses of her admirers into mirrors of her own creative consciousness, Marina again illustrates the link between art and power.

It is only when Serezha catches sight of his stepmother honing her image that Marina's artistic process is exposed: "Before him lay a woman wrapped in a sheet. Her face was thickly coated with a pale purple porridge. It ran when the masseuse plunged her manicured hands into it. And then the face stirred and unstuck its eyelids. 'What are you doing here, Serezha? Don't be frightened. You don't recognize me? It's me, Marina.'"⁵⁴ Anticipating how he will later expose his own aestheticization of reality, the author-narrator uses defamiliarizing language to convey Serezha's renewed awareness. In a similar disruption of Marina's reflective control, after months of wooing the elusive beauty, the defense attorney Karlinskii is unable to perform sexually after Marina insists that the room be darkened. Having deconstructed her appearance through his defamiliarizing sense of touch, Karlinskii finds that it is only by invoking his visual memory of a pile of pornographic photographs that can rekindle his desire.⁵⁵ Shortly thereafter, Marina notices cracks in her façade in a shop window she passes on the street: "There, as if in a bad mirror, she caught a glimpse of herself. People walked across her, trolleybuses drove across her, pierced by vials of perfume and pyramids of multicolored soap. 'You can ruin your looks with all these products,' she thought, frowning at her reflection."⁵⁶ Where Marina once expertly conflated art and life, the external world has begun to interfere. The uneven glass defamiliarizes her reflection by crisscrossing it with the discordant images of the passersby outside and the beauty products within. Previously disdainful of cosmetics, she resigns herself to using them from now on. The breakdown of her reflection demands that she rebuild her illusion by still more interventional means.

If Marina idealizes the reality of her mirror image, then the NKVD agents Vitia and Tolia shape citizens' perception of reality by actively regulating their private thoughts. To do this, they invent a range of instruments for harnessing the consciousnesses of Soviet citizens to the state's conception of existence. Aware that people often flush their unsanctioned manuscripts down the toilet when their homes are searched, for instance, Tolia proposes installing a sewage net.[57] Vitia, however, has a better idea: He suggests installing a "psychoscope" in each district "so that even those who don't speak a word and don't express themselves on paper can be automatically controlled."[58] Dissenting thoughts would be overseen at a central office such that the authorities could step in and say: "Greetings, citizen. What were you thinking about four minutes and seventeen seconds ago? All is known to us. If you don't trust us, we can show you the film."[59] As Globov's dream sequence goes on to show, the regime seeks to replace the diversity of individual awareness with the unity of conforming to an overarching creative consciousness:

> Over the pneumatic door shone a quotation from the Master's works:
> GREAT AIMS GIVE RISE TO GREAT ENERGY.
> Behind the quotation was an empty space, in its center was a glass jar, and in the jar was a preserved brain, as tightly wound as the crust of the earth. Its hemispheres slowly throbbed.[60]

Encased in its semireflective coating of glass, the brain recalls Siniavskii's characterization of Lenin in "A Point of Departure" as both the brain of Bolshevism and the scientific scaffolding behind Stalin's aestheticized reality. Here, however, that brain is poised on the brink of insanity, as Rabinovich warns Globov in the latter's dream: "'I fear, Citizen Prosecutor, that it will go mad from all this constant contemplating.'"[61] When the state's consciousness imposes itself on existence and the millions of consciousnesses that reflect it in kind, society gives way to creative madness.

Such is the trajectory of Globov's transformation from the rational voice of law at the novella's beginning to the people's irrational scourge at its end. Globov initially appears as the positive hero whom the author-narrator is meant to depict: "The man was standing by his window, gazing at the sleeping City. He buttoned his uniform and raised his hand. It looked small and weak beside the right hand of God. But its gesture was just as fearsome and just as glorious."[62] The reflective positioning of Globov's and the Master's respective fists on opposite sides of a window conflates art and life by transforming the hero into a mirror of his creator. And indeed, Globov mimics the Master by idealizing reality through trials so scripted that Globov can rehearse them as if all of the necessary participants were present.⁶³ That the legal process treats life as art is further emphasized when the NKVD agent interrogating Serezha instructs the boy to look out the window: "Serezha saw the square he used to frequent, he saw the entrance to the metro with the tiny people diving inside, the little trolleybuses and cars filled with people, and each person was going where he wanted. And from above fell snow, real live snow."⁶⁴ What Serezha briefly glimpses through the building's window is a similarly aestheticized image of reality to the one Globov saw when, standing at his own window beside a bust of the Master, he observed the policeman conducting absent traffic. It is the same idealized view that Vitia and Tolia hope to disseminate by using a psychoscope to control citizens' minds. And it is the same amalgam of art and life that the author-narrator glimpses when the Master turns one wall of his apartment into a delusory window on the city. In a society that fails to impose limits on its own aestheticizing impulse, reflection becomes a mechanism of political power.

Order gives way to chaos, however, when the artistic force overseeing the display loses sight of any reality outside itself. At the end of the novella, the Master dies and unleashes his malevolent spirit on the mourners lining up to view his body. Significantly, it is Globov's own body that he transforms into a tool for wreaking havoc by clenching it in his enormous fist and using it to pummel the helpless crowd.⁶⁵ Globov's protests are to no avail; despite his claim to rationality, the prosecutor has become unable to control his compulsion to root out enemies of the state. In the privacy of his apartment, he takes a saber to his personal belongings, convinced that the state's enemies must be concealing themselves there: "Bouncing off the wall, the saber hit him hard on the head and shattered the chandelier. But even in the darkness, wet with blood, he continued striking out at the air, the emptiness—everywhere where they could be hiding."⁶⁶ Globov continues to seek out enemies even after extinguishing the light that would logically be necessary for finding them. His dismissal of the reality that actually surrounds him indicates his submission to an aestheticized reality that can no longer be contained.

By contrast with Globov, Vitia, Tolia, and Marina, two characters—the fictional author-narrator and the Jewish physician Rabinovich—illustrate to varying degrees the dissenting stance of defamiliarization. The author-narrator initially embraces his role as a prism for the Master's vision of reality only to defamiliarize that reality by exposing the creative process by which it is put together. At the beginning of the central narrative, for instance, he conceals both his own and the Master's input and thus the fact that their consciousnesses are determining the reader's perception of existence. By the end of the central narrative, however, his increasingly frequent first-person commentaries begin to disrupt that conflation of art and life. The result is a *skaz*-like storyteller who, like Siniavskii's Pasternak, reveals rather than conceals his self-elimination. In the Epilogue, the state arrests the author-narrator and relocates him to a camp at the periphery of the empire. The punishment merely reinforces the author-narrator's defamiliarized perspective, however. As opposed to the view of the idealized city that the author-narrator enjoyed from his vertiginous vantage point in the Prologue, the Epilogue takes place at the bottom of a ditch that confines the author-narrator's vision to the reality that he himself perceives. Significantly, this reality includes the characters Serezha and Rabinovich, calling into question their fictional status. Is the Epilogue the unvarnished truth behind the central narrative's idealization, or is the reality of the Epilogue itself also idealized? That *The Trial Begins* never fully resolves this question promotes a more acute awareness of its own conflation of art and life.

Yet the author-narrator remains far from unequivocal in his support of defamiliarization. Fearing the freedom of outright dissent, he interrupts the central text with a declaration of loyalty to the Master:

> Somewhere or other you can already hear someone whining.
> "Let's live freely and prance around like wolves."
> But I know, I know only too well, what swill these sellouts swallowed earlier, these poodles, these lapdogs, these pugs. And I don't want freedom. I need a Master.[67]

For the writer who devotes his artistic energy to transmitting an idealized reality imposed from above, defamiliarization appears to bring delusion and chaos. After the court attributes his own defamiliarized stance to the excesses of an "unchecked imagination," then, the author-narrator dutifully promises to correct his thinking.[68] Moreover, he mimics the state's diagnostic rhetoric by accusing Rabinovich, the one character whose view of reality is more defamiliarized than his own, of either succumbing to or simulating insanity:

> Lately something strange had been happening to [Rabinovich]. Perhaps he had lost his mind from that business of the doctor murderers who were declared innocent. It was on that matter that he had been convicted, after all, and somehow they had forgotten to rehabilitate him. But most likely he was simply feigning

abnormality, recalling with that usual Jewish slyness that in our country we are lenient toward the mentally ill and often release them into madhouses.[69]

Reasoning in tandem with the state, the author-narrator interprets Rabinovich's dissenting views as possible grounds for psychiatric diagnosis. Yet by giving Rabinovich the last word and having him utter it with both fists in the air, the novella inverts the Master and Globov's earlier postures to highlight the awareness that comes with maintaining a defamiliarized perspective:

> Grabbing the sword in both hands, [Rabinovich] lifted it like an umbrella and poked it at the sky hanging over our ditch.
> "In the name of God! With the help of God! In place of God! Against God!" he repeated like an actual madman. "And now there is no God. All that remains is the dialectic. It's time to forge a new sword for a new aim!"[70]

Communism is merely the latest in a series of aestheticized visions of reality, the Jew notes in a highly ironic tone that establishes him as the modern-day superfluous man who incites diagnosis or accusations of feigning. The literary implications are significant in light of the Jewish nature of Siniavskii's own pseudonym. As Terts confirmed in 1974: "Every Russian writer (of Russian heritage) who does not feel like writing by the book is a Jew. He is a degenerate and enemy of the people."[71] In *The Trial Begins*, it is Rabinovich who best illustrates the pathologizability of defamiliarization and dissent.

SELF-PATHOLOGIZATION IN "GRAPHOMANIACS"

The psychiatric implications of reflection and defamiliarization resurface in Terts's 1960 tale "Graphomaniacs (Stories from My Life)." The story's own fictional author-narrator, Pavel Straustin, is an unsuccessful novelist who, in accordance with Siniavskii's critique of reflection theory, conflates art and life to the point of creative madness while considering himself both brilliant and sane. But when Straustin discovers that his latest Socialist Realist opus, *In Search of Joy*, will not be published, he joins forces with a similarly unsuccessful poet named Semen Galkin who cultivates a more defamiliarized aesthetic that does distinguish art from life. The fact that defamiliarization preserves sanity and awareness is evident not least in the ironic tone with which Galkin, unlike Straustin, can pathologize himself:

Graphomania! The psychiatrists say it is an illness. An incurable, spiteful urge to produce poems, plays, novels, whether people like it or not. What talent, what genius, pray tell, what genius has not suffered from this noble malady? And every graphomaniac—this is key!—the mangiest and tiniest little graphomaniac believes in his trembling heart of hearts that he is a genius.[72]

Galkin's self-pathologization is tongue-in-cheek, but Straustin, who as an aspiring Socialist Realist writer has no ear for the double-voicedness of irony, takes it all too literally. Casting a diagnostic glance around him, he quickly decides that he is the only true genius among a crowd of graphomaniacs ranging from his little son Pavlik, who composes a fairytale about shock-worker dwarves; to the sanctioned writers who pursue money and fame; to the unsanctioned writers who spout their modernist logorrhea at Galkin's soirees; to the thousands of citizens who scribble their self-proclaimed works of genius at night. As the narrative progresses, however, Straustin acquires a level of awareness that culminates with his own ironic self-pathologization and composition of a work called "Graphomaniacs (Stories from My Life)." The repetition of Terts's title suggests that the story that has just ended may in fact have been penned by Straustin, highlighting the aestheticized nature of its vision of reality. By registering its own created status, "Graphomaniacs" draws defamiliarizing attention to the ease with which art may be taken for life.

Galkin's ironic comparison of writing to madness launches Straustin on an anguished reconsideration of his own psychological state. According to Galkin, the government is to blame for society's graphomania, since censorship entitles any writer to play the undiscovered genius. Galkin, however, commands the awareness to call himself a graphomaniac. "For instance, you have drunks, you have perverts, sadists, drug addicts ... As for me, I am a graphomaniac! Like Pushkin, like Leo Tolstoy!" he says.[73] Svetlana Boym has stressed the metaphorical nature of Galkin's self-diagnosis; where graphomania conveys a psychiatric meaning in the West, she writes, in Russia it is viewed as a "cultural illness."[74] But for Straustin the psychiatric meaning of graphomania is real and frightening. Here is Straustin quite clinically observing Galkin's retreats into that self-eliminating state that Galkin associates with creative health but Straustin associates with insanity: "From time to time he went silent and, his puffy lips slack, sat motionless for some fifteen minutes like an idiot, the perfect copy of a sheep or, to be precise, a ram. [...] A thread of spittle dangled onto his collar from his bulging lower lip."[75] Though Galkin presents his strategy of self-elimination as an aspect of the artistic process that he ironically calls graphomania, Straustin interprets it as actual madness.

Creativity, for Straustin, is that reflective process whereby life and art bleed into each other through a kind of hypertrophied self-expression: "In the air you could feel the breath of a coming storm," Straustin muses about the actual weather before borrowing the phrase for his magnum opus: "I liked the sound of that. I should remember it, make use of it. 'In the air you could feel the breath of a coming storm.' I'll use that line to end my novel *In Search of Joy*."[76] Straustin treats art as a reflection of life, on the one hand, and life as a reflection of art, on the other. Existence thus becomes a canvas onto which the hero can pathologically project his own creative consciousness. Shortly after Straustin has a daydream about the gray suit he would buy if his novel were ever to be published, his more successful classmate B. appears dressed in such a gray suit.[77] Straustin's son Pavlik meanwhile shares not only his father's name but also his pathological compulsion to write, while the heroine of *In Search of Joy* is an idealized mirror of Straustin's own wife Zinaida: "After all it was her image, full of impetuousness and passion, with wind-blown hair the color of ripe corn, that my memory fixed in the image of Tat'iana Krechet, changing only the name so that readers wouldn't guess, and placing her in a different historical setting."[78] The delusory power of the image is such that, for Straustin, it supplants reality itself: "I can't help but wonder when I see Zinaida: Can this unfamiliar, aging, unattractive woman—drained by female maladies, dressed in whatever came to hand, and always rushing one place or another—can she really be my wife?"[79] Reflective self-expression paves the way toward delusion in the absence of a defamiliarized perspective.

As was the case in *The Trial Begins*, Straustin's lack of artistic awareness is confirmed by way of semi-reflective surfaces such as his own unseeing eyes:

> I dreamed that, while I was sleeping, a piece of paper riddled with printed characters wormed its way through the back of my head and cerebellum and into my brainpan. Turning my eyes to the back of my head, I looked at this piece of paper and strained to read what was written there, and it was as if my entire fate depended on what I discovered. But the opaque paragraphs would appear before me for a moment and then grow dark, then reappear, then again grow dark, and nothing came of it.[80]

When Straustin looks at himself through the mirror of his own eyes, he cannot understand the reflection he sees. Nor can he make sense of his surroundings. Wandering through the city at night, he similarly turns the city's windows into reflections of himself:

> Having nothing better to do, I glanced into the lit windows on the first floors and in the basements and, when the curtains were not tightly drawn, one and the same picture appeared before me.
>
> It was late at night—the graphomaniac's favorite hour—and in every hole I saw, someone was writing. It was as if the city were teeming with writers, and all of them, from great to small, were pushing their fountain pens across the paper.[81]

Framed like a "picture" within each window is a graphomaniac with a fountain pen, the delusory connotations of which are further emphasized by the term Straustin uses for "fountain pen": *avtomaticheskaia ruchka*, or "automatic pen." Just as the heroes of *The Trial Begins* came to believe their delusory view of reality in the absence of defamiliarization, Straustin has turned the city's windows into pathological reflections of himself. His creative solipsism is such that, when he suddenly notices similarities between his writings and those of the literary "greats" Aleksandr Fadeev and Mikhail Sholokhov, he fails to realize that it is he who is unconsciously assimilating their language and instead accuses them of plagiarizing him.

By contrast, Galkin retains that artistic awareness that enables him to keep his creative impulse contained. The title page of his self-published book of poems duly acknowledges his role in shaping the reality that the book depicts: "Editor: S. Galkin. Graphic artist: S. Galkin. Technical editor: S. Galkin. Typesetter: S. Galkin. Circulation: 1 copy."[82] If Straustin's novel promotes delusion by concealing its reflective self-expression behind both an omniscient voice and the claim to accurately reflect life, Galkin's book draws attention to its aestheticization of reality by exposing the self that it eliminates. Anticipating how Siniavskii would later describe Pasternak, Straustin summarizes Galkin's credo as follows:

> The writer blathers with friends, goes on and on in manuscripts, repeats trite phrases, trips himself up, talks utter gibberish. And suddenly he spits it out! Spits out whatever popped into his head and made its way to the tip of his tongue. And

that's the point: You blather on until you cough up that unexpected word that henceforth, as Galkin liked to bombastically declare, the world will view as its perfect synonym.[83]

Galkin forgoes the madness of reflection by cultivating a more defamiliarized awareness of the irrational process of artistic creation. The self-eliminating stance that elicits diagnosis acts as his safeguard of creative health.

Where Straustin loses himself within reflection, then, Galkin places his creative impulse at a defamiliarizing remove. "They're always talking about 'leaving a mark' and 'expressing yourself,' he says. "But the way I see it, writers are concerned with one thing: self–e–li–mi–na–tion!"[84] What looks to Straustin like Galkin's insanity is in fact the creative health of the artist who eliminates his "I" in order to more accurately channel reality. As Galkin exclaims: "This thing here isn't worth anything because you wrote it, but that thing there isn't yours at all, and you wouldn't dare, you don't have the right to do anything to it—whether it's changing or improving it. It's not your property!"[85] Galkin embraces self-elimination as a path toward artistic awareness, but it is only toward the story's end that Straustin comes to understand and accept the same:

> Suddenly it seemed to me that I wasn't walking down the street on my own, but someone's fingers were moving me like a pencil is moved across paper. I walked in cramped, uneven handwriting, I hurried for dear life after the movement of the hand that composed and recorded everything on the asphalt: these deserted streets, and these buildings with their still-lit windows here and there, and myself—me and all my long, long unlucky life.[86]

Whereas previously Straustin had insisted that existence answer to his own consciousness, now he perceives that creativity entails becoming an empty vessel for reality itself. The realization terrifies him but also offers relief, suggesting as it does that the self-eliminating condition that he previously pathologized in Galkin is indicative of sanity and awareness. Upon returning to his apartment, Straustin embraces his graphomania and urges little Pavlik to ironically pathologize himself, as well. "Let them laugh at you, let them call you a graphomaniac," he declares. "They're graphomaniacs themselves. It's graphomaniacs as far as the eye can see."[87] "Graphomaniacs" concludes with Straustin sitting down to write a new work whose title—"Graphomaniacs

(Stories from My Life)"—defamiliarizes the story as a whole by transforming it into a narrative of its own genesis. Doubling back to emphasize the aestheticized nature of the reality that has been represented so far, the ending invites the reader to partake in Straustin's newfound awareness of the distinction between art and life.

Reality as Fantasy in *Liubimov*

The novella *Liubimov* (1962–63) stands as Siniavskii's most sustained comparison of reflection and defamiliarization and their implications for creative health. Like the Prologue and Epilogue of *The Trial Begins* and like the recurring title that folds "Graphomaniacs" back on itself, the Prologue and Epilogue of *Liubimov* expose the central narrative's idealized view of reality. Similarly defamiliarizing is the novella's movement among its *skaz*-like author-narrators. The two most dominant of these are Savelii Kuz'mich Proferansov, a librarian and amateur historian in the titular town Liubimov, and his ghostly ancestor Samson Samsonovich Proferansov, who regularly commandeers Savelii Kuz'mich's pen and endows a bicycle repairman named Leonid Tikhomirov with the power to control other people's minds. Reading Samson Samsonovich's *The Psychic Magnet* alongside Friedrich Engels' *The Dialectics of Nature*, Tikhomirov argues in a direct parody of reflection theory that the proposition that "consciousness is the highest product of matter" does not preclude the idea that "consciousness must also change and manufacture some sort of material product ..."[88] Tikhomirov puts his own creative consciousness to work by overthrowing the government of Liubimov and proclaiming the arrival of an illusory utopia in which water tastes like vodka, pickles taste like sausages, and even the dead might come back to life. As he falls ever further under the spell of his reality, however, the townspeople of Liubimov gradually break free. The novella ends with Tikhomirov's downfall and the town gearing up for a show trial that suggests that the literary and psychiatric questions raised have legal ramifications, as well.

A typical Soviet backwater, Liubimov is remarkable in one respect: its citizens harbor dreams of the fame and glory that sidestepped their town and are therefore ripe for psychological manipulation. The ghost of Samson Samsonovich arrives in Liubimov just before dawn to find the townspeople aestheticizing reality within their dreams: "What do you think is going on there, inside of them, under the cover of their brows, where they've cloistered themselves with bated breath since dawn? It's a holiday in there, all bustling and hustling, passions aflame, glasses clinking, and some anemic pauper leading a world revolution atop the governor's daughter for the umpteenth time."⁸⁹ If Liubimov's citizens are individually capable of idealizing reality within their dreams, then the power they collectively generate could conceivably alter the reality they actually share. Samson Samsonovich therefore promises them a leader who will harness that power and use it to remake existence itself. At the same time, he blurs the line between night and day so that their dreamlike state carries over through dawn: "It was as if huge pumps stationed everywhere were siphoning the reserves of blood out of these spacious nighttime refuges and onto the foggy mirrored surface of the day. But the reflection was more powerful than the original, and the colors that had faded there now lit up here, their strength increased tenfold."⁹⁰ By inviting Tikhomirov to turn reality into a mirror of the townspeople's dreams, Samson Samsonovich licenses him to reshape it in irrationally artistic ways.

Just as mirrors, windows, and other characters' eyes aestheticized the reality they claimed to reflect in Terts's earlier works of fiction, the eyes of Tikhomirov—known as the Squint-Eyed One—become semireflective surfaces for asserting power by conflating art and life: "It was as if his eyes, fixed at a distance, beyond the town limits, were sending terrible bluish flares out into space."⁹¹ Pledging his allegiance to Tikhomirov's vision early in the central narrative, Savelii Kuz'mich exposes its reflective underpinnings by imagining a utopian future wherein consciousness will have so domesticated existence that man will be able to satisfy each of his desires by pushing a button. To be sure, Savelii Kuz'mich notes, dissenting voices will continue to whine: "I'd rather rot away all covered with lice, I'd rather be in a primitive state and swing upside down from a eucalyptus branch, hanging by my tail."⁹² According to Savelii Kuz'mich, however, such expressions of resistance will also be overcome when Tikhomirov succeeds in reinventing consciousness itself:

> To prevent this from happening, it is necessary to reinvent it entirely: the old consciousness must be forced out and a new one put into place. And this reinvented man will, of his own accord, set off down the path to perfection and will even be grateful to you for all that science, and this is exactly what Lenia Tikhomirov understood and counted on.¹ What he, Lenia, was guessing was that bourgeois technology alone would get him nowhere unless he bolstered it from within by the reinvention of consciousness.²
>
>   1. He calculated wrongly.
>   2. His guessing was flawed.⁹³

Casting himself as a spokesman for Tikhomirov, Savelii Kuz'mich points to the fact that the end-stage of the leader's imposition of his own consciousness on existence is the reinvention of those myriad consciousnesses that form in reflection of his vision. That another outcome is more likely emerges, however, through Samson Samsonovich's insertion of the two dissenting footnotes. As was the case with the people and trolleybuses that disruptively crisscrossed Marina's reflection in *The Trial Begins*, Samson Samsonovich's footnotes testify both to the error of Tikhomirov's thinking and to the constructed nature of Savelii Kuz'mich's own depiction of reality. The central narrative thus traces the town historian's move away from an aesthetic rooted in reflection theory and toward the awareness of Samson Samsonovich's more defamiliarized perspective.

By contrast, Tikhomirov begins the central narrative with an awareness of the excesses of creativity before himself giving way to the creative madness he has spread. Gazing at his illusory wedding feast upon seizing power, he thinks, "Or maybe I alone fell under my hypnosis and the rest of them are healthy, sober, and only I, drunk with my mad dream, am seeing these tables wind their way around town, and that whooping by the river, and this wedding jaunt, and this easy victory over the heart of a woman who just recently was so indifferent to my sincerest professions ..."[94] Tikhomirov's clarity is short-lived, however; by the end of the novella, the leader has fallen prey to his own imaginings. Significantly, his creative madness brings a loss of vision. Tikhomirov "spun around before me, a scrawny, squint-eyed whippersnapper playing at king, and, trying in the darkness to inspect something that resisted optical measurement, gathered his courage in desperation," Samson Samsonovich writes.[95] The leader of the town has aestheticized reality to the point where he can no longer separate the real from the ideal. Echoing the critique of reflection theory that resonates throughout Siniavskii and Terts's essays and early fiction, the author-narrator proceeds to lodge a protest:

> How dare man in his blindness violate the harmony of existence with his senseless din? How dare he divert the great waterways and topple centuries-old trees that have been nourished for the highest aims? It's all well and good to change your own consciousness, to turn the whole congregation into cogs and castors. But the trees! But the stones! But the old women—your wretched mothers, do you hear me? the mothers!—should not be touched ...[96]

As is shortly confirmed by an explanatory footnote identifying Tikhomirov as the blind man in question, when consciousness imposes itself on other consciousnesses by reshaping the existence that they reflect, the consequence is creative madness.

Rather than cultivate the defamiliarized perspective of Galkin in "Graphomaniacs," then, Tikhomirov hews closer to the early Straustin by pathologically conflating art and life. His thoughts, "like ants in a disturbed anthill, swarmed in his brain and rapidly erected multistoried structures"— fantasies of world domination that directly echo the language used to describe the idealized city of *The Trial Begins* while similarly situating him at their center.[97] Tikhomirov "envisioned mankind in the form of a colossus, with the vigorous torso of a fighter on which the half-turned, proud head of a thinker was sculpted—was that not his own, Tikhomirov's, ministerial head?"[98] Once again Terts invokes the image of the centralizing brain, only here it is not Lenin's or the Master's creative consciousness but Tikhomirov's own consciousness that shapes existence. The bicycle repairman aims at nothing less than complete control—a goal that he finally achieves precisely as he loses his mind: "Never had Tikhomirov commanded such power to rule the masses and to charge them with untold reserves of energy. Only his own thoughts were beyond his control, and the smallest thoughtlet, the slightest mental tic, whatever nonsense popped into his head was at once brought to life by those around him."[99] Tikhomirov's unhinged psychic powers so overwhelm the town of Liubimov that, even when the leader manages to immobilize the chaos in a theatrical tableau, a stray thought is enough to set it going again: "The director's own nerves gave way before this forest of uplifted, twisted joints. A voice whispered to him: 'And what if that old man over there, the one pretending to be a dog, yaps anyway . . .' And at this involuntary thought the old man yapped, and Lenia lost his focus, and the silence exploded in a new bout of rabid fury [*beshenstva*] . . ."[100] As is stressed by the combination of the theatrical term "director" and the diagnostic label "rabid fury," Tikhomirov's creative impulse has taken on a life of its own.

The return to sanity demands defamiliarization and thus retreat from Tikhomirov's sphere of psychic influence, be it the external emigration of physical flight or the internal emigration of deviance and dissent. By the end of the central narrative, so many citizens have fled Liubimov that the town is a mere shadow of its former self. Yet even at the height of Tikhomirov's power, the townspeople actively withdraw by beginning to cultivate pathologizable behaviors. "And man will take to drink from sheer misery, as an act of protest. He'll start stealing government-regulated spirits, vodka, drugs," Savelii Kuz'mich predicts.[101] Standing over the body of one such citizen toward the end of the central narrative, Tikhomirov struggles to understand why a thief whom he had released from prison should have then proceeded to drink himself to death. "You wanted your freedom?" he asks. "What more freedom could you have wanted when you had all that your heart desired?"[102] Wandering around the town, Tikhomirov encounters a society that is rapidly sliding backward in time: half-built monuments, citizens high on home-brewed vodka, a man unabashedly urinating in the street. A local girl miscarries a fetus that boasts a full-grown penis, mustache, and beard; this is not Tikhomirov's prophecy of rational evolution but the chaos of degeneration and dissent. Turning back the clock of historical progress that Tikhomirov sped up, the people of Liubimov reject their leader's vision of reality.

To the extent that Tikhomirov's hypnotic hold does manage to subdue the population for a time, however, its reflective underpinnings testify to the link between art and power that *The Trial Begins* also emphasized. Shortly after completing his coup, the former bicycle repairman mimics the Master of *The Trial Begins* by anointing Savelii Kuz'mich his literary prophet: "Your task as a writer, as the town historian, is to ceaselessly examine reality in its unswerving development and to provide each fact with its truthful reflection. Be our mirror, our Leo Tolstoy; it isn't for nothing that the people call him 'the mirror of the Revolution,' after all."[103] Tikhomirov constructs his spokesman's remit from canonical texts that argue in part for consciousness' capacity to shape the existence it reflects—here, a parodic combination of the Writers' Union 1934 statute and Lenin's 1908 essay "Leo Tolstoy as a Mirror of the Russian Revolution."[104] The aesthetic nature of Tikhomirov's newfound rule is accordingly emphasized by Savelii Kuz'mich's designation of Liubimov as a work of art: the town, Savelii Kuz'mich proclaims, has now become "a picture worthy of a painter's brush."[105]

Savelii Kuz'mich begins the central narrative as a believer in reflection theory, only to acquire the critical distance and artistic awareness that a more defamiliarized perspective on reality provides. The end-stage of this process is evident in the Prologue and Epilogue, both of which describe his state of mind in the wake of Tikhomirov's downfall. Creative health, Savelii Kuz'mich has now begun to realize just as Straustin of "Graphomaniacs" did before him, entails self-consciously eliminating the self as a way of more faithfully absorbing reality:

> You write without any understanding of what is happening to you and where these words are coming from—words that you yourself never heard and never thought to put in writing, and now, on their own, they have suddenly bobbed to the surface from under your pen and, gosling-like, set off swimming across the paper like veritable ducks, like geese, like veritable black-winged Australian swans...[106]

Whereas much of the novella's central narrative recalls Savelii Kuz'mich's resistance to Samson Samsonovich's direction of his pen, the clarity of hindsight enables the historian to embrace his creative impulse with a greater measure of artistic awareness. "Let's put our heads together like we used to and pitch in to give the wheel of history one more spin," he plaintively begs his now-departed ancestor in the Epilogue.[107] Though Savelii Kuz'mich still longs to aestheticize reality, he now demonstrates an increased awareness of how art can irrationally crowd out life.

Yet as Savelii Kuz'mich observes, in a stark echo of the author-narrator's diagnosis of Rabinovich in *The Trial Begins*, the writer who defamiliarizes reality is likely to be accused of simulating or even succumbing to mental illness. "Are you trying to pass yourself off as a holy fool?" Tikhomirov responds in the central narrative when the disaffected Savelii Kuz'mich regales him with an irony-laced ode.[108] To a leader who reflectively conflates art and life, Savelii Kuz'mich's newly defamiliarized and double-voiced aesthetic smacks of deviance and even insanity. Tikhomirov, who continues to hold Savelii Kuz'mich responsible just as the state would do with Siniavskii himself, concludes that the historian must be feigning his symptoms. Yet as Savelii Kuz'mich strategically reasons after Tikhomirov's demise, the same association between defamiliarization and madness may work to the benefit of the dissenting writer who does seek to avoid being held responsible for his crimes. "If they lock my poor little hands and feet in iron shackles on Judgment Day, I tell you now: I'll deny it all, you better believe I'll deny it. 'Oho,' I'll say, 'Citizen Judges! They tricked me, they led me astray. Shoot me, if you like, but I'm not guilty!'"[109] Assuming that he can avoid the charge of feigning, the literary criminal may indeed take refuge in the state's pathologization of his self-elimination and dissent.

The chronicler's path toward artistic awareness suggests an antidote to Tikhomirov's lack of such awareness—an antidote that reverberates on a formal level through the structure of the novella itself. Savelii Kuz'mich's narration is accordingly ringed by several other *skaz*-like voices that ripple outward from the ancestral author Samson Samsonovich, to what appears to be yet another unnamed author-narrator, to the pseudonym Abram Terts, to the biographical author Andrei Siniavskii, himself.[110] These narrative voices grow ever more aware as they proliferate, highlighting both the constructed nature of the novella and the increasing rationality of their purpose. "*Skaz* is a deviation from the average, generally accepted literary norm," Siniavskii later commented about *Liubimov*. "Its words can sound strange, wild, at odds with their surroundings, and even exotic to the reader's ear. As a result, the word in *skaz* becomes philologically palpable and physiologically palpable."[111] What *Liubimov* ultimately suggests is that the reflective logic of creative madness can be kept in check by the artistic awareness that defamiliarization brings. Yet so do *The Trial Begins* and "Graphomaniacs": works of fiction that, as if illustrating Terts's claims about the state's conflation of art and life, would be taken as reflections of Siniavskii himself during the latter's trial.

Siniavskii on Trial

Siniavskii's attitude toward the state's aestheticization of reality was deeply ambivalent. On the one hand, the author welcomed the artistic energy that, in his view, the Soviet project had unleashed. On the other hand, he suggested that Stalin's treatment of life as art had condemned society to creative madness. For Siniavskii, the reflective tenets of sanctioned culture had vaulted a fundamentally subjective view of reality to the status of objective truth. Emphasizing the pathological results of this process, Siniavskii proposed a defamiliarized credo of irony, *skaz*, and self-elimination that aimed to more self-consciously channel that fantastical aestheticization of reality. Following Siniavskii's 1965 arrest for anti-Soviet agitation and propaganda, a team of psychiatrists found the defendant imputable and declared that the court could prosecute him as charged. At the same time, a team of literary experts examined Terts's works and confirmed that Siniavskii was indeed their author. These evaluations were followed by newspaper articles and a prosecutorial strategy that equated the author with his fictional heroes while dismissing his diagnostically provocative aesthetic and his courtroom argument for art's exemption from legal prosecution as strategic devices for evading punishment. Psychiatric, literary, and legal discourses came together to affirm Siniavskii's responsibility for the words and actions of his fictional characters, thereby illustrating what the author had himself pathologized as the state's conflation of life and art.

Siniavskii, who described Terts as a literary "criminal," was acutely aware of both the cultural tendency to link unsanctioned creativity with insanity and the pathologizable nature of his alter ego's aesthetic. While literary deviance had long been viewed through a diagnostic lens, Nikita Khrushchev arguably pathologized literary crime, specifically, in a 1959 speech to the Writers' Union. According to Khrushchev: "A crime is a deviation from the generally accepted norms of behavior in society, often caused by mental disorders. Can there be diseases, mental disorders among certain people in a communist society? It appears there can be. If so, then there can also be offenses that are characteristic of people with abnormal minds."[112] Soviet and Western critics would later describe Khrushchev's comment as a top-down sanction of the psychiatric repression of dissidents.[113] That Khrushchev addressed his words to members of the Writers' Union should not be overlooked, however, since if the Soviet leader was indeed pathologizing criminals, then he was pathologizing literary criminals high among them.

Khrushchev's speech was printed across the first three pages of *Pravda*, making it likely that Siniavskii read these words. Yet even if the author only encountered them upon joining the Writers' Union the following year, he was already well aware of the diagnostically provocative nature of Terts's "criminal" texts. Addressing his investigators in a statement dated November 30, 1965, Siniavskii recalled how an acquaintance had once "expressed the opinion that the hero of [one of Terts's stories] was clearly psychologically abnormal and that everything was happening only in his imagination, and had then begun recalling similar cases from his own medical practice."[114] In another deposition dated December 16, Siniavskii reiterated that, "in content and style (their predilection for the supernatural fantastic, their interest in people with manic personalities, their formal refinement of language and so on), my works differed noticeably from the literature of the time when I was writing."[115] Indeed, Siniavskii informed his investigators, it was precisely the pathologies of creativity that interested him; his goal in composing "Graphomaniacs" had been to explore the "passion for writing, which reaches manic proportions and consumes the genius and the hack alike."[116] In light of this interest, he had drawn inspiration from Nikolai Gogol's fantastic tales "Nevskii Prospect," "The Nose," and "Notes of a Madman"—stories that thematize the relationship between creativity and insanity.[117] Siniavskii thus built Terts's body of work with an eye to its diagnostically provocative nature.

The state and Siniavskii were in full agreement that the author should be held responsible for his actions. Yet whereas Siniavskii's assumption of responsibility stemmed from his view of art as the rational deployment of literary devices, the state's ascription of responsibility testified to what Siniavskii had himself identified as its irrational adherence to reflection theory. When it came to evaluating Siniavskii's psychological condition, for instance, the court used psychiatric discourse to present his consciousness as capable of accurately reflecting existence. Siniavskii's mental health having thus been established, Terts's distortions of reality could then be presented as a choice for which Siniavskii himself must be held to legal account. But making this argument entailed dismissing the alternate possibility that Terts's pathologizable aesthetic might be read as a mirror of Siniavskii's own pathologies and thus nonimputability. This dismissal unfolded as follows: On December 18, a Serbskii Institute team of physicians headed by Daniil Lunts found the author imputable and released him to the court for prosecution. But the team also dwelled in detail on the diagnostically provocative nature of Siniavskii's stance:

> On this basis, the commission has reached the conclusion that SINIAVSKII A. D. does not suffer from mental illness. He displays psychopathic traits of character that express themselves in timidity, in an internal striving toward solitude, and in a heightened sensitivity, in experiences such as a subjective feeling of "mental aging," and in a certain tendency toward symbolic reasoning and conceptualization that leaves intellectual functioning intact.[118]

Situating Siniavskii's defamiliarizing approach to life and Terts's defamiliarizing approach to art within a reflective relationship, the psychiatrists commented: "The subject's unique worldview formed slowly and gradually over time and expressed itself, in his words, in the perception of the world as 'forever new and mysterious.' This sort of worldview is reflected in his creative work, particularly in his description of artistic images."[119] Reflection theory might thus have licensed the psychiatrists to evaluate Terts's diagnostically provocative fiction as a mirror of Siniavskii's state of mind. Yet Lunts and his colleagues ultimately dismissed this possibility by foregrounding another reflective relationship: that between the author's consciousness and existence itself. By indicating that Siniavskii's consciousness was indeed capable of reflecting existence despite the author's "psychopathic traits of character" and despite what they described as his deliberate choice to distort reality instead, the physicians affirmed his imputability and determined that he could be prosecuted as charged.

Psychiatry was not the only discursive parameter through which the court established Siniavskii's ability to reflect reality, however; the state also sought out literary expertise. When Siniavskii was arrested on September 8, 1965, he initially denied having read Terts's works.[120] That first denial evidently put his investigators on guard even though Siniavskii acknowledged just a few days later that he and Terts were one and the same.[121] On November 22, the KGB therefore presented a team of literary experts with a pair of questions: Had the works attributed to Terts been written by one individual? And could that individual be identified as Siniavskii?[122] These questions were apparently aimed at preventing Siniavskii from ever being able to renounce the content of Terts's writings. But from the perspective of a literary culture that equated creative sanity with a reflective unity of author, narrator, and hero, they also enabled the court to argue that Siniavskii had cultivated his "split personality" precisely in order to disrupt that unity. In their December 14 report, the literary experts accordingly drew attention to Siniavskii's diagnostically provocative use of such "devices as hallucination, dreams, and delirium that are supposedly meant to achieve a deeper understanding of the psychological state of his main characters, the depiction of scenes where his heroes undergo 'epiphanies,' split personalities, and so on."[123] Yet they also responded positively to the questions put before them, thereby setting the stage for Siniavskii's "split personality" to be dismissed as a façade. Literary discourse and psychiatric discourse together confirmed the author's identity and responsibility for his actions.

In the weeks leading up to the trial, a series of articles by journalists and critics explained Siniavskii's actions to a wider audience in similar terms that further laid bare the conflation of art and life that the author had long pathologized. A January 13, 1966, piece for *Izvestiia* by Dmitrii Eremin, the secretary of the Moscow section of the Union of Soviet Writers, thus noted about *Liubimov* that "it is not always easy in the delirious phantasmagoria of this lampoon to find one's way to the real-life prototypes. But the ideological-political essence is utterly obvious. This is an unrestrained mockery of the laws of history, of those who gave their lives in the struggle for our great aims. It is a mockery of our country and people."[124] For Eremin, *Liubimov* was indeed meant to function as a reflection of Soviet reality, making Terts's "delirious" aesthetic nothing more than a mechanism for disguising Siniavskii's responsibility for his crimes. Writing for *Literaturnaia gazeta* on January 22, the critic Zoia Kedrina also depicted what she called the author's "incoherent rambling" as a cover-up. "A. Terts's extreme entanglement of form is nothing more than a colorful camouflage for his 'basic ideas,' and when you strip it away and throw it aside, the naked formula is shocking at first: Is that all there is?! Two or three worn-out theses of anti-Soviet propaganda, familiar from time immemorial," she wrote.[125] Siniavskii was perfectly capable of reflecting reality as it truly was, Kedrina's article suggests in concert with Eremin's critique; his distortion of reality therefore constituted a deliberate choice, while his "entanglement of form" was merely a means of evasion. Coupled with the psychiatric and literary experts' twin admissions of the pathologizable nature of the author's aesthetic,

Kedrina and Eremin's articles illustrate the allegation that Siniavskii had sought to conceal his crimes by writing in diagnostically provocative ways.

Siniavskii himself countered such reflective readings by highlighting his commitment to both defamiliarization and an essentially Formalist notion of art as device. His primary object of representation had not, in fact, been Soviet reality, he told investigators before the trial. Rather, it had been the fantastic reality that emerged by way of contrast with the everyday:

> My fantastic images and plots play out not in some imaginary land but in the conditions of actual reality, the everyday grind, which contrasts with the elevated, fantastic level and, at the same time, acts as its artistic confirmation by authenticating the verisimilitude of the most unlikely occurrences. This second (realistic) level never interested me in and of itself, and usually played an instrumental role in my works rather than being the main object of representation.[126]

To the extent that he did seek to portray Soviet existence, Siniavskii confirmed, his purpose was decidedly not reflective: What interested him was not existence itself but rather its fantastically aestheticized representation. For Siniavskii, depicting the fantastic encouraged artistic awareness by cutting through the delusions of lived reality. For the state, however, that lived reality was indeed Siniavskii's object of representation, and the defendant's defamiliarized aesthetic therefore a diagnostically provocative façade. Writing for *Sovetskaia Rossiia* on February 13, 1966, the journalist I. Konetko thus accused Siniavskii of inventing a "new literary credo, some sort of mishmash of teleology and mysticism, and calling it all Fantastic Realism. 'My works are complicated, tangled up,' Siniavskii repeats again and again. 'It's hard to put your finger on the logical essence of the images. Even I don't know what they mean.'"[127] For Konetko, as for Eremin and Kedrina, Terts's pathologizable aesthetic amounted to a disguise for Siniavskii's politically motivated distortion of reality.

Drawing a similarly reflective link between Terts's art and Siniavskii's life, Konetko went on to compare the defendant's self-eliminating aesthetic and behavior on the stand to that of a common criminal who simulates insanity in order to be declared nonimputable:

> Criminals caught red-handed at the scene of the crime often pretend to be criminally nonimputable. Something similar is happening here. Only this time the criminal is a man of letters and his defense consists of literary arguments—a new

theory, supposedly thought up by him and rooted in the almost mystical notion that the author was unaware of what and how he was writing, and therefore need not answer for anything.[128]

What Konetko was evidently referring to was Siniavskii's praise for self-elimination and his courtroom argument that art should be exempted from political oversight and legal action. "A work of art does not express political views," the defendant had informed the court on February 11.[129] Later that day, he had extended the argument to legal practice: "I think it is impossible to analyze artistic texts from a legal perspective. Because it is impossible to describe the meaning of an artistic text in the univocal terms of law."[130] As Murav and Nepomnyashchy have noted about this statement, Siniavskii was expressing his concern about the state's subordination of literary language to political demands as articulated through law.[131] Yet this argument only bolstered charges that Siniavskii was simulating nonimputability. Writing for *Pravda* on February 15, the journalist T. Petrov alleged that Siniavskii and Daniel' had "attempted to present everything they had written as the creation of fantastical, psychological, and other such situations that had nothing to do with politics, as a selfless and fervent ministration to 'pure' art, trying at all costs to avoid answering the questions put before them."[132] Siniavskii's insistence on art's apolitical nature was little more than a means of evasion, Petrov wrote: "Grown men try to present themselves as naïve boys, to make it seem as if they did not know what they were doing. But no ruse can help the accused avoid responsibility for their crimes."[133] By implying that the authors were mimicking minors who, like mentally ill adults, were considered "incompetent" by civil law, Petrov reiterated Konetko's claim that the defendants were simulating nonimputability.

Psychiatric discourse combined with state-sanctioned literary discourse to present Terts's pathologizable aesthetic as a form of obfuscation that reflected Siniavskii's alleged propensity for feigning. Whereas the state did in fact diagnose and hospitalize dissidents such as Aleksandr Vol'pin and Vladimir Bukovskii, as discussed in chapter 2, in Siniavskii's case its representatives implied that the author was merely simulating and that therefore he should be held responsible not just for his own utterances but also for those of his fictional creations. What Siniavskii had pathologized as the state's tendency to conflate art and life thus became the very means by which the state depathologized his "split personality." During the trial itself, the court followed this reflective reasoning to present Terts's heroes and narrators as fictional extensions of Siniavskii himself. Whereas

Siniavskii had distanced himself from these figures by way of *skaz*, irony, and self-elimination, the prosecutor dismissed these devices as convenient subterfuges and claimed that his characters spoke for him. Siniavskii was quick to disagree. "This isn't the author speaking. There is no authorial speech in *Liubimov*," he said on February 11 after the prosecutor attributed to him the views expressed in one of the novella's footnotes.[134] For Siniavskii, both the footnotes and the novella's *skaz*-like delivery had been literary devices for defamilarizing reality. The court, however, portrayed them as mechanisms for disguising the overlap between Terts's characters and Siniavskii himself. "Siniavskii and Daniel''s reminders that authors and heroes are not identical were beside the point," Petrov wrote in *Pravda*. "The court irrefutably proved that the anti-Soviet statements, the anti-Soviet essence of the heroes and their authors coincided in this instance."[135] By depicting the allegedly anti-Soviet content of Terts's fiction as a mirror of Siniavskii's views, Petrov added ammunition to the charge that the defendant's alleged evasion of responsibility was feigned.

The possibility that being conflated with his psychologically deviant heroes might lessen Siniavskii's punishment seems not to have escaped the author's staunchest supporters, however. Called in for questioning on October 16, 1965, Siniavskii's former professor Viktor Duvakin assured investigators that the author was indeed a "normal Soviet person."[136] Yet on October 20, Duvakin attributed the defendant's aesthetic to "a soul that was terribly sick with irony (which A. Blok called the terrible sickness of the century), or perhaps a soul that had temporarily undergone a terrifying crisis."[137] One of the stories had reportedly so alarmed Duvakin that he decided that "the right person to analyze it was not a critic or investigator, but a psychiatrist."[138] Highlighting the fantastic orientation of Terts's stories, Duvakin raised the possibility that it might shed light on the defendant's state of mind. Read through this benevolently reflective lens, Straustin's urge to write in "Graphomaniacs" might therefore indicate the compulsive nature of Siniavskii's own creative urge. "It seems to me that Siniavskii was taken in by his maniacal love for the word as such and by his 'graphomaniacal' desire to see his writing in print, no matter what happened," the interrogation transcript records Duvakin as saying.[139]

Seizing on this line of argument during the trial itself, Siniavskii's lawyer, Ernest Kogan, prompted Duvakin, who appeared as a witness for the defense, to repeat his comparison between Siniavskii and Straustin.[140] Moreover, he implied during his closing statement that the defendant might not be imputable, after all. "Siniavskii suffers from the graphomaniacal mania to write and see himself in print," Kogan argued in a direct extension of Duvakin's statements.[141] The lawyer then supplemented his own diagnosis with reference to Siniavskii's psychiatric report:

> Siniavskii's fantastical, mystical state of mind is confirmed by the evidence in his psychiatric report. The end of the report talks about his tendency toward exaggeration, toward the fantastic, toward fantastic constructions. It talks about how Siniavskii is a person who lives partly in an unreal world of his own design. Therefore, what the prosecution calls slander can also be seen as a unique perspective particular to his psychological type. With regard to his personality, Siniavskii is certainly not pathological, but he does have certain quirks within the bounds of the norm.[142]

Prioritizing the Serbskii Institute psychiatrists' diagnostic caveats over their actual finding of imputability, Kogan attempted to convince the court that Siniavskii's actions might indeed have been beyond his evaluation and control.

Yet whatever benefits such a legal strategy might have afforded in his case, Siniavskii himself continued to insist on the fundamental separation of his own life from the fictional world he had constructed as Terts. In his closing statement, then, Siniavskii reiterated the importance of distinguishing between himself and Terts's hero Straustin. "Take, for instance, the commentary on the literary greats in 'Graphomaniacs,'" he said. "You can't conclude that the author hates the literary greats just because the story is narrated in first person, from the perspective of a graphomaniac failure who, perhaps, has certain autobiographical traits. That would be the thinking of an uneducated person who has only lately begun learning how to read."[143] For Siniavskii, the court's "uneducated" conflation of author and hero was yet another example of the state's tendency to irrationally conflate life and art. And indeed, what Siniavskii presented as the value and even necessity of defamiliarization was interpreted by the state as a ruse to deny his status as a biographical reflection of Terts's writing. By emphasizing Siniavskii's sanity, the state laid bare the author's diagnosis of its own creative madness.

CULTIVATING ARTISTIC AWARENESS

The court's use of sanctioned literary and psychiatric discourses to conflate Siniavskii's life and art confirms what the author had long suggested: the state evaluated creative health in keeping with reflection theory, which claimed not only that existence determines consciousness but also that consciousness might shape existence through the creative nature of social practice. For Siniavskii, Stalin's implementation of reflection theory had condemned society to a madness that expressed itself through a pathological inability to distinguish between art and life. Replete with images of reflective surfaces that distort the very reality they claim to mirror, Siniavskii and Terts's writings model a more defamiliarized perspective that maintains an awareness of the artifice of art.

During his closing statement at his trial, Siniavskii drew attention to Terts's prescience by suggesting that the proceedings had starkly illustrated Soviet society's conflation of art and life. "It's as if we've entered some kind of fog, an especially electrified atmosphere where reality ends and the unnatural begins—almost like in a work by Arzhak or Terts," he said before concluding: "Here, the artistic image truly loses its conventional nature and is literalized in a very frightening and unexpected way, as the court proceedings pick up where the text left off and form its natural continuation."[144] If Terts had focused primarily on the state's compulsion to realize its own ideological metaphors, Siniavskii now suggests that it is Terts's writings that the state has transformed into lived realities. It may thus have been with an eye to the court's own mental clarity that Siniavskii urged his prosecutors to draw a clearer line between art and life: "The artistic image is a convention; the author is not identical to the hero," he said. "These are elementary ideas, and we tried to touch on them. But the prosecution stubbornly rejects them as a figment of the imagination, as a means of taking cover, as a means of deception."[145] What for Siniavskii constituted the responsibility of a defamiliarized aesthetic looked to the court like the feigned irresponsibility of a writer who was denying his reflective relationship with both reality and his literary works. Siniavskii, however, attributed the court's assertion of that relationship to the state's own lack of artistic awareness—an awareness that defamiliarization alone could restore. "Generally speaking, it could be said that all art is 'defamiliarization,'" Siniavskii commented in 1988 in his essay "In Praise of Emigration," deploying Shklovskii's term. "Art looks at the world with new eyes, as if not recognizing it, and strives again and again to discover its essence."[146] It was by concealing rather than revealing reality's essence, Siniavskii and Terts suggested, that the state had driven society mad.

CHAPTER 5

MADNESS AS MASK: THE CASE OF VENEDIKT EROFEEV

Few dissenters of the post-Stalin period explored the pathological extremes of creativity more immersively than the writer Venedikt Erofeev. In both his first extant effort, *Notes of a Psychopath* (1956–57), and his *samizdat* prose poem *Moscow–Petushki* (1969–70), Erofeev introduced his readers to socially deviant heroes who bore his own name, thereby implying that they might be autobiographical extensions of himself. At the same time, he behaved in ways that suggestively echoed those heroes' chaotic way of life: he dropped out of university, frequently changed jobs and places of residence, and drank to the point of eventually requiring treatments in psychiatric hospitals. The madman's persona that Erofeev described in a late interview was thus an all-encompassing amalgam of literary expression and lived behavior:

—So you began writing in the children's home, or already in school?
—I began even before I started school.
—And what were you writing at such a tender age?
—"Notes of a Madman."
—And who was the madman?
—Why, me, of course.
—What, at the age of six?
—One can be a madman at any time.
—How is that, to feel like a madman at the age of six?
—It's very interesting.

—Do you mean that was how you felt, or that it was a mask you created for yourself?
—Naturally, a mask.[1]

Dating what this chapter terms his "mask of madness" to the moment he began to write, Erofeev, who was born in 1938, presents his entire literary career as an exercise in pretending to be insane. In much the same way as it became increasingly common in the post-Stalin period for citizens to feign mental illness for practical purposes, some dissenters preserved and expressed themselves by dramatizing insanity in life and on the page. Having long cultivated his own mask of madness, however, Erofeev subjected it to trenchant critique in his 1985 drama *Walpurgis Night, or The Steps of the Commander*. Set in a psychiatric hospital and centered on a hero, Gurevich, who is arguably also pretending to be insane, the play depicts the erosion of the line between theatricality and reality and the loss of reason that ensues.

Erofeev's mask of madness may be characterized as one writer's take on two increasingly common phenomena: "dissimulation," or the feigning of mental health, and "simulation," or the feigning of mental illness. During the post-Stalin period, psychiatrists registered a spike in the number of Soviet citizens who were prepared to theatrically manipulate diagnostic categories if and when the need arose. And the need for pretending to be well evidently did arise for people in danger of being registered as addicts or as suffering from major mental illnesses. Though the registration system offered access to medical treatment, it also threw up hurdles in everyday life. Many people who were in genuine need of psychiatric care therefore dissimulated by feigning health.[2] Simulators, by contrast, feigned mental illness primarily in order to evade such sanctions and duties as criminal prosecution or military conscription. "While the scientific world was caught up debating sluggish schizophrenia, conducting research and writing treatises, Moscow's gangsters quickly discerned its advantages," the dissident Vladimir Bukovskii recalled in his memoir. "All of them had at some point been in the camps and weren't exactly itching to go back there; let those fools cut down trees, only fools and horses work. A clever man only needed one evaluation in the Kashchenko Hospital to secure himself a solid diagnosis for the rest of his life."[3] Reifying the perceived overlap between insanity and *inakomyslie*, or "thinking differently," certain citizens accused of nonpolitical crimes pretended to be dissidents in order to provoke psychiatric evaluations that might lead to hospitalization rather than to imprisonment. "One common method [of simulation] is to 'spout a political diatribe' in court or hand out pamphlets. And alas, it produces the desired result!" the dissident poet Viktor Nekipelov recalled.[4] Nekipelov, who in 1974 spent two months in the V. P. Serbskii Institute for Forensic Psychiatry in connection with his own political activities, estimates in his memoir that 95 percent of his fellow patients in the institute's Fourth Section were sane, and that, of those eventually certified as mentally ill, as many as two thirds were of sound mind.[5]

Moving beyond historical questions, this chapter examines Erofeev's transformation of simulation and dissimulation into self-consciously theatrical arts. Much as Gurevich simulates insanity within *Walpurgis Night*, Erofeev's mask of madness served to shore up the boundary between two possible poles of insanity: one which was theatricalized and controllable and one which was real and therefore out of control. Gurevich, by contrast, loses sight of that line, allowing his mask to permanently stick. Paradoxically, *Walpurgis Night* also suggests that simulation is in fact the behavioral norm throughout Soviet society. Even as Gurevich's physician continues to pathologize deviations from medical standards, madness exerts such a powerful tug that everyone—from the patients to the hospital staff—either goes insane or feigns insanity. What dissenters diagnosed as Soviet society's madness thus acquires a theatrical edge against the psychiatric backdrop of *Walpurgis Night*.

Andrei Siniavskii countered Soviet society's conflation of life and art in part by drawing a line between himself and his alter ego Abram Terts. Erofeev, by contrast, increased awareness of that line by producing what this chapter terms an "implied authorial persona" that pointedly straddled lived and literary expression. This implied authorial persona asserted himself within Erofeev's fiction through the accentuated presence of that "implied author" who, as Wayne C. Booth has argued, may be inferred from a given text.[6] But he also manifested himself outside the fiction through Erofeev's cultivation of an "authorial persona," or, to use the Formalist critic Boris Tomashevskii's term, that "biographical legend" that writers develop both in life and on the page.[7] Mikhail Epstein has discussed how Erofeev and his acquaintances together promoted a "myth" of Erofeev that drew partly on the author's actual behavior and partly on his heroes' semiautobiographical escapades.[8] Erofeev's authorial persona and implied author accordingly came together as that very implied authorial persona who had simulated madness since the age of six. As the poet Ol'ga Sedakova wrote about her friend: "Venia was himself more significant than his works. That is, if they became significant, it was precisely due to his personality's presence in the text, behind the text, above the text."⁹ Yet this chapter presents the character Gurevich as Erofeev's means of reevaluating his career-long blurring of art and life. By dramatizing his hero's slide into madness, the implied authorial persona separates theatricality from reality and affirms his own reason and self-control.

Scholars noting the theatricality of madness in Erofeev's work have generally explained it with reference to the *iurodivyi*, or holy fool, who cleanses the world by antagonizing it through dramatic displays of insanity.¹⁰ But while holy foolishness is certainly significant for Erofeev's oeuvre, and for *Moscow–Petushki* in particular, it overlooks the psychiatric and political subtexts of feigning insanity specific to the post-Stalin period. Nor does it provide sufficient justification for the mortal harm that Gurevich brings to his fellow patients. Though he may style himself as a holy fool, Gurevich undermines his idealistic claims of deliverance with the brutal and irreversible trail of destruction that he ultimately leaves in his wake. His irresponsible behavior charts his lack of that self-control that Erofeev's implied authorial persona is able to exert. And indeed, as Epstein has observed, artistic representations of madness provide their creators with an imaginative canvas for testing the limits of their own systems of thought: "Every learned person, every intellectual, every creator or distributor of ideas needs *the self-critique of pure reason*, the ability to recognize the curve of his own model of the world before it turns into complete gibberish."¹¹ *Walpurgis Night* captures the risks of simulating madness in an irrational world of ever more meaningless diagnostic categories. Surrounded by madmen who feign mental health and healthy individuals who feign insanity, only the most self-conscious of simulators will remain aware of where to draw the line.

SIMULATION, DISSIMULATION, AND SELF-CREATION

The consumption of alcohol and its social and medical consequences serving as the symptomatic framework of his own mask of madness, Erofeev built his implied authorial persona in part from personal experience. According to the artist and journalist Andrei Bil'zho, who observed the author's treatment while working as a psychiatrist at Moscow's Psychiatric Hospital No. 1, or the Kashchenko Hospital, the author never lost sight of the creative possibilities that issued from drinking. "All those things he drank, they were experiments, of course. It wasn't just alcoholism, the way he made up and mixed together those cocktails and tried them out on himself," Bil'zho said, referring to the famously unpotable recipes of *Moscow–Petushki* and noting that Erofeev sampled such recipes in life, as well.¹² As Epstein has observed, the author's capacity for self-control was itself heavily mythologized by his friends and family.¹³ But Erofeev was likewise ready to mythologize his experience of psychiatric treatment. According to the author's friend Lidiia Liubchikova, "much of *Walpurgis Night* is pure delirium that he wrote at the [Kashchenko Hospital]. He was, of course, in the so-called 'sanatorium' section, but clearly there were also such disturbed individuals there."¹⁴ If Erofeev approached his stays in hospital in part as a source of literary material, then Petr Vail' and Aleksandr Genis underplay the play's psychiatric setting with their assertion that "Erofeev's medical personnel are not the subjects of action, but the condition. One does not speak to or argue with them, just as there is nothing to talk about with a flood."¹⁵ The psychiatric specificities of the hospital setting and of Gurevich's simulative stance inform Erofeev's critique of the mask of madness.

Reportedly often reticent in social settings, Erofeev nevertheless possessed a theatrical flair that embellished his implied authorial persona. "Those who got close to him became the objects of almost taunting experiments," the author's friend Vladimir Murav'ev recalls. "His life was a constant performance that he himself directed—one part scripted, one part improvised—and everyone took part in that performance."¹⁶ By incorporating others into his own theatrical mask of madness, Erofeev raised the possibility that the simulation he practiced was widespread and therefore more the norm than the exception. Yet he also made dissimulation central to his persona by repeatedly describing both himself and his heroes as actual madmen pretending to be sane. "It was as if he never took his eyes off the avalanche of brutality, stupidity, and desecration committed by his people," Sedakova writes. "Faced with such a spectacle, one could go even madder than Hamlet and spend the rest of one's time 'simulating imputability' [*simulirovat' vmeniaemost'*], as Venichka referred to his own behavior."¹⁷ Sedakova's comment illustrates one of the central paradoxes of Erofeev's mask of madness: The dissimulative claim to feigning "imputability"—that legal category for Soviet citizens deemed capable of evaluating and controlling their criminal actions—asserts an underlying nonimputability that may itself be simulated. Sedakova suggests this likelihood by comparing Erofeev to William Shakespeare's Hamlet, an iconic simulator whom Erofeev invokes throughout *Walpurgis Night*. Dissimulation hints at simulation in a world where diagnostic categories have been stripped of meaning and where madness, or feigning madness, has become the norm.

Sanity and insanity are thus both theatricalized in *Notes of a Psychopath*, an early work whose titular allusion to Nikolai Gogol's story "Notes of a Madman" brings the literary tradition of psychiatric narratives into active dialogue with contemporary psychiatric discourse.[18] Narrated by the hero, Venedikt Erofeev, this fictionalized account of Erofeev's own university years has been described by Murav'ev as "a test of the pen twelve years before [Erofeev] found his prose."[19] Many of Erofeev's stylistic signatures first surface here: his predilection for neologisms, punning, and syntactic innovation; his clashes and shifts of register; his interlayering of metatextual and intertextual references; his interpolation of multiple voices; the neurotic self-consciousness of the narrating hero. But it is also here that Erofeev's implied authorial persona first uses a semiautobiographical hero to model the link between dissimulation and simulation and to explore how they together form the creative individual's mask of madness. A family friend warns the university-bound Venedikt to be wary of showing his true colors to his peers. According to the friend, their norm will be one of insincerity: "The main thing is to always avoid sincerity with them. Show a little sincerity and they'll call you heartless, filthy, crazy..."[20] Survival depends on concealing oneself behind a mask of sanity, as the unmasked individual will be declared insane.

Where Venedikt departs from his friend's analysis is in his readiness to incur diagnosis and his refusal to accept that what psychiatry calls sanity is in fact the most pressing behavioral norm. For Venedikt, it is precisely by simulating madness that individuals adapt to a generally mad society:

> And in the madhouses! Have you seen!? The madhouses! What's going on there? Eh?! At least they used to lock up smart people! They discovered things, they read, they wrote—that's why they went out of their minds! And now? Now any bastard falls down in the street and waves his legs in the air! Just to get into the [Kashchenko Hospital], the dog, that's all he wants, so he doesn't have to think about anything!...[21]

Madness being the norm in Soviet society, the individual who has yet to lose his mind would be well advised to simulate insanity. Toward the end of *Notes of a Psychopath*, another character echoes the thought: "Why is every other man an alcoholic these days? Why is the Kashchenko Hospital running out of beds for madmen?" The character answers his own question by founding an organization for performing social deviance and naming Venedikt an honorary member: "In that case, down with quietness and all that deathly calmness! We are the defenders of moral progress! In the first stage, our main task is to smash windows! (stormy applause) [...] Our second task is to sow noise and disorder wherever quietness is required! Let's take pride in being cannon fodder! No one will dare to silence us! (applause)."[22] Mimicking the scripted quality of Party congress reports right down to their obligatory audience responses, the implied authorial persona suggests that the madness performed by Venedikt and his friends is endemic to society.

Erofeev wrote *Moscow–Petushki* more than a decade after completing *Notes of a Psychopath*, yet the connected arts of simulation and dissimulation resurface here in the hero Venichka's theatricalization of madness. Partway through the *poema*, Venichka (a diminutive of Venedikt) punctuates his narrative with a self-diagnostic query: "And when, Venichka, did you first realize you were a fool?" The hero replies that he took note of his foolishness when he was accused of both boringness and frivolity. He then explains:

> Because I'm sick in the head, though I don't let people know. Because ever since I can remember, the only thing I've ever done is simulate mental health, at every moment, and this uses up all of my intellectual and physical and other energy, down to the very last drop. So that's why I'm boring. Everything you talk about, everything that concerns you is eternally alien to me. Yes. And as to that which does concern me, I won't breathe a word about it to anyone, not ever.[23]

Dissimulation is a means of adaptation, Venichka declares in evident agreement with the friend of the narrator of *Notes of a Psychopath*. Yet because Venichka's display of health is predicated on a claim to being "sick in the head," the hero's declaration also acts as a simulation of insanity. The same duality of simulation and dissimulation provides explanatory context for Sedakova's description of Erofeev's own habit of "simulating imputability": the claim to sanity assumes a claim to insanity that shields the dissenting individual. Emerging at the juncture of hero and author, the implied authorial persona builds his mask from a complex blend of dissimulation and simulation.

What, then, lies behind the mask of madness? One key passage points to the "universal faintheartedness" (*vseobshchee malodushie*) that drinking and subsequent withdrawal can also bring: that revelatory state of humility, timidity, and reticence that Venichka extols in Christian terms as the "salvation from all misfortunes":

> Why are they all so crude? Well? And they're crude, so crude exactly at those moments when one shouldn't be crude, when a person has got a hangover and

his nerves are all exposed, when he is fainthearted and quiet! Why must it be that way?! Oh, if only the whole world, if only everyone in the world could be as I am right now: quiet and fearful and also unsure of anything—of oneself, of the importance of one's place under the sun—how good it would be! No enthusiasts, no great feats, no obsessiveness—just universal faintheartedness.[24]

Echoing a line from the state-sanctioned writer Maksim Gor'kii's 1895 story "The Old Woman Izergil'" ("In life, you know, there is always a place for great feats"), Venichka criticizes the senselessly heroic tenor of everyday discourse.[25] It is this "crude" and indeed irrational bluster that Venichka's drinking parodically simulates; retreating from that state of mind reveals his *malodushie* and must therefore be concealed through still more drinking. That Erofeev himself expressed a similar admiration for faintheartedness is evident in another of Sedakova's reminiscences. "He often spoke not only about the excusability, but also about the normality and even laudability of faintheartedness, about how a person should not be tried by extreme trials," she writes. "Was it a rebellion against communist stoicism, against courage and the 'madness of the brave' to which not only the brave and insane had to pay their dues, but also millions of the sane and unbrave?"[26] Citing yet another psychiatrically themed line from Gor'kii ("The madness of the brave—that's the wisdom of life!" is from Gor'kii's 1894 story "Song of a Falcon"), Sedakova's comment indicates that Erofeev, like Venichka, equated faintheartedness with the "normality" and "sanity" that society had lost.[27]

The implied authorial persona who emerged at the juncture of Venichka and Erofeev was similarly skeptical of Soviet psychiatry. "I'm no fool," Venichka notes in *Moscow–Petushki*. "I understand that in this world there is also psychiatry, there is extragalactic astronomy. All that is true! But when you think about it, none of it is ours, it was all forced on us by Peter the Great and Nikolai Kibal'chich, and when you think about it, our calling is not here at all, our calling is somewhere else entirely!" Suggesting that his countrymen leave "psychiatry to the Germans," Venichka dismisses psychiatric discourse as incapable of capturing the spiritual essence of man.[28] Erofeev himself deepened his interest in psychiatry in the years following his composition of *Moscow–Petushki*. In 1975, he recorded in his notebooks reading a *samizdat* copy of one of the dissident military officer Petro Grigorenko's psychiatric reports. The entry he wrote in response illustrates his attention to the discursive mechanisms by which *inakomyslie* was then being pathologized:

"From the Grigorenko report: 'idea of reformism,' 'delusion of truth-seeking' and so on."[29] Making literary use of psychiatric discourse in another notebook entry that year, Erofeev folded the surname of the prominent psychiatrist Andrei Snezhnevskii into a mockingly alliterative tongue-twister composed entirely of medical and theatrical dignitaries: "Snezhnevskii, Smoktunovskii, and Sklifosovskii."[30] By 1976, the author was evidently collecting *samizdat* reports on the punitive hospitalization of Soviet dissenters. One reading list enumerates Bukovskii's *samizdat* works, highlighting his and Semen Gluzman's "Manual on Psychiatry for Differently Thinking People." Another mentions the dissenting writer Valerii Tarsis's *Ward No. 7*, an account of punitive psychiatry that itself invokes a literary tradition of psychiatric narratives by recalling Anton Chekhov's story "Ward No. 6."[31]

Yet even as Erofeev's implied authorial persona questioned Soviet psychiatry through an amalgam of art and life, the biographical author evidently found himself in ever-increasing need of medical care. Three years after completing *Moscow–Petushki*, Erofeev was treated in the 31st section of the Kashchenko Hospital for what Soviet physicians termed alcoholic delirium, also known as delirium tremens and, in the colloquial Russian, as "white fever" (*belaia goriachka*).[32] The disorientation, agitation, and visual and auditory hallucinations that had previously given structure to the first-person narrative of *Moscow–Petushki* were now shaping the author's lived reality.[33] Treatments followed at both the Kashchenko Hospital and the Mental Health Research Center of the Soviet Academy of Medical Sciences.[34] On December 25, 1979, for instance, Erofeev was hospitalized with symptoms that he reportedly described as follows: "Radio on all night to drown out the singing in the wall. The snowstorm makes faces in the window. People in the cupboard, a mole rat on the ceiling lamp. A panopticon."[35] In 1983, he was back in the Kashchenko Hospital. "Venedikt took this compulsory hospitalization very hard," recalls Igor' Avdiev, who, together with another friend of Erofeev, spirited into the ward a bottle of vodka disguised as compote. The trio drank the vodka surrounded by the staff and patients in a scene that may have inspired the bacchanalian fest with which *Walpurgis Night* ends.[36] As yet another friend, Mark Freidkin, has emphasized, the author genuinely needed the treatment he received: "Venia's clinical case was by no means a habit and certainly not an act of devotion, but a serious and essentially incurable illness."[37] If the mask of madness had previously confined itself to Erofeev's implied authorial persona, by the mid-1980s the pathological state that it theatrically simulated was threatening to become real.

Patients treated for alcoholic delirium in the 1970s and 1980s were generally exposed to a combination of short-term and long-term medical treatments. The first stage typically involved the administration of solutions such as glucose and piracetam, while the second stage focused on instilling a more lasting aversion to alcohol.[38] Conditioned-reflex therapies involved the coordinated ingestion of alcohol and nausea-inducing substances that were meant to provoke negative associations with drinking.[39] Sensitizing therapies entailed the administration of drugs such as disulfiram, often in the form of injected "torpedoes" that triggered a violent reaction to alcohol and, theoretically, a healthy dose of fear.[40] Suggestion-based therapies sought to instill aversion through a combination of hypnosis and the theatrically spoken word.[41] One particularly popular suggestion-based therapy was emotional-stress psychotherapy, or *kodirovanie*, whereby physicians followed a set script of words and gestures to convince patients that they had been "coded" to die if they drank. The operative principle behind *kodirovanie* was the theatrical force of the physician's persona.[42] "Innumerable instances from the practice of medical psychotherapy have shown that elements of dramatization can reveal the possible negative consequences of the patient's violation of sobriety in vividly concrete, emotional, and convincing ways," the method's founder Aleksandr Dovzhenko wrote in 1988.[43]

Psychiatrists of the post-Stalin period, to continue chapter 1's application of J. L. Austin's terms, positioned their diagnoses as "constative utterances" that objectively affirmed the presence or absence of a psychiatric disorder. But to the extent that those diagnoses subjectively altered the patient's reality through the verbal application of psychiatric categories, they also operated as "performative utterances." In his monograph *How to Do Things with Words*, Austin maintains that performative utterances are incommensurate with theatrical performance: "A performative utterance will, for example, be *in a peculiar way* hollow or void if said by an actor on the stage, or if introduced in a poem, or spoken in soliloquy." Language that is "used not seriously" becomes "*parasitic* upon its normal use," Austin writes.[44] Questioning Austin's exclusion of theatrical performance from performative utterances, however, the philosopher Jacques Derrida argues that performatives acquire their authority precisely from their theatrical ritualization: "For, ultimately, isn't it true that what Austin excludes as anomaly, exception, 'non-serious,' *citation* (on stage, in a poem, or a soliloquy) is the determined modification of a general citationality—or rather, a general iterability—without which there would not even be a 'successful' performative?"[45] For Derrida, performative utterances are always in some sense theatrically repeated performances, while theatrical performances themselves wield linguistic and therefore performative power by generating new realities through words. Following Derrida's argument, this chapter describes both psychiatric diagnosis and Erofeev's mask of madness as "performative" in the linguistic as well as theatrical senses of the term.[46]

During the post-Stalin period, psychiatrists seeking to uncover simulation alerted each other to the evidentiary value of excessively dramatic behavior. The more gifted simulators in turn took care to curb the visible theatricality of their displays. "The task demanded maximum simplicity and naturalness of behavior, calmness, restraint," Nekipelov recalled.[47] For Nekipelov, the most effective feigners of mental illness were those who kept their dramatizations controlled. In much the same way, the success or failure of Erofeev's mask proves contingent on whether the simulator can continue to distinguish between madness as a theatrical display and madness as a lived reality. Simulation may be viewed as a linguistic utterance that launches what Austin might have termed a performative momentum toward actual illness. But by the same token it may cement the artistic awareness that, as in Joseph Brodsky and Andrei Siniavskii's work, protects creative and mental health. This process is not dissimilar to the contemporary practice of "autosuggestion," by which patients being treated for alcoholism would be taught to repeat such formulae as "I am utterly indifferent to vodka, wine, beer" and "I will always withstand temptations and efforts at persuasion, even if people force me to drink."[48] Autosuggestion was intended to act upon the patient just as psychiatrist-led suggestion therapies were meant to do, only here it was the patient who took charge of constructing his or her own theater of words. In *Walpurgis Night*, the theatrical arts of dissimulation and simulation not only expose and challenge the performativity of diagnosis; they also give the patient the performative power to precipitate a state of madness or health.

The same holds true for Erofeev's implied authorial persona, through whom Erofeev shored up the border between theatricality and reality by dramatizing madness in life and on the page. As Erofeev's friend Natal'ia Shmel'kova recorded in her diary in March 1988, "I promised to come over with a cake, but he asked me to bring champagne. 'You'll drink it with Galina [Erofeev's wife], and I'll spend the evening at my writing desk. I'm not the kind to implant myself with all sorts of torpedoes. I can quit drinking whenever I want. I can even flirt with death.'"[49] In May of that year, Shmel'kova recorded Erofeev responding similarly to a doctor's offer of antidepressants: "My condition isn't depression; it's fatalism, and I can battle my bad mood on my own. That's what books and favorite records are for."[50] For the implied authorial persona whom Erofeev projected through such lived behavior as well as literary expression, madness was a mask that was only as durable as the artistic commitment and awareness of its wearer. If, in *Walpurgis Night*, Gurevich irrationally blurs the line between theatricality and reality, the implied authorial persona affirms the rational limits of his own dramatic display. The play thus marks a significant departure from previous works by Erofeev. In *Moscow–Petushki*, for instance, the implied authorial persona conflated art and life by claiming in the foreword to have deleted a string of obscenities that may have never existed, and in the postscript to have, like his hero Venichka, worked for a time laying telephone cable.[51] *Walpurgis Night*, by contrast, introduces an implied authorial persona who sets himself apart from his hero's loss of mind, thereby highlighting his own ability to distinguish the reality of madness from its theatrical representation.

The Literary Intertexts of *Walpurgis Night*

Though Erofeev explored simulation and dissimulation throughout his work, nowhere did he do so more directly, and with greater attention to contemporary psychiatric practices, than in his play *Walpurgis Night*. Speaking to Shmel'kova, Erofeev attributed the work's genesis to having "not that long ago been in the Kashchenko Hospital and seen how on May 1 they arranged a dance party for the patients in the men's and women's wards."[52] In an interview with *Literaturnaia gazeta*, however, Erofeev said that the idea had come when several acquaintances asked him to taste what they suspected might be lethal methanol. Testifying to his awareness of the implied authorial persona that he projected in life and art, Erofeev attributed their request to the fact that, "ever since *Petushki*, I've had the reputation for being a great specialist." Although he immediately realized that the drink was potable, Erofeev recalled, he took the opportunity to consolidate that reputation:

> I told them: "Pour me a second!" And tossed it back. They watched me closely and, though they were shaking with impatience, there was no way they were going to get close. The rationalism of the fool. Ever since then I've hated it.
>
> And then at night, while my insomnia had me tossing and turning, I thought about it and the idea of the play came to me. It took me a month to pull it off.[53]

In addition to highlighting the theatricality of the implied authorial persona's mask of madness, this story captures the theatrical mechanism by which Erofeev cultivated that persona in reality. Confronted in life by people who appeared willing to sacrifice his welfare for their own, Erofeev evened the playing field through dramatic display. He then quite literally dramatized the scene through the production of the play itself. Art and life combined to flesh out that implied authorial persona through whom Erofeev placed limits on the feigning of madness.[54]

Written in March and April of 1985, *Walpurgis Night* was first published later that year in the émigré journal *Kontinent*.[55] Performances of excerpts took place in 1988, followed by full productions at Moscow's Theater on Malaia Bronnaia in March 1989 and the Student Theater of Moscow State University in October 1989.[56] Set in the same Kashchenko Hospital where Erofeev had been treated, the play begins when Gurevich is brought to the hospital and examined by a physician and his assistants. Among them are a sadistic nurse named Tamarochka and a brutish orderly named Boren'ka whose resemblance to the orderly Nikita in Chekhov's "Ward No. 6" links the play with the literary tradition of psychiatric narratives that dissenters often referenced. Gurevich is revealed to be an alcoholic, a poet, and, on his father's side, a Jew—three facts repeatedly noted by the physician. Prescribed a combination of glucose and piracetam, Gurevich is transferred to Ward No. 3. There he witnesses one patient, Prokhorov, putting another patient on trial for a range of absurd crimes, the physician conducting electroshock therapy as a means of punishment, and Tamarochka administering the antipsychotic drug Aminazine. Gurevich punches Boren'ka and is rewarded with a beating, a debilitating injection of Sulfozine, and a challenge to join Boren'ka for dinner, if he is physically capable. Only a dose of hard alcohol will counteract the pain of the injection, Prokhorov declares, so Gurevich filches the keys to the supply closet from his former lover, the nurse Natalie. Returning with a bucket of lethal methanol, he ladles it out as philosophizing and merriment ensue. During the final act, Gurevich mines his Jewish and Russian Orthodox heritages to unveil a prophecy of universal deliverance that both realizes and undermines itself with the patients' ensuing deaths from alcohol poisoning. The curtain descends on Boren'ka beating Gurevich, presumably also to death.

Walpurgis Night has received little attention by comparison with *Moscow–Petushki*, and much of the existing criticism highlights the formal and thematic features that the two texts share. These include the play's examination of the spiritual isolation of the individual in a totalitarian society; its engagement with holy foolishness and the carnivalesque; its citation and parody of political, cultural, religious, and other discourses; and its juxtaposition of the chaos of reality with the transcendence of the word. Of particular interest for this discussion, however, is the difference in critical opinion as to whether Gurevich is in fact aware of his actions and who should be blamed for the patients' deaths. Naum Leiderman and Mark Lipovetsky present Gurevich as a holy fool figure who asserts his freedom through poetic language only to be suppressed by external forces, while Vail' and Genis hold Soviet society chiefly responsible for the massacre.[57] Alexander Burry argues that it is the hero's own embrace of poetry's destructive power that prevents him from achieving "a sufficient distance from the Soviet reality, culture, and clichés [that he] parodies" and thus from bringing the salvation he promises.[58] Yet if Gurevich does lose sight of the dividing line between the theatricality and reality of madness, then ultimately even he cannot be held responsible for his own destructive actions. In a world where diagnostic categories have become meaningless and insanity is the social norm, there is little to prevent the feigner of madness from following his simulation over the brink.

The literary lineage of *Walpurgis Night* points most directly to the Walpurgisnacht scenes in Johann Wolfgang von Goethe's *Faust*, when the title character joins the witches' revelry after selling his soul to Mephistopheles.[59] Yet whereas Faust submits to demonic possession, Gurevich assumes a theatrical role that only later takes on a life of its own. While Erofeev roots his play in the literary tradition of fictional works such as Chekhov's "Ward No. 6," moreover, the cynicism with which Gurevich feigns madness also recalls the cynical bent of contemporary attitudes toward psychiatry. Gurevich's madness is not the madness that is commonly depicted by Gogol, who explores the hazy border between sanity and insanity but does not dwell on whether the madness that he does depict is feigned. Nor is it the insanity found in the works of Fyodor Dostoevsky, whose self-destructive characters tend to fervently believe in their delusions even when they are theatrically exaggerating them. Madness in *Walpurgis Night* is a more deliberate enterprise: a theatrical mask that facilitates both self-expression and self-preservation while ideally keeping actual insanity at bay. And indeed, it is precisely this model of madness that surfaces in two of the dramatic works most heavily referenced in Erofeev's play: Aleksandr Pushkin's *The Stone Guest* (1830) and Shakespeare's *Hamlet*. Both of these plays feature vengeful protagonists who arguably, like Gurevich, simulate madness while exploiting the opportunities that come with being judged not responsible for their actions. By citing these two theatrical portrayals of madness within his own theatrical work about the theatrical portrayal of madness, Erofeev explores simulation and dissimulation on textual, intertextual, and metatextual levels.

The first of *Walpurgis Night*'s many references to Pushkin's dramatization of the Don Juan tale appears in its subtitle, which repeats the title of Aleksandr Blok's similarly themed poem "The Steps of the Commander" (1910–12).[60] The resulting intertextual dialogue between Erofeev and Pushkin highlights Gurevich's simulation of madness. Just as the hero adapts his simulation of insanity to the physician's diagnostic prompts, Don Juan appeals to Dona Anna by assuming the role of the proverbial desperate lover whom passion has driven out of his mind:

> Dona Anna
> You must have lost your mind.
>
> Don Juan
>   Oh Dona Anna
> Is wishing for the end a mark of madness?
> Were I a madman, I would surely want
> To stay among the living, I would hope
> That with my gentle love I'd touch your heart;
> Were I a madman, I would doubtless be
> Beneath your balcony from dusk till dawn,
> Preventing you from sleeping with my song,
> I would not hide myself in any way,
> Instead you'd always see me by your side,
> Were I a madman, I would never have
> Allowed myself to suffer silently...[61]

Despite the fact that Don Juan claims to be sane, his seduction of Dona Anna perfectly accords with his own definition of insanity. Dissimulation and simulation thus combine to produce a mask of madness that serves Don Juan's strategic purposes. Though the hero's behavior may be self-contradictory, rhetorically it serves its aim of convincing Dona Anna that he cannot control his feelings. Don Juan's implication that he is indeed not responsible for his actions provides an intertextual model for the simulative nature of Gurevich's mask of madness.

Simulated madness likewise features prominently in *Hamlet*, to which Erofeev gestures through such overt allusions as Gurevich's use of "Shakespearean iambs" and his own implied authorial persona's description of the work as a "tragedy in five acts" on the frontispiece and reference to the hospital staff as "Fortinbrases" in the concluding stage directions.[62] Even the tableau of dead bodies discovered by the hospital personnel recalls the vision of "purposes mistook / Fall'n on th' inventors' heads" that is encountered by Fortinbras at the end of Shakespeare's play: the poisoned characters scattered about the room, agents as much as victims of their demise.[63] As was the case with Don Juan, however, Gurevich also resembles Hamlet in that both characters turn madness into a strategically motivated theatrical display. As Polonius famously says about the Danish prince, "Though this be madness, yet there is method in't."[64] Hamlet simulates insanity in full awareness of how he might profit from the perception of his insanity. By capitalizing on his presumed condition, for instance, Hamlet is able to convince his uncle Claudius to attend a dramatic reenactment of the latter's murder of the late king. Theater and the theatrical simulation of madness further Hamlet's aims much as Gurevich seeks to reap the benefits of diagnosis by forging and donning his mask of madness.

Erofeev conceived *Walpurgis Night* as the second of three plays that, had the trilogy ever been completed, would evidently have also referenced the historical and cultural traditions of feigning insanity.[65] The third play, which was meant to be set in an Orthodox church on Christmas Eve, never did materialize. But the theatricalization of madness proves central to the extant draft of the first play, *The Dissidents, or Fanny Kaplan*, which Erofeev sketched out after writing *Walpurgis Night*. Set on Ivan Kupala Day in a bottle-drop station, the play was to have unfolded "at the end of [the station owner's] second day of white fever" and to have featured a holy fool named Vitalik; a girl who suffers from a "congenital yet touching idiotism" and who bears the historically auspicious name of Lenin's attempted assassin Fanny Kaplan; and a crowd of "dissidents at very different levels of mental prostration," according to the cast list. The list concludes with a pointed aside from the implied authorial persona that Erofeev projects: "Not a single hero—apart from Fanny—not one is in a rational state of mind." Also worthy of note is the inclusion of two characters called False Dimitrii I and False Dimitrii II; both are said to be "half-witted," but the genuineness of their madness is cast into doubt by their connection to the cultural trope of the royal pretender and its historically catastrophic consequences.[66] Simulation acquires political overtones as the two False Dimitriis pretend to be the seventeenth-century insurgents who claimed the Russian throne by pretending to be the murdered son of Tsar Ivan IV. Erofeev's characters seek out the "real Dimitrii" only to conclude that it would be impossible to tell him apart from the "real False Dimitrii" as "everything real and everything false comes from the same place."[67] The implication for the play's depiction of madness is clear: In a world where diagnosis has become an ever more meaningless display, the line between theatricality and reality blurs to the point where it disappears.

SIMULATION AS THEATRICAL PERFORMANCE

As in *The Dissidents*, the projected trilogy's second play, *Walpurgis Night*, presents mental illness and alcoholism as norms throughout post-Stalinist society. The play thus conflates two theatricalized rituals: the patients' unofficial celebration of the pagan holiday of Walpurgisnacht on the night leading from April 30 to May 1, when witches and spirits are said to celebrate the coming of spring, and the staff's celebration of International Labor Day, the official revelry of which is set to begin in the morning. While the patients imbibe Gurevich's methanol, the hospital staff act in much the same way by drinking to excess in a room offstage. Nor is it just the psychiatric personnel who mirror their patients; the inmates imitate their overseers by parodying their ideological rhetoric and subjecting each other to nonsensical renditions of the state's repressive tactics. Gurevich, for instance, demands that the other patients bow to his utopian vision—a vision that itself entails subordinating humanity to his dictatorial will. Prokhorov similarly puts his fellow patients on trial for political crimes such as plotting to sell the Bolshoi Ballet and the Moscow Metro to the enemy.[68] Asked by Gurevich why his latest victim is tied to a bed, Prokhorov declares that the patient in question has been found guilty of "delirium tremens. He betrayed his homeland in thought and intention. In short, he doesn't drink and he doesn't smoke."[69] By using the state's authoritarian methods to administer their own alcoholic regime that parodically imitates the madness of Soviet society, Gurevich and Prokhorov suggest a continuity between life inside and life outside the walls of the psychiatric hospital.

As the distinction between sanity and insanity dissolves, diagnostic categories become empty vessels for theatrical display, and "normality" becomes an arbitrary designation. "Today we mark the Walpurgian festival of strength, beauty, and grace!" Prokhorov says. "Let the normal people mark May Day, that is, not the normal people, but the staff who attend to *us*."[70] And indeed, madness—or, at least, the dramatic display of madness—is so ubiquitous in *Walpurgis Night* that citizens who display no psychiatric symptoms at all are simply assumed to be faking mental health. With dissimulation paradoxically constituting the exception, simulation becomes the surest way of adapting to society's norms. As Gurevich's physician wryly observes:

> Just between us, lately we've even been hospitalizing people who, at first glance, don't present a single symptom of psychological disturbance. But we should not forget these invalids' capacity for involuntary or well considered dissimulation. These people, as a rule, go through their whole lives without committing a single antisocial act, not a single criminal deed, not even the slightest hint of nervous imbalance. But that is precisely what makes them dangerous and why they should be sent for treatment. At the very least, because of their inner disinclination toward social adaptation.[71]

The physician admits to diagnosing sane individuals based on the expectation that they must be feigning health—a possible allusion to the punitive hospitalization of Soviet dissidents.[72] And indeed, as was demonstrated in chapter 1, psychiatrists who engaged in the pathologization of *inakomyslie* sometimes substantiated their diagnoses by dismissing displays of sanity as efforts at dissimulation. In Erofeev's tragedy, by contrast, the social norm is one of either insanity or pretending to be insane. Mental health thus becomes a pathology, while diagnostic categories are stripped of meaning. Madness being the status quo, those who appear sane are automatically assumed to be dissimulating, while those who appear insane are considered to be adapting in adequate ways. If society is insane, or at least simulating insanity, then there is nothing more abnormal than sane behavior.

According to Victor Kuperman and Josef Zislin, simulation situates the psychiatrist and the patient within a single "semiotic sphere" of psychiatric terms: "That which the simulator deems significant for the outward identification of a disease is rigidly predetermined by the structure of the nosological classification of his time."[73] The psychiatrist is trained to assume the authenticity of behavior that conforms to diagnostic categories, while the patient subverts the meaning of those categories by turning them into a manual for faking. In response, Kuperman and Zislin write, the psychiatrist abandons his or her diagnostic logic and adopts "the logic of a so-called 'police' examination, wherein evaluative categories such as true/false, sincere/insincere come to the foreground."[74] The physician in *Walpurgis Night* accordingly assumes that all of his patients are either mad or pretending to be mad. Gurevich meanwhile takes psychiatric discourse as a readymade script for dramatizing insanity, starkly inverting the theatrical script for sanity that Bukovskii and Gluzman proposed in their "Manual on Psychiatry for Differently Thinking People." Throughout his examination, Gurevich uses the physician's questions as prompts for perfecting his madman's mask. These questions reflect psychiatric norms that, in keeping with the critique of Soviet psychiatry laid out by such dissidents as Bukovskii and Gluzman, are either hopelessly politicized or violated in daily practice. The doctor is duly pleased with Gurevich's theatrical performance. "You have a beautifully presented syndrome," he says.[75] Yet Gurevich's mask of madness is far from benign, functioning as it does to aggressively unveil both the ubiquity of madness and the emptiness of psychiatric discourse itself. In a society where insanity is the norm, the physician's claim to diagnostic authority is revealed to be as much of a theatrical and linguistic charade as Gurevich's own performance of psychiatric symptoms.

Constructed as they are from both the physician's statements and the general madness that Gurevich mirrors, the hero's "symptoms" expose the fact that it is society that has lost its mind. Gurevich's irrational statements about space and time accordingly act to theatrically parody the physician's grasp of those categories. When Gurevich alludes to Lord Byron by informing the physician that he and his father once swam across the Hellespont, for instance, the physician notes that Gurevich could not have visited a body of water that lies beyond the closed border. In the course of registering that quite rational protest, however, the physician betrays his own ideologically determined theory of Soviet world domination. "After all, if my knowledge of geography doesn't deceive me, it's *not yet* our territory," the physician says. Gurevich seizes on the physician's expansionist rhetoric by folding it into his simulation of madness: "Well, how shall I put it? All territory is ours. Or rather, it will be ours. It's just that they don't let us in to wander around, most likely in the interest of peace, so that we content ourselves with a sixth of the earth's surface."[76] By parodying the oft-repeated slogan that the Soviet Union covers a sixth of the earth's surface, Gurevich pathologizes the state and society's compulsive ideologization of geographical space. Shortly thereafter, the physician shifts the topic to time and a similar exchange ensues. "And what day is it out there? What year? What month?" the physician asks. Gurevich once again replies by parodying ideological rhetoric. "What difference does it make? After all, for Russia these things are all a bit petty—days, millennia . . ."[77] Though psychiatric discourse may still demand that citizens measure history in rational units such as days and years, Gurevich dramatizes the fact that Soviet society instead adheres to a pathologically ideologized understanding of time.

Normality, for the physician, means harboring a paranoid perception of the outside world and being prepared to give one's life for one's country even when no sacrifice is needed. "Well, and what if worse comes to worst for our Motherland?" the physician asks. "After all, it's no secret that our foes have only one thought in their heads: to destabilize us, and then once and for all . . ."[78] The physician's reverent praise for great feats stands in stark contrast to the universal faintheartedness that Venichka of *Moscow–Petushki* proposed as a sane and far more spiritually enlightened alternative to society's insanity and crudeness. And indeed, Gurevich echoes Venichka by parodying the physician's bombastically heroic rhetoric: "If my Homeland were to find herself on the brink of disaster, if She were to say: 'Leva! Quit drinking, arise and emerge from nonexistence'— well, then . . ."[79] Lest he appear to too closely mimic the physician's commitment to heroic feats, however, Gurevich exposes his own theatricality through frequent forays into dramatic declamation: "Every normal citizen should be a valiant warrior, just like all normal urine should be light amber in color. (Quotes with inspiration from Kheraskov.)"[80] As the implied authorial persona's stage directions explain with reference to the eighteenth-century poet and playwright Mikhail Kheraskov, the controlled simulation of insanity is that which underscores its own theatricality.

Gurevich comes closest to lifting his mask in conversation with Natalie. "Just think about it," he informs his lover. "I am my own magnificent infirmary, I am my own shot of piracetam in the bottom."[81] After Natalie tells Gurevich to avoid bursting into tears, as the physician sees it as symptomatic of illness, Gurevich admits that he used to earn money by weeping on demand. Then, as if illustrating his claim to this theatrical talent, he begins to speak in iambic pentameter:

> You realize, Natalie, how I would wail?
> Without the slightest cause. Just by demand.
> In time they all found out I had *this* talent.
> They'd come and say to me, "Gurevich, wail!"
> Amid our bacchanalian affairs,
> "Gurevich, wail in streams of thirty-three."

> And I would wail. Each stream at 50 kopecks.
> And, Natalie, you see what I am saying?
> At any time! By popular demand![82]

Rather than maintain his symptomatic charade, Gurevich admits his penchant for simulation and highlights its theatrical nature by doing so in meter. Moreover, he insists to Natalie that the other patients are in fact as "normal" as he:

> Gurevich: Good Lord! Then why am I here?! That's what I don't understand. And the other patients, too. Why?
> They're all quite normal, everyone you see here,
> They're little cuttlefish, no more than children,
> It's only that they sank into a stupor.[83]

If the rest of the patients are as "normal" as Gurevich, then they too may be simulating insanity. But interpreted in light of the physician's admission that the state is also ready to pathologize people who show no psychiatric symptoms, even Gurevich's claim to sanity may be said to hone the contours of his madman's mask. Sanity and insanity being indistinguishable in a world where madness is the norm, the only certainty is the theatricality with which both categories manifest themselves.

Gurevich's simulation of insanity parodies psychiatric discourse to suggest that diagnosis is itself performative in both the theatrical and the linguistic senses. When Gurevich responds to the physician's request that he evaluate his health by suggesting that the latter evaluate his own, the doctor says: "I've asked you, patient, to confine yourself to answering my questions; I'll answer yours when you're completely cured."[84] The psychiatric script dictates that the physician be the only one to ask the questions and that the patient respond in such a way as to bolster the authority of psychiatry itself. Followed to the letter, that script utilizes diagnostic labels such as "patient" to situate both the patient and the physician within a ritualized power hierarchy. By exposing the ritual and questioning the physician's authority, however, Gurevich turns that hierarchy around. After the doctor carries out several physical tests ("Get up. Move your feet. Narrow your eyes. Stretch your arms forward."), for instance, Gurevich follows his interlocutor's diagnostic logic to complain of the following condition: "I found that when I lifted my left foot, I couldn't lift my right one at the same time. That really threw me."[85] By exposing the meaninglessness of the physician's methods through mimicry and exaggeration, Gurevich questions their authority.

Told by the physician to show his respect for psychiatry, then, the hero accedes in such a way as to mirror the physician's empty rhetoric:

> Gurevich: [. . .] You were speaking about our medical sciences, and whether I respect them? But "respect" is really too dull a word, so . . . commonplace . . .
> For I, for I'm in love with it, and say this
> Without a trace of mockery or grimace.
> In love with all its risings and its fallings,
> With all its labor pains of therapeutics
> And weaknesses of body and of soul,
> With its dominion of the Universe,
> With its unfading Reason, with its eyes
> And with its tail, and mane, and with its lips,
> And with . . .[86]

Gurevich exposes the performativity of psychiatric discourse by mirroring it in theatrical ways. To use Austin's term, the "non-seriousness" of his dramatic engagement with psychiatry violates the seriousness on which diagnosis relies. The more obviously theatrical Gurevich's simulation, then, the more antagonized the physician becomes:

> Doctor (frowning, interrupts him): I believe I already told you more than once to not play the fool. You're not onstage. You're in a doctor's office. I'd advise you to speak in human language, without those . . . those . . .
> Zinaida Nikolaevna (prompts): Those Shakespearean iambs . . .[87]

The physician pathologizes Gurevich's detours into poetry as the antics of a simulated "fool," indicating that, from the state's perspective, the hero's self-definition as a poet itself amounts to simulating madness. Aware that Gurevich's declamations provoke the physician, Natalie advises the patient to henceforth avoid speaking in verse: "And you know what else, Gurevich? Stay away from those five-footed iambs, especially around the doctors. They'll think you're making fun of them. They'll start treating you with Sulfozine or something even worse."[88] By "making fun" of psychiatry through the art of simulation, the dissenter reverses the diagnostic gaze to pathologize society.

Simulation as Performative Utterance

Yet even as it reveals the theatrical and linguistic performativity of diagnosis, Gurevich's dramatization of mental illness launches its own performative momentum toward actual insanity. Simulating madness makes madness happen, like an Austinian speech act whose pronouncement not only describes a change in state but also brings that change about. Moreover, it makes that madness happen through words that are themselves performative in their delusory animation of alternate realities. The patient Prokhorov accordingly renames Moscow's landmarks based on the idea that "contemporary dissidence, as represented by Alekha, overlooks the fact that first you have to pull things out by their roots, and only then can everything else be pulled out along with those rancid roots; we must rename our streets and squares."[89] This "Alekha" is Alekha the Dissident, a patient who acquired his nickname and diagnosis for shooting streams of snot onto officials' neckties. For Prokhorov, however, such "dissidence" is evidently not enough; true dissidence means reforming reality through the power of language itself. Another patient named Serezha Kleinmikhel' illustrates that approach by using words to inaugurate a series of utopian projects with Soviet-style titles such as "Book Factory for Cultured Pilots" and "Cosmic Exhibit of Happy Love and Secret Joys of All the Happy Cosmonauts of the Happy Cosmosis [*veselogo Kosmusa*]."[90] Meanwhile, the patient Stasik repurposes the discursive detritus of Soviet life to ensconce himself within an imaginary garden filled with flowers such as "Savvy Bellballs," "Tender Tax Police" and "Birdbrained Plenum."[91] Prokhorov, Serezha, and Stasik's renaming of the world recalls the naming of things in the Garden of Eden. Within every patient is a creative Adam who actively reshapes reality through words. As Prokhorov tells Stasik: "Those little flowers—they're within us. Isn't that so, Gurevich? Well? What's the point of flowers on the outside?"[92] The mask of madness frees the creative individual to remake the world by way of language.

Yet if the performative power of language enables the construction of alternate worlds, then it also launches a drive toward the irrational conviction that those worlds are not theatrical but real. Gurevich thus convinces himself that he can do away with the hospital workers simply by speaking them out of existence—workers who will later affirm their presence by physically beating him to a pulp: "After all, they don't really exist . . . We're psychos, see . . . and they, those phantasmagorias in white, they appear to us from time to time . . . Sure, it gets a bit nauseating, but what can you do? One minute they're here ... the next they're gone ... and they pass themselves off as full-blooded people who know how to live ..."[93] If it is true that words are capable of single-handedly altering Moscow's streets and inventing new types of flowers, then language is presumably also enough to dismiss the reality of the hospital staff and launch a new "era of Enlightenment":

> Prokhorov: [...] Shall we not begin the era of Enlightenment in Russia before it is too late?
> Gurevich: But we have already begun it. For now, within the confines of Ward No. 3. And as for out there, who knows ...[94]

Gurevich supplies the patients with alcohol as part of his aim to liberate them from the hospital regime. Yet alcohol is only one of his means: if reality is to be reinvented, it will have to be primarily through language. Erofeev's exploration of the irrational extremes of creativity directly addresses this study's wider concern with the pathological consequences of reinventing reality by way of words. Whereas Brodsky suggested that the poet's habit of materializing "parts of speech" might pave the way from creativity to insanity, Siniavskii depicted Soviet society's realization of ideological metaphors as a creative madness in its own right. In *Walpurgis Night*, Erofeev comes to a similar conclusion: The mask of madness becomes a self-fulfilling prophecy when its words performatively create a new reality that dispenses with reality as it is.

Gurevich accordingly gives free rein to his mask by using language to wipe off the map not only the hospital where he is currently confined but also Germany, Britain, America, the Arab world, Scandinavia, and all of East Asia. "Just the sound of the word 'Lisbon' makes me sick," he tells the patients. "My bile rises when I hear people say 'Lisbon.' And should a person's bile have to rise? No, it should not have to rise ... Which means that Lisbon should not exist!"[95] Gurevich polls the patients as to whether they need Lisbon and, upon establishing for himself that they do not, proceeds to cancel out Lisbon, as well. Gurevich's evident belief that Lisbon can be erased through language points to the hero's mounting irrationality. But it also speaks to the destructive impulse that underlies his prophecy of deliverance. It is not long before Gurevich uses language to annihilate the Russian nation itself: "Having caught all the maladies of the defeated, [the Russians] will wither away, and nothing will remain of their one-time gigantism, and they will scatter like dust on the face of the earth."[96]

Having linguistically dispensed with the majority of the world's population, Gurevich inaugurates a new messianic age:

> Gurevich (still more animated): All hail Eretz Israel up to the Euphrates!
> Prokhorov:
> > Why limit it? The *Nile* to the Euphrates!
>
> Gurevich:
> > Why think so small? The Nile to the Euphrates—
> > All that is well and good but still small-minded.
> > Begin at the Euphrates and head east . . .—
> > Until you reach the Nile again![97]

Gurevich's reinvention of reality culminates with the expansion of Israel across the planet, with Cana in the Galilee—where Jesus turned water into wine—serving as Israel's capital. While outwardly this hybrid messianic vision most immediately reflects Gurevich's half-Jewish, half-Russian Orthodox heritage, its underlying utopianism and expansionist impulse also mirror the physician's own rhetoric. Gurevich, like the society that provided the point of departure for his parodic mask of madness, has spun a fantasy of world domination that claims deliverance while spreading destruction.

The tragedy of *Walpurgis Night* thus ultimately lies in Gurevich's loss of contact with reality.[98] What now drives the hero's vision is not the faintheartedness of Venichka in *Moscow–Petushki* but an uncritical assimilation of society's cult of great feats:

> Gurevich: [. . .] But come what may, we must always be on guard and prepare ourselves for a great feat! What about you: Are you preparing yourself for a great feat?
> Potbellied Vitia: You bet we're preparing![99]

Where Gurevich once parodically pathologized the bombastic rhetoric of the physician, he now adopts that heroic fervor to the point of presenting it as an end in itself. Only by carrying out great feats will Russia fulfill its higher destiny, he declares; what those feats specifically entail is unimportant by comparison. "Well, what were the Russian people before we came along?" Gurevich asks. "Sluggish demonism, depressive folly. Daredevilry spun together from yawns. No lordship, no honor, not even the slightest bit of excellency in anyone. And let's not even begin to speak of highness or majesty."¹⁰⁰ Yet feats devoid of meaningful content bring no deliverance; instead, they become vessels for irresponsibility and destruction. Quoting from the German lullaby "Sleep, My Joy, Go to Sleep," in which a baby is urged not to heed the sighs behind the wall, Gurevich says of the Russian people: "No, we are not like [the Germans]. Others' misfortunes are our misfortunes. Every sigh matters to us, and there's no time to sleep. We've already achieved such vigilance and all-powerfulness in this regard that we can deprive whomever we want not only of sighs, of heavy sighs behind the wall, but also of inhalations and exhalations. We won't sleep a wink!"¹⁰¹ If Gurevich once parodied the physician's rhetoric, he now uncritically assimilates it. As his violent reading of the lullaby reveals in stark anticipation of the patients' deaths, the mask of madness can compromise even the most benevolent of aims.

When Prokhorov charges Gurevich with having intended to murder his fellow patients, then, his accusation fails to take account of the hero's slide into actual madness:

> Prokhorov: What were you thinking? . . . And when half the ward had already croaked, were you still *thinking*? (Maliciously.) You had a sche-eme [*um-mysel*]. A sche-eme. You people can't do without a sche-eme . . .
> Gurevich: Yes, I had a scheme: to unite the scattered. To pacify the embittered . . . to give them a bit of joy . . . to bring dawn to the twilight of these souls that are caged here until the end of their days . . . I had no other scheme . . .¹⁰²

Prokhorov invokes anti-Semitic canards to accuse the half-Jewish Gurevich of destructive intent, while Gurevich defends himself by claiming to have intended deliverance. But matters of intent are beside the point in cases of actual insanity. With the breakdown of the theatrical boundaries that previously kept his simulation of madness in check, the hero has become as irresponsible for his actions as the society that surrounds him. Merging with his madman's mask, Gurevich deconstructs the theatrical frame of the play itself:

> Today, this very night, I'll tear to shreds
> This tragedy where iambs can't be heard.
> In short, tonight I will blow up this *home*!¹⁰³

Gurevich vows to destroy not only the hospital but also the dramatic scaffolding that previously kept his madness confined. This process plays out thematically as Gurevich's mask becomes a reality, but it also unfolds on a formal level as the play spills over its theatrical frame. Speaking to Natalie in Act III, Gurevich says: "Up to this point I've yet to lose my marbles. / But *we shall see about that in Act V* . . ."[104] And indeed, the play's concluding act graphically captures the onset of madness.

As Gurevich blurs the line between theatricality and reality, the play enacts that process on the viewer through stage directions that destroy what little remains of the boundary between the actors and the audience. Just as Gurevich and Prokhorov succumb to the methanol's effect and note that the room is darkening, for instance, the implied authorial persona's directions stipulate that "the light in the ward—for no apparent reason—begins to fade" from the audience's point of view, as well.[105] The lowering of the lights equates the perspective of the audience with that of the characters, incorporating the former into the events onstage. This process culminates in the final lines with an extended stage direction that erases the division between actors and audience by issuing commands to the theatergoers themselves:

> The curtain has already fallen and, for all intents and purposes, the audience can disperse. But there, on the other side of the curtain, the same thing continues without respite. Gurevich's howls become ever more deathly. From there—from the ward, through the curtain—a sack of bedclothes flies out at the audience; on its heels a nightstand, which breaks into smithereens. Then the cage with the parrot, which has already kicked the bucket from *all of this*. No applause.[106]

The curtain may have dropped, but as the stage direction suggests by continuing to address the audience, what previously was theatrically simulated has now become an actuality. The implied authorial persona incorporates the theatergoers into the play by instructing them to disperse if they so wish and, if they remain, to refrain from applause. Meanwhile, the curtain is repeatedly breached by the sound of Gurevich's screams and the sight of objects flying out at the audience. The fourth wall between the onstage madhouse and the madhouse of post-Stalinist life collapses in palpable illustration of Gurevich's own loss of theatrical control.

Simulation as Safeguard of Sanity

Creativity turns out to be just a step from insanity in a world where the madman's mask leads to both the realization of alternate realities and the onset of madness itself. With madmen readily casting themselves as sane and healthy people pretending to be mad, the line between simulated and actual insanity wears thin. Yet Erofeev provides his own alternative to Gurevich's slide into madness in the form of the implied authorial persona Venedikt Erofeev—a revised and reconsidered rendition of that implied authorial persona who surfaced both in and around Erofeev's earlier works and who, as Erofeev would later say, had been simulating madness since the age of six. By erecting a more resilient boundary between an insanity that is theatricalized and an insanity that is real, the implied authorial persona who emerges through *Walpurgis Night* uses his own mask to affirm his sanity.

Gurevich fails to distinguish the theatrical from the real in part as a result of his general rejection of concrete markers of identity. Asked by the physician to state his name, he replies: "No documents. I don't like them."[107] And indeed, there is ultimately little substance behind his simulative façade. "It's as if you're occupied," Gurevich tells the physician. "And occupied for some purpose, in connection with some treaty on mutual aid or close alliance—but still you're occupied ... and such a ... a harassment-by-nothingness, but at the same time a crucifixion-on-nothingness ... a puking-from-nowhereness. In short, it's like you're in God's grace, and yet *not there at all* ... it's like ... being inside your stepmother's womb ..."[108] Unlike the implied authorial persona, who remains clearly identifiable, Gurevich can only define himself in terms of what he is not. At the same time, Gurevich resorts so regularly to the same aesthetic devices and alludes so predictably to the same literary influences that any possibility of genius fizzles out.[109] Even his poetic identity turns out to be an exercise in imitation and pretending:

> Doctor: [...] And whom do you imitate? Who is your favorite?
> Gurevich: Martynov, of course ...
> Zinaida Mikhailovna: Leonid Martynov?
> Gurevich: Certainly not. Nikolai Martynov ... and Georges d'Anthès.[110]

Burry notes that Gurevich's allegiance to d'Anthès and Martynov, killers of the poets Pushkin and Mikhail Lermontov, respectively, underlines both his role as a destroyer of poetry and the destructive nature of poetry itself.[111] But viewed as an extension of his penchant for feigning, Gurevich's admission of derivativeness also suggests that even the hero's poetic identity is a theatrical and thus simulative display. Despite the fact that he used to write poems in his own style, Gurevich admits, he now only copies the work of others. He is not a true poet but a poetic pretender whose language is devoid of substance and meaning. Simulation leaves Gurevich with no identity to fall back on when the mask of madness finally becomes fixed.

If Gurevich's words are powerless to halt the drive toward madness, however, the same is not true of the implied authorial persona, who asserts his control both extratextually, through Erofeev's lived behavior, and textually, within the play itself. Like Gurevich, Erofeev projected an implied authorial persona who avoided affiliation and documentation. Yet whereas Gurevich's fluid identity breeds insanity, Erofeev's implied authorial persona plays at such fluidity without ever losing its underlying form. As Avdiev retrospectively commented about the stabilizing role that he believed Erofeev to have fulfilled within their circle of friends:

> You sit there unimprinted, like a kiss in the air, and unprintable, like an obscene word. And unindexed by a single stamp, even in your documents, because you don't have any documents either. And without documents in the USSR, either there is no you, or ... within you there is no USSR. Your native land disappears beneath your feet. And then comes a comforting thought: But Venia exists! And he also has no documents, no USSR, no land beneath his feat; he's also unimprinted, unprintable. And you rush to Venia as if toward proof of your existence and consciousness.[112]

Where Gurevich fails to sustain a mode of expression that would counteract his loss of reason, the implied authorial persona whom Erofeev projected through lived behavior kept his mask of madness in check. *Walpurgis Night* thus contrasts the hero's loss of control over his mask with the implied authorial persona's separation of theatricalized insanity from actual delusion.

Beyond his extratextual manifestations, Erofeev's implied authorial persona also asserts his control within the textual bounds of the play. He does this most immediately by pointing to differences between himself and his increasingly deranged protagonist. Unlike the eponymous protagonists of *Notes of a Psychopath* and *Moscow–Petushki*, for instance, the hero of *Walpurgis Night* does not bear Erofeev's name. Nor do Gurevich's half-Jewish origins align with the Christian worldview of Erofeev's earlier writing. In addition to separating himself from the madman Gurevich, the implied authorial persona demonstrates his sanity by dotting the text with stage directions that testify to his critical perspective. "Still the same Ward No. 3, several hours later. Everything is so changed that it's stupid to even talk about it," a stage direction notes at the start of Act V.[113] Drawing attention to their distance from the events unfolding onstage, the directions self-consciously refer to each other through asides such as "More on him later" and "More on that below."[114] Taken together, they insistently invoke an implied author—and, in conjunction with Erofeev's behavior outside of the text, an implied authorial persona—whose presence serves to shore up the divide between theatricality and reality. By the final scenes, the implied authorial persona has affirmed his sanity to the point where his voice is able to dominate over the voice of Gurevich himself:

> Gurevich (lifting himself up from his chair with great difficulty, having clutched at the nightstand for his life—the main thing is not to fall, not to fall): As long as I've got some vision left, I'll make it to you [...] I'll get there. I'll crawl there ... (How does he do it? Again he rises to his full height. Feeling out the space before him with his hands, he takes another five steps—and he is already by the door.) Just a minute ... I'll rest a bit—and then down the hallway, along the wall, along the wall ...[115]

Interspersed among Gurevich's dying gasps, the parenthetical stage directions draw attention to the implied authorial persona's artistic awareness and control. Whereas both Gurevich and the play's audience have lost their power of vision—the former due to his alcohol poisoning and the latter due to the lowering of lights—the implied authorial persona continues to bear witness and describes the hero's movements in minute detail. Where Gurevich's eloquence is rapidly fading, moreover, the implied authorial persona has become more articulate than ever. The same performative momentum that impelled Gurevich from simulation to madness has, in the case of the implied authorial persona, reaffirmed the boundaries of theatrical display.

But because *Walpurgis Night* is a dramatic work that is meant to be staged, the implied authorial persona's voice risks disappearing in the transition from written text to action. The stage directions compensate by specifying a musical soundtrack that is designed to be as conspicuous and intrusive as possible, from the "five minutes of pounding and bad music" that the implied authorial persona requests to the "5 to 7 minutes" of cacophony "that sounds like nothing at all and anything you like."[116] Forcing themselves on the viewer, these bursts of music suggest the continued oversight of a creative figure who never melds with the events onstage and therefore retains his critical distance. The importance of the musical directions must not be underestimated, the implied authorial persona adds in an afterword dedicated to the topic:

> *A Tiny Afterword*
> "Music above all else," there's no other way. Beyond the authorial notations already planted throughout the text, one might use (as quietly as possible) Russian folksongs like "The Paths were Overgrown," "On the Road to Murom," ideally orchestral variations on these themes (in the third act). The Russian song "At Dawn, At First Light" (in the first half of the fourth act). The first movement of Mahler's Symphony No. 3, very muted, in the first act. One of Bruckner's most restrained and dreary andantes in the fifth. And so on.[117]

Supplementing the many other musical directions that are scattered throughout the tragedy, the afterword ensures that the implied authorial persona will be sensed on the stage as well as the page, ensuring the durability of his own mask of madness.

Where *Notes of a Psychopath* and *Moscow–Petushki* gave freer rein to the simulation of madness by blurring the boundary between hero and implied authorial persona, *Walpurgis Night* investigates the consequences of feigning by distinguishing the theatrical from the real. Though at first glance it reads somewhat tongue in cheek, then, Erofeev's characterization of himself as a faithful pupil of Nicolas Boileau's 1674 versification manual *The Art of Poetry* may in fact be taken seriously. Writing to Murav'ev upon completing *Walpurgis Night*, Erofeev promised with regard to the trilogy's other plays that "all of Boileau's canons will be meticulously followed."[118] And indeed, Boileau's proposition of a "rhyme" that not only bolsters but also violates "reason" coincides with Erofeev's critique of the mask of madness:

> Whate'er you write of pleasant or sublime,
> Always let sense accompany your rhyme:
> Vainly they seem two different ways to draw;
> Rhyme must be made to close with reason's law.
> And when to conquer her you bend your force,
> The mind will triumph in the noble course;
> To reason's yoke she quickly will incline,

> Which, far from hurting, renders her divine:
> But, if neglected, will as easily stray,
> And master reason, which she should obey.[119]

Rhyme and reason present an unstable dichotomy not only in Boileau's Enlightenment-era text, but also in Erofeev's implied authorial persona. "Venichka lived and thought according to the rules of reason, and not simply on a whim," Murav'ev recalled. "His evident anarchism simply indicates that he did not live by reason's dictation."[120] Erofeev struck a balance between rhyme and reason by piecing together an implied authorial persona who was capable of controlling his madman's mask.

Beyond the Mask

Preoccupied like many of his nonconformist contemporaries with the variable meanings of madness, Erofeev defined insanity through a dissenting lens. He did so even though he was no activist and his own hospitalizations were certainly not punitive; Erofeev's need for treatment was evidently all too real, and the author is reported to have respected his physicians.[121] When it came to developing his mask of madness, however, Erofeev proved ready to imbue his own experiences of hospitalization with the politically charged imagery of punitive diagnosis and simulation. The pathological world of *Walpurgis Night* is one wherein the terms "sanity" and "insanity" have become so hollowed out, so interchangeable and, indeed, so feignable that dissimulation and simulation are all that remain. How, then, is the dissenter who takes refuge in them to maintain an awareness of the distinction between theatricalized and actual madness? "I dare say Venichka was as free in his life as he was in his writing," Murav'ev recalled of his friend. "But he didn't go around with his head in the clouds. He could see the border that he crossed where others halted."[122] It was by constructing an implied authorial persona who could simulate insanity while resisting its pathological tug that Erofeev brought that border to light.

CONCLUSION

In the decades after Joseph Stalin's death, Soviet dissenters converged on the claim that reform had merely scratched the surface of what was still an authoritarian regime. For them, the state's authoritarianism was self-evident; why, then, were they the only ones who recognized that fact? It was by making literary use of psychiatric discourse to diagnose a chronically deluded society that the dissenters profiled in this study answered this question for themselves. The Soviet state was in a state of madness, they suggested through lived behavior and literary expression that reversed the diagnostic gaze that was simultaneously being trained on them. Curing, or at least containing, that state of madness therefore demanded that they validate a norm of *inakomyslie*, or "thinking differently." As Vladimir Bukovskii and Semen Gluzman observed in their "Manual on Psychiatry for Differently Thinking People," dissenters were like the child in Hans Christian Andersen's 1837 story "The Emperor's New Clothes." While the rest of the emperor's subjects irrationally praise the clothing of their ruler despite the fact that it does not exist, the child displays his rationality by pointing out its illusory nature.[1]

Yet in a society where pretending to see the emperor's clothes is the norm, it is the child laughing at the naked monarch who is declared abnormal and pathologized. As Gluzman wrote in the 1980s with renewed reference to Andersen's tale: "Confirming that the naked emperor is dressed is a sign of conformism; pointing out that the emperor has no clothes is, in a 'similarly thinking' society, a clear demonstration of *inakomyslie*."[2] While Stalin had formerly punished dissenters with arbitrary arrest and execution, Gluzman suggested, his like-minded successors had been unable to do so because of their public commitment to reform. The solution they settled upon to control dissent embodied the emptiness of that commitment and illustrated the normative tug of the madness to which the state and society had both succumbed:

> Yet execution is impossible. So exhausted totalitarianism looks for another route: to punish him in such a way as to put off others. "Millions of people don't see,

and yet he saw ... There are millions of others who don't see. So why was he the only one who saw? Why? ... He's just one person and still he fears neither us nor the crowd ... How can that be? ... Only madmen act that way! Yes, he must be a madman ... Call in the experts!"³

For Gluzman and many of the other dissenters whose words and actions this study has analyzed, the pathologization of dissent and the phenomenon of state-sponsored punitive psychiatry ran counter to such rational principles of liberal modernity as the rule of law and the freedom of the arts and sciences from political agendas. It therefore undermined the state's own claim to have corrected its course since Stalin's death. If even psychiatrists could not or would not "see" that the emperor was not clothed but naked, then legality, rationality, and indeed modernity remained distant prospects indeed.

Manipulating psychiatric discourse in literary ways in the documentary and imaginative works they unofficially disseminated, dissenters pathologized both society and the state. At the same time, they characterized psychiatric abuse as the subjective art of manipulating diagnostic categories for political purposes. Psychiatrists also used the term "art" to describe the masterful physician's expertise at implementing objective methods of diagnosis. Yet when psychiatrists constructed narratives of disease that flexibly accommodated dissidents' life stories, and when they equated sanity with the patient's own production of artworks that adhered to or violated state-sanctioned norms, they, like dissenters, were bringing together psychiatric and literary discourses. Psychiatry and dissent thus entered a discursive exchange that sometimes centered on conceptual flash points such as the "antipsychiatric" critique of psychiatric practices that had arisen in the West. By the late 1960s and early 1970s, as noted in chapter 2, antipsychiatry had already begun reaching the ears of informed Soviet citizens. Dissenters proved ready to apply these ideas to their own country's psychiatric policies but usually dismissed them with regard to the West. By contrast, Soviet psychiatrists tended to claim that antipsychiatry could have no purchase on a medical culture like their own—one that was rooted in the objective tenets of Marxist-Leninist theory and clinical practice.

Yet in a telling demonstration of their own receptivity to dissenters' rhetoric, some Soviet psychiatrists drew on ethically cognate ideas when it came to describing their Western counterparts. "The perversity of antipsychiatric arguments is not difficult to demonstrate," the psychiatrist Erikh Shternberg wrote in 1973. "At the same time, it would be an exercise in self-complacency to fail to note the defects of modern psychiatry that foster such tendencies."⁴ By "defects of modern psychiatry," Shternberg was referring to what he described as those West German hospitals that engaged in the "unthinking, across-the-board administration of large doses of psychotropic drugs that turn patients into passive, sluggish, apathetic 'vegetables.'"[5] Yet Shternberg's suggestion that the discipline as a whole might be vulnerable to abuse echoed the rhetoric of dissenters. Similarly mirroring that rhetoric with reference to Western psychiatry, in 1983 the legal expert Rudol'f Mikheev published a monograph that cited the West German case of a woman who had been wrongfully hospitalized for thirteen years. Moreover, he noted, some eight hundred healthy individuals had been unjustly hospitalized in the Italian city of Turin: "Criminal experiments on mentally ill people and the pronouncement of healthy people nonimputable are typical aspects of many foreign states, and, in the first instance, of the United States, England, and other capitalist countries."[6] What was "typical" for foreign systems was "inadmissible" in a society that adhered to the letter of socialist law, Mikheev duly noted. Yet even as Mikheev affirmed his support for Soviet psychiatric practices, his critique of Western practices testifies to the spread of dissenting arguments years before perestroika began.

When allegations of punitive hospitalization first gained traction in the 1970s, prominent Soviet psychiatrists dismissed them outright. As the psychiatrist Ruben Nadzharov told *Izvestiia* in August 1973: "There can be no doubt that talk in the West of the 'compulsory placement in psychiatric hospitals' of certain 'differently thinking' members of the intelligentsia is an integral part of that anti-Soviet propaganda campaign that certain circles are attempting to launch with the basest of political aims."[7] In 1977, following a successful campaign against Soviet practices at the World Psychiatric Association's (WPA) congress in Honolulu, a journalist writing for the same newspaper also characterized criticism of Soviet psychiatry as political propaganda:

> This entire fraud would easily be dispelled by the publication of the case histories of all those mentally ill criminals whom the Western propagandists present with such remarkable persistence as "healthy differently thinking people," from V[iktor] Fainberg to V[ladimir] Bukovskii to that very L[eonid] Pliushch whom these enemies of professional cooperation and de-escalation dragged to Honolulu. But our specialists believed and continue to believe that publishing these reports in the general press would violate medical confidentiality.[8]

The conflict over whether to release the psychiatric records of dissidents who had been declared insane demonstrated, according to the journalist, the ethical superiority of the Soviet delegation to the congress. Several months later, the *S. S. Korsakov Journal of Neuropathology and Psychiatry* echoed this argument in its summary of the Honolulu proceedings: "The Soviet delegate's lecture [on ethics] set itself apart from all the other lectures in the plenary meeting in that it was rooted in actual legislative measures and real statistics from the practical work of the Soviet psychiatric organization, whereas the other lectures essentially amounted to catalogues of what the authors deemed to be ethical themes."[9] For the *Korsakov Journal*, and presumably for its editor, Andrei Snezhnevskii, the ethical standards of the Soviet delegation were rooted in the objective bases of Soviet psychiatry itself.

Allegations of mistreatment became assertions of power as Soviet physicians, journalists, and jurists mirrored dissenters in staking out a sphere of medical ethics and using it to criticize psychiatrists abroad. In 1976, the broadsheet *Literaturnaia gazeta* published a series of articles titled "Are You Being Critical? Off to the Madhouse with You!" The first one, a special report from Italy, detailed the hospitalization of those eight hundred residents of Turin to whom Mikheev would subsequently allude in his monograph.[10] The second article shifted the scene to Washington, DC, by narrating the fate of a taxi driver who had been summarily confined to St. Elizabeths Hospital after trying to deliver a letter of protest to the U.S. president himself. Like dissenters who often used irony to make their points and who defended those points with reference to human rights, the article's author ironically noted the hospital's location on Martin Luther King Jr. Avenue. "Having done in the great civil rights activist, now they have given his name to the road that leads to the hell of this 'madhouse' [*zheltyi dom*]," he wrote. Like dissenters who redefined insanity as *inakomyslie*, moreover, the author portrayed such Western detainees as victims of a system that persecuted individuals who thought and spoke differently. "Over the course of many decades, bourgeois 'democracy' had developed quite a number of devices and methods for battling the dissatisfied and suppressing differently thinking people [*inakomysliashchie*]," he commented. "But today the achievements of chemical therapy, psychosurgery, and electronics have placed a new weapon in the hands of those in power."[11] Though journalists and physicians responding to allegations of Soviet abuse generally put quotation marks around words such as *inakomyslie* and *inakomysliashchie*, here the author mirrors the rhetoric of *samizdat* by leaving them out when alleging equivalent crimes by Western psychiatrists.[12]

The state's measured criticism of Western psychiatry signals the reciprocity of Cold War tensions. More importantly, however, it constitutes a tacit admission of something that Soviet practitioners only rarely acknowledged: their discipline's subjectivity and susceptibility to abuse. Even as psychiatrists continued to insist upon their scientific objectivity, the 1970s saw them begin to couch that insistence within the framework of deontology, a field that aimed to study both medical ethics and the doctor's duties to patients and their families. In 1971, the Presidium of the Supreme Soviet declared that all graduating medical students were henceforth to pronounce the Oath of the Physician of the USSR. In addition to pledging to care for patients and to further the cause of science, doctors now promised "to be guided in all my actions by the principles of communist morality" and "to always remember the high calling of the Soviet physician and my responsibility to the People and to the Soviet state."[13] But political loyalty was not the only lesson that Soviet psychiatrists drew from the nascent field of deontology. As the psychiatrist Nikolai Timofeev argued in a 1974 *Korsakov Journal* article on the subject, the best guarantee of ethical practices was the physician's philosophical and clinical objectivity:

> At the theoretical root of Soviet psychiatry is the philosophy of dialectical materialism with its unity of theory and method. This helps the psychiatrist on an everyday level to follow the principles of socialist humanism to their fullest (including the readaptation of mentally ill people and, among them, those who have been compulsorily hospitalized because they have committed dangerous or criminal acts), and not to turn humanistic ideas into slogans that are merely intoned while being stripped of any material basis.[14]

Unlike capitalist physicians whose humanism was based on subjective research and therefore deeply fallible, Timofeev argued, socialist psychiatrists drew their ethical principles from the objective bases of Marxism-Leninism and clinical practice. For Timofeev and his colleagues, Soviet psychiatry's claim to objectivity was its guarantee of morality.

Yet the advent of both deontology and attacks on Western practices indicates that, well before perestroika brought reforms to the discipline, Soviet psychiatry was already discursively engaging with the ethical issues that defined the rhetoric of dissent. In late 1971, activists at the WPA congress in Mexico City agitated to obtain a condemnation of Soviet practices.[15] By 1977, that campaign came to fruition with resolutions at the WPA congress in Honolulu condemning Soviet practices and founding a committee to monitor the misuses of psychiatry. Facing suspension or expulsion from the WPA, the Soviet delegation withdrew from the international body in 1983.[16] By 1982, however, Leonid Brezhnev's death had initiated a decline in punitive hospitalizations that would continue with the 1985 ascension of Mikhail Gorbachev and the launching of perestroika shortly thereafter.[17] In March 1988, following Snezhnevskii's death, the Ministry of Health issued a raft of legislation limiting the autonomy of clinicians, clarifying the criteria for compulsory hospitalization, and elucidating the administration of psychiatric treatment, among other reforms. By the end of the year, the *Korsakov Journal* had acquainted its readers with the texts of these instructions, as well.[18]

The liberalization of Soviet society under Gorbachev and the collapse of communism in 1991 initiated a period of disciplinary self-examination as psychiatrists joined dissenters in confronting the potential subjectivity of a science that had formerly emphasized its objectivity. Yet the discursive exchange of psychiatry and dissent went both ways in the post-Stalin period. If the state countered allegations of abuse in part by applying dissenters' arguments to Western practices, then dissenters made literary use of psychiatric rhetoric to pathologize the state and to consider the implications of its insanity for society and individuals. Joseph Brodsky incorporated the Soviet psychiatric establishment's discussion of the relationship between existence and consciousness into a poetic examination of the creative dissenter's own susceptibility to madness. Venedikt Erofeev suggested that insanity was now so ubiquitous that simulation had become the norm. And Andrei Siniavskii diagnosed in both society and the state a pathological tendency to aestheticize reality while modeling in its place a more acute awareness of the artifice of art. In Siniavskii's novella *Liubimov*, written under the pseudonym Abram Terts, the upstart ruler Leonid Tikhomirov enslaves the townspeople to an aestheticized reality wherein, among other miracles, water tastes like vodka. Tellingly, the character who maintains sufficient awareness to perceive that the vodka is in fact water turns out to be an invalid. "'But why shouldn't we weep, brother?' the war hero groaned and continued in a whisper: 'After all, you know, our tsar is a sorcerer.'"[19] However mesmerizing Tikhomirov's artistic mirage may be, the word of an invalid—like the word of Andersen's child and, indeed, like the word of anyone who invites pathologization by thinking and speaking differently—is capable of exposing its delusory nature.

For dissenters, a society that could not see that its emperor was naked was a society that had lost its mind. Yet this madness did not perpetuate itself, dissenters reiterated; it was the state that disseminated it by using psychiatric discourse to validate its own irrationality and authoritarianism. "In our country's conditions," the dissident Viktor Fainberg wrote in a 1970 account of his own hospitalization, "the fig leaf of psychiatry offers a reliable cover for the indefinite confinement of differently thinking people."[20] Fainberg's metaphor of the psychiatric "fig leaf" echoes through the pages of *samizdat* and *tamizdat*, testifying to the intertextuality of dissenters' psychiatric narratives. Describing the treatment of Leonid Pliushch several years later, for instance, the dissident linguist Tat'iana Khodorovich used the very same metaphor to lambaste the expediency of psychiatric diagnoses. "This is not the act of a group of scientific gangsters who seize someone in order to perform some kind of experiment," she wrote. "It is a governmental undertaking that cloaks itself—though only just barely—with the fig leaf of justice and psychiatry."[21] Deepening the metaphor, Khodorovich listed eleven subsidiary "fig leaves" through which the state had allegedly covered up Pliushch's abuse, from the smokescreen of diagnostic jargon to the closed doors of the trial at which Pliushch had been declared irresponsible for his actions. For dissenters, Soviet psychiatry did more than conceal the irrational authoritarianism of society and the state; as the arbiter of diagnostic standards, it also validated that mentality as the norm.

Circulating through *samizdat* and *tamizdat*, metaphors such as Fainberg's fig leaf and allusions to literary works such as Andersen's tale of the naked emperor united dissidents and dissenting writers who presumably shared these frames of reference. What might once have appeared to be a benign cultural association between creativity and madness was now, with the rise of punitive diagnosis and hospitalization, an all-too-threatening reality. Dissenters responded by making literary use of psychiatric discourse to both validate themselves and challenge the authority of the state. The impact of their essays, transcripts, poems, and works of fiction may have seemed limited within the isolation and silence of their psychiatric wards and unpublished exchanges. Yet the diagnosis they pronounced on Soviet society would resound with ever more prescience and clarity in the tumultuous decades to come.

Abbreviations

Archival and *samizdat* documents are individually cited and abbreviated in the notes as follows:

ACRC: Amherst Center for Russian Culture, Amherst College
    PGFP: Petr (Petro) Grigorenko (Hrykorenko) and his Family Papers

BRBML: Beinecke Rare Book and Manuscript Library, Yale University
    JBP: Joseph Brodsky Papers

GARF: State Archive of the Russian Federation, Moscow
    Fond R8131: *Prokuratura SSSR*

HIA: Hoover Institution Archives, Stanford University
    ASP: A. (Andrei) Siniavskii Papers

MSA: Memorial Society Archive, Moscow
    Fond 120: A. Esenin-Vol'pin
    Fond 163: *Rabochaia komissiia po rassledovaniiu ispol'zovaniia psikhiatrii v politicheskikh tseliakh*

SDS: *Sobranie dokumentov samizdata*
    AS: *Arkhiv samizdata*

Notes

Introduction

1. SDS, vol. 9, 30 vols. (Munich: Radio Liberty, 1972-78), AS 658 (Roi Medvedev, "'Informatsiia dlia druz'ei' (ezhednevnyi biulleten', posviashchennyi prinuditel'noi gospitalizatsii Zhoresa Medvedeva), 30 maia-6 iiunia 1970 g.").

2. Zhores Medvedev and Roi Medvedev, *Kto sumasshedshii?* (London: Macmillan, 1971), 121-22.

3. A. P. Chekhov, "Palata No. 6," in *Sochineniia v chetyrekh tomakh*, vol. 2, 4 vols. (Moscow: Pravda, 1984), 328.

4. Several scholars have proposed overarching terms for Soviet opposition that, like this study, draw attention to questions of the unity or diversity of thought. Vladimir Kozlov argues that what united dissenters was chiefly the *kramola*, or "religious rebellion," ascribed to them by an orthodox state. See V. A. Kozlov and S. V. Mironenko, eds., *Kramola: Inakomyslie v SSSR pri Khrushcheve i Brezhneve, 1953-1982 gg.: Rassekrechennye dokumenty Verkhovnogo suda i Prokuratury SSSR* (Moscow: Materik, 2005), 5-64. Boris Firsov argues for society's gravitation toward *raznomyslie*, or "diversity of thinking." See B. M. Firsov, *Raznomyslie v SSSR, 1940-1960-e gg: Istoriia, teoriia i praktika* (St. Petersburg: Evropeiskii dom, 2008). Alexei Yurchak challenges the binary of "official" and "unofficial" culture with the term "being *vnye*": a style of living both inside and outside the system. See Alexei Yurchak, *Everything Was Forever, Until It Was No More: The Last Soviet Generation* (Princeton: Princeton University Press, 2006), 126-57. On these debates, see also Ann Komaromi, "Samizdat and Soviet Dissident Publics," *Slavic Review* 71, no. 1 (Spring 2012): 70-90; Benjamin Nathans and Kevin M. F. Platt, "Socialist in Form, Indeterminate in Content: The Ins and Outs of Late Soviet Culture," *Ab Imperio*, no. 2 (2011): 301-24.

5. "dissent, v." OED Online. June 2017. Oxford University Press. http://www.oed.com/view/Entry/55410?result=2&rskey=TMI5Mm& (accessed October 13, 2017).

6. "dissidence, n." OED Online. http://www.oed.com/view/Entry/55457?result=1&rskey=bszHfi& (accessed October 13, 2017).

7. SDS, vol. 25, AS 1420 (Initsiativnaia gruppa po zashchite prav Cheloveka v SSSR, "Otkrytoe pis'mo v zashchitu chlena Leonida Pliushcha s 2-mia prilozheniiami (AS 1420-a i -b), (Moskva), bez daty, no mezhdu 15 i 25.1.73"), 1.

8. Vladimir Bukovskii, *I vozvrashchaetsia veter ... : Avtobiografiia* (Moscow: Zakharov, 2007), 184.

9. In exploring the literary interaction of psychiatry and dissent in the post-Stalin period, this study describes not an empirical reality about which all participants and observers were themselves necessarily aware, intentional or in vocal agreement, but rather what it determines to be a mutual effort by psychiatrists and dissenters to assert their authority by discursive means.

10. Bukovskii, *I vozvrashchaetsia veter* ..., 224.

11. In addition to Zhores Medvedev's mention of "Ward No. 6," this study discusses the references to Chekhov's story that appear in Joseph Brodsky's poem "New Year at the Kanatchikova Dacha" and in Venedikt Erofeev's play *Walpurgis Night, or The Steps of the Commander*. See also Valerii Tarsis's *Ward No. 7*, first published in Russian as Valerii Tarsis, *Palata No. 7* (Frankfurt am Main: Posev, 1966). For post-Soviet cinematic retellings of Chekhov's tale, see Kirill Serebrennikov's *Ragin* (2004) and Karen Shakhnazarov's *Palata No. 6* (2009).

12. Chekhov, "Palata No. 6," in *Sochineniia v chetyrekh tomakh*, vol. 2, 287.

13. On holy foolery, see chapter 1, note 22. On Ivan the Fool, see Andrei Siniavskii, *Ivan-durak: Ocherk russkoi narodnoi very* (Moscow: Agraf, 2001), 36–48.

14. A. S. Pushkin, "Ne dai mne bog soiti s uma ...," in *Polnoe sobranie sochinenii*, vol. 3, 17 vols. (Leningrad: Akademiia nauk SSSR, 1937–59), 322–23.

15. Gary Rosenshield, *Pushkin and the Genres of Madness: The Masterpieces of 1833* (Madison: University of Wisconsin Press, 2003), 9–18, 25–26.

16. N. V. Gogol', "Zapiski sumasshedshego," in *Sobranie sochinenii*, vol. 3, 8 vols. (Moscow: Terra-Knizhnyi klub, 2001), 150–67.

17. F. M. Dostoevskii, *Dvoinik. Peterburgskaia poema*, in *Polnoe sobranie sochinenii*, vol. 1, 30 vols. (Leningrad: Nauka, 1972–90), 109–229.

18. V. M. Garshin, "Krasnyi tsvetok," in *Sochineniia* (Moscow: Gosudarstvennoe izdatel'stvo khudozhestvennoi literatury, 1963), 225.

19. Andrei Belyi, *Peterburg*, in *Sobranie sochinenii*, vol. 2, 6 vols. (Moscow: Terra-Knizhnyi klub, 2003).

20. Aleksei Kruchenykh, "O bezumii v iskusstve," *Novyi den'*, May 26, 1919. Cited and translated in Gerald Janecek, *Zaum: The Transrational Poetry of Russian Futurism* (San Diego: San Diego State University Press, 1996), 255–56.

21. On the resurgence of interest in modernism, see, for example, Ann Komaromi, *Uncensored: Samizdat Novels and the Quest for Autonomy in Soviet Dissidence* (Evanston: Northwestern University Press, 2015), 8-9; Jane A. Sharp, "After Malevich—Variations on the Return to the Black Square," in *Picturing Russia: Explorations in Visual Culture*, ed. Valerie A. Kivelson and Joan Neuberger (New Haven: Yale University Press, 2008), 233–38; Michael Wachtel, "Heirs of Mayakovsky: The Poet and the Citizen," in *The Development of Russian Verse: Meter and Its Meanings* (Cambridge: Cambridge University Press, 1998), 206–38.

22. Felman also emphasizes literature's ability to subvert the rhetoric of madness through a "madness of rhetoric" that defers meaning. Shoshana Felman, *Writing and Madness: (Literature / Philosophy / Psychoanalysis)*, trans. Martha Noel Evans, Shoshana Felman, and Brian Massumi (Ithaca: Cornell University Press, 1985).

23. M. M. Rozental', S. M. Tretiakov, and I. K. Luppol, eds., *Pervyi vsesoiuznyi s″ezd sovetskikh pisatelei 1934: Stenograficheskii otchet* (Moscow: Khudozhestvennaia literatura, 1934), 17.

24. N. S. Khrushchev, "O kul'te lichnosti i ego posledstviiakh," *Izvestiia TsK KPSS*, no. 3 (1989): 160. I am grateful to Susan Larsen for highlighting this passage.

25. Abram Terts, "Chto takoe sotsialisticheskii realizm," in *Literaturnyi protsess v Rossii: Literaturno-kriticheskie raboty raznykh let*, by Andrei Siniavskii and Abram Terts (Moscow: Rossiiskii gosudarstvennyi gumanitarnyi universitet, 2003), 139–75.

26. Andrei Siniavskii, "Stalin—geroi i khudozhnik stalinskoi epokhi," *Sintaksis*, no. 19 (1987): 124. On the artistic underpinnings of Stalinism, see also Boris Groys, *The Total*

Art of Stalinism: Avant-Garde, Aesthetic Dictatorship, and Beyond, trans. Charles Rougle (London: Verso, 2011).

27. Felman, *Writing and Madness*, 252. Italics in the original.

28. Khrushchev, "O kul'te lichnosti," 133-34. On the state's claims to legality under Stalin and Khrushchev and dissident responses to those claims, see Benjamin Nathans, "Soviet Rights-Talk in the Post-Stalin Era," in *Human Rights in the Twentieth Century*, ed. Stefan-Ludwig Hoffman (Cambridge: Cambridge University Press, 2011), 166-90.

29. SDS, vol. 2, AS 133 (P. G. Grigorenko and A. E. Kosterin, "Otkrytoe pis'mo o restalinizatsii, priblizitel'no mart 1968 g."), 1.

30. Michel Foucault, *Madness and Civilization: A History of Insanity in the Age of Reason*, trans. Richard Howard (New York: Pantheon Books, 1965), x.

31. Ibid., 246.

32. Laura Engelstein, "Combined Underdevelopment: Discipline and the Law in Imperial and Soviet Russia," *American Historical Review* 98, no. 2 (April 1993): 344, 351, 353.

33. Medvedev and Medvedev, *Kto sumasshedshii?*, 140. Italics in the original.

34. Founded in 1921, the V. P. Serbskii Institute for Forensic Psychiatry was named for Vladimir Petrovich Serbskii (1858-1917), a founder of Russian forensic psychiatry.

35. Viktor Nekipelov, *Institut durakov: Dokumental'naia povest' "Institut durakov" i izbrannye stikhotvoreniia* (Barnaul: Pomoshch' postradavshim ot psikhiatrov, 2005), 21.

36. Bukovskii, *I vozvrashchaetsia veter...*, 195-96.

37. For an overview of the Medical Humanities, see Victoria Bates, Alan Bleakley, and Sam Goodman, eds., *Medicine, Health and the Arts: Approaches to the Medical Humanities* (London: Routledge, 2014), 3-13. Consonant approaches to Russian medicine and psychiatry include Konstantin Bogdanov, *Vrachi, patsienty, chitateli: Patograficheskie teksty russkoi kul'tury XVIII-XIX vekov* (Moscow: OGI, 2005); Konstantin Bogdanov, Iurii Murashov, and Rikkardo Nikolozi, eds., *Russkaia literatura i meditsina: Telo, predpisaniia, sotsial'naia praktika* (Moscow: Novoe izdatel'stvo, 2005); Angela Brintlinger, "Writing about Madness: Russian Attitudes toward Psyche and Psychiatry, 1887-1907," in *Madness and the Mad in Russian Culture*, ed. Angela Brintlinger and Ilya Vinitsky (Toronto: University of Toronto Press, 2007), 173-91; Cathy Popkin, "Hysterical Episodes: Case Histories and Silent Subjects," in *Self and Story in Russian History*, ed. Laura Engelstein and Stephanie Sandler (Ithaca: Cornell University Press, 2000), 189-216; Irina Sirotkina, *Diagnosing Literary Genius: A Cultural History of Psychiatry in Russia, 1880-1930* (Baltimore: Johns Hopkins University Press, 2002).

38. Sirotkina, *Diagnosing Literary Genius*, 7-8.

39. Concurrent and retrospective analyses of Soviet punitive psychiatry include Olga Bertelsen, "Rethinking Psychiatric Terror against Nationalists in Ukraine: Spatial Dimensions of Post-Stalinist State Violence," *Kyiv-Mohyla Humanities Journal*, no. 1 (2014): 27-76; Sidney Bloch and Peter Reddaway, *Psychiatric Terror: How Soviet Psychiatry Is Used to Suppress Dissent* (New York: Basic Books, 1977); Sidney Bloch and Peter Reddaway, *Soviet Psychiatric Abuse: The Shadow Over World Psychiatry* (London: V. Gollancz, 1984); Bartłomiej Brążkiewicz, *Psychiatria radziecka jako instrument walki z opozycją polityczną w latach 1918-1984* (Toruń: Wydawnictwo Adam Marszałek, 2004); Semyon Gluzman, *On Soviet Totalitarian Psychiatry* (Amsterdam: International Association on the Political Use of Psychiatry, 1989); Harvey Fireside, *Soviet Psychoprisons* (New York: W. W. Norton, 1979); K. W. Fulford, A. Y. Smirnov, and E. Snow, "Concepts of Disease and the Abuse of Psychiatry in the USSR," *The British Journal of Psychiatry* 162, no. 6 (June 1993): 801-10;

A. Korotenko and N. Alikina, *Sovetskaia psikhiatriia: Zabluzhdeniia i umysel* (Kiev: Sfera, 2002); Walter Reich, "The Spectrum Concept of Schizophrenia: Problems for Diagnostic Practice," *Archives of General Psychiatry* 32 (April 1975): 489–98; Theresa C. Smith and Thomas A. Oleszczuk, *No Asylum: State Psychiatric Repression in the Former USSR* (New York: New York University Press, 1996); Robert Van Voren and Sidney Bloch, eds., *Soviet Psychiatric Abuse in the Gorbachev Era* (Amsterdam: International Association on the Political Use of Psychiatry, 1989); Robert Van Voren, *On Dissidents and Madness: From the Soviet Union of Leonid Brezhnev to the "Soviet Union" of Vladimir Putin* (Amsterdam: Rodopi, 2009); Robert Van Voren, *Cold War in Psychiatry: Human Factors, Secret Actors* (Amsterdam: Rodopi, 2010).

40. On madness in Russian culture, see Bartłomiej Brążkiewicz, *Choroba psychiczna w literaturze i kulturze rosyjskiej* (Krakow: Wydawnictwo Księgarnia Akademicka, 2011); Angela Brintlinger, "The Hero in the Madhouse: The Post-Soviet Novel Confronts the Soviet Past," *Slavic Review* 63, no. 1 (2004): 43–65; Brintlinger and Vinitsky, eds., *Madness and the Mad in Russian Culture*; Priscilla Hart Hunt and Svitlana Kobets, eds., *Holy Foolishness in Russia: New Perspectives* (Bloomington: Slavica Publishers, 2011); Harriet Murav, *Holy Foolishness: Dostoevsky's Novels and the Poetics of Cultural Critique* (Stanford: Stanford University Press, 1992); Oliver Ready, *Persisting in Folly: Russian Writers in Search of Wisdom, 1963-2013* (Oxford: Peter Lang, 2017); Rosenshield, *Pushkin and the Genres of Madness*. As Ready published his illuminating analysis of foolishness in post-Stalinist culture when this book was already in production, the following notes cite his earlier articles.

41. On Russian and Soviet psychology and psychiatry, see Julie Vail Brown, "The Professionalization of Russian Psychiatry: 1857–1911" (PhD diss., University of Pennsylvania, 1981); Paul Calloway, *Russian/Soviet and Western Psychiatry: A Contemporary Comparative Study* (New York: John Wiley & Sons, 1993); D. D. Fedotov, *Ocherki po istorii otechestvennoi psikhiatrii* (Moscow: Institut psikhiatrii, 1957); T. I. Iudin, *Ocherki istorii otechestvennoi psikhiatrii* (Moscow: Gosudarstvennoe izdatel'stvo meditsinskoi literatury, 1951); David Joravsky, *Russian Psychology: A Critical History* (Oxford: Blackwell, 1989); Sarah Marks and Mat Savelli, eds., *Psychiatry in Communist Europe* (London: Palgrave Macmillan, 2015); Daniel P. Todes, *Ivan Pavlov: A Russian Life in Science* (Oxford: Oxford University Press, 2014); Benjamin Zajicek, "Scientific Psychiatry in Stalin's Soviet Union: The Politics of Modern Medicine and the Struggle to Define 'Pavlovian' Psychiatry, 1939–1953" (PhD diss., University of Chicago, 2009).

42. On Soviet and East European dissidence, see Ludmilla Alexeyeva, *Soviet Dissent: Contemporary Movements for National, Religious, and Human Rights* (Middletown: Wesleyan University Press, 1985); Jonathan Bolton, *Worlds of Dissent: Charter 77, the Plastic People of the Universe, and Czech Culture Under Communism* (Cambridge: Harvard University Press, 2012); Philip Boobbyer, *Conscience, Dissent and Reform in Soviet Russia* (London: Routledge, 2005); Firsov, *Raznomyslie v SSSR*; Robert Hornsby, *Protest, Reform and Repression in Khrushchev's Soviet Union* (Cambridge: Cambridge University Press, 2013); Komaromi, "Samizdat and Soviet Dissident Publics"; Komaromi, *Uncensored*; Kozlov and Mironenko, eds., *Kramola*; Benjamin Nathans, "The Disenchantment of Socialism: Soviet Dissidents, Human Rights, and the New Global Morality," in *The Breakthrough: Human Rights in the 1970s*, ed. Jan Eckel and Samuel Moyn (Philadelphia: University of Pennsylvania Press, 2014), 33–48; Joshua Rubenstein, *Soviet Dissidents: Their Struggle for Human Rights* (Boston: Beacon Press, 1985); Sesil' Vess'e, *Za vashu i nashu svobodu:*

Dissidentskoe dvizhenie v Rossii, trans. E. Baevskaia, N. Kislova, and N. Mavlevich (Moscow: Novoe literaturnoe obozrenie, 2015).

43. On de-Stalinization, see Miriam Dobson, *Khrushchev's Cold Summer: Gulag Returnees, Crime, and the Fate of Reform After Stalin* (Ithaca: Cornell University Press, 2009); Polly Jones, *Myth, Memory, Trauma: Rethinking the Stalinist Past in the Soviet Union, 1953–70* (New Haven: Yale University Press, 2013); Polly Jones, ed., *The Dilemmas of De-Stalinization: Negotiating Cultural and Social Change in the Khrushchev Era* (London: Routledge, 2006). On post-Stalinist society and culture, see Stephen V. Bittner, *The Many Lives of Khrushchev's Thaw* (Ithaca: Cornell University Press, 2008); Anne E. Gorsuch and Diane P. Koenker, eds., *The Socialist Sixties: Crossing Borders in the Second World* (Bloomington: Indiana University Press, 2013); Denis Kozlov, *The Readers of Novyi Mir: Coming to Terms with the Stalinist Past* (Cambridge: Harvard University Press, 2013); Denis Kozlov and Eleonory Gilburd, eds., *The Thaw: Soviet Society and Culture During the 1950s and 1960s* (Toronto: University of Toronto Press, 2013); Petr Vail' and Aleksandr Genis, *60-e: Mir sovetskogo cheloveka* (Moscow: Novoe literaturnoe obozrenie, 1996).

44. Mikhail Bakhtin, "Discourse in the Novel," in *The Dialogic Imagination: Four Essays*, ed. Michael Holquist, trans. Caryl Emerson and Michael Holquist (Austin: University of Texas Press, 2004), 324–25.

45. Viktor Shklovskii, "Iskusstvo kak priem," in *Gamburgskii schet: Stat'i—vospominaniia—esse (1914-1933)* (Moscow: Sovetskii pisatel', 1990), 58–72.

46. Roman Iakobson, "Noveishaia russkaia poeziia. Nabrosok pervyi: Podstupy k Khlebnikovu," in *Raboty po poetike* (Moscow: Progress, 1987), 279. Cited and translated in Svetlana Boym, *Death in Quotation Marks: Cultural Myths of the Modern Poet* (Cambridge: Harvard University Press, 1991), 21. For later, non-Russian arguments in this vein, see Roland Barthes, "The Death of the Author," in *The Norton Anthology of Theory and Criticism*, ed. Vincent B. Leitch (New York: W. W. Norton, 2001), 1466–70; Michel Foucault, "What Is an Author?," in Leitch, ed., *The Norton Anthology of Theory and Criticism*, 1622–36.

47. B. Tomashevskii, "Literatura i biografiia," *Kniga i revoliutsiia: Ezhemesiachnyi kritiko-bibliograficheskii zhurnal*, no. 4 (1923): 6–9.

48. Boym, *Death in Quotation Marks*, 20–26.

CHAPTER 1

1. Anonymous, "Andrei Vladimirovich Snezhnevskii," *Zhurnal nevropatologii i psikhiatrii imeni S. S. Korsakova*, no. 10 (1987): 1441.

2. Ibid., 1442.

3. Ibid., 1441.

4. Anonymous, "K chitateliam 'Zhurnala nevropatologii i psikhiatrii im. S. S. Korsakova,'" *Zhurnal nevropatologii i psikhiatrii imeni S. S. Korsakova*, no. 1 (1988): 3.

5. Ibid., 4.

6. Anonymous, "Andrei Vladimirovich Snezhnevskii," 1444.

7. Leonid Zagal'skii, "Sumasshestvie: Zametki na poliakh istorii bolezni otechestvennoi psikhiatrii," *Literaturnaia gazeta*, June 28, 1989.

8. On the press coverage of psychiatric abuse in the perestroika era, see Robert Van Voren, "Soviet Psychiatry Criticized in the Soviet Press," in Van Voren and Bloch, eds., *Soviet Psychiatric Abuse in the Gorbachev Era*, 62–72.

9. Bukovskii, *I vozvrashchaetsia veter*..., 349.

10. SDS, vol. 5, AS 345 (P. G. Grigorenko, "'Sravnenie dvukh ekspertiz'" (6 avgusta i 22 oktiabria), bez daty, veroiatno, konets oktiabria 1969 g."), 3.

11. Medvedev and Medvedev, *Kto sumasshedshii?*, 146; Nekipelov, *Institut durakov*, 133; Aleksandr Podrabinek, *Karatel'naia meditsina* (New York: Khronika, 1979), 168–73.

12. Vladimir Bukovskii, *Moskovskii protsess*, vol. 1, 2 vols. (Paris, Moscow: Russkaia mysl', 1996), 161.

13. Ibid., 150, 162.

14. Ibid., 161.

15. See, for instance, many of the accounts described in chapter 2 and in Bloch and Reddaway, *Psychiatric Terror*, 43–47.

16. See, for instance, ibid., 31–33, 220–57; Korotenko and Alikina, *Sovetskaia psikhiatriia*, 80–82; Reich, "The Spectrum Concept of Schizophrenia," 489–98.

17. Fulford, Smirnov, and Snow, "Concepts of Disease and the Abuse of Psychiatry in the USSR," 808. On these debates, see also Helen Lavretsky, "The Russian Concept of Schizophrenia: A Review of the Literature," *Schizophrenia Bulletin* 24, no. 4 (January 1998): 550.

18. Nekipelov, *Institut durakov*, 131.

19. O. V. Kerbikov, M. V. Korkina, R. A. Nadzharov, A. V. Snezhnevskii, *Psikhiatriia* (Moscow: Meditsina, 1968), 124–25.

20. Ibid., 126.

21. V. Ivanova, "Zalog dushevnogo zdorov'ia," *Literaturnaia gazeta*, January 24, 1967.

22. On holy foolishness, see Hunt and Kobets, eds., *Holy Foolishness in Russia*; S. A. Ivanov, *Blazhennye pokhaby: Kul'turnaia istoriia iurodstva* (Moscow: Iazyki slavianskikh kul'tur, 2005); D. S. Likhachev and A. M. Panchenko, *Smekhovoi mir Drevnei Rusi* (Leningrad: Nauka, 1984), 91–183; Ewa M. Thompson, *Understanding Russia: The Holy Fool in Russian Culture* (Lanham: University Press of America, 1987).

23. On shriekers, see Julie V. Brown, "Female Sexuality and Madness in Russian Culture: Traditional Values and Psychiatric Theory," *Social Research* 53 (Summer 1986): 380–82; Christine Worobec, *Possessed: Women, Witches, and Demons in Imperial Russia* (DeKalb: Northern Illinois University Press, 2001).

24. Brown, "The Professionalization of Russian Psychiatry," 45–46.

25. Ibid.," 43–44, 48–50, 58–64; T. I. Iudin, *Ocherki istorii otechestvennoi psikhiatrii*, 15–16, 25, 34–36.

26. Brown, "The Professionalization of Russian Psychiatry," 64; Iudin, *Ocherki istorii otechestvennoi psikhiatrii*, 58; A. A. Lebedev, *Chaadaev* (Moscow: Molodaia gvardiia, 1965), 173–74; Richard Tempest, "Madman or Criminal: Government Attitudes to Petr Chaadaev in 1836," *Slavic Review* 43, no. 2 (Summer 1984): 281–87.

27. Brown, "The Professionalization of Russian Psychiatry," 68–70, 74, 99, 105; Iudin, *Ocherki istorii otechestvennoi psikhiatrii*, 93–101, 109–10, 114.

28. Bloch and Reddaway, *Psychiatric Terror*, 51–53; Smith and Oleszczuk, *No Asylum*, 3; Vess'e, *Za vashu i nashu svobodu*, 55–56.

29. Sirotkina, *Diagnosing Literary Genius*, 7.

30. Brintlinger, "Writing about Madness," in Brintlinger and Vinitsky, eds., *Madness and the Mad in Russian Culture*, 181.

31. Popkin, "Hysterical Episodes," in Engelstein and Sandler, eds., *Self and Story in Russian History*, 189–216.

32. On modernity and the Russian and Soviet human sciences, see Daniel Beer, *Renovating Russia: The Human Sciences and the Fate of Liberal Modernity, 1880-1930* (Ithaca: Cornell University Press, 2008); Laura Engelstein, *The Keys to Happiness: Sex and the Search for Modernity in Fin-De-Siècle Russia* (Ithaca: Cornell University Press, 1992); David L. Hoffmann, *Cultivating the Masses: Modern State Practices and Soviet Socialism, 1914-1939* (Ithaca: Cornell University Press, 2011), 70-180.

33. On psychiatry's response to war and revolution, see Julie V. Brown, "Revolution and Psychosis: The Mixing of Science and Politics in Russian Psychiatric Medicine, 1905-13," *Russian Review* 46, no. 3 (July 1987): 283-302; Jacqueline Lee Friedlander, "Psychiatrists and Crisis in Russia, 1880-1917" (PhD diss., University of California, Berkeley, 2007); Dan Healey, *Bolshevik Sexual Forensics: Diagnosing Disorder in the Clinic and Courtroom, 1917-1939* (DeKalb: Northern Illinois University Press, 2009); Irina Sirotkina, "Toward a Soviet Psychiatry: War and the Organization of Mental Health Care in Revolutionary Russia," in *Soviet Medicine: Culture, Practice, and Science,* ed. Frances Lee Bernstein, Christopher Burton, and Dan Healey (DeKalb: Northern Illinois University Press, 2010), 27-48.

34. On psychoanalysis in Russia and the Soviet Union, see Alexander Etkind, *Eros of the Impossible: The History of Psychoanalysis in Russia,* trans. Noah and Maria Rubins (Boulder: Westview Press, 1997); Martin A. Miller, *Freud and the Bolsheviks: Psychoanalysis in Imperial Russia and the Soviet Union* (New Haven: Yale University Press, 1998), 96, 100-110. On social and biological theories, see Loren R. Graham, *Science, Philosophy, and Human Behavior in the Soviet Union* (New York: Columbia University Press, 1987), 221-44; Zajicek, "Scientific Psychiatry in Stalin's Soviet Union," 228-308.

35. Translation adapted from Karl Marx and Friedrich Engels, *The Marx-Engels Reader,* ed. Robert C. Tucker (New York: W.W. Norton, 1978), 4.

36. V. I. Lenin, "Materializm i empiriokrititsizm," in *Polnoe sobranie sochinenii,* vol. 18, 55 vols. (Moscow: Izdatel'stvo politicheskoi literatury, 1967-70), 7-384.

37. Benjamin Zajicek, "Soviet Madness: Nervousness, Mild Schizophrenia, and the Professional Jurisdiction of Psychiatry in the USSR, 1918-1936," *Ab Imperio,* no. 4 (2014): 174-79. See also Kenneth M. Pinnow, *Lost to the Collective: Suicide and the Promise of Soviet Socialism, 1921-1929* (Ithaca: Cornell University Press, 2010), 99-139.

38. Beer, *Renovating Russia,* 182-89, 197-201.

39. Zajicek, "Soviet Madness," 180.

40. Benjamin Zajicek, "Soviet Psychiatrists and the Schizophrenia Diagnosis, 1918-1948", unpublished paper, 8-9.

41. Zajicek, "Soviet Madness," 183, 191; Zajicek, "Soviet Psychiatrists and the Schizophrenia Diagnosis," 30.

42. Lavretsky, "The Russian Concept of Schizophrenia," 540; Zajicek, "Scientific Psychiatry in Stalin's Soviet Union," 369-409. On Pavlov's social and political legacies and his impact on the development of the mind sciences, see Todes, *Ivan Pavlov;* Daniel Philip Todes, "From Radicalism to Scientific Convention: Biological Psychology in Russia From Sechenov to Pavlov" (PhD diss., University of Pennsylvania, 1981).

43. Ivanova, "Zalog dushevnogo zdorov'ia."

44. Anonymous, "Andrei Vladimirovich Snezhnevskii," 1443. On the psychiatric schools, see Joravsky, *Russian Psychology,* 438; Lavretsky, "The Russian Concept of Schizophrenia," 541.

45. Akademiia meditsinskikh nauk SSSR and Vsesoiuznoe nauchnoe meditsinskoe obshchestvo nevropatologov i psikhiatrov, *Fiziologicheskoe uchenie akademika I. P. Pavlova*

v psikhiatrii i nevropatologii: Materialy stenograficheskogo otcheta ob"edinennogo zasedaniia rasshirennogo Prezidiuma AMN SSSR i plenuma Pravleniia Vsesoiuznogo obshchestva nevropatologov i psikhiatrov, 11–15 oktiabria 1951 g. (Moscow: Gosudarstvennoe izdatel'stvo meditsinskoi literatury, 1952), 41.

46. Joravsky, *Russian Psychology*, 429.

47. Versions of the diagrams appear in A. V. Snezhnevskii, "O nozologicheskoi spetsifichnosti psikhopatologicheskikh sindromov," *Zhurnal nevropatologii i psikhiatrii imeni S. S. Korsakova*, no. 1 (1960): 98; A. V. Snezhnevskii, "Mesto kliniki v issledovanii prirody shizofrenii," *Zhurnal nevropatologii i psikhiatrii imeni S. S. Korsakova*, no. 9 (1975): 1342–1343; A. V. Snezhnevskii, ed., *Rukovodstvo po psikhiatrii*, vol. 1, 2 vols. (Moscow: Meditsina, 1983), 83, 85.

48. The 1960 image of positive syndromes is also reproduced and discussed in Joravsky, *Russian Psychology*, plate 18. On the totalizing implications of the diagrams, see ibid., 431; Lavretsky, "The Russian Concept of Schizophrenia," 542.

49. A. V. Snezhnevskii, ed., *Spravochnik po psikhiatrii* (Moscow: Meditsina, 1974), 6.

50. Edward Shorter, *A History of Psychiatry: From the Era of the Asylum to the Age of Prozac* (New York: John Wiley & Sons, 1997), 103–107.

51. Lavretsky, "The Russian Concept of Schizophrenia," 546; Shorter, *A History of Psychiatry*, 106, 298–305.

52. Bloch and Reddaway, *Psychiatric Terror*, 246–48; Fulford, Smirnov, and Snow, "Concepts of Disease and the Abuse of Psychiatry in the USSR," 806–807; Korotenko and Alikina, *Sovetskaia psikhiatriia*, 80–82; Reich, "The Spectrum Concept of Schizophrenia," 492.

53. Fulford, Smirnov, and Snow, "Concepts of Disease and the Abuse of Psychiatry in the USSR," 804; Reich, "The Spectrum Concept of Schizophrenia," 493–96.

54. A. V. Snezhnevskii, ed., *Shizofreniia: Mul'tidistsiplinarnoe issledovanie* (Moscow: Meditsina, 1972), 31; Snezhnevskii, ed., *Rukovodstvo po psikhiatrii*, vol. 1, 305. On the frequency of sluggish forms of schizophrenia, see ibid., 334.

55. Natalya Gorbanevskaya, *Selected Poems, With a Transcript of Her Trial and Papers Relating to Her Detention in a Prison Psychiatric Hospital*, trans. Daniel Weissbort (Oxford: Carcanet Press, 1972), 144.

56. Kerbikov et al., *Psikhiatriia*, 126.

57. Ia. M. Kalashnik and G. V. Morozov, eds., *Sudebnaia psikhiatriia* (Moscow: Iuridicheskaia literatura, 1967), 46.

58. Ibid., 47.

59. SDS, vol. 8, AS 561 (G. V. Morozov, D. R. Lunts, T. P. Pechernikova, Martynenko, and I. K. Ianushevskii, "'Zakliuchenie komissii pod predsedatel'stvom gorodskogo psikhiatra I. K. Ianushevskogo o sostoianii N. E. Gorbanevskoi, 19 noiabria 1969g' and 'Zakliuchenie meditsinskoi komissii Instituta im. Serbskogo o nevmeniaemosti N. E. Gorbanevskoi, 6 aprelia 1970g.'"), 2.

60. Ibid.
61. Ibid.
62. Ibid., 3.
63. Ibid.
64. Ibid. On Gorbanevskaia's own account of this experience, see chapter 2.
65. Ibid., 4.

66. Ibid. The protest in question was the well-known August 25, 1968, demonstration against the Soviet invasion of Czechoslovakia. For Gorbanevskaia's account of the ensuing events, see Natal'ia Gorbanevskaia, *Polden': Delo o demonstratsii na Krasnoi ploshchadi 25 avgusta 1968 goda* (Moscow: Novoe izdatel'stvo, 2007).

67. SDS, vol. 8, AS 561 ("Zakliuchenie"), 5.

68. The report does not mention that, just one month prior to her latest arrest, yet another team of psychiatrists had dismissed Gorbanevskaia's schizophrenia diagnosis and diagnosed her with a "psychopathic personality with signs of hysteria and a tendency to decompensation." See ibid., 1.

69. Snezhnevskii, ed., *Shizofreniia*, 33.

70. Ibid.

71. Ibid.

72. Ibid.

73. Ibid., 34.

74. Ibid.

75. Ibid.

76. On paranoiac and paranoid syndromes, see Kerbikov et al., *Psikhiatriia*, 96–97.

77. Ibid., 47–48.

78. Snezhnevskii, ed., *Shizofreniia*, 36.

79. On Bukovskii's dissident activities and psychiatric history, see chapter 2 and Philip Boobbyer, "Vladimir Bukovskii and Soviet Communism," *Slavonic and East European Review* 87, no. 3 (July 2009): 454–56.

80. GARF, f. R8131, op. 31, d. 95676, l. 16 (V. M. Morozov and G. A. Rotshtein, "Akt 20/s," April 18, 1966).

81. Ibid.

82. Ibid.

83. Ibid, l. 17.

84. Kerbikov et al., *Psikhiatriia*, 379.

85. Ibid., 382–83.

86. Ibid., 388.

87. SDS, vol. 8, AS 560 (G. V. Morozov, V. M. Morozov, D. R. Lunts, Z. G. Turova, and M. M. Mal'tseva, "Zakliuchenie meditsinskoi komissii Instituta im. Serbskogo o nevmeniaemosti P. G. Grigorenko, 19 noiabria 1969 g."), 9.

88. Ibid., 2–3.

89. Ibid., 5.

90. Ibid., 9.

91. N. M. Zharikov et al., "Diagnosticheskie trudnosti pri sudebnopsikhiatricheskoi ekspertize bol'nykh shizofreniei (kliniko-psikhopatologicheskii aspekt)," *Zhurnal nevropatologii i psikhiatrii imeni S. S. Korsakova*, no. 1 (1976): 124.

92. Snezhnevskii, ed., *Spravochnik po psikhiatrii*, 4.

93. Snezhnevskii, ed., *Shizofreniia*, 10.

94. V. M. Shumakov, "K sistematike form techeniia shizofrenii i obshchei kharakteristike bol'nykh, sovershaiushchikh obshchestvenno opasnye deistviia," *Zhurnal nevropatologii i psikhiatrii imeni S. S. Korsakova*, no. 2 (1969): 272.

95. V. M. Shumakov, S. B. Shesterneva, E. D. Sokolova, and K. F. Efremenko, "Kliniko-psikhopatologicheskie osobennosti bol'nykh shizofreniei, sovershavshikh

obshchestvenno opasnye deistviia," *Zhurnal nevropatologii i psikhiatrii imeni S. S. Korsakova*, no. 12 (1976): 1866.

96. V. M. Shumakov, E. D. Sokolova, and Ia. E. Svirinovskii, "O klinicheskikh kriteriiakh obshchestvennoi opasnosti bol'nykh shizofreniei (psikhopatopodobnye sostoianiia)," *Zhurnal nevropatologii i psikhiatrii imeni S. S. Korsakova*, no. 1 (1980): 112-13.

97. Z. N. Serebriakova, B. P. Shchukin, and Iu. O. Musaev, "O vozmozhnosti prognozirovaniia obshchestvenno opasnykh deistvii psikhicheski bol'nykh," in *Problemy prinuditel'nogo lecheniia psikhicheski bol'nykh (sbornik nauchnykh trudov)*, ed. G. V. Morozov (Moscow: Ministerstvo zdravookhraneniia SSSR: Tsentral'nyi ordena trudovogo krasnogo znameni nauchno-issledovatel'skii institut sudebnoi psikhiatrii im. prof. V. P. Serbskogo, 1978), 145.

98. Bakhtin, "Discourse in the Novel," in Holquist, ed., *The Dialogic Imagination*, 259-422.

99. Kerbikov et al., *Psikhiatriia*, 114.

100. Snezhnevskii, ed., *Spravochnik po psikhiatrii*, 10.

101. Kerbikov et al., *Psikhiatriia*, 124.

102. Ibid., 115.

103. Ibid., 118.

104. Ibid., 114.

105. Ia. I. Khurgin and P. G. Nikiforova, "O perspektivakh diagnostiki zabolevanii psikhicheskikh," *Zhurnal nevropatologii i psikhiatrii imeni S. S. Korsakova*, no. 3 (1966): 462.

106. Kalashnik and Morozov, eds., *Sudebnaia psikhiatriia*, 47.

107. Ibid., 46.

108. Kerbikov et al., *Psikhiatriia*, 126.

109. Ministerstvo iustitsii RSFSR, *Ugolovnyi kodeks RSFSR: Ofitsial'nyi tekst s izmeneniiami na 1 avgusta 1962 g. i s prilozheniem postateino sistematizirovannykh materialov* (Moscow: Gosudarstvennoe izdatel'stvo iuridicheskoi literatury, 1962), 9-10.

110. Iuridicheskaia komissiia soveta ministrov RSFSR, *Grazhdanskii kodeks RSFSR: Ofitsial'nyi tekst* (Moscow: Iuridicheskaia literatura, 1964), 11-13.

111. E. M. Kholodkovskaia, *Deesposobnost' psikhicheski bol'nykh v sudebno-psikhiatricheskoi praktike* (Moscow: Meditsina, 1967), 97.

112. D. R. Lunts, *Problema nevmeniaemosti v teorii i praktike sudebnoi psikhiatrii* (Moscow: Meditsina, 1966), 112.

113. Ibid., 179-81.

114. Kalashnik and Morozov, eds., *Sudebnaia psikhiatriia*, 47.

115. Applications of Austin's speech-act theory to diagnosis include Kazem Sadegh-Zadeh, *Handbook of Analytic Philosophy of Medicine*, Philosophy and Medicine 113 (Dordrecht: Springer, 2012), 55-58, 354-56; Peter J. Schulz, "The Communication of Diagnostic Information by Doctors to Patients in the Consultation," in *Bordering Biomedicine*, ed. Vera Kalitzkus and Peter Twohig (Amsterdam, New York: Rodopi, 2006), 103-15. On speech acts in Soviet and post-Soviet alcoholism therapy, see Eugene Raikhel, "Placebos or Prostheses for the Will?: Trajectories of Alcoholism Treatment in Russia," in *Addiction Trajectories*, ed. Eugene Raikhel and William Garriott (Durham: Duke University Press, 2013), 201.

116. J. L. Austin, *How to Do Things with Words* (Cambridge: Harvard University Press, 1975), 3-6.

117. Lunts, *Problema nevmeniaemosti v teorii i praktike sudebnoi psikhiatrii*, 77, 206, 208. See also D. R. Lunts, "O sudebno-psikhiatricheskom znachenii psikhicheskikh

anomalii, ne iskliuchaiushchikh vmeniaemosti (po povodu stat'i S. F. Semenova 'K voprosu ob ogranichennoi (umen'shennoi) vmeniaemosti')," *Zhurnal nevropatologii i psikhiatrii imeni S. S. Korsakova*, no. 4 (1967): 605.

118. Austin, *How to Do Things with Words*, 8.

119. For the 1961 and 1971 Instructions, see Podrabinek, *Karatel'naia meditsina*, 177–79, 180–81.

120. E. A. Babaian, "Zakonodatel'stvo SSSR i nekotorykh zarubezhnykh stran po psikhiatrii," *Zhurnal nevropatologii i psikhiatrii imeni S. S. Korsakova*, no. 11 (1969): 1618.

121. M. F. Tal'tse and Ia. L. Landau, "Mery meditsinskogo kharaktera i kriterii izmeneniia ikh v otnoshenii s medlenno-progredientnoi paranoidnoi shizofrenii," in *Problemy prinuditel'nogo lecheniia psikhicheski bol'nykh (sbornik nauchnykh trudov)*, ed. G. V. Morozov (Moscow: Ministerstvo zdravookhraneniia SSSR, Tsentral'nyi ordena trudovogo krasnogo znameni nauchno-issledovatel'skii institut sudebnoi psikhiatrii im. prof. V. P. Serbskogo, 1978), 61.

122. SDS, vol. 8, AS 574 (Ia. L. Landau, D. R. Lunts, and G. V. Morozov, "Zakliuchenie meditsinskoi komissii Instituta im. Serbskogo o nevmeniaemosti V. E. Fainberga, 10 oktiabria 1968 g."), 5.

123. GARF, f. R8131, op. 36, d. 5502, l. 19 (D. E. Melekhov, R. A. Nadzharov, A. K. Kachaev, M. F. Tal'tse, and A. G. Azamatov, "Akt No. 28/s," April 20, 1972).

124. SDS, vol. 8, AS 560 ("Zakliuchenie"), 7.

125. Ibid., 8.

126. SDS, vol. 8, AS 561 ("Zakliuchenie"), 4.

127. Ibid., 4.

128. E. A. Babaian et al., *Izobrazitel'nyi iazyk bol'nykh shizofrenii* (Basel: Sandoz, 1982), unpaginated; references are by my own count from the first page of full text [13]. There was a significant pedigree to Soviet psychiatry's marked emphasis on analyzing patients' art. On the psychiatrist Lev Rozenshtein's work in the 1930s, for example, see Zajicek, "Soviet Madness," 186. See also Brintlinger, "Writing about Madness," in Brintlinger and Vinitsky, eds., *Madness and the Mad in Russian Culture*; Sirotkina, *Diagnosing Literary Genius*.

129. Katerina Clark, *The Soviet Novel: History as Ritual* (Bloomington: Indiana University Press, 2000).

130. Evgeny Dobrenko, *Political Economy of Socialist Realism*, trans. Jesse M. Savage (New Haven: Yale University Press, 2007), xii.

131. Rozental', Tretiakov, and Luppol, eds., *Pervyi vsesoiuznyi s"ezd sovetskikh pisatelei 1934*, 712.

132. Clark, *The Soviet Novel*, 16.

133. Snezhnevskii, ed., *Spravochnik po psikhiatrii*, 11.

134. Babaian et al., *Izobrazitel'nyi iazyk bol'nykh shizofrenii*, [11].

135. Ibid., [17].

136. Ibid., [14, 16].

137. E. A. Babaian et al., *Izobrazitel'nyi iazyk bol'nogo paranoiei* (Basel: Sandoz, 1986), unpaginated; references are by my own count from the first page of full text [26–27].

138. E. A. Babaian et al., *Izobrazitel'nyi iazyk bol'nykh shizofrenii s bredovymi i sverkhtsennymi obrazovaniiami* (Basel: Sandoz, 1985), unpaginated; references are by my own count from the first page of full text [12].

139. Babaian et al., *Izobrazitel'nyi iazyk bol'nogo paranoiei*, [27].

140. Ibid., [24].

141. Ibid., [36].
142. Ibid., [27].
143. Ibid., [33].
144. Ibid., [29].
145. Ibid., [52].
146. Ibid., [34].
147. V. E. Pelipas, *Simuliatsiia psikhicheskikh rasstroistv i ee raspoznavanie pri sudebno-psikhiatricheskoi ekspertize (metodicheskie rekomendatsii)* (Moscow: Ministerstvo zdravookhraneniia SSSR, 1983), 3.
148. Ibid., 11.
149. D. R. Lunts, "Dissimuliatsiia u psikhicheski bol'nykh," in *Problemy kliniki, sudebnopsikhiatricheskoi ekspertizy, patofiziologii i immunologii shizofrenii,* No. 3, ed. G. V. Morozov, Nauchnye trudy vyp. 15 (Moscow: Ministerstvo zdravookhraneniia SSSR: Tsentral'nyi nauchno-issledovatel'skii institut sudebnoi psikhiatrii im. prof. V. P. Serbskogo, 1964), 314–15.
150. Kalashnik and Morozov, eds., *Sudebnaia psikhiatriia,* 205.
151. Iakhimovich's diagnoses of paranoiac development of personality followed an examination at a Riga dispensary that reached a tentative finding of paranoid schizophrenia. For the Riga evaluations, see SDS, vol. 8, AS 562 (A. A. Brishke, L. A. Ligure, Z. R. Vshtenberg, Rusinova, Markis, and Krasnianskii, "Predvaritel'nyi diagnoz, postavlennyi I.A. Iakhimovichu v Respublikanskom nevrologicheskom dispansere g. Rigi, 1 aprelia 1969g. Zakliuchenie statsionarnoi sudebno-psikhiatricheskoi ekspertnoi komissii Rizhskoi respublikanskoi psikhiatricheskoi bol'nitsy o nevmeniaemosti I. A. Iakhimovicha, 3 iiunia 1969g.").
152. SDS, vol. 8, AS 563 (T. P. Pechernikova, D. R. Lunts, M. F. Tal'tse, and Tabanova, "Zakliuchenie meditsinskoi komissii Instituta im. Serbskogo o nevmeniaemosti I. A. Iakhimovicha, 12 ianvaria 1970g."), 6.
153. Ibid., 7.
154. Pelipas, *Simuliatsiia psikhicheskikh rasstroistv i ee raspoznavanie pri sudebno-psikhiatricheskoi ekspertize,* 5.
155. Ibid., 12.
156. Ibid., 6, 10.
157. Ibid., 14. On the cultural contingency of simulative displays and their feedback into cultural texts that depict simulation, see Viktor Kuperman and Iosif Zislin, "Simuliatsiia psikhoza: Semiotika povedeniia," in Bogdanov, Murashov, and Nikolozi, eds., *Russkaia literatura i meditsina,* 290–302; Victor Kuperman, "Narratives of Psychiatric Malingering in Works of Fiction," *Medical Humanities* 32, no. 2 (2006): 67–72.
158. Pelipas, *Simuliatsiia psikhicheskikh rasstroistv i ee raspoznavanie pri sudebno-psikhiatricheskoi ekspertize,* 14.
159. Kalashnik and Morozov, eds., *Sudebnaia psikhiatriia,* 395–96.

CHAPTER 2

1. Bukovskii, *I vozvrashchaetsia veter* ..., 190; Petro Grigorenko, *V podpol'e mozhno vstretit' tol'ko krys* ... (Moscow: Zven'ia, 1997), 542; Podrabinek, *Karatel'naia meditsina,* 85.

2. SDS, vol. 8, AS 575 (Viktor Fainberg, "Obrashchenie k organizatsiiam, zashchishchaiushchim prava Cheloveka, s opisaniem Leningradskoi spetsial'noi psikhiatricheskoi bol'nitsy, iiul' 1970 g."), 4.

3. Leonid Pliushch, *Na karnavale istorii* (London: Overseas Publications Interchange, 1979), 8. On dissident memoirs, see Benjamin Nathans, "Talking Fish: On Soviet Dissident Memoirs," *Journal of Modern History* 87, no. 3 (September 2015): 579–614.

4. Podrabinek, *Karatel'naia meditsina*, 8.

5. V. Bukovskii and S. Gluzman, "Posobie po psikhiatrii dlia inakomysliashchikh," *Khronika zashchity prav v SSSR*, no. 13 (January-February 1975): 41.

6. In addition to the psychiatric narratives analyzed in this chapter, see SDS, vol. 9, AS 666 (Vladimir Gershuni, "Zapiski iz Orlovskoi spetspsikhbol'nitsy, 9–19 marta 1971 g."); Valeriia Novodvorskaia, *Po tu storonu otchaianiia* (Moscow: Novosti, 1993); G. M. Shimanov, "Zapiski iz krasnogo doma," in *Zapiski iz krasnogo doma* (Moscow: Tipografiia IPO profsoiuov Profizdat, 2006), 51–92; Tarsis, *Palata No. 7*.

7. Podrabinek, *Karatel'naia meditsina*, 10.

8. Bukovskii, *I vozvrashchaetsia veter...*, 185.

9. Yuri Glazov, *The Russian Mind Since Stalin's Death* (Dordrecht: D. Reidel, 1985), 11–13.

10. Ibid., 76.

11. On dissidents' "mimetic resistance" to authority, see Serguei Alex. Oushakine, "The Terrifying Mimicry of Samizdat," *Public Culture* 13, no. 2 (April 2001): 191–214.

12. R. D. Laing, *The Divided Self: A Study of Sanity and Madness* (Chicago: Quadrangle Books, 1960); Thomas S. Szasz, *The Myth of Mental Illness: Foundations of a Theory of Personal Conduct* (New York: Hoeber-Harper, 1961).

13. Erving Goffman, *Asylums: Essays on the Social Situation of Mental Patients and Other Inmates* (New Brunswick: Aldine Transaction, 2007).

14. Foucault, *Madness and Civilization*. Foucault's ideas are further discussed in the introduction to this study, while the Soviet psychiatric establishment's response to antipsychiatry is discussed in the conclusion.

15. T. Papodopulos, review of *Madness and Civilization: A History of Insanity in the Age of Reason*, by Michel Foucault, *Zhurnal nevropatologii i psikhiatrii imeni S. S. Korsakova* 1973, no. 4 (1973): 602.

16. Ibid., 596.

17. Iu. S. Savenko and L. Vinogradova, "Latentnye formy antipsikhiatrii kak glavnaia opasnost," *Nezavisimyi psikhiatricheskii zhurnal*, no. 4 (2005): 12; Iurii Savenko, interview by Rebecca Reich, Moscow, Russia, April 15, 2009; Iurii Savenko, interview by Benjamin Zajicek, Moscow, Russia, July 3, 2003. I am grateful to Benjamin Zajicek for sharing his notes.

18. Bukovskii and Gluzman, "Posobie po psikhiatrii dlia inakomysliashchikh," 43.

19. Iu. S. Savenko, "Perebolet' Fuko," *Novoe literaturnoe obozrenie*, no. 49 (2001): 89.

20. On antipsychiatry and the work of Iurii Mamleev, see Oliver Ready, "'Questions to Which Reason Has No Answer': Iurii Mamleev's Irrationalism in European Context," in *Facets of Russian Irrationalism between Art and Life: Mystery inside Enigma*, ed. Olga Tabachnikova (Leiden: Brill Rodopi, 2016), 511–15.

21. S. F. Gluzman, "Zloupotreblenie psikhiatriei: Sotsial'nye i iuridicheskie istoki," *Filosofskaia i sotsiologicheskaia mysl'*, no. 7 (1990): 71.

22. Savenko and Vinogradova, "Latentnye formy antipsikhiatrii kak glavnaia opasnost," 13–14.

23. Podrabinek, *Karatel'naia meditsina*, 108. Podrabinek's source is E. Ia. Shternberg, review of *Antipsikhiatriia. Kritika psikhiatrii*, by I. Glatsel', *Zhurnal nevropatologii i psikhiatrii imeni S. S. Korsakova*, no. 8 (1976): 1264–66.

24. Podrabinek, *Karatel'naia meditsina*, 108.

25. Bukovskii, *I vozvrashchaetsia veter...*, 232.

26. MSA, f. 120, op. 1, d. 13, ll. 1–2, 7, 11–12 (Aleksandr Vol'pin, "Fragment vospominanii o detstve. Chernovoi avtograf," May 1949).

27. Aleksandr Vol'pin, interview by Rebecca Reich, Revere, MA, September 2, 2009.

28. MSA, f. 120, op. 1, d. 14, ll. 53–54 ("Opredelenie SKUD Verkhovnogo suda SSSR").

29. Benjamin Nathans, "The Dictatorship of Reason: Aleksandr Vol'pin and the Idea of Rights under 'Developed Socialism,'" *Slavic Review* 66, no. 4 (Winter 2007): 639; Vol'pin, interview.

30. Nathans, "The Dictatorship of Reason," 651–52.

31. A. S. Esenin-Vol'pin, "Grazhdanskoe obrashchenie," in *Filosofiia. Logika. Poeziia. Zashchita prav cheloveka: Izbrannoe* (Moscow: Rossiiskii gosudarstvennyi gumanitarnyi universitet, 1999), 313. The poetry and other materials cited from this volume are reproduced with permission from Rossiiskii gosudarstvennyi gumanitarnyi universitet.

32. HIA, ASP, Box 5, Folder 10, "Dokladyvaiu, chto 5 dekabria...," December 6, 1965, pp. 1–2. Page references to the A. (Andrei) Siniavskii Papers refer to individual documents rather than to the folder as a whole.

33. HIA, ASP, Box 5, Folder 10, "V noiabre s.g...," December 6, 1965, pp. 1, 3.

34. MSA, f. 120, op. 1, d. 13, ll. 89ob-91 (Aleksandr Vol'pin, "Istekaet 44-ii god moei zhizni...," May 12, 1968).

35. MSA, f. 120, op. 1, d. 16, ll. 23–23ob (Aleksandr Vol'pin, "Opisanie A. S. Eseninym-Vol'pinym svoego nasil'stvennogo pomeshcheniia v psikhiatricheskuiu bol'nitsu," 1968, hereafter cited as "Opisanie 1"). For Articles 126 and 178, see Ministerstvo iustitsii RSFSR, *Ugolovnyi kodeks RSFSR*, 70, 91.

36. MSA, f. 120, op. 1, d. 16, l. 1 (Aleksandr Vol'pin, "Pis'mo A. S. Esenina-Vol'pina V. B. Vol'pin po povodu svoei nasil'stvennoi gospitalizatsii," February 14, 1968).

37. MSA, f. 120, op. 1, d. 16, l. 23ob ("Opisanie 1").

38. Ibid., l. 23ob–24.

39. Vol'pin, interview.

40. Esenin-Vol'pin, "Iuridicheskaia pamiatka," in *Izbrannoe*, 356–72; Nathans, "The Dictatorship of Reason," 637, 647, 662–63. On Vol'pin's legalism as defamiliarization, see Svetlana Boym, *Another Freedom: The Alternative History of an Idea* (Chicago: University of Chicago Press, 2010), 236–37.

41. GARF, f. R8131, op. 31, d. 89189b, l. 4 (G. V. Morozov, D. R. Lunts, R. A. Nadzharov, and Burno, "Zakliuchenie," March 6, 1968).

42. Esenin-Vol'pin, "Obrashchenie k druz'iam," in *Izbrannoe*, 331.

43. MSA, f. 120, op. 1, d. 3, l. 7 (Aleksandr Vol'pin, "Pis'mo N. S. Khrushchevu v sviazi s kampaniei vokrug publikatsii sbornika 'Vesennii list'. Variant 1. Chernovoi avtograf," December 22, 1962).

44. Esenin-Vol'pin, "Svobodnyi filosofskii traktat," in *Izbrannoe*, 40.

45. Aleksandr Sergeyevich Yesenin-Volpin, *A Leaf of Spring* (*Vesennii list*), trans. George Reavey. (New York: Praeger, 1961), 2. All quotations from this bilingual edition are my own translations from the original Russian.

46. Esenin-Vol'pin, "Shizofreniia," in *Izbrannoe*, 248.

47. M. Iu. Lermontov, "Dva velikana," in *Sochineniia*, vol. 2, 6 vols. (Leningrad: Akademiia nauk SSSR, 1954–57), 51; Pushkin, "Napoleon," in *Polnoe sobranie sochinenii*, vol. 2, 213–16.

48. Esenin-Vol'pin, "Ot otsa rodnogo li rozhden ...," in *Izbrannoe*, 255–56.

49. On Esenin's psychiatric history and the impact of his suicide, see Gordon McVay, *Esenin: A Life* (Ann Arbor: Ardis, 1976), 146, 201; Anne Nesbet, "Suicide as Literary Fact in the 1920s," *Slavic Review* 50, no. 4 (Winter 1991): 830; Pinnow, *Lost to the Collective*, 48–49, 224–25; Constantin V. Ponomareff, *Sergey Esenin* (Boston: Twayne Publishers, 1978), 65, 154–61.

50. Nadezhda Vol'pin, "Svidanie s drugom," in *Moi Esenin: Vospominaniia sovremennikov*, ed. L. P. Bykov (Ekaterinburg: U-Faktoriia, 2008), 329.

51. Joseph Warren Dauben, *Georg Cantor: His Mathematics and Philosophy of the Infinite* (Cambridge: Harvard University Press, 1979), 271–99.

52. MSA, f. 120, op. 1, d. 3, l. 51 (Aleksandr Vol'pin, "Variant pis'ma N. S. Khrushchevu v sviazi s kampaniei vokrug publikatsii sbornika 'Vesennii list'. Chernovoi avtograf," January 10, 1963, or after).

53. Esenin-Vol'pin, "Fronda," in *Izbrannoe*, 261.

54. Esenin-Vol'pin, "Svobodnyi filosofskii traktat," in *Izbrannoe*, 40.

55. Ibid.

56. Yesenin-Volpin, *A Leaf of Spring*, 2. On Vol'pin's rejection of literature's moral authority, see Ann Komaromi, "The Unofficial Field of Late Soviet Culture," *Slavic Review* 66, no. 4 (Winter 2007): 622–23; Komaromi, *Uncensored*, 41; Nathans, "The Dictatorship of Reason," 647, 654.

57. Esenin-Vol'pin, "Svobodnyi filosofskii traktat," in *Izbrannoe*, 36–37. Italics in the original.

58. Ibid., 41.

59. MSA, f. 120, op. 1, d. 6, l. 30 (Aleksandr Vol'pin, "Iskovoe zaiavlenie A. S. Esenina-Vol'pina o narushenii pravil sanitarnogo zakonodatel'stva i ob imushchestvennom ushcherbe," 1968).

60. MSA, f. 120, op. 1, d. 16, ll. 14–15 (Aleksandr Vol'pin, "Opisanie A. S. Eseninym-Vol'pinym psikhiatricheskoi komissii, kotoraia ego posetila 06.03.1968," March 6, 1968, hereafter cited as "Opisanie 2").

61. MSA, f. 120, op. 1, d. 16, ll. 24ob-25 ("Opisanie 1").

62. Esenin-Vol'pin, "Ob antitraditsionnoi (ul'traintuitsionistskoi) programme osnovanii matematiki i estestvenno-nauchnom myshlenii," in *Izbrannoe*, 101.

63. Bukovskii, *I vozvrashchaetsia veter ...*, 223.

64. Vol'pin, interview.

65. Aleksandr Solzhenitsyn, "Zhit' ne po lzhi!," in *Sobranie sochinenii v deviati tomakh*, vol. 7, 9 vols. (Moscow: Terra–Knizhnyi klub, 2001), 95–99.

66. Viktoriia Vol'pina, "Iz vospominanii Viktorii Vol'pinoi," in Esenin-Vol'pin, *Izbrannoe*, 314–15. See also Nathans, "The Dictatorship of Reason," 655.

67. Esenin-Vol'pin, "O logike nravstvennykh nauk," in *Izbrannoe*, 227.

68. Esenin-Vol'pin, "Iuridicheskaia pamiatka," in *Izbrannoe*, 368.

69. Bukovskii, *I vozvrashchaetsia veter ...*, 217.

70. Ibid., 34; Vladimir Bukovskii, interview by Rebecca Reich, Cambridge, UK, March 27, 2012.

71. On Bukovskii's dissident activities in the Soviet Union, see Boobbyer, "Vladimir Bukovskii and Soviet Communism," 454–59.

242 NOTES TO CHAPTER 2

72. SDS, vol. 8, AS 571 (Vladimir Bukovskii, "Otkrytoe pis'mo vracham-psikhiatram SShA, Anglii, Gollandii, Kanady i Izraelia s prilozheniem kopii i vyderzhek iz zakliuchenii sudebno-psikhiatricheskikh ekspertiz i drugikh dokumentov o liudiakh, priznannykh nevmeniaemymi, 28 ianvaria 1971 g."), 1.

73. Ibid., 2. On Bukovskii's founding role in the dissident campaign against psychiatric abuse, see Vess'e, *Za vashu i nashu svobodu*, 211–12.

74. S. F. Gluzman, *Risunki po pamiati, ili vospominaniia otsidenta* (Kiev: Izdatel'skii dom Dmitriia Burago, 2012), 460–61, 464–65, 478–82.

75. Ibid., 481.

76. Ibid., 464.

77. SDS, vol. 24, AS 1243 (Troe sov. anonimnykh psikhiatra, "Psikhiatricheskaia zaochnaia ekspertiza po delu P. G. Grigorenko v Komitet prav Cheloveka, akad. Sakharovu, v KGB pri SM SSSR, dr. vysshim sov. instantsiiam i ko vsei obshchestvennosti, bez mesta i daty, no do 15.11.72"), 29.

78. Ibid., 3. On Grigorenko's psychiatric reports, see also chapter 1.

79. Ibid., 13.

80. Ibid., 14.

81. Ibid., 19–20.

82. Ibid., 21.

83. Ibid., 27–29, 32–33, 37.

84. Ibid., 22, 33, 35–37, 39.

85. Ibid., 34.

86. Ibid., 25.

87. Ibid., 23–24.

88. Ibid., 24.

89. Ibid., 26.

90. Ibid., 20, 37.

91. Ibid., 23.

92. Bukovskii, interview.

93. Semen Gluzman, interview by Rebecca Reich, Kiev, Ukraine, May 22, 2009.

94. Bukovskii, interview; Gluzman, interview; Gluzman, *Risunki po pamiati*, 210–13, 302–304.

95. Bukovskii and Gluzman, "Posobie po psikhiatrii dlia inakomysliashchikh," 55.

96. Gluzman, interview.

97. Bukovskii and Gluzman, "Posobie po psikhiatrii dlia inakomysliashchikh," 58.

98. Bukovskii, interview.

99. Bukovskii and Gluzman, "Posobie po psikhiatrii dlia inakomysliashchikh," 47–48.

100. Ibid., 57.

101. Ibid., 51–53.

102. Gluzman's poems from the 1970s and 1980s appear in his *Psalmy i skorbi* (Khar'kov: Folio, 1994). For references to madness in his verse, see "Gel'derlin" and "Ia v sotvoren'i mira—prakh . . .," 90–91, 109.

103. Bukovskii and Gluzman, "Posobie po psikhiatrii dlia inakomysliashchikh," 57.

104. Ibid., 51.

105. Ibid., 42.

106. Ibid., 50.

107. Ibid., 48.
108. Ibid., 49–50.
109. Ibid., 50.
110. Gluzman, interview.
111. Bukovskii, interview.
112. Bukovskii, *I vozvrashchaetsia veter* ..., 362–63. On the limits of Bukovskii's willingness to compromise, see Boobbyer, "Vladimir Bukovskii and Soviet Communism," 459–61.
113. Bukovskii and Gluzman, "Posobie po psikhiatrii dlia inakomysliashchikh," 53.
114. Tat'iana Khodorovich and Iurii Orlov, "Leonida Pliushcha prevrashaiut v sumasshedsego. Zachem?," *Russkaia mysl'*, May 15, 1975.
115. Pliushch, *Na karnavale istorii*, 624.
116. Foucault, *Madness and Civilization*, x–xi.
117. Ibid., 262.
118. Bakhtin, "Discourse in the Novel," in Holquist, ed., *The Dialogic Imagination*, 259–422.
119. MSA, f. 120, op. 1, d. 16, l. 16 ("Opisanie 2").
120. Tat'iana Khodorovich, ed., *Istoriia bolezni Leonida Pliushcha* (Amsterdam: Fond im. Gertsena, 1974), 160. See also Podrabinek, *Karatel'naia meditsina*, 10.
121. Aleksandr Podrabinek, *Dissidenty* (Moscow: AST, 2014), 228–31; Aleksandr Podrabinek, interview by Rebecca Reich, Moscow, Russia, April 10, 2009. See also Bloch and Reddaway, *Soviet Psychiatric Abuse*, 75–110; Vess'e, *Za vashu i nashu svobodu*, 213–16, 224–28.
122. SDS, vol. 2, AS 153 (N. Gorbanevskaia, "Ocherk 'Besplatnaia meditsinskaia pomoshch'," mart 1968 g."), 4. Gorbanevskaia's essay and the interpolated poem "Locked inside the madhouse..." are reproduced with permission from the Natal'ia Gorbanevskaia Estate.
123. Ibid., 11.
124. Ibid., 21–22.
125. Ibid.
126. Medvedev and Medvedev, *Kto sumasshedshii?*, 106–107.
127. Ibid., 106.
128. Ibid., 36.
129. SDS, vol. 5, AS 345 ("'Sravnenie dvukh ekspertiz'"), 3.
130. Grigorenko, *V podpol'e mozhno vstretit' tol'ko krys* ..., 422.
131. SDS, vol. 5, AS 344 (P. G. Grigorenko, "Vtoraia ekspertiza, 20–25 noiabria 1969 g."), 13.
132. Gluzman, "Zloupotreblenie psikhiatriei," 69.
133. Ibid., 67.
134. For other references to Chaadaev in dissidents' psychiatric narratives, see Bukovskii, *I vozvrashchaetsia veter* ..., 350; Gluzman, *Risunki po pamiati*, 283; Grigorenko, *V podpol'e mozhno vstretit' tol'ko krys* ..., 397; Medvedev and Medvedev, *Kto sumasshedshii?*, 130–31, 141–42; Pliushch, *Na karnavale istorii*, 658; Podrabinek, *Karatel'naia meditsina*, 15–17; SDS, vol. 6, AS 386 (Aleksandr Solzhenitsyn, "'Vot kak my zhivem', zaiavlenie v sviazi s nasil'stvennym pomeshcheniem Zh. Medvedeva v psikhbol'nitsu, 15 iunia 1970g"), 1.
135. Bukovskii and Gluzman, "Posobie po psikhiatrii dlia inakomysliashchikh," 36. The epigraph is taken from Andrei Platonov's play *The Lycée Pupil*, though in the original,

the word "servitude" (*rabstvo*) appears in place of "equality" (*ravenstvo*). Andrei Platonov, *Uchenik litseia*, in *Noev kovcheg* (Moscow: Vagrius, 2006), 334.

136. Pushkin, "Ne dai mne bog soiti s uma ...," in *Polnoe sobranie sochinenii*, vol. 3, 322–23.

137. ACRC, PGFP, Series II, Box 5, Folder 43, Vol'pin to Grigorenko, June 23, 1970, pp. 1–1ob. Page references to the Petr (Petro) Grigorenko (Hrykorenko) and his Family Papers refer to individual documents rather than to the folder as a whole.

138. ACRC, PGFP, Series I, Box 1, Folder 3, Grigorenko to Grigorenko, June 30, 1970, p. 1.

139. SDS, vol. 6, AS 406 (A. S. Vol'pin, "'Vechnuiu ruchku Petru Grigor'evichu Grigorenko!'—otkrytoe pis'mo A. I. Solzhenitsynu 20 iiulia 1970 g."), 3.

140. Ibid., 6.

141. Ibid., 12.

142. MSA, f. 163, op. 1, d. 9 (Aleksandr Podrabinek and Viktor Nekipelov, ed., "Iz zheltogo bezmolviia: Sbornik vospominanii i statei politzakliuchennykh psikhiatricheskikh bol'nits," 1977), l. 1.

143. Ibid., l. 3.

Chapter 3

1. Joseph Brodsky, "Less Than One," in *Less Than One: Selected Essays* (New York: Farrar, Straus and Giroux, 1986), 3. Joseph Brodsky's works are reproduced with permission from the Joseph Brodsky Estate as follows: "Less Than One," by Joseph Brodsky, Copyright © 1986; "The Condition We Call Exile," by Joseph Brodsky, Copyright © 1995; "Gorbunov and Gorchakov," by Joseph Brodsky, Copyright © 2011; "A Part of Speech," by Joseph Brodsky, Copyright © 2011, used by permission of The Wylie Agency (UK) Limited; and selected works by Joseph Brodsky, Copyright © Selected Work by Joseph Brodsky 2016, used by permission of The Wylie Agency (UK) Limited.

2. Brodsky, "Less Than One," in *Less Than One*, 3.

3. Ibid., 13.

4. Ibid., 3.

5. Iosif Brodskii, "Men'she edinitsy," trans. V. Golyshev, *Inostrannaia literatura*, no. 10 (1992): 234.

6. Brodsky, "Less Than One," in *Less Than One*, 21.

7. Christina Daub and Mike Hammer. "Joseph Brodsky: An Interview," in *Joseph Brodsky: Conversations*, ed. Cynthia L. Haven (Jackson: University Press of Mississippi, 2002), 154.

8. Brodsky, "Less Than One," in *Less Than One*, 6.

9. Shklovskii, "Iskusstvo kak priem," in *Gamburgskii schet*, 58–72. This chapter builds on the work of Svetlana Boym and Cristina Vatulescu to explore the biographical implications of defamiliarization. See Boym, *Another Freedom*, 201–53; Svetlana Boym, "Estrangement as a Lifestyle: Shklovsky and Brodsky," in *Exile and Creativity: Signposts, Travelers, Outsiders, Backward Glances*, ed. Susan Rubin Suleiman (Durham: Duke University Press, 1998), 241–62; Cristina Vatulescu, *Police Aesthetics: Literature, Film, and the Secret Police in Soviet Times* (Stanford: Stanford University Press, 2010), 161–86; Cristina Vatulescu, "The Politics of Estrangement: Tracking Shklovsky's Device through Literary

and Policing Practices," *Poetics Today* 27, no. 1 (Spring 2006): 35-66. On defamiliarization as a literary device, see chapter 4.

10. Boym, "Estrangement as a Lifestyle," in Suleiman, ed., *Exile and Creativity*, 254.

11. Daub and Hammer, "Joseph Brodsky: An Interview," in Haven, ed., *Joseph Brodsky: Conversations*, 152-53.

12. Joseph Brodsky, "The Condition We Call Exile, or Acorns Aweigh," in *On Grief and Reason: Essays* (New York: Farrar, Straus and Giroux, 1995), 32.

13. Daub and Hammer, "Joseph Brodsky: An Interview," in Haven, ed., *Joseph Brodsky: Conversations*, 155.

14. Joseph Brodsky, "Poetry as a Form of Resistance to Reality," *PMLA* 107, no. 2 (March 1992): 224.

15. Tomas Ventslova, "Chuvstvo perspektivy," in *Iosif Brodskii: Bol'shaia kniga interv'iu*, ed. Valentina Polukhina (Moscow: Zakharov, 2000), 343.

16. David Betea, "Naglaia propoved' idealizma," in Polukhina, ed., *Iosif Brodskii: Bol'shaia kniga interv'iu*, 537-38. I am grateful to David M. Bethea, Gleb Shul'piakov, and Valentina Polukhina for directing me to and providing me with the original English quoted here.

17. Ibid., 538.

18. Frida Vigdorova, "Sudilishche," *Ogonek*, no. 49 (1988): 26.

19. David M. Bethea, *Joseph Brodsky and the Creation of Exile* (Princeton: Princeton University Press, 1994), 11-12, 17. Boym likewise problematizes the concept of the biography-less poet in Russia, where writers have actively cultivated their authorial personae and where the idea of the "death of the author" acquired lethal connotations. See Svetlana Boym, *Death in Quotation Marks*, 9-10.

20. Brodsky, "Poetry as a Form of Resistance to Reality," 220.

21. Dzhon Kopper, "Amkherst kolledzh: 1974-1975," in *Iosif Brodskii: Trudy i dni*, ed. Lev Losev and Petr Vail' (Moscow: Nezavisimaia gazeta, 1998), 53; GARF, f. R8131, op. 31, d. 99616, l. 58ob (N. N. Timofeev, N. E. Isaevich, T. D. Kasharova, E. I. Sokolova, and L. A. Petrov, "Statsionarnaia ekspertiza," March 11, 1964).

22. Lev Losev, *Iosif Brodskii: Opyt literaturnoi biografii* (Moscow: Molodaia gvardiia, 2006), 80, 86. Loseff also discusses Brodsky's psychiatric history in Lev Loseff, "On Hostile Ground: Madness and Madhouse in Joseph Brodsky's 'Gorbunov and Gorchakov,'" in Brintlinger and Vinitsky, eds., *Madness and the Mad in Russian Culture*, 90-100; Lev Losev, "Shchit Perseia: Literaturnaia biografiia Iosifa Brodskogo," in *Stikhotvoreniia i poemy*, by Iosif Brodskii, vol. 1, 2 vols., Novaia biblioteka poeta (St. Petersburg: Vita Nova, 2011), 45-110.

23. GARF, f. R8131, op. 31, d. 99616, ll. 58ob.-59 ("Statsionarnaia ekspertiza").

24. Losev, *Iosif Brodskii: Opyt literaturnoi biografii*, 86.

25. Vigdorova, "Sudilishche," 26.

26. GARF, f. R8131, op. 31, d. 99616, l. 21 (K. Grubskii, "Spravka po administrativnomu delu," February 24, 1964).

27. GARF, f. R8131, op. 31, d. 99616, l. 59ob. ("Statsionarnaia ekspertiza").

28. Ibid.

29. Ibid.

30. Ibid., l. 59.

31. Ibid., l. 59ob.

32. Ia. M. Kalashnik, *Sudebnaia psikhiatriia* (Moscow: Gosudarstvennoe izdatel'stvo iuridicheskoi literatury, 1961), 305.

33. Ibid., 307–08.
34. Ibid., 316.
35. Vladimir Lupandin, "Karatel'naia psikhiatriia. Vospominaniia ochevidtsa," *Moskovskie novosti*, August 12, 1990, cited in Loseff, "On Hostile Ground," in Brintlinger and Vinitsky, eds., *Madness and the Mad in Russian Culture*, 92.
36. Losev, *Iosif Brodskii: Opyt literaturnoi biografii*, 140.
37. Vigdorova, "Sudilishche," 28.
38. GARF, f. R8131, op. 31, d. 99616, l. 6 (Komissiia po rabote s molodymi avtorami pri Leningradskom otdelenii Soiuza pisatelei RSFSR, "Spravka," February 15, 1964).
39. Losev, *Iosif Brodskii: Opyt literaturnoi biografii*, 57–59.
40. Vigdorova, "Sudilishche," 29.
41. Ibid.
42. GARF, f. R8131, op. 31, d. 99616, l. 13 (Vigdorova to Rudenko, February 20, 1964).
43. GARF, f. R8131, op. 31, d. 99616, l. 9 (Chaikovskaia to Rudenko, February 25, 1964).
44. Vigdorova, "Sudilishche," 30.
45. GARF, f. R8131, op. 31, d. 99617, l. 19 (Brodskii and Vol'pert to Kravtsov, October 17, 1964).
46. Quoted in Loseff, "On Hostile Ground," in Brintlinger and Vinitsky, eds., *Madness and the Mad in Russian Culture*, 91.
47. Vigdorova, "Sudilishche," 26.
48. Losev, *Iosif Brodskii: Opyt literaturnoi biografii*, 73, 86.
49. Ibid., 141.
50. Helen Benedict, "Flight from Predictability: Joseph Brodsky," *Antioch Review* 43, no. 1 (Winter 1985): 13–14.
51. Lars Kleberg and Svante Veiler, "Ia pozvolial sebe vse, krome zhalob," in Polukhina, ed., *Iosif Brodskii: Bol'shaia kniga interv'iu*, 429. The phrase "violation of proportions" appears in Brodsky's telling of this anecdote in Solomon Volkov, *Dialogi s Iosifom Brodskim: Literaturnye biografii* (Moscow: Nezavisimaia Gazeta, 1998), 71.
52. For Brodsky's remark on his psychiatric experiences, see Jane B. Katz, *Artists in Exile* (New York: Stein and Day, 1983), 52. On the poet's habit of self-pathologization see Losev, *Iosif Brodskii: Opyt literaturnoi biografii*, 21.
53. Iosif Brodskii, "Novyi god na Kanatchikovoi dache," in *Sochineniia Iosifa Brodskogo*, vol. 2, 7 vols. (St. Petersburg: Pushkinskii fond, 1997–2001), 10–11.
54. On the cultural impact of "Ward No. 6," see also the introduction.
55. William Mills Todd III, "Pushkin and Society: Post-1966 Perspectives," in *The Pushkin Handbook*, ed. David M. Bethea (Madison: University of Wisconsin Press, 2005), 364. I am grateful to Angela Brintlinger for suggesting this allusion.
56. Brodsky, "Less Than One," in *Less Than One*, 21.
57. Carl R. Proffer, "A Stop in the Madhouse: Brodsky's 'Gorbunov and Gorchakov,'" *Russian Literature Triquarterly*, no. 1 (Fall 1971): 344.
58. Ibid., 347.
59. Loseff, "On Hostile Ground," in Brintlinger and Vinitsky, eds., *Madness and the Mad in Russian Culture*, 94, 99; Proffer, "A Stop in the Madhouse," 344.
60. Loseff, "On Hostile Ground," in Brintlinger and Vinitsky, eds., *Madness and the Mad in Russian Culture*, 94–95.
61. Ibid., 97–98. On the post-Stalin interest in Bakhtin, see also Komaromi, *Uncensored*, 12–13.

62. BRBML, JBP, Box 11, Folder 315, Brodsky to Proffer, November 6, 1971, p. 1. Page references to the Joseph Brodsky Papers refer to individual documents rather than to the folder as a whole.
63. Brodskii, "Gorbunov i Gorchakov," in *Stikhotvoreniia i poemy*, vol. 1, 222.
64. Valentina Polukhina, *Joseph Brodsky: A Poet for Our Time* (Cambridge: Cambridge University Press, 1989), 242.
65. Brodskii, "Gorbunov i Gorchakov," in *Stikhotvoreniia i poemy*, vol. 1, 225–26.
66. Birgit Fait, "U menia net printsipov, est' tol'ko nervy . . .," in Polukhina, ed., *Iosif Brodskii: Bol'shaia kniga interv'iu*, 567.
67. On Brodsky's criticism of Marx and Freud, see Bethea, *Joseph Brodsky and the Creation of Exile*, 42; Losev, *Iosif Brodskii: Opyt literaturnoi biografii*, 99–100, 143, 162, 173; Polukhina, *Joseph Brodsky: A Poet for Our Time*, 55, 100.
68. Brodskii, "Gorbunov i Gorchakov," in *Stikhotvoreniia i poemy*, vol. 1, 217.
69. Ibid.
70. Ibid., 218.
71. Ibid., 223.
72. Ibid., 223–24.
73. Ibid., 236.
74. Ibid., 228–29.
75. BRBML, JBP, Box 11, Folder 315, Brodsky to Proffer, November 6, 1971, p. 1ob. On Brodsky's medical procedure, see Losev, *Iosif Brodskii: Opyt literaturnoi biografii*, 352.
76. Brodskii, "Gorbunov i Gorchakov," in *Stikhotvoreniia i poemy*, vol. 1, 232.
77. Ibid., 233.
78. Ibid., 225.
79. Ibid.
80. Ibid., 230.
81. Ibid.
82. Ibid., 219.
83. Ibid., 222. On how the words "cranberry syrup" recall the poet Aleksandr Blok, who lived on the embankment where the Priazhka Hospital stands, and whose play *The Little Showbooth* features a clown who claims to be "bleeding cranberry juice," see Brodskii, *Stikhotvoreniia i poemy*, vol. 1, 514; Aleksandr Blok, *Balaganchik*, in *Sobranie sochinenii v vos'mi tomakh*, vol. 4, 8 vols. (Moscow: Gosudarstvennoe izdatel'stvo khudozhestvennoi literatury, 1960–63), 19.
84. Benedict, "Flight from Predictability," 13; Losev, *Iosif Brodskii: Opyt literaturnoi biografii*, 140.
85. Brodskii, "Gorbunov i Gorchakov," in *Stikhotvoreniia i poemy*, vol. 1, 222.
86. Ibid., 244.
87. Losev, *Iosif Brodskii: Opyt literaturnoi biografii*, 100.
88. Brodskii, "Gorbunov i Gorchakov," in *Stikhotvoreniia i poemy*, vol. 1, 236.
89. Ibid.
90. Ibid., 237.
91. Ibid., 239.
92. I am grateful to Angela Brintlinger for this observation.
93. Ibid., 240.
94. Ibid., 232.
95. Ibid., 237.
96. Brodsky, "Less Than One," in *Less Than One*, 31.

97. Brodsky, "The Condition We Call Exile, or Acorns Aweigh," in *On Grief and Reason*, 32.
98. Ibid.
99. Brodsky, "Poetry as a Form of Resistance to Reality," 221.
100. Ibid., 222.
101. BRBML, JBP, Box 11, Folder 315, Brodsky to Proffer, November 6, 1971, p. 1.
102. Loseff, "On Hostile Ground," in Brintlinger and Vinitsky, eds., *Madness and the Mad in Russian Culture*, 96.
103. Barry Scherr, "False Starts: A Note on Brodsky's Poetics," *Toronto Slavic Annual*, no. 1 (Summer 2003): 197–204. On Brodsky's turn to the *dol'nik* in emigration and for a metrical analysis of "A Part of Speech," see G. S. Smith, "The Development of Joseph Brodsky's Dol'nik Verse, 1972–1976," *Russian Literature* 52, no. 4 (November 2002): 471–92.
104. George L. Kline, "Variations on the Theme of Exile," in *Brodsky's Poetics and Aesthetics*, ed. Lev Loseff and Valentina Polukhina (London: Macmillan, 1990), 58.
105. Brodskii, "V ozernom kraiu," in *Stikhotvoreniia i poemy*, vol. 1, 336.
106. Losev, *Iosif Brodskii: Opyt literaturnoi biografii*, 196.
107. Brodskii, "Niotkuda s liubov'iu . . .," in *Stikhotvoreniia i poemy*, vol. 1, 363.
108. Brodskii, "Sever kroshit metal . . .," in *Stikhotvoreniia i poemy*, vol. 1, 364.
109. Brodskii, "Eto—riad nabliudenii . . .," in *Stikhotvoreniia i poemy*, vol. 1, 364.
110. Brodskii, "Potomu chto kabluk . . .," in *Stikhotvoreniia i poemy*, vol. 1, 364–65.
111. Plato, *The Republic of Plato*, trans. Allan Bloom (New York: Basic Books, 1991), 193–98. I am grateful to Benjamin Nathans for suggesting this allusion.
112. Brodskii, "Vsegda ostaetsia vozmozhnost' . . .," in *Stikhotvoreniia i poemy*, vol. 1, 368.
113. Brodskii, ". . . i pri slove 'griadushchee' . . .," in *Stikhotvoreniia i poemy*, vol. 1, 369.
114. Losev, *Iosif Brodskii: Opyt literaturnoi biografii*, 141.
115. Brodsky, "The Condition We Call Exile, or Acorns Aweigh," in *On Grief and Reason*, 32.
116. Brodskii, "Ia ne to chto skhozhu s uma . . .," in *Stikhotvoreniia i poemy*, vol. 1, 369.
117. Brodskii, "Gorbunov i Gorchakov," in *Stikhotvoreniia i poemy*, vol. 1, 243.
118. Brodsky, "Less Than One," in *Less Than One*, 11–12.

CHAPTER 4

1. Abram Terts, "Literaturnyi protsess v Rossii," *Kontinent*, no. 1 (1974): 150.
2. Catharine Theimer Nepomnyashchy, *Abram Tertz and the Poetics of Crime* (New Haven: Yale University Press, 1995).
3. For biographical background, see Walter F. Kolonosky, *Literary Insinuations: Sorting Out Sinyavsky's Irreverence* (Lanham: Lexington Books, 2003), 1–10; Eugenie Markesinis, *Andrei Siniavskii: A Hero of His Time?* (Boston: Academic Studies Press, 2013); Nepomnyashchy, *Abram Tertz*, 1–39.
4. Z. Kedrina, "Nasledniki Smerdiakova," *Literaturnaia gazeta*, January 22, 1966.
5. Aleksandr Ginzburg, ed., *Belaia kniga po delu A. Siniavskogo i Iu. Danielia* (Frankfurt am Main: Posev, 1967), 241.
6. Andrei Siniavskii, "Dissidentstvo kak lichnyi opyt," *Sintaksis*, no. 15 (1985): 132.

7. The links between Siniavskii and Terts also extend over time. On Siniavskii's consistency, see Jane Grayson, "Picture Windows: The Art of Andrei Siniavskii," in *Russian Literature, Modernism and the Visual Arts*, ed. Catriona Kelly and Stephen Lovell (Cambridge: Cambridge University Press, 2000), 92.

8. Nepomnyashchy, *Abram Tertz*, 2, 11.

9. Harriet Murav, *Russia's Legal Fictions* (Ann Arbor: University of Michigan Press, 1998), 216.

10. Ibid., 228.

11. On reflection theory and its implications for creativity, see Zeev Katvan, "Reflection Theory and the Identity of Thinking and Being," *Studies in Soviet Thought* 18, no. 2 (May 1978): 87–109.

12. Lenin, "Materializm i empiriokrititsizm," in *Polnoe sobranie sochinenii*, vol. 18, 198.

13. Rozental', Tretiakov, and Luppol, eds., *Pervyi vsesoiuznyi s"ezd sovetskikh pisatelei 1934*, 712.

14. On reflection theory and reflex theory, see Katvan, "Reflection Theory and the Identity of Thinking and Being," 91–92; K. B. Madsen, *A History of Psychology in Metascientific Perspective* (Amsterdam: North-Holland, 1988), 445–46.

15. Akademiia meditsinskikh nauk SSSR et al., *Fiziologicheskoe uchenie akademika I. P. Pavlova*, 298.

16. Kalashnik and Morozov, eds., *Sudebnaia psikhiatriia*, 56.

17. HIA, ASP, Box 41, Folder 5, "Tetrad' no. 6," "Teoriia otrazheniia," pp. 1–2. Page references to the A. (Andrei) Siniavskii Papers refer to individual documents rather than to the folder as a whole.

18. Shklovskii, "Iskusstvo kak priem," in *Gamburgskii schet*, 58–72.

19. HIA, ASP, Box 46, Folder 5, "Zaniatie o 'Liubimove,'" undated, p. 1.

20. Shklovskii, "Iskusstvo kak priem," in *Gamburgskii schet*, 63. Analyses of defamiliarization in Terts's work most frequently focus on the story "Pkhents." See Margaret Dalton, *Andrei Siniavskii and Julii Daniel': Two Soviet Heretical Writers* (Würzburg: Jal-Verlag, 1973), 93–95; Andrew R. Durkin, "Narrator, Metaphor, and Theme in Sinjavskij's Fantastic Tales," *Slavic and East European Journal* 24, no. 2 (Summer 1980): 134–35; Richard Lourie, *Letters to the Future: An Approach to Sinyavsky-Tertz* (Ithaca: Cornell University Press, 1975), 152–53; Kevin Reese, "Imagination and Realism in Soviet Science Fiction: Siniavsky's 'Bez skidok' and Terts's 'Pkhents,'" *Slavic and East European Journal* 52, no. 3 (October 2008): 447, 449.

21. Ginzburg, ed., *Belaia kniga*, 224.

22. Siniavskii, "Dissidentstvo kak lichnyi opyt," 132–33.

23. Ibid., 133.

24. For yet another telling of this anecdote, see Abram Terts, "Iskusstvo i deistvitel'nost'," *Sintaksis*, no. 2 (1978): 117–18.

25. As dates of composition for Terts's *tamizdat* works vary across sources, this chapter follows those in Abram Terts, *Sobranie sochinenii v dvukh tomakh*, 2 vols. (Moscow: SP "Start," 1992) and in Siniavskii and Terts, *Literaturnyi protsess v Rossii*. On Siniavskii's essayistic work, see T. E. Rat'kina, *Nikomu ne zadolzhav: Literaturnaia kritika i esseistika A. D. Siniavskogo* (Moscow: Sovpadenie, 2010).

26. Terts, "Chto takoe sotsialisticheskii realizm," in Siniavskii and Terts, *Literaturnyi protsess v Rossii*, 140–41.

27. Ibid., 175.

28. HIA, ASP, Box 52, Folder 9, "Tochka otscheta," undated, p. 15. The date of composition provided here follows Siniavskii's testimony in HIA, ASP, Box 4, Folder 13, "Protokol doprosa," December 27, 1965, p. 2.

29. Terts, "Literaturnyi protsess v Rossii," 161-62. On Siniavskii's attention to Stalin's artistry, see Sara Fenander, "Author and Autocrat: Tertz's Stalin and the Ruse of Charisma," *Russian Review* 58, no. 2 (April 1999): 289.

30. On Siniavskii and Terts's concept of the realized metaphor, see Murav, *Russia's Legal Fictions*, 208-12; Nepomnyashchy, *Abram Tertz*, 15.

31. Siniavskii, "Stalin—geroi i khudozhnik stalinskoi epokhi," 114, 124-25.

32. A. D. Siniavskii, "Poeziia Pasternaka," in *Stikhotvoreniia i poemy*, by B. L. Pasternak (Leningrad: Sovetskii pisatel', 1965), 27. On the publication history of the Pasternak collection and Siniavskii's introduction, see Komaromi, "The Unofficial Field of Late Soviet Culture," 610-19; Komaromi, *Uncensored*, 28-39.

33. Siniavskii, "Poeziia Pasternaka," in Pasternak, *Stikhotvoreniia i poemy*, 24. See also Komaromi, *Uncensored*, 34.

34. Terts, "Literaturnyi protsess v Rossii," 178-79.

35. Siniavskii, "Poeziia Pasternaka," in Pasternak, *Stikhotvoreniia i poemy*, 19.

36. On self-elimination in Siniavskii and Terts's writings, see also Mikhail Epshtein, "Siniavskii kak myslitel'," *Zvezda*, no. 2 (1998): 151-71; Aleksandr Genis, "Archaic Postmodernism: The Aesthetics of Andrei Sinyavsky," in *Russian Postmodernism: New Perspectives on Post-Soviet Culture*, ed. Mikhail Epstein, Aleksandr Genis, and Slobodanka Vladiv-Glover (Providence: Berghahn Books, 1999), 185-97; Beth Holmgren, "The Transfiguring of Context in the Work of Abram Terts," *Slavic Review* 50, no. 4 (Winter 1991): 968-69; Nepomnyashchy, *Abram Tertz*, 102-103, 107, 142-43.

37. Terts, "Mysli vrasplokh," in *Sobranie sochinenii v dvukh tomakh*, vol. 1, 314.

38. Ibid., 338.

39. On *skaz*, see B. M. Eikhenbaum, "Illiuziia skaza," in *Skvoz' literaturu: Sbornik statei* (Leningrad: Akademiia, 1924), 152-56.

40. Terts, "Chto takoe sotsialisticheskii realizm," in Siniavskii and Terts, *Literaturnyi protsess v Rossii*, 164.

41. Ibid., 160.

42. Ibid., 175.

43. Lourie, *Letters to the Future*, 131.

44. Andrei Siniavskii, "Prostranstvo prozy," *Sintaksis*, no. 21 (1988): 29.

45. Ibid.

46. Terts, *Sud idet*, in *Sobranie sochinenii v dvukh tomakh*, vol. 1, 253.

47. Ibid., 260.

48. Ibid., 287.

49. Ibid., 251.

50. Ibid.

51. Ibid., 262.

52. Ibid., 261.

53. Ibid., 276.

54. Ibid., 275.

55. Ibid., 307.

56. Ibid., 308.

57. Ibid., 297.
58. Ibid., 297-98.
59. Ibid., 298.
60. Ibid., 284.
61. Ibid., 285.
62. Ibid., 252.
63. Ibid., 275.
64. Ibid., 301.
65. Ibid., 308.
66. Ibid., 305.
67. Ibid., 306.
68. Ibid., 309-10.
69. Ibid., 311.
70. Ibid., 312.
71. Terts, "Literaturnyi protsess v Rossii," 188.
72. Terts, "Grafomany (Iz rasskazov o moei zhizni)," in *Sobranie sochinenii v dvukh tomakh*, vol. 1, 155-56.
73. Ibid., 156.
74. Svetlana Boym, *Common Places: Mythologies of Everyday Life in Russia* (Cambridge: Harvard University Press, 1994), 171.
75. Terts, "Grafomany" (Iz rasskazov o moei zhizni)," in *Sobranie sochinenii v dvukh tomakh*, vol. 1, 168.
76. Ibid., 154.
77. Ibid., 158, 160.
78. Ibid., 164.
79. Ibid.
80. Ibid., 174.
81. Ibid., 175-76.
82. Ibid., 167.
83. Ibid., 168.
84. Ibid.
85. Ibid.
86. Ibid., 177.
87. Ibid., 179.
88. Terts, *Liubimov*, in *Sobranie sochinenii v dvukh tomakh*, vol. 1, 34.
89. Ibid., 39.
90. Ibid., 41.
91. Ibid., 57.
92. Ibid., 29.
93. Ibid.
94. Ibid., 52.
95. Ibid., 75.
96. Ibid., 74.
97. Ibid., 69.
98. Ibid., 70.
99. Ibid., 104.
100. Ibid., 105.

101. Ibid., 29.
102. Ibid., 55.
103. Ibid., 52.
104. Lenin, "Lev Tolstoi, kak zerkalo russkoi revoliutsii," in *Polnoe sobranie sochinenii*, vol. 17, 206-13.
105. Terts, *Liubimov*, in *Sobranie sochinenii v dvukh tomakh*, vol. 1, 53.
106. Ibid., 18.
107. Ibid., 111.
108. Ibid., 100.
109. Ibid., 18.
110. On these levels of narration, see Vladimir E. Alexandrov, "Typographical Intrusion and the Transcendent in Bely's *Petersburg* and Sinyavsky's *Lyubimov*," *Slavonic and East European Review* 62, no. 2 (April 1984): 174-77; Erika Haber, "In Search of the Fantastic in Tertz's Fantastic Realism," *Slavic and East European Journal* 42, no. 2 (Summer 1998): 256-61; Murav, *Russia's Legal Fictions*, 200; Nepomnyashchy, *Abram Tertz*, 141-46.
111. HIA, ASP, Box 46, Folder 5, "Zaniatie o 'Liubimove,'" p. 3.
112. N. S. Khrushchev, "Sluzhenie narodu—vysokoe prizvanie sovetskikh pisatelei. Rech' tovarishcha N. S. Khrushcheva na III s"ezde pisatelei 22 maia 1959 goda," *Pravda*, May 24, 1959.
113. Bukovskii, *Moskovskii protsess*, vol. 1, 144, 163, 168; Bloch and Reddaway, *Psychiatric Terror*, 62; Brintlinger and Vinitsky, eds., *Madness and the Mad in Russian Culture*, 4.
114. HIA, ASP, Box 4, Folder 13, "Zaiavlenie Siniavskogo," November 30, 1965, p. 2.
115. HIA, ASP, Box 4, Folder 13, "Sobstvennoruchnye pokazaniia Siniavskogo," December 16, 1965, p. 6.
116. Ibid., p. 2.
117. Ibid.
118. HIA, ASP, Box 5, Folder 3, D. R. Lunts, Z. G. Turova, and M. F. Tal'tse, "Akt No. 15/a sudebno-psikhiatricheskoi ekspertizy na ispytuemogo Siniavskogo Andreia Donatovicha," December 18, 1965, p. 3. I am grateful to Benjamin Nathans for sharing this document.
119. Ibid., p. 1.
120. HIA, ASP, Box 4, Folder 12, "Protokol doprosa svidetelia Siniavskogo," September 8, 1965, p. 9; HIA, ASP, Box 4, Folder 12, "Protokol doprosa podozrevaemogo," September 9, 1965, p. 3.
121. HIA, ASP, Box 4, Folder 12, "Sobstvennoruchnye pokazaniia Siniavskogo," September 11, 1965, p. 1.
122. HIA, ASP, Box 5, Folder 3, "Postanovlenie o naznachenii ekspertizy," November 22, 1965, p. 2.
123. HIA, ASP, Box 5, Folder 3, V. V. Vinogradov, V. G. Kostomarov, F. G. Biriukov, E. I. Prokhorov, "Zakliuchenie," December 14, 1965, p. 3.
124. D. Eremin, "Perevertyshi," *Izvestiia*, January 13, 1966.
125. Kedrina, "Nasledniki Smerdiakova."
126. HIA, ASP, Box 4, Folder 13, "Sobstvennoruchnye pokazaniia Siniavskogo," December 16, 1965, p. 4.
127. Ginzburg, ed., *Belaia kniga*, 311.
128. Ibid.
129. Ibid., 224.

130. Ibid., 251.
131. Murav, *Russia's Legal Fictions*, 213; Nepomnyashchy, *Abram Tertz*, 14.
132. T. Petrov, "Prigovor klevetnikam," *Pravda*, February 15, 1966.
133. Ibid.
134. Ginzburg, ed., *Belaia kniga*, 231.
135. Petrov, "Prigovor klevetnikam."
136. HIA, ASP, Box 5, Folder 1, "Protokol doprosa svidetelia Duvakina Viktora Dmitrievicha," October 16, 1965, p. 5.
137. HIA, ASP, Box 5, Folder 1, "Sobstvennoruchnoe pokazanie Duvakina Viktora Dmitrievicha," October 20, 1965, p. 6.
138. Ibid., p. 3.
139. Ibid., p. 8. On Duvakin and Siniavskii's relationship, see Markesinis, *Andrei Siniavskii*, 32–33; N. N. Rubinshtein, ed., *Progulki s Andreem Siniavskim* (Moscow: Tsentr knigi "Rudomino," 2011), 118–27; Terts, *Sobranie sochinenii v dvukh tomakh*, vol. 2, 579–80.
140. Ginzburg, ed., *Belaia kniga*, 277.
141. HIA, ASP, Box 6, Folder 2, "Protokol sudebnogo zasedaniia verkhovnogo suda RSFSR," p. 84. This official transcript includes passages not transcribed in the *samizdat* transcript quoted elsewhere.
142. Ginzburg, ed., *Belaia kniga*, 297.
143. Ibid., 303.
144. Ibid., 301. See also Murav, *Russia's Legal Fictions*, 210; Nepomnyashchy, *Abram Tertz*, 15–16.
145. Ginzburg, ed., *Belaia kniga*, 302. See also Murav, *Russia's Legal Fictions*, 212; Nepomnyashchy, *Abram Tertz*, 15–16.
146. Andrei Siniavskii, "Pokhvala emigratsii," *Sintaksis*, no. 24 (1988): 40.

CHAPTER 5

1. Leonid Prudovskii, "Sumasshedshim mozhno byt' v liuboe vremia," *Kontinent*, no. 65 (1990): 413. On this passage, see also Claudia Criveller, "Madness as an Aesthetic and Social Act in Russian Autobiographical Prose: The Case of Venedikt Erofeev's *Memoirs of a Psychopath*," *Toronto Slavic Quarterly*, no. 36 (Spring 2011): 52.
2. On the registration system, see G. V. Morozov, V. E. Rozhnov, and E. A. Babaian, eds., *Alkogolizm: Rukovodstvo dlia vrachei* (Moscow: Meditsina, 1983), 375–400; Eugene Raikhel, "Institutional Encounters: Identification and Anonymity in Russian Addiction Treatment (and Ethnography)," in *Being There: The Fieldwork Encounter and the Making of Truth*, ed. John Borneman and Abdellah Hammoudi (Berkeley: University of California Press, 2009), 223; Eugene Raikhel, *Governing Habits: Treating Alcoholism in the Post-Soviet Clinic* (Ithaca: Cornell University Press, 2016), 70–72. On narcology's status as a subfield of psychiatry and on the continued role of the psychiatric hospital in alcoholism treatment after the narcological system's establishment as a separate discipline in 1975, see ibid., 55–56, 64–70.
3. Bukovskii, *I vozvrashchaetsia veter* ..., 245. On the allure of simulation, see Kuperman and Zislin, "Simuliatsiia psikhoza," in Bogdanov, Murashov, and Nikolozi, eds., *Russkaia literatura i meditsina*, 291.
4. Nekipelov, *Institut durakov*, 27.

5. Ibid., 21.
6. Wayne C. Booth, *The Rhetoric of Fiction* (Chicago: University of Chicago Press, 1983), 71–76.
7. Tomashevskii, "Literatura i biografiia."
8. Mikhail Epshtein, "Posle karnavala, ili Vechnyi Venichka," in *Ostav'te moiu dushu v pokoe: Pochti vse*, by Venedikt Erofeev (Moscow: Kh.G.S., 1995), 3–30.
9. Ol'ga Sedakova, "Ol'ga Sedakova (Pechat' minuvshego. Neskol'ko monologov o Venedikte Erofeeve)," *Teatr*, no. 9 (September 1991): 102.
10. There is an extensive critical literature on holy foolishness in Erofeev. See Epshtein, "Posle karnavala," in Erofeev, *Ostav'te moiu dushu v pokoe*; Svetlana Gaiser-Shnitman, *Venedikt Erofeev: "Moskva–Petushki" ili "The rest is silence"* (Bern: Peter Lang, 1989), 116–21; Komaromi, *Uncensored*, 108; Mark Lipovetsky, "From an Otherworldly Point of View: Venedikt Erofeev's 'Moscow to the End of the Line,'" in *Russian Postmodernist Fiction: Dialogue with Chaos*, ed. Eliot Borenstein (Armonk: M. E. Sharpe, 1999), 66–82; I. V. Moteiunaite, "Ven. Erofeev i iurodstvo: Zametki k teme," in *"Moskva–Petushki" Ven. Erofeeva. Materialy Tret'ei mezhdunarodnoi konferentsii "Literaturnyi tekst: problemy i metody issledovaniia" 18–21 maia 2000 goda, Tver'*, ed. Iu. V. Domanskii (Tver': Tverskoi gosudarstvennyi universitet, 2000), 142–45; Natalia Ottovordemgentschenfelde, *Jurodstvo: eine Studie zur Phänomenologie und Typologie des Narren in Christo: Jurodivyj in der postmodernen russischen Kunst: Venedikt Erofeev Die Reise nach Petuški, Aktionismus Aleksandr Breners und Oleg Kuliks* (Frankfurt am Main: Peter Lang, 2004); Ol'ga Sedakova, "Neskazannaia rech' na vechere Venedikta Erofeeva," *Druzhba narodov*, no. 12 (1991): 264–65; Irina Sluzhevskaia, "Poslednyi iurodivyi (o tvorchestve Venedikta Erofeeva)," *Word—Slovo*, no. 10 (1991): 88–92. On the limitations of the holy-foolishness reading, see Ivanov, *Blazhennye pokhaby*, 380–81; Mark Lipovetsky, *Charms of the Cynical Reason: The Trickster's Transformations in Soviet and Post-Soviet Culture* (Boston: Academic Studies Press, 2011), 188; Oliver Ready, "In Praise of Booze: 'Moskva–Petushki' and Erasmian Irony," *Slavonic and East European Review* 88, no. 3 (July 2010): 441.
11. Mikhail Epstein, "Methods of Madness and Madness as a Method," in Brintlinger and Vinitsky, eds., *Madness and the Mad in Russian Culture*, 280. Italics in the original.
12. Andrei Bil'zho, interview by Rebecca Reich, Moscow, July 22, 2009. Bil'zho also discusses Erofeev's treatment in Igor' Shevelev, "Petrovich segodnia—eto Leonardo vchera," *Vremia MN*, June 10, 2000. On alcohol and the carnivalesque, see Epshtein, "Posle karnavala," in Erofeev, *Ostav'te moiu dushu v pokoe*, 16–17; Andrei Zorin, "Prigorodnyi poezd dal'nego sledovaniia," *Novyi mir*, no. 5 (1989): 256–57. On alcohol as spiritual and social escape, see Irina Paperno and Boris Gasparov, "V stan' i idi," *Slavica Hierosolymitana*, no. 5–6 (1981): 387–400; Karen L. Ryan-Hayes, *Contemporary Russian Satire: A Genre Study* (Cambridge: Cambridge University Press, 1995), 88; Cynthia Simmons, *Their Fathers' Voice: Vassily Aksyonov, Venedikt Erofeev, Eduard Limonov, and Sasha Sokolov* (New York: Peter Lang, 1993), 63–72, 84–86.
13. Epshtein, "Posle karnavala," in Erofeev, *Ostav'te moiu dushu v pokoe*, 12. On Erofeev's capacity for self-control, see Igor' Avdiev, "Igor' Avdiev (Pechat' minuvshego. Neskol'ko monologov o Venedikte Erofeeve)," *Teatr*, no. 9 (September 1991): 104, 109; Elena Ignatova, "Venedikt," *Neva*, no. 1 (1993): 217; Lidiia Liubchikova, "Lidiia Liubchikova (Pechat' minuvshego. Neskol'ko monologov o Venedikte Erofeeve)," *Teatr*, no. 9 (September 1991): 82.
14. Ibid., 85.

15. Petr Vail' and Aleksandr Genis, "Vo chreve machekhi," *Grani*, no. 139 (1985): 146.
16. Vladimir Murav'ev, "Vladimir Murav'ev (Pechat' minuvshego. Neskol'ko monologov o Venedikte Erofeeve)," *Teatr*, no. 9 (September 1991): 94.
17. Sedakova, "Ol'ga Sedakova," 102.
18. As dates of composition for Erofeev's works vary across sources, this chapter follows those presented in Venedikt Erofeev, *Sobranie sochinenii*, 2 vols. (Moscow: Vagrius, 2007), 25.
19. Murav'ev, "Vladimir Murav'ev," 92.
20. Erofeev, *Zapiski psikhopata*, in *Sobranie sochinenii*, vol. 2, 40. On this passage, see also Oliver Ready, "From Aleshkovsky to Galkovsky: The Praise of Folly in Russian Prose Since the 1960s" (PhD diss., University of Oxford, 2007), 63.
21. Erofeev, *Zapiski psikhopata*, in *Sobranie sochinenii*, vol. 2, 114.
22. Ibid., 149.
23. Erofeev, *Moskva-Petushki*, in *Sobranie sochinenii*, vol. 1, 54. See also Ready, "From Aleshkovsky to Galkovsky," 63, 65.
24. Erofeev, *Moskva-Petushki*, in *Sobranie sochinenii*, vol. 1, 30.
25. Maksim Gor'kii, "Starukha Izergil'," in *Polnoe sobranie sochinenii*, vol. 1, 24 vols. (Moscow: Nauka, 1968-76), 87. On this passage and on Venichka and Erofeev's rejection of great feats, see also Epshtein, "Posle karnavala," in Erofeev, *Ostav'te moiu dushu v pokoe*, 12-13.
26. Sedakova, "Ol'ga Sedakova," 101.
27. Gor'kii, "Pesnia o sokole," in *Polnoe sobranie sochinenii*, vol. 2, 47.
28. Erofeev, *Moskva-Petushki*, in *Sobranie sochinenii*, vol. 1, 71-72.
29. Venedikt Erofeev, *Zapisnye knizhki: Kniga vtoraia* (Moscow: Zakharov, 2007), 117.
30. Ibid., 151. Erofeev's other references are evidently to the actor Innokentii Smoktunovskii and the physiologist Nikolai Sklifosovskii.
31. Ibid., 186, 377.
32. Valerii Berlin, ed., "Khibini-Moskva-Petushki: Venedikt Erofeev (1938-1990). Letopis' zhizni i tvorchestva Venedikta Erofeeva," *Zhivaia Arktika: Istoriko-kraevedcheskii almanakh*, no. 1 (2005): 61.
33. Morozov, Rozhnov, and Babaian, eds., *Alkogolizm*, 225-307.
34. Berlin, ed., "Khibini-Moskva-Petushki," 61, 77-78, 82-84, 89-90, 95-96; Bil'zho, interview.
35. Berlin, ed., "Khibini-Moskva-Petushki," 76-77.
36. Ibid., 84.
37. Mark Freidkin, "O Venedikte Erofeeve," *TextOnly*, no. 26 (2008), accessed February 12, 2016. http://textonly.ru/case/?issue=26&article=27417.
38. On the uses of piracetam, see G. M. Entin, *Lechenie alkogolizma* (Moscow: Meditsina, 1990), 130-31; Morozov, Rozhnov, and Babaian, eds., *Alkogolizm*, 335.
39. On the conditioned-reflex therapies, see Entin, *Lechenie alkogolizma*, 176-201; Morozov, Rozhnov, and Babaian, eds., *Alkogolizm*, 321-25.
40. On the sensitizing therapies, see Entin, *Lechenie alkogolizma*, 201-26; Morozov, Rozhnov, and Babaian, eds., *Alkogolizm*, 325-30. Soviet narcologists frequently administered placebos in place of disulfiram; see Entin, *Lechenie alkogolizma*, 173; A. Ia. Ialovoi, "Zamena alkogol'no-antabusnoi proby pri lechenii alkogolizma platsebo," *Zhurnal nevropatologii i psikhiatrii imeni S. S. Korsakova*, no. 4 (1968): 593-96; Raikhel, "Placebos

or Prostheses for the Will?" in Raikhel and Garriott, eds., *Addiction Trajectories*; Raikhel, *Governing Habits*, 104-49.

41. On the suggestion-based therapies, see Entin, *Lechenie alkogolizma*, 156-76; Morozov, Rozhnov, and Babaian, eds., *Alkogolizm*, 342-49.

42. On the theatricality and ritualism of *kodirovanie*, see Raikhel, "Placebos or Prostheses for the Will?" in Raikhel and Garriott, eds., *Addiction Trajectories*, 200-203; Raikhel, *Governing Habits*, 129-32.

43. A. R. Dovzhenko, A. F. Artemchuk, Z. N. Bolotova, T. M. Vorob'eva, Iu. A Manuilenko, A. I. Minko, L. A. Kurilko, and V. A. Dovzhenko, "Stressopsikhoterapiia bol'nykh alkogolizmom v ambulatornykh usloviiakh," *Zhurnal nevropatologii i psikhiatrii imeni S. S. Korsakova*, no. 2 (1988): 95.

44. Austin, *How to Do Things with Words*, 22.

45. Jacques Derrida, "Signature Event Context," in *Limited Inc*, trans. Jeffrey Melman and Samuel Weber (Evanston: Northwestern University Press, 1988), 17.

46. On the link between linguistic performativity and theatrical performance, see Andrew Parker and Eve Kosofsky Sedgwick, "Introduction: Performativity and Performance," in *Performativity and Performance* (New York: Routledge, 1995), 1-18. For alternate analyses of the implications of Parker and Sedgwick's analysis for performativity and performance in Erofeev's *Moscow-Petushki*, see Ann Komaromi, "Venedikt Erofeev's *Moskva-Petushki*: Performance and Performativity in the Late Soviet Text," *Slavic and East European Journal* 55, no. 3 (Fall 2011): 418-38; Komaromi, *Uncensored*, 102-28. On the implications of Austin and Derrida's debate for Siniavskii, see Murav, *Russia's Legal Fictions*, 223-25.

47. Nekipelov, *Institut durakov*, 129.

48. Entin, *Lechenie alkogolizma*, 175. See also Morozov, Rozhnov, and Babaian, eds., *Alkogolizm*, 348.

49. Natal'ia Shmel'kova, *Vo chreve machekhi, ili Zhizn'—diktatura krasnogo* (St. Petersburg: Limbus Press, 1999), 68.

50. Ibid., 80-81.

51. Erofeev, *Moskva-Petushki*, in *Sobranie sochinenii*, vol. 1, 21, 166. See also E. A. Smirnova, "Venedikt Erofeev glazami gogoloveda," *Russkaia literatura*, no. 3 (1990): 65.

52. Shmel'kova, *Vo chreve machekhi*, 32-33.

53. Irina Tosunian, "Ot Moskvy do samykh Petushkov," *Literaturnaia gazeta*, January 3, 1990.

54. Despite similarities between *Walpurgis Night* and *One Flew Over the Cuckoo's Nest* (1975), it was evidently only in 1988 that Erofeev first watched Miloš Forman's film. See Venedikt Erofeev, *Moi ochen' zhiznennyi put'* (Moscow: Vagrius, 2003), 433; Ignatova, "Venedikt," 229; Shmel'kova, *Vo chreve machekhi*, 60. On the Soviet and post-Soviet reception of *One Flew Over the Cuckoo's Nest*, see Rebecca Reich, "Over the Cuckoo's Nest: Russian Variations on a Psychiatric Theme," in Marks and Savelli, eds., *Psychiatry in Communist Europe*, 196-215.

55. Venedikt Erofeev, "Val'purgieva noch', ili 'Shagi komandora,'" *Kontinent*, no. 45 (1985): 96-185.

56. Berlin, ed., "Khibini-Moskva-Petushki," 117, 119, 125, 130.

57. N. L. Leiderman and M. N. Lipovetskii, *Sovremennaia russkaia literatura*, vol. 3, 3 vols. (Moscow: Editorial URSS, 2001), 68-70; Vail' and Genis, "Vo chreve machekhi."

58. Alexander Burry, "The Poet's Fatal Flaw: Venedikt Erofeev's Don Juan Subtext in *Walpurgis Night, or The Steps of the Commander*," *Russian Review* 64, no. 1 (January 2005): 75.

59. Johann Wolfgang von Goethe, *Faust: A Tragedy*, trans. Walter W. Arndt (New York: W. W. Norton, 1976).

60. Blok, "Shagi komandora," in *Sobranie sochinenii v vos'mi tomakh*, vol. 3, 80–81. On the Don Juan intertext, see O. Iu. Bagdasarian, "Siuzhet o Don Zhuane v russkoi dramaturgii 1980-kh gg. ('Don Zhuan' V. Kazakova—'Val'purgieva noch', ili Shagi Komandora' Ven. Erofeeva)," *Filologicheskii klass*, no. 31 (2013): 132–37; Burry, "The Poet's Fatal Flaw."

61. Pushkin, *Kamennyi gost'*, in *Polnoe sobranie sochinenii*, vol. 7, 156.

62. Erofeev, *Val'purgieva noch', ili Shagi Komandora*, in *Sobranie sochinenii*, vol. 1, 167, 274. On the *Hamlet* intertext, see also Vail' and Genis, "Vo chreve machekhi," 148.

63. William Shakespeare, *Hamlet, Prince of Denmark*, in *The Riverside Shakespeare* (Boston: Houghton Mifflin Company, 1974), 1185.

64. Ibid., 1155.

65. Erofeev, *Val'purgieva noch'*, in *Sobranie sochinenii*, vol. 1, 169.

66. Erofeev, *Dissidenty, ili Fanni Kaplan*, in *Ostav'te moiu dushu v pokoe*, 258. On pretending and its cultural representations, see Caryl Emerson, "Pretenders to History: Four Plays for Undoing Pushkin's *Boris Godunov*," *Slavic Review* 44, no. 2 (Summer 1985): 257–79; Maureen Perrie, *Pretenders and Popular Monarchism in Early Modern Russia: The False Tsars of the Time of Troubles* (Cambridge: Cambridge University Press, 1995); B. A. Uspenskii, "Tsar' i samozvanets: Samozvanchestvo v Rossii kak kul'turno-istoricheskii fenomen," in *Izbrannye trudy*, vol. 1, 3 vols. (Moscow: Gnozis, 1994), 75–109.

67. Erofeev, *Dissidenty, ili Fanni Kaplan*, in *Ostav'te moiu dushu v pokoe*, 266.

68. Erofeev, *Val'purgieva noch'*, in *Sobranie sochinenii*, vol. 1, 192.

69. Ibid., 199.

70. Ibid., 254. Italics in the original.

71. Ibid., 183–84.

72. Burry, "The Poet's Fatal Flaw," 64.

73. Kuperman and Zislin, "Simuliatsiia psikhoza," in Bogdanov, Murashov, and Nikolozi, eds., *Russkaia literatura i meditsina*, 300.

74. Ibid., 299.

75. Erofeev, *Val'purgieva noch'*, in *Sobranie sochinenii*, vol. 1, 183.

76. Ibid., 173.

77. Ibid., 175.

78. Ibid., 178.

79. Ibid.

80. Ibid., 179.

81. Ibid., 224.

82. Ibid., 222–23. Italics in the original.

83. Ibid., 223.

84. Ibid., 180.

85. Ibid., 174, 176.

86. Ibid., 181–82.

87. Ibid., 181.

88. Ibid., 223.

89. Ibid., 209.

90. Ibid., 242.
91. Ibid., 234.
92. Ibid., 237.
93. Ibid., 212.
94. Ibid., 258.
95. Ibid., 263.
96. Ibid., 267.
97. Ibid., 268–69.
98. T. L. Rybal'chenko, "Krizis kul'turnykh modelei v soznanii cheloveka ('Val'purgieva noch', ili Shagi Komandora' Ven. Erofeeva)," *Filologicheskii klass*, no. 21 (2009): 8.
99. Erofeev, *Val'purgieva noch'*, in *Sobranie sochinenii*, vol. 1, 259.
100. Ibid., 258.
101. Ibid., 260.
102. Ibid., 271. Italics in the original.
103. Ibid., 225. Italics in the original.
104. Ibid., 229. Italics in the original.
105. Ibid., 270.
106. Ibid., 275. Italics in the original.
107. Ibid., 172.
108. Ibid., 180–81. Italics in the original.
109. Burry, "The Poet's Fatal Flaw," 75.
110. Erofeev, *Val'purgieva noch'*, in *Sobranie sochinenii*, vol. 1, 184.
111. Burry, "The Poet's Fatal Flaw," 73, 75.
112. Avdiev, "Igor' Avdiev," 103.
113. Erofeev, *Val'purgieva noch'*, in *Sobranie sochinenii*, vol. 1, 250.
114. Ibid., 172, 206.
115. Ibid., 273.
116. Ibid., 189, 250.
117. Ibid., 276.
118. Ibid., 169.
119. Nicolas Boileau, *Art of Poetry*, trans. Sir William Soames and John Ozell (Richmond: Alma Classics, 2008), 3. The translation is reproduced with kind permission from Alma Classics Ltd.
120. Murav'ev, "Vladimir Murav'ev," 93.
121. Bil'zho, interview; Tamara Gushchina, "Venedikt Erofeev: Pis'ma k sestre," *Teatr*, no. 9 (September 1992): 144.
122. Murav'ev, "Vladimir Murav'ev," 94.

Conclusion

1. Bukovskii and Gluzman, "Posobie po psikhiatrii dlia inakomysliashchikh," 50; Hans Christian Andersen, "The Emperor's New Clothes," in *The Complete Stories*, trans. Jean Hersholt (London: British Library, 2005), 67–71.
2. Gluzman, "Zloupotreblenie psikhiatriei," 67.
3. Ibid., 70. Bukovskii and Gluzman were not alone in investing Andersen's tale with political meaning. For a Stalin-era retelling that was published and staged at Moscow's

Sovremennik Theater in 1960, see Evgenii Shvarts, *Golyi korol'*, in *Klad. Snezhnaia koroleva. Golyi korol'. Ten'. Drakon. Dva klena. Obyknovennoe chudo. Povest' o molodykh suprugakh. Zolushka. Don Kikhot.* (Moscow: Sovetskii pisatel', 1960), 89-164. See also Vladimir Voinovich, "Novaia skazka o golom korole," in *Skazki dlia vzroslykh* (Moscow: Vagrius, 1996), 413-19. On Andersen's tale, Voinovich's story, and the dissident campaign to expose the "myths" of the Soviet system, see also Vess'e, *Za vashu i nashu svobodu*, 310, 335-57, 439.

4. E. Ia. Shternberg, "O nekotorykh raznovidnostiakh sovremennogo antipsikhiatricheskogo techeniia," *Zhurnal nevropatologii i psikhiatrii imeni S. S. Korsakova*, no. 4 (1973): 606.

5. Ibid. See also M. S. Kel'ner, "Antipsikhiatriia: Filosofskie i sotsial'no-ideologicheskie aspekty," *Zhurnal nevropatologii i psikhiatrii imeni S. S. Korsakova*, no. 8 (1978): 1262.

6. R. I. Mikheev, *Problemy vmeniaemosti i nevmeniaemosti v sovetskom ugolovnom prave* (Vladivostok: Izdatel'stvo dal'nevostochnogo universiteta, 1983), 8-9.

7. R. A. Nadzharov, "Fal'shivki i deistvitel'nost': Beseda s professorom-psikhiatrom R. A. Nadzharovym," *Izvestiia*, August 10, 1973.

8. V. Kassis, "Neukliuzhaia zateia intriganov: Chto pokazal kongress psikhiatrov v Gonolulu," *Izvestiia*, October 17, 1977.

9. Anonymous, "VI Vsemirnyi psikhiatricheskii kongress," *Zhurnal nevropatologii i psikhiatrii imeni S. S. Korsakova*, no. 4 (1978): 608.

10. V. Malyshev, "Ty kritikuesh'? V sumasshedshii dom!," *Literaturnaia gazeta*, April 28, 1976.

11. M. Andronov, "Ty kritikuesh'? V sumasshedshii dom!," *Literaturnaia gazeta*, September 29, 1976.

12. Such quotation marks cast doubt on the legitimacy of Soviet *inakomyslie* in, for instance, Kassis, "Neukliuzhaia zateia intriganov"; Nadzharov, "Fal'shivki i deistvitel'nost'"; N. N. Timofeev, "Deontologicheskii aspekt raspoznavaniia bol'nykh shizofreniei," *Zhurnal nevropatologii i psikhiatrii imeni S. S. Korsakova*, no. 7 (1974): 1070.

13. Prezidium VS SSSR, "Ukaz Prezidiuma VS SSSR ot 26.03.1971 'Ob utverzhdenii teksta prisiagi vracha Sovetskogo Soiuza i Polozheniia o poriadke prineseniia prisiagi,'" March 26, 1971. On deontology, see Ralph Crawshaw, "Medical Deontology in the Soviet Union," *Archives of Internal Medicine* 134, no. 3 (September 1974): 592-94; D. I. Pisarev, *Osnovnye problemy vrachebnoi etiki i meditsinskoi deontologii* (Moscow: Meditsina, 1969).

14. Timofeev, "Deontologicheskii aspekt raspoznavaniia bol'nykh shizofreniei," 1068.

15. Bloch and Reddaway, *Psychiatric Terror*, 79-92.

16. Bloch and Reddaway, *Soviet Psychiatric Abuse*, 197.

17. Smith and Oleszczuk, *No Asylum*, 3-4, 157-158.

18. See *Zhurnal nevropatologii i psikhiatrii imeni S. S. Korsakova*, nos. 9-11 (1988).

19. Terts, *Liubimov*, in *Sobranie sochinenii v dvukh tomakh*, vol. 1, 92.

20. SDS, vol. 8, AS 575 (Viktor Fainberg, "Obrashchenie k organizatsiiam, zashchishchaiushchim prava Cheloveka, s opisaniem Leningradskoi spetsial'noi psikhiatricheskoi bol'nitsy, iiul' 1970 g."), 1-2.

21. Khodorovich, ed., *Istoriia bolezni Leonida Pliushcha*, 167.

Bibliography

Akademiia meditsinskikh nauk SSSR, and Vsesoiuznoe nauchnoe meditsinskoe obshchestvo nevropatologov i psikhiatrov. *Fiziologicheskoe uchenie akademika I. P. Pavlova v psikhiatrii i nevropatologii: Materialy stenograficheskogo otcheta ob"edinennogo zasedaniia rasshirennogo Prezidiuma AMN SSSR i plenuma Pravleniia Vsesoiuznogo obshchestva nevropatologov i psikhiatrov, 11-15 oktiabria 1951 g.* Moscow: Gosudarstvennoe izdatel'stvo meditsinskoi literatury, 1952.

Alexandrov, Vladimir E. "Typographical Intrusion and the Transcendent in Bely's *Petersburg* and Sinyavsky's *Lyubimov*." *Slavonic and East European Review* 62, no. 2 (April 1984): 161-79.

Alexeyeva, Ludmilla. *Soviet Dissent: Contemporary Movements for National, Religious, and Human Rights.* Middletown: Wesleyan University Press, 1985.

Andersen, Hans Christian. *The Complete Stories*, translated by Jean Hersholt. London: British Library, 2005.

Andronov, M. "Ty kritikuesh'? V sumasshedshii dom!" *Literaturnaia gazeta*, September 29, 1976.

Anonymous. "Andrei Vladimirovich Snezhnevskii." *Zhurnal nevropatologii i psikhiatrii imeni S. S. Korsakova*, no. 10 (1987): 1441-44.

———. "K chitateliam 'Zhurnala nevropatologii i psikhiatrii im. S. S. Korsakova.'" *Zhurnal nevropatologii i psikhiatrii imeni S. S. Korsakova*, no. 1 (1988): 3-4.

———. "VI Vsemirnyi psikhiatricheskii kongress." *Zhurnal nevropatologii i psikhiatrii imeni S. S. Korsakova*, no. 4 (1978): 607-25.

Austin, J. L. *How to Do Things with Words*. Cambridge: Harvard University Press, 1975.

Avdiev, Igor'. "Igor' Avdiev (Pechat' minuvshego. Neskol'ko monologov o Venedikte Erofeeve)." *Teatr*, no. 9 (September 1991): 103-16.

Babaian, E. A. "Zakonodatel'stvo SSSR i nekotorykh zarubezhnykh stran po psikhiatrii." *Zhurnal nevropatologii i psikhiatrii imeni S. S. Korsakova*, no. 11 (1969): 1617-23.

Babaian, E. A., G. V. Morozov, V. M. Morkovkin, and A. B. Smulevich. *Izobrazitel'nyi iazyk bol'nykh shizofrenii*. Basel: Sandoz, 1982.

———. *Izobrazitel'nyi iazyk bol'nykh shizofrenii s bredovymi i sverkhtsennymi obrazovaniiami*. Basel: Sandoz, 1985.

———. *Izobrazitel'nyi iazyk bol'nogo paranoiei*. Basel: Sandoz, 1986.

Bagdasarian, O. Iu. "Siuzhet o Don Zhuane v russkoi dramaturgii 1980-kh gg. ('Don Zhuan' V. Kazakova—'Val'purgieva noch', ili Shagi Komandora' Ven. Erofeeva)." *Filologicheskii klass*, no. 31 (2013): 132-37.

Bakhtin, M. M. *The Dialogic Imagination: Four Essays*, edited by Michael Holquist, translated by Caryl Emerson and Michael Holquist. Austin: University of Texas Press, 2004.

Barthes, Roland. "The Death of the Author." In *The Norton Anthology of Theory and Criticism*, edited by Vincent B. Leitch, 1466-70. New York: W. W. Norton, 2001.

Bates, Victoria, Alan Bleakley, and Sam Goodman, eds. *Medicine, Health and the Arts: Approaches to the Medical Humanities*. London: Routledge, 2014.
Beer, Daniel. *Renovating Russia: The Human Sciences and the Fate of Liberal Modernity, 1880–1930*. Ithaca: Cornell University Press, 2008.
Belyi, Andrei. *Sobranie sochinenii*. 6 vols. Moscow: Terra–Knizhnyi klub, 2003.
Benedict, Helen. "Flight from Predictability: Joseph Brodsky." *Antioch Review* 43, no. 1 (Winter 1985): 9–21.
Berlin, Valerii, ed. "Khibini–Moskva–Petushki: Venedikt Erofeev (1938–1990). Letopis' zhizni i tvorchestva Venedikta Erofeeva." *Zhivaia Arktika: Istoriko-kraevedcheskii almanakh*, no. 1 (2005): 1–148.
Bertelsen, Olga. "Rethinking Psychiatric Terror against Nationalists in Ukraine: Spatial Dimensions of Post-Stalinist State Violence." *Kyiv-Mohyla Humanities Journal*, no. 1 (2014): 27–76.
Bethea, David M. *Joseph Brodsky and the Creation of Exile*. Princeton: Princeton University Press, 1994.
Bil'zho, Andrei. Interview by Rebecca Reich. Moscow, July 22, 2009.
Bittner, Stephen V. *The Many Lives of Khrushchev's Thaw*. Ithaca: Cornell University Press, 2008.
Bloch, Sidney, and Peter Reddaway. *Psychiatric Terror: How Soviet Psychiatry Is Used to Suppress Dissent*. New York: Basic Books, 1977.
———. *Soviet Psychiatric Abuse: The Shadow over World Psychiatry*. London: V. Gollancz, 1984.
Blok, Aleksandr. *Sobranie sochinenii v vos'mi tomakh*. 8 vols. Moscow: Gosudarstvennoe izdatel'stvo khudozhestvennoi literatury, 1960–63.
Bogdanov, Konstantin. *Vrachi, patsienty, chitateli: Patograficheskie teksty russkoi kul'tury XVIII–XIX vekov*. Moscow: OGI, 2005.
Bogdanov, Konstantin, Iurii Murashov, and Rikkardo Nikolozi, eds. *Russkaia literatura i meditsina: Telo, predpisaniia, sotsial'naia praktika*. Moscow: Novoe izdatel'stvo, 2005.
Boileau, Nicolas. *Art of Poetry*, translated by Sir William Soames and John Ozell. Richmond: Alma Classics, 2008.
Bolton, Jonathan. *Worlds of Dissent: Charter 77, the Plastic People of the Universe, and Czech Culture Under Communism*. Cambridge: Harvard University Press, 2012.
Boobbyer, Philip. *Conscience, Dissent and Reform in Soviet Russia*. London: Routledge, 2005.
———. "Vladimir Bukovskii and Soviet Communism." *Slavonic and East European Review* 87, no. 3 (July 2009): 452–87.
Booth, Wayne C. *The Rhetoric of Fiction*. Chicago: University of Chicago Press, 1983.
Boym, Svetlana. *Death in Quotation Marks: Cultural Myths of the Modern Poet*. Cambridge: Harvard University Press, 1991.
———. *Common Places: Mythologies of Everyday Life in Russia*. Cambridge: Harvard University Press, 1994.
———. "Estrangement as a Lifestyle: Shklovsky and Brodsky." In *Exile and Creativity: Signposts, Travelers, Outsiders, Backward Glances*, edited by Susan Rubin Suleiman, 241–62. Durham: Duke University Press, 1998.
———. *Another Freedom: The Alternative History of an Idea*. Chicago: University of Chicago Press, 2010.
Brążkiewicz, Bartłomiej. *Psychiatria radziecka jako instrument walki z opozycją polityczną w latach 1918–1984*. Toruń: Wydawnictwo Adam Marszałek, 2004.

---. *Choroba psychiczna w literaturze i kulturze rosyjskiej.* Krakow: Wydawnictwo Księgarnia Akademicka, 2011.
Brintlinger, Angela. "The Hero in the Madhouse: The Post-Soviet Novel Confronts the Soviet Past." *Slavic Review* 63, no. 1 (2004): 43–65.
---. "Writing about Madness: Russian Attitudes toward Psyche and Psychiatry, 1887–1907." In *Madness and the Mad in Russian Culture*, edited by Angela Brintlinger and Ilya Vinitsky, 173–91. Toronto: University of Toronto Press, 2007.
Brintlinger, Angela, and Ilya Vinitsky, eds. *Madness and the Mad in Russian Culture.* Toronto: University of Toronto Press, 2007.
Brodskii, Iosif. "Men'she edinitsy," translated by V. Golyshev. *Inostrannaia literatura*, no. 10 (1992): 234–42.
---. *Sochineniia Iosifa Brodskogo.* 7 vols. St. Petersburg: Pushkinskii fond, 1997–2001.
---. *Stikhotvoreniia i poemy.* 2 vols. Novaia biblioteka poeta. St. Petersburg: Vita Nova, 2011.
Brodsky, Joseph. *Less Than One: Selected Essays.* New York: Farrar, Straus and Giroux, 1986.
---. "Poetry as a Form of Resistance to Reality." *PMLA* 107, no. 2 (March 1992): 220–25.
---. *On Grief and Reason: Essays.* New York: Farrar, Straus and Giroux, 1995.
Brown, Julie V. "Female Sexuality and Madness in Russian Culture: Traditional Values and Psychiatric Theory." *Social Research* 53 (Summer 1986): 369–85.
---. "Revolution and Psychosis: The Mixing of Science and Politics in Russian Psychiatric Medicine, 1905–13." *Russian Review* 46, no. 3 (July 1987): 283–302.
Brown, Julie Vail. "The Professionalization of Russian Psychiatry: 1857–1911." PhD diss., University of Pennsylvania, 1981.
Bukovskii, Vladimir. *Moskovskii protsess.* 2 vols. Paris, Moscow: Russkaia mysl', 1996.
---. *I vozvrashchaetsia veter...: Avtobiografiia.* Moscow: Zakharov, 2007.
---. Interview by Rebecca Reich. Cambridge, UK, March 27, 2012.
Bukovskii, V., and S. Gluzman. "Posobie po psikhiatrii dlia inakomysliashchikh." *Khronika zashchity prav v SSSR*, no. 13 (January-February 1975): 36–60.
Burry, Alexander. "The Poet's Fatal Flaw: Venedikt Erofeev's Don Juan Subtext in *Walpurgis Night, or The Steps of the Commander*." *Russian Review* 64, no. 1 (January 2005): 62–76.
Calloway, Paul. *Russian/Soviet and Western Psychiatry: A Contemporary Comparative Study.* New York: John Wiley & Sons, 1993.
Chekhov, A. P. *Sochineniia v chetyrekh tomakh.* 4 vols. Moscow: Pravda, 1984.
Clark, Katerina. *The Soviet Novel: History as Ritual.* Bloomington: Indiana University Press, 2000.
Crawshaw, Ralph. "Medical Deontology in the Soviet Union." *Archives of Internal Medicine* 134, no. 3 (September 1974): 592–94.
Criveller, Claudia. "Madness as an Aesthetic and Social Act in Russian Autobiographical Prose: The Case of Venedikt Erofeev's *Memoirs of a Psychopath*." *Toronto Slavic Quarterly*, no. 36 (Spring 2011): 52–65.
Dalton, Margaret. *Andrei Siniavskii and Julii Daniel': Two Soviet Heretical Writers.* Würzburg: Jal-Verlag, 1973.
Dauben, Joseph Warren. *Georg Cantor: His Mathematics and Philosophy of the Infinite.* Cambridge: Harvard University Press, 1979.
Derrida, Jacques. "Signature Event Context." In *Limited Inc*, translated by Jeffrey Melman and Samuel Weber, 1–23. Evanston: Northwestern University Press, 1988.

Dobrenko, Evgeny. *Political Economy of Socialist Realism,* translated by Jesse M. Savage. New Haven: Yale University Press, 2007.
Dobson, Miriam. *Khrushchev's Cold Summer: Gulag Returnees, Crime, and the Fate of Reform After Stalin.* Ithaca: Cornell University Press, 2009.
Dostoevskii, Fedor. *Polnoe sobranie sochinenii.* 30 vols. Leningrad: Nauka, 1972–90.
Dovzhenko, A. R., A. F. Artemchuk, Z. N. Bolotova, T. M. Vorob'eva, Iu. A Manuilenko, A. I. Minko, L. A. Kurilko, and V. A. Dovzhenko. "Stressopsikhoterapiia bol'nykh alkogolizmom v ambulatornykh usloviiakh." *Zhurnal nevropatologii i psikhiatrii imeni S. S. Korsakova,* no. 2 (1988): 94–97.
Durkin, Andrew R. "Narrator, Metaphor, and Theme in Sinjavskij's *Fantastic Tales.*" *Slavic and East European Journal* 24, no. 2 (Summer 1980): 133–44.
Eikhenbaum, B. M. *Skvoz' literaturu: Sbornik statei.* Leningrad: Akademiia, 1924.
Emerson, Caryl. "Pretenders to History: Four Plays for Undoing Pushkin's *Boris Godunov.*" *Slavic Review* 44, no. 2 (Summer 1985): 257–79.
Engelstein, Laura. *The Keys to Happiness: Sex and the Search for Modernity in Fin-De-Siècle Russia.* Ithaca: Cornell University Press, 1992.
——. "Combined Underdevelopment: Discipline and the Law in Imperial and Soviet Russia." *American Historical Review* 98, no. 2 (April 1993): 338–53.
Entin, G. M. *Lechenie alkogolizma.* Moscow: Meditsina, 1990.
Epshtein, Mikhail. "Posle karnavala, ili Vechnyi Venichka." In *Ostav'te moiu dushu v pokoe: Pochti vse,* by Venedikt Erofeev, 3–30. Moscow: Kh.G.S., 1995.
——. "Siniavskii kak myslitel'." *Zvezda,* no. 2 (1998): 151–71.
Epstein, Mikhail. "Methods of Madness and Madness as a Method." In *Madness and the Mad in Russian Culture,* edited by Angela Brintlinger and Ilya Vinitsky, 263–82. Toronto: University of Toronto Press, 2007.
Eremin, D. "Perevertyshi." *Izvestiia,* January 13, 1966.
Erofeev, Venedikt. "Val'purgieva noch', ili 'Shagi komandora.'" *Kontinent,* no. 45 (1985): 96–185.
——. *Ostav'te moiu dushu v pokoe: Pochti vse.* Moscow: Kh.G.S., 1995.
——. *Moi ochen' zhiznennyi put'.* Moscow: Vagrius, 2003.
——. *Zapisnye knizhki: Kniga vtoraia.* Moscow: Zakharov, 2007.
——. *Sobranie sochinenii.* 2 vols. Moscow: Vagrius, 2007.
Esenin-Vol'pin, A. S. *Filosofiia. Logika. Poeziia. Zashchita prav cheloveka: Izbrannoe.* Moscow: Rossiiskii gosudarstvennyi gumanitarnyi universitet, 1999.
Etkind, Alexander. *Eros of the Impossible: The History of Psychoanalysis in Russia,* translated by Noah and Maria Rubins. Boulder: Westview Press, 1997.
Fedotov, D. D. *Ocherki po istorii otechestvennoi psikhiatrii.* Moscow: Institut psikhiatrii, 1957.
Felman, Shoshana. *Writing and Madness: (Literature / Philosophy / Psychoanalysis),* translated by Martha Noel Evans, Shoshana Felman, and Brian Massumi. Ithaca: Cornell University Press, 1985.
Fenander, Sara. "Author and Autocrat: Tertz's Stalin and the Ruse of Charisma." *Russian Review* 58, no. 2 (April 1999): 286–97.
Fireside, Harvey. *Soviet Psychoprisons.* New York: W. W. Norton, 1979.
Firsov, B. M. *Raznomyslie v SSSR, 1940–1960-e gg: Istoriia, teoriia i praktika.* St. Petersburg: Evropeiskii dom, 2008.
Foucault, Michel. *Madness and Civilization: A History of Insanity in the Age of Reason,* translated by Richard Howard. New York: Pantheon Books, 1965.

———. "What Is an Author?" In *The Norton Anthology of Theory and Criticism*, edited by Vincent B. Leitch, 1622–36. New York: W. W. Norton, 2001.
Freidkin, Mark. "O Venedikte Erofeeve." *TextOnly*, no. 26 (2008). http://textonly.ru/case/?issue=26&article=27417.
Friedlander, Jacqueline Lee. "Psychiatrists and Crisis in Russia, 1880–1917." PhD diss., University of California, Berkeley, 2007.
Fulford, K. W., A. Y. Smirnov, and E. Snow. "Concepts of Disease and the Abuse of Psychiatry in the USSR." *British Journal of Psychiatry* 162, no. 6 (June 1993): 801–10.
Gaiser-Shnitman, Svetlana. *Venedikt Erofeev: "Moskva–Petushki" ili "The rest is silence."* Bern: Peter Lang, 1989.
Garshin, V. M. *Sochineniia*. Moscow: Gosudarstvennoe izdatel'stvo khudozhestvennoi literatury, 1963.
Genis, Aleksandr. "Archaic Postmodernism: The Aesthetics of Andrei Sinyavsky." In *Russian Postmodernism: New Perspectives on Post-Soviet Culture*, edited by Mikhail Epstein, Aleksandr Genis, and Slobodanka Vladiv-Glover, 185–97. Providence: Berghahn Books, 1999.
Ginzburg, Aleksandr, ed. *Belaia kniga po delu A. Siniavskogo i Iu. Danielia*. Frankfurt am Main: Posev, 1967.
Glazov, Yuri. *The Russian Mind Since Stalin's Death*. Dordrecht: D. Reidel, 1985.
Gluzman, Semen. *Psalmy i skorbi*. Khar'kov: Folio, 1994.
———. Interview by Rebecca Reich. Kiev, Ukraine, May 22, 2009.
Gluzman, Semyon. *On Soviet Totalitarian Psychiatry*. Amsterdam: International Association on the Political Use of Psychiatry, 1989.
Gluzman, S. F. "Zloupotreblenie psikhiatriei: Sotsial'nye i iuridicheskie istoki." *Filosofskaia i sotsiologicheskaia mysl'*, no. 7 (1990): 66–78.
———. *Risunki po pamiati, ili vospominaniia otsidenta*. Kiev: Izdatel'skii dom Dmitriia Burago, 2012.
Goethe, Johann Wolfgang von. *Faust: A Tragedy*, translated by Walter W. Arndt. New York: W. W. Norton, 1976.
Goffman, Erving. *Asylums: Essays on the Social Situation of Mental Patients and Other Inmates*. New Brunswick: Aldine Transaction, 2007.
Gogol', Nikolai. *Sobranie sochinenii*. 8 vols. Moscow: Terra–Knizhnyi klub, 2001.
Gorbanevskaia, Natal'ia. *Polden': Delo o demonstratsii na Krasnoi ploshchadi 25 avgusta 1968 goda*. Moscow: Novoe izdatel'stvo, 2007.
Gorbanevskaya, Natalya. *Selected Poems, With a Transcript of Her Trial and Papers Relating to Her Detention in a Prison Psychiatric Hospital*, translated by Daniel Weissbort. Oxford: Carcanet Press, 1972.
Gor'kii, Maksim. *Polnoe sobranie sochinenii*. 24 vols. Moscow: Nauka, 1968–76.
Gorsuch, Anne E., and Diane P. Koenker, eds. *The Socialist Sixties: Crossing Borders in the Second World*. Bloomington: Indiana University Press, 2013.
Graham, Loren R. *Science, Philosophy, and Human Behavior in the Soviet Union*. New York: Columbia University Press, 1987.
Grayson, Jane. "Picture Windows: The Art of Andrei Siniavskii." In *Russian Literature, Modernism and the Visual Arts*, edited by Catriona Kelly and Stephen Lovell, 88–118. Cambridge: Cambridge University Press, 2000.
Grigorenko, Petro. *V podpol'e mozhno vstretit' tol'ko krys . . .* Moscow: Zven'ia, 1997.
Groys, Boris. *The Total Art of Stalinism: Avant-Garde, Aesthetic Dictatorship, and Beyond*, translated by Charles Rougle. London: Verso, 2011.

Gushchina, Tamara. "Venedikt Erofeev: Pis'ma k sestre." *Teatr*, no. 9 (September 1992): 122–44.
Haber, Erika. "In Search of the Fantastic in Tertz's Fantastic Realism." *Slavic and East European Journal* 42, no. 2 (Summer 1998): 254–67.
Haven, Cynthia L., ed. *Joseph Brodsky: Conversations*. Jackson: University Press of Mississippi, 2002.
Healey, Dan. *Bolshevik Sexual Forensics: Diagnosing Disorder in the Clinic and Courtroom, 1917–1939*. DeKalb: Northern Illinois University Press, 2009.
Hoffmann, David L. *Cultivating the Masses: Modern State Practices and Soviet Socialism, 1914–1939*. Ithaca: Cornell University Press, 2011.
Holmgren, Beth. "The Transfiguring of Context in the Work of Abram Terts." *Slavic Review* 50, no. 4 (Winter 1991): 965–77.
Hornsby, Robert. *Protest, Reform and Repression in Khrushchev's Soviet Union*. Cambridge: Cambridge University Press, 2013.
Hunt, Priscilla Hart, and Svitlana Kobets, eds. *Holy Foolishness in Russia: New Perspectives*. Bloomington: Slavica Publishers, 2011.
Iakobson, Roman. *Raboty po poetike*. Moscow: Progress, 1987.
Ialovoi, A. Ia. "Zamena alkogol'no-antabusnoi proby pri lechenii alkogolizma platsebo." *Zhurnal nevropatologii i psikhiatrii imeni S. S. Korsakova*, no. 4 (1968): 593–96.
Ignatova, Elena. "Venedikt." *Neva*, no. 1 (1993): 217–34.
Iudin, T. I. *Ocherki istorii otechestvennoi psikhiatrii*. Moscow: Gosudarstvennoe izdatel'stvo meditsinskoi literatury, 1951.
Iuridicheskaia komissiia soveta ministrov RSFSR. *Grazhdanskii kodeks RSFSR: Ofitsial'nyi tekst*. Moscow: Iuridicheskaia literatura, 1964.
Ivanov, S. A. *Blazhennye pokhaby: Kul'turnaia istoriia iurodstva*. Moscow: Iazyki slavianskikh kul'tur, 2005.
Ivanova, V. "Zalog dushevnogo zdorov'ia." *Literaturnaia gazeta*, January 24, 1967.
Janecek, Gerald. *Zaum: The Transrational Poetry of Russian Futurism*. San Diego: San Diego State University Press, 1996.
Jones, Polly, ed. *The Dilemmas of De-Stalinization: Negotiating Cultural and Social Change in the Khrushchev Era*. London: Routledge, 2006.
———. *Myth, Memory, Trauma: Rethinking the Stalinist Past in the Soviet Union, 1953–70*. New Haven: Yale University Press, 2013.
Joravsky, David. *Russian Psychology: A Critical History*. Oxford: Blackwell, 1989.
Kalashnik, Ia. M. *Sudebnaia psikhiatriia*. Moscow: Gosudarstvennoe izdatel'stvo iuridicheskoi literatury, 1961.
Kalashnik, Ia. M., and G. V. Morozov, eds. *Sudebnaia psikhiatriia*. Moscow: Iuridicheskaia literatura, 1967.
Kassis, V. "Neukliuzhaia zateia intriganov: Chto pokazal kongress psikhiatrov v Gonolulu." *Izvestiia*, October 17, 1977.
Katvan, Zeev. "Reflection Theory and the Identity of Thinking and Being." *Studies in Soviet Thought* 18, no. 2 (May 1978): 87–109.
Katz, Jane B. *Artists in Exile*. New York: Stein and Day, 1983.
Kedrina, Z. "Nasledniki Smerdiakova." *Literaturnaia gazeta*, January 22, 1966.
Kel'ner, M. S. "Antipsikhiatriia: Filosofskie i sotsial'no-ideologicheskie aspekty." *Zhurnal nevropatologii i psikhiatrii imeni S. S. Korsakova*, no. 8 (1978): 1257–65.
Kerbikov, O. V., M. V. Korkina, R. A. Nadzharov, and A. V. Snezhnevskii. *Psikhiatriia*. Moscow: Meditsina, 1968.

Khodorovich, Tat'iana, ed. *Istoriia bolezni Leonida Pliushcha*. Amsterdam: Fond im. Gertsena, 1974.

Khodorovich, Tat'iana, and Iurii Orlov. "Leonida Pliushcha prevrashaiut v sumasshedsego. Zachem?" *Russkaia mysl'*, May 15, 1975.

Kholodkovskaia, E. M. *Deesposobnost' psikhicheski bol'nykh v sudebno-psikhiatricheskoi praktike*. Moscow: Meditsina, 1967.

Khrushchev, N. S. "Sluzhenie narodu—vysokoe prizvanie sovetskikh pisatelei. Rech' tovarishcha N. S. Khrushcheva na II s"ezde pisatelei 22 maia 1959 goda." *Pravda*, May 24, 1959.

———. "O kul'te lichnosti i ego posledstviiakh." *Izvestiia TsK KPSS*, no. 3 (1989): 128–70.

Khurgin, Ia. I., and P. G. Nikiforova. "O perspektivakh diagnostiki zabolevanii psikhicheskikh." *Zhurnal nevropatologii i psikhiatrii imeni S. S. Korsakova*, no. 3 (1966): 462–63.

Kolonosky, Walter F. *Literary Insinuations: Sorting Out Sinyavsky's Irreverence*. Lanham: Lexington Books, 2003.

Komaromi, Ann. "The Unofficial Field of Late Soviet Culture." *Slavic Review* 66, no. 4 (Winter 2007): 605–29.

———. "Venedikt Erofeev's *Moskva-Petushki*: Performance and Performativity in the Late Soviet Text." *Slavic and East European Journal* 55, no. 3 (Fall 2011): 418–38.

———. "Samizdat and Soviet Dissident Publics." *Slavic Review* 71, no. 1 (Spring 2012): 70–90.

———. *Uncensored: Samizdat Novels and the Quest for Autonomy in Soviet Dissidence*. Evanston: Northwestern University Press, 2015.

Korotenko, A., and N. Alikina. *Sovetskaia psikhiatriia: Zabluzhdeniia i umysel*. Kiev: Sfera, 2002.

Kozlov, Denis. *The Readers of Novyi Mir: Coming to Terms with the Stalinist Past*. Cambridge: Harvard University Press, 2013.

Kozlov, Denis, and Eleonory Gilburd, eds. *The Thaw: Soviet Society and Culture During the 1950s and 1960s*. Toronto: University of Toronto Press, 2013.

Kozlov, V. A., and S. V. Mironenko, eds. *Kramola: Inakomyslie v SSSR pri Khrushcheve i Brezhneve, 1953–1982 gg.: Rassekrechennye dokumenty Verkhovnogo suda i Prokuratury SSSR*. Moscow: Materik, 2005.

Kruchenykh, Aleksei. "O bezumii v iskusstve." *Novyi den'*, May 26, 1919.

Kuperman, Victor. "Narratives of Psychiatric Malingering in Works of Fiction." *Medical Humanities* 32, no. 2 (2006): 67–72.

Kuperman, Viktor, and Iosif Zislin. "Simuliatsiia psikhoza: Semiotika povedeniia." In *Russkaia literatura i meditsina: Telo, predpisaniia, sotsial'naia praktika*, edited by Konstantin Bogdanov, Iurii Murashov, and Rikkardo Nikolozi, 290–302. Moscow: Novoe izdatel'stvo, 2005.

Laing, R. D. *The Divided Self: A Study of Sanity and Madness*. Chicago: Quadrangle Books, 1960.

Lavretsky, Helen. "The Russian Concept of Schizophrenia: A Review of the Literature." *Schizophrenia Bulletin* 24, no. 4 (January 1998): 537–57.

Lebedev, A. A. *Chaadaev*. Moscow: Molodaia gvardiia, 1965.

Leiderman, N. L., and M. N. Lipovetskii. *Sovremennaia russkaia literatura*. 3 vols. Moscow: Editorial URSS, 2001.

Lenin, V. I. *Polnoe sobranie sochinenii*. 55 vols. Moscow: Izdatel'stvo politicheskoi literatury, 1967–70.

Lermontov, M. Iu. *Sochineniia*. 6 vols. Leningrad: Akademiia nauk SSSR, 1954–57.

Likhachev, D. S., and A. M. Panchenko. *Smekhovoi mir Drevnei Rusi*. Leningrad: Nauka, 1984.
Lipovetsky, Mark. "From an Otherworldly Point of View: Venedikt Erofeev's 'Moscow to the End of the Line.'" In *Russian Postmodernist Fiction: Dialogue with Chaos*, edited by Eliot Borenstein, 66–82. Armonk: M. E. Sharpe, 1999.
———. *Charms of the Cynical Reason: The Trickster's Transformations in Soviet and Post-Soviet Culture*. Boston: Academic Studies Press, 2011.
Liubchikova, Lidiia. "Lidiia Liubchikova (Pechat' minuvshego. Neskol'ko monologov o Venedikte Erofeeve)." *Teatr*, no. 9 (September 1991): 80–86.
Loseff, Lev. "On Hostile Ground: Madness and Madhouse in Joseph Brodsky's 'Gorbunov and Gorchakov.'" In *Madness and the Mad in Russian Culture*, edited by Ilya Vinitsky and Angela Brintlinger, 90–100. Toronto: University of Toronto Press, 2007.
Loseff, Lev, and Valentina Polukhina, eds. *Brodsky's Poetics and Aesthetics*. London: Macmillan, 1990.
Losev, Lev. *Iosif Brodskii: Opyt literaturnoi biografii*. Moscow: Molodaia gvardiia, 2006.
Losev, Lev, and Petr Vail', eds. *Iosif Brodskii: Trudy i dni*. Moscow: Nezavisimaia gazeta, 1998.
Lourie, Richard. *Letters to the Future: An Approach to Sinyavsky-Tertz*. Ithaca: Cornell University Press, 1975.
Lunts, D. R. "Dissimuliatsiia u psikhicheski bol'nykh." In *Problemy kliniki, sudebnopsikhiatricheskoi ekspertizy, patofiziologii i immunologii shizofrenii*, No. 3, edited by G. V. Morozov, 309–22. Nauchnye trudy vyp. 15. Moscow: Ministerstvo zdravookhraneniia SSSR: Tsentral'nyi nauchno-issledovatel'skii institut sudebnoi psikhiatrii im. prof. V. P. Serbskogo, 1964.
———. *Problema nevmeniaemosti v teorii i praktike sudebnoi psikhiatrii*. Moscow: Meditsina, 1966.
———. "O sudebno-psikhiatricheskom znachenii psikhicheskikh anomalii, ne iskliuchaiushchikh vmeniaemosti (po povodu stat'i S. F. Semenova 'K voprosu ob ogranichennoi (umen'shennoi) vmeniaemosti')." *Zhurnal nevropatologii i psikhiatrii imeni S. S. Korsakova*, no. 4 (1967): 605–8.
Lupandin, Vladimir. "Karatel'naia psikhiatriia. Vospominaniia ochevidtsa." *Moskovskie novosti*, August 12, 1990.
Madsen, K. B. *A History of Psychology in Metascientific Perspective*. Amsterdam: North-Holland, 1988.
Malyshev, V. "Ty kritikuesh'? V sumasshedshii dom!" *Literaturnaia gazeta*, April 28, 1976.
Markesinis, Eugenie. *Andrei Siniavskii: A Hero of His Time?* Boston: Academic Studies Press, 2013.
Marks, Sarah, and Mat Savelli, eds. *Psychiatry in Communist Europe*. London: Palgrave Macmillan, 2015.
Marx, Karl, and Friedrich Engels. *The Marx-Engels Reader*. Edited by Robert C. Tucker. New York: W. W. Norton, 1978.
McVay, Gordon. *Esenin: A Life*. Ann Arbor: Ardis, 1976.
Medvedev, Zhores, and Roi Medvedev. *Kto sumasshedshii?* London: Macmillan, 1971.
Mikheev, R. I. *Problemy vmeniaemosti i nevmeniaemosti v sovetskom ugolovnom prave*. Vladivostok: Izdatel'stvo dal'nevostochnogo universiteta, 1983.
Miller, Martin A. *Freud and the Bolsheviks: Psychoanalysis in Imperial Russia and the Soviet Union*. New Haven: Yale University Press, 1998.

Ministerstvo iustitsii RSFSR. *Ugolovnyi kodeks RSFSR: Ofitsial'nyi tekst s izmeneniiami na 1 avgusta 1962 g. i s prilozheniem postateino sistematizirovannykh materialov.* Moscow: Gosudarstvennoe izdatel'stvo iuridicheskoi literatury, 1962.
Morozov, G. V., V. E. Rozhnov, and E. A. Babaian, eds. *Alkogolizm: Rukovodstvo dlia vrachei.* Moscow: Meditsina, 1983.
Moteiunaite, I. V. "Ven. Erofeev i iurodstvo: Zametki k teme." In *"Moskva-Petushki" Ven. Erofeeva. Materialy Tret'ei mezhdunarodnoi konferentsii "Literaturnyi tekst: Problemy i metody issledovaniia" 18–21 maia 2000 goda, Tver'*, edited by Iu. V. Domanskii, 142–45. Tver': Tverskoi gosudarstvennyi universitet, 2000.
Murav, Harriet. *Holy Foolishness: Dostoevsky's Novels and the Poetics of Cultural Critique.* Stanford: Stanford University Press, 1992.
———. *Russia's Legal Fictions.* Ann Arbor: University of Michigan Press, 1998.
Murav'ev, Vladimir. "Vladimir Murav'ev (Pechat' minuvshego. Neskol'ko monologov o Venedikte Erofeeve)." *Teatr*, no. 9 (September 1991): 90–95.
Nadzharov, R. A. "Fal'shivki i deistvitel'nost': Beseda s professorom-psikhiatrom R. A. Nadzharovym." *Izvestiia*, August 10, 1973.
Nathans, Benjamin. "The Dictatorship of Reason: Aleksandr Vol'pin and the Idea of Rights under 'Developed Socialism.'" *Slavic Review* 66, no. 4 (Winter 2007): 630–63.
———. "Soviet Rights-Talk in the Post-Stalin Era." In *Human Rights in the Twentieth Century*, edited by Stefan-Ludwig Hoffman, 166–90. Cambridge: Cambridge University Press, 2011.
———. "The Disenchantment of Socialism: Soviet Dissidents, Human Rights, and the New Global Morality." In *The Breakthrough: Human Rights in the 1970s*, edited by Jan Eckel and Samuel Moyn, 33–48. Philadelphia: University of Pennsylvania Press, 2014.
———. "Talking Fish: On Soviet Dissident Memoirs." *Journal of Modern History* 87, no. 3 (September 2015): 579–614.
Nathans, Benjamin, and Kevin M. F. Platt. "Socialist in Form, Indeterminate in Content: The Ins and Outs of Late Soviet Culture." *Ab Imperio*, no. 2 (2011): 301–24.
Nekipelov, Viktor. *Institut durakov: Dokumental'naia povest' "Institut durakov" i izbrannye stikhotvoreniia.* Barnaul: Pomoshch' postradavshim ot psikhiatrov, 2005.
Nepomnyashchy, Catharine Theimer. *Abram Tertz and the Poetics of Crime.* New Haven: Yale University Press, 1995.
Nesbet, Anne. "Suicide as Literary Fact in the 1920s." *Slavic Review* 50, no. 4 (Winter 1991): 827–35.
Novodvorskaia, Valeriia. *Po tu storonu otchaianiia.* Moscow: Novosti, 1993.
OED Online. June 2017. Oxford University Press.
Ottovordemgentschenfelde, Natalia. *Jurodstvo: eine Studie zur Phänomenologie und Typologie des Narren in Christo: Jurodivyj in der postmodernen russischen Kunst: Venedikt Erofeev Die Reise nach Petuški, Aktionismus Aleksandr Breners und Oleg Kuliks.* Frankfurt am Main: Peter Lang, 2004.
Oushakine, Serguei Alex. "The Terrifying Mimicry of Samizdat." *Public Culture* 13, no. 2 (April 2001): 191–214.
Paperno, Irina, and Boris Gasparov. "Vstan' i idi." *Slavica Hierosolymitana*, no. 5–6 (1981): 387–400.

Papodopulos, T. Review of *Madness and Civilization: A History of Insanity in the Age of Reason*, by Michel Foucault. *Zhurnal nevropatologii i psikhiatrii imeni S. S. Korsakova* 1973, no. 4 (1973): 595–602.
Parker, Andrew, and Eve Kosofsky Sedgwick, eds. *Performativity and Performance.* New York: Routledge, 1995.
Pelipas, V. E. *Simuliatsiia psikhicheskikh rasstroistv i ee raspoznavanie pri sudebnopsikhiatricheskoi ekspertize (metodicheskie rekomendatsii).* Moscow: Ministerstvo zdravookhraneniia SSSR, 1983.
Perrie, Maureen. *Pretenders and Popular Monarchism in Early Modern Russia: The False Tsars of the Time of Troubles.* Cambridge: Cambridge University Press, 1995.
Petrov, T. "Prigovor klevetnikam." *Pravda*, February 15, 1966.
Pinnow, Kenneth M. *Lost to the Collective: Suicide and the Promise of Soviet Socialism, 1921–1929.* Ithaca: Cornell University Press, 2010.
Pisarev, D. I. *Osnovnye problemy vrachebnoi etiki i meditsinskoi deontologii.* Moscow: Meditsina, 1969.
Plato. *The Republic of Plato*, translated by Allan Bloom. New York: Basic Books, 1991.
Platonov, Andrei. *Noev kovcheg.* Moscow: Vagrius, 2006.
Pliushch, Leonid. *Na karnavale istorii.* London: Overseas Publications Interchange, 1979.
Podrabinek, Aleksandr. *Karatel'naia meditsina.* New York: Khronika, 1979.
———. Interview by Rebecca Reich. Moscow, Russia, April 10, 2009.
———. *Dissidenty.* Moscow: AST, 2014.
Polukhina, Valentina. *Joseph Brodsky: A Poet for Our Time.* Cambridge: Cambridge University Press, 1989.
———, ed. *Iosif Brodskii: Bol'shaia kniga interv'iu.* Moscow: Zakharov, 2000.
Ponomareff, Constantin V. *Sergey Esenin.* Boston: Twayne Publishers, 1978.
Popkin, Cathy. "Hysterical Episodes: Case Histories and Silent Subjects." In *Self and Story in Russian History*, edited by Laura Engelstein and Stephanie Sandler, 189–216. Ithaca: Cornell University Press, 2000.
Prezidium VS SSSR. "Ukaz Prezidiuma VS SSSR ot 26.03.1971 'Ob utverzhdenii teksta prisiagi vracha Sovetskogo Soiuza i Polozheniia o poriadke prineseniia prisiagi,'" March 26, 1971.
Proffer, Carl R. "A Stop in the Madhouse: Brodsky's 'Gorbunov and Gorchakov.'" *Russian Literature Triquarterly*, no. 1 (Fall 1971): 342–51.
Prudovskii, Leonid. "Sumasshedshim mozhno byt' v liuboe vremia." *Kontinent*, no. 65 (1990): 411–30.
Pushkin, A. S. *Polnoe sobranie sochinenii.* 17 vols. Leningrad: Akademiia nauk SSSR, 1937–59.
Raikhel, Eugene. "Institutional Encounters: Identification and Anonymity in Russian Addiction Treatment (and Ethnography)." In *Being There: The Fieldwork Encounter and the Making of Truth*, edited by John Borneman and Abdellah Hammoudi, 201–36. Berkeley: University of California Press, 2009.
———. "Placebos or Prostheses for the Will?: Trajectories of Alcoholism Treatment in Russia." In *Addiction Trajectories*, edited by Eugene Raikhel and William Garriott, 188–212. Durham: Duke University Press, 2013.
———. *Governing Habits: Treating Alcoholism in the Post-Soviet Clinic.* Ithaca: Cornell University Press, 2016.
Rat'kina, T. E. *Nikomu ne zadolzhav: Literaturnaia kritika i esseistika A. D. Siniavskogo.* Moscow: Sovpadenie, 2010.

Ready, Oliver. "From Aleshkovsky to Galkovsky: The Praise of Folly in Russian Prose since the 1960s." PhD diss., University of Oxford, 2007.
———. "In Praise of Booze: 'Moskva–Petushki' and Erasmian Irony." *Slavonic and East European Review* 88, no. 3 (July 2010): 437–67.
———. "'Questions to Which Reason Has No Answer': Iurii Mamleev's Irrationalism in European Context." In *Facets of Russian Irrationalism between Art and Life: Mystery inside Enigma*, edited by Olga Tabachnikova, 496–518. Leiden: Brill Rodopi, 2016.
———. *Persisting in Folly: Russian Writers in Search of Wisdom, 1963–2013*. Oxford: Peter Lang, 2017.
Reese, Kevin. "Imagination and Realism in Soviet Science Fiction: Siniavsky's 'Bez Skidok' and Terts's 'Pkhents.'" *Slavic and East European Journal* 52, no. 3 (October 2008): 439–53.
Reich, Rebecca. "Over the Cuckoo's Nest: Russian Variations on a Psychiatric Theme." In *Psychiatry in Communist Europe*, edited by Sarah Marks and Mat Savelli, 196–215. London: Palgrave Macmillan, 2015.
Reich, Walter. "The Spectrum Concept of Schizophrenia: Problems for Diagnostic Practice." *Archives of General Psychiatry* 32 (April 1975): 489–98.
Rosenshield, Gary. *Pushkin and the Genres of Madness: The Masterpieces of 1833*. Madison: University of Wisconsin Press, 2003.
Rozental', M. M., S. M. Tretiakov, and I. K. Luppol, eds. *Pervyi vsesoiuznyi s"ezd sovetskikh pisatelei 1934: Stenograficheskii otchet*. Moscow: Khudozhestvennaia literatura, 1934.
Rubenstein, Joshua. *Soviet Dissidents: Their Struggle for Human Rights*. Boston: Beacon Press, 1985.
Rubinshtein, N. N., ed. *Progulki s Andreem Siniavskim*. Moscow: Tsentr knigi "Rudomino," 2011.
Ryan-Hayes, Karen L. *Contemporary Russian Satire: A Genre Study*. Cambridge: Cambridge University Press, 1995.
Rybal'chenko, T. L. "Krizis kul'turnykh modelei v soznanii cheloveka ('Val'purgieva noch', ili Shagi Komandora' Ven. Erofeeva)." *Filologicheskii klass*, no. 21 (2009): 4–11.
Savenko, Iurii. Interview by Benjamin Zajicek. Moscow, Russia, July 3, 2003.
———. Interview by Rebecca Reich. Moscow, Russia, April 15, 2009.
Savenko, Iu. S. "Perebolet' Fuko." *Novoe literaturnoe obozrenie*, no. 49 (2001): 89–94.
Savenko, Iu. S., and L. Vinogradova. "Latentnye formy antipsikhiatrii kak glavnaia opasnost'." *Nezavisimyi psikhiatricheskii zhurnal*, no. 4 (2005): 12–16.
Sedakova, Ol'ga. "Ol'ga Sedakova (Pechat' minuvshego. Neskol'ko monologov o Venedikte Erofeeve)." *Teatr*, no. 9 (September 1991): 98–102.
———. "Neskazannaia rech' na vechere Venedikta Erofeeva." *Druzhba narodov*, no. 12 (1991): 264–65.
Sadegh-Zadeh, Kazem. *Handbook of Analytic Philosophy of Medicine*. Philosophy and Medicine 113. Dordrecht: Springer, 2012.
Scherr, Barry. "False Starts: A Note on Brodsky's Poetics." *Toronto Slavic Annual*, no. 1 (Summer 2003): 197–204.
Schulz, Peter J. "The Communication of Diagnostic Information by Doctors to Patients in the Consultation." In *Bordering Biomedicine*, edited by Vera Kalitzkus and Peter Twohig, 103–15. Amsterdam, New York: Rodopi, 2006.
Serebriakova, Z. N., B. P. Shchukin, and Iu. O. Musaev. "O vozmozhnosti prognozirovaniia obshchestvenno opasnykh deistvii psikhicheski bol'nykh." In *Problemy prinuditel'nogo lecheniia psikhicheski bol'nykh (sbornik nauchnykh trudov)*, edited by

G. V. Morozov, 144-50. Moscow: Ministerstvo zdravookhraneniia SSSR: Tsentral'nyi ordena trudovogo krasnogo znameni nauchno-issledovatel'skii institut sudebnoi psikhiatrii im. prof. V. P. Serbskogo, 1978.

Shakespeare, William. *The Riverside Shakespeare.* Boston: Houghton Mifflin Company, 1974.

Sharp, Jane A. "After Malevich—Variations on the Return to the Black Square." In *Picturing Russia: Explorations in Visual Culture,* edited by Valerie A. Kivelson and Joan Neuberger, 233-38. New Haven: Yale University Press, 2008.

Shevelev, Igor'. "Petrovich segodnia—eto Leonardo vchera." *Vremia MN,* June 10, 2000.

Shimanov, G. M. *Zapiski iz krasnogo doma.* Moscow: Tipografiia IPO profsoiuov Profizdat, 2006.

Shklovskii, Viktor. *Gamburgskii schet: Stat'i—vospominaniia—esse (1914-1933).* Moscow: Sovetskii pisatel', 1990.

Shmel'kova, Natal'ia. *Vo chreve machekhi, ili Zhizn'—diktatura krasnogo.* St. Petersburg: Limbus Press, 1999.

Shorter, Edward. *A History of Psychiatry: From the Era of the Asylum to the Age of Prozac.* New York: John Wiley & Sons, 1997.

Shternberg, E. Ia. "O nekotorykh raznovidnostiakh sovremennogo antipsikhiatricheskogo techeniia." *Zhurnal nevropatologii i psikhiatrii imeni S. S. Korsakova,* no. 4 (1973): 602-6.

———. Review of *Antipsikhiatriia. Kritika psikhiatrii,* by I. Glatsel'. *Zhurnal nevropatologii i psikhiatrii imeni S. S. Korsakova,* no. 8 (1976): 1264-66.

Shumakov, V. M. "K sistematike form techeniia shizofrenii i obshchei kharakteristike bol'nykh, sovershaiushchikh obshchestvenno opasnye deistviia." *Zhurnal nevropatologii i psikhiatrii imeni S. S. Korsakova,* no. 2 (1969): 268-74.

Shumakov, V. M., S. B. Shesterneva, E. D. Sokolova, and K. F. Efremenko. "Kliniko-psikhopatologicheskie osobennosti bol'nykh shizofreniei, sovershavshikh obshchestvenno opasnye deistviia." *Zhurnal nevropatologii i psikhiatrii imeni S. S. Korsakova,* no. 12 (1976): 1860-66.

Shumakov, V. M., E. D. Sokolova, and Ia. E. Svirinovskii. "O klinicheskikh kriteriiakh obshchestvennoi opasnosti bol'nykh shizofreniei (psikhopatopodobnye sostoianiia)." *Zhurnal nevropatologii i psikhiatrii imeni S. S. Korsakova,* no. 1 (1980): 107-14.

Shvarts, Evgenii. *Klad. Snezhnaia koroleva. Golyi korol'. Ten'. Drakon. Dva klena. Obyknovennoe chudo. Povest' o molodykh suprugakh. Zolushka. Don Kikhot.* Moscow: Sovetskii pisatel', 1960.

Simmons, Cynthia. *Their Fathers' Voice: Vassily Aksyonov, Venedikt Erofeev, Eduard Limonov, and Sasha Sokolov.* New York: Peter Lang, 1993.

Siniavskii, A. D. "Poeziia Pasternaka." In *Stikhotvoreniia i poemy,* by B. L. Pasternak, 9-62. Leningrad: Sovetskii pisatel', 1965.

Siniavskii, Andrei. "Dissidentstvo kak lichnyi opyt." *Sintaksis,* no. 15 (1985): 131-47.

———. "Stalin—geroi i khudozhnik stalinskoi epokhi." *Sintaksis,* no. 19 (1987): 106-25.

———. "Prostranstvo prozy." *Sintaksis,* no. 21 (1988): 25-31.

———. "Pokhvala emigratsii." *Sintaksis,* no. 24 (1988): 39-42.

———. *Ivan-durak: Ocherk russkoi narodnoi very.* Moscow: Agraf, 2001.

Siniavskii, Andrei, and Abram Terts. *Literaturnyi protsess v Rossii: Literaturno-kriticheskie raboty raznykh let.* Moscow: Rossiiskii gosudarstvennyi gumanitarnyi universitet, 2003.

Sirotkina, Irina. *Diagnosing Literary Genius: A Cultural History of Psychiatry in Russia, 1880-1930*. Baltimore: Johns Hopkins University Press, 2002.

———. "Toward a Soviet Psychiatry: War and the Organization of Mental Health Care in Revolutionary Russia." In *Soviet Medicine: Culture, Practice, and Science*, edited by Frances Lee Bernstein, Christopher Burton, and Dan Healey, 27-48. DeKalb: Northern Illinois University Press, 2010.

Sluzhevskaia, Irina. "Poslednyi iurodivyi (o tvorchestve Venedikta Erofeeva)." *Word— Slovo*, no. 10 (1991): 88-92.

Smirnova, E. A. "Venedikt Erofeev glazami gogoloveda." *Russkaia literatura*, no. 3 (1990): 58-66.

Smith, G. S. "The Development of Joseph Brodsky's Dol'nik Verse, 1972-1976." *Russian Literature* 52, no. 4 (November 2002): 471-92.

Smith, Theresa C., and Thomas A. Oleszczuk. *No Asylum: State Psychiatric Repression in the Former USSR*. New York: New York University Press, 1996.

Snezhnevskii, A. V. "O nozologicheskoi spetsifichnosti psikhopatologicheskikh sindromov." *Zhurnal nevropatologii i psikhiatrii imeni S. S. Korsakova*, no. 1 (1960): 91-108.

———, ed. *Shizofreniia: Mul'tidistsiplinarnoe issledovanie*. Moscow: Meditsina, 1972.

———, ed. *Spravochnik po psikhiatrii*. Moscow: Meditsina, 1974.

———. "Mesto kliniki v issledovanii prirody shizofrenii." *Zhurnal nevropatologii i psikhiatrii imeni S. S. Korsakova*, no. 9 (1975): 1340-45.

———, ed. *Rukovodstvo po psikhiatrii*. 2 vols. Moscow: Meditsina, 1983.

Solzhenitsyn, Aleksandr. *Sobranie sochinenii v deviati tomakh*. 9 vols. Moscow: Terra-Knizhnyi klub, 2001.

Szasz, Thomas S. *The Myth of Mental Illness: Foundations of a Theory of Personal Conduct*. New York: Hoeber-Harper, 1961.

Tal'tse, M. F., and Ia. L. Landau. "Mery meditsinskogo kharaktera i kriterii izmeneniia ikh v otnoshenii s medlenno-progredientnoi paranoidnoi shizofrenii." In *Problemy prinuditel'nogo lecheniia psikhicheski bol'nykh (sbornik nauchnykh trudov)*, edited by G. V. Morozov, 53-62. Moscow: Ministerstvo zdravookhraneniia SSSR, Tsentral'nyi ordena trudovogo krasnogo znameni nauchno-issledovatel'skii institut sudebnoi psikhiatrii im. prof. V. P. Serbskogo, 1978.

Tarsis, Valerii. *Palata No. 7*. Frankfurt am Main: Posev, 1966.

Tempest, Richard. "Madman or Criminal: Government Attitudes to Petr Chaadaev in 1836." *Slavic Review* 43, no. 2 (Summer 1984): 281-87.

Terts, Abram. "Literaturnyi protsess v Rossii." *Kontinent*, no. 1 (1974): 143-90.

———. "Iskusstvo i deistvitel'nost'." *Sintaksis*, no. 2 (1978): 111-19.

———. *Sobranie sochinenii v dvukh tomakh*. 2 vols. Moscow: SP "Start," 1992.

Thompson, Ewa M. *Understanding Russia: The Holy Fool in Russian Culture*. Lanham: University Press of America, 1987.

Timofeev, N. N. "Deontologicheskii aspekt raspoznavaniia bol'nykh shizofrenii." *Zhurnal nevropatologii i psikhiatrii imeni S. S. Korsakova*, no. 7 (1974): 1064-70.

Todd, William Mills, III. "Pushkin and Society: Post-1966 Perspectives." In *The Pushkin Handbook*, edited by David M. Bethea, 364-78. Madison: University of Wisconsin Press, 2005.

Todes, Daniel P. *Ivan Pavlov: A Russian Life in Science*. Oxford: Oxford University Press, 2014.

Todes, Daniel Philip. "From Radicalism to Scientific Convention: Biological Psychology in Russia From Sechenov to Pavlov." PhD diss., University of Pennsylvania, 1981.
Tomashevskii, B. "Literatura i biografiia." *Kniga i revoliutsiia: Ezhemesiachnyi kritiko-bibliograficheskii zhurnal*, no. 4 (1923): 6–9.
Tosunian, Irina. "Ot Moskvy do samykh Petushkov." *Literaturnaia gazeta*, January 3, 1990.
Uspenskii, B. A. *Izbrannye trudy*. 3 vols. Moscow: Gnozis, 1994.
Vail', Petr, and Aleksandr Genis. "Vo chreve machekhi." *Grani*, no. 139 (1985): 137–50.
———. *60-e: Mir sovetskogo cheloveka*. Moscow: Novoe literaturnoe obozrenie, 1996.
Van Voren, Robert. *On Dissidents and Madness: From the Soviet Union of Leonid Brezhnev to the "Soviet Union" of Vladimir Putin*. Amsterdam: Rodopi, 2009.
———. *Cold War in Psychiatry: Human Factors, Secret Actors*. Amsterdam: Rodopi, 2010.
Van Voren, Robert, and Sidney Bloch, eds. *Soviet Psychiatric Abuse in the Gorbachev Era*. Amsterdam: International Association on the Political Use of Psychiatry, 1989.
Vatulescu, Cristina. "The Politics of Estrangement: Tracking Shklovsky's Device through Literary and Policing Practices." *Poetics Today* 27, no. 1 (Spring 2006): 35–66.
———. *Police Aesthetics: Literature, Film, and the Secret Police in Soviet Times*. Stanford: Stanford University Press, 2010.
Vess'e, Sesil'. *Za vashu i nashu svobodu: Dissidentskoe dvizhenie v Rossii*, translated by E. Baevskaia, N. Kislova, and N. Mavlevich. Moscow: Novoe literaturnoe obozrenie, 2015.
Vigdorova, Frida. "Sudilishche." *Ogonek*, no. 49 (1988): 26–31.
Voinovich, Vladimir. *Skazki dlia vzroslykh*. Moscow: Vagrius, 1996.
Volkov, Solomon. *Dialogi s Iosifom Brodskim: Literaturnye biografii*. Moscow: Nezavisimaia Gazeta, 1998.
Vol'pin, Aleksandr. Interview by Rebecca Reich. Revere, MA, September 2, 2009.
Vol'pin, Nadezhda. "Svidanie s drugom." In *Moi Esenin: Vospominaniia sovremennikov*, edited by L. P. Bykov, 293–452. Ekaterinburg: U-Faktoriia, 2008.
Wachtel, Michael. "Heirs of Mayakovsky: The Poet and the Citizen." In *The Development of Russian Verse: Meter and Its Meanings*, 206–38. Cambridge: Cambridge University Press, 1998.
Worobec, Christine. *Possessed: Women, Witches, and Demons in Imperial Russia*. DeKalb: Northern Illinois University Press, 2001.
Yesenin-Volpin, Aleksandr Sergeyevich. *A Leaf of Spring* (*Vesennii list*), translated by George Reavey. New York: Praeger, 1961.
Yurchak, Alexei. *Everything Was Forever, Until It Was No More: The Last Soviet Generation*. Princeton: Princeton University Press, 2006.
Zagal'skii, Leonid. "Sumasshestvie: Zametki na poliakh istorii bolezni otechestvennoi psikhiatrii." *Literaturnaia gazeta*, June 28, 1989.
Zajicek, Benjamin. "Scientific Psychiatry in Stalin's Soviet Union: The Politics of Modern Medicine and the Struggle to Define 'Pavlovian' Psychiatry, 1939–1953." PhD diss., University of Chicago, 2009.
———. "Soviet Madness: Nervousness, Mild Schizophrenia, and the Professional Jurisdiction of Psychiatry in the USSR, 1918–1936." *Ab Imperio*, no. 4 (2014): 167–94.
———. "Soviet Psychiatrists and the Schizophrenia Diagnosis, 1918–1948." Unpublished paper.

Zharikov, N. M., D. R. Lunts, S. M. Gerasimova, M. S. Rakhmanova, M. F. Tal'tse, and Z. G. Turova. "Diagnosticheskie trudnosti pri sudebnopsikhiatricheskoi ekspertize bol'nykh shizofreniei (kliniko-psikhopatologicheskii aspekt)." *Zhurnal nevropatologii i psikhiatrii imeni S. S. Korsakova*, no. 1 (1976): 121–26.

Zorin, Andrei. "Prigorodnyi poezd dal'nego sledovaniia." *Novyi mir*, no. 5 (1989): 256–58.

INDEX

Academy of Medical Sciences, 32, 193
Akutagawa, Ryūnosuke, 63
Alexander II, 30
All-Union Congress of Neuropathologists and Psychiatrists (1936), 32
All-Union Society of Neuropathologists and Psychiatrists, 24, 32
American Psychiatric Association, 35
Andersen, Hans Christian: "The Emperor's New Clothes," 217–18, 222–23, 258–59n3
antipsychiatry, 28, 64–66, 218–19. *See also* Foucault, Michel
Arzamas, 115
Arzhak, Nikolai. *See* Daniel', Iulii
Austin, J. L., 47, 194–95, 206–7. *See also* performativity
Avdiev, Igor', 193, 213

Babaian, Eduard, 47–49, 51–56
Bakhtin, Mikhail, 17–18, 43–44, 93, 117
Batshev, Vladimir, 68
Belyi, Andrei: *Petersburg* [*Peterburg*], 8
Bethea, David M., 104–5
Bil'zho, Andrei, 188
Bleuler, Eugen, 32
Blok, Aleksandr, 157, 182, 199, 247n83
Boileau, Nicolas: *The Art of Poetry* [*L'Art poétique*], 215–16
Booth, Wayne C., 187
Borodino, Battle of, 72
Boym, Svetlana, 21, 103, 166, 245n19
Brezhnev, Leonid, 17, 221–22
Brintlinger, Angela, 31
Brodsky, Joseph: and "art of estrangement," 20, 101–5, 118, 133–34, 145; and awareness, 20, 103, 195; and consciousness and existence, 19–20, 101–8, 114–41, 144–47, 151–53, 222; and defamiliarization, 20, 103, 153; and dialogue or dialogism, 19, 103–5, 115–23, 127–43, 146, 153; and emigration, 19–20, 103–4, 133–40, 143, 146–47; hospitalizations of, 19, 102–11, 115, 122–23, 127–29, 135, 146; and literary tradition, 114–16, 137; and "parts of speech," 129–33, 137–39, 142–46, 155, 208; and psychiatric discourse, 110–11, 115, 119–22, 126–27, 132–33; psychiatric evaluations of, 105–10; self-evaluation of, 20, 102–6, 109–11, 115–16, 122, 132, 147, 222; trial of, 19, 105–110
Brodsky, Joseph, works of: "... and at the word 'future'..." ["i pri slove 'griadushchee'..."], 142–43; "The Condition We Call Exile," 103–4, 134, 140, 143; "From nowhere with love..." ["Niotkuda s liubov'iu..."], 136–37; "Gorbunov and Gorchakov" ["Gorbunov i Gorchakov"], 19, 102–4, 116–35, 139, 142–43, 145–47; "In the Lake District" ["V ozernom kraiu"], 135; "It's not that I'm losing my mind..." ["Ia ne to chto skhozhu s uma..."], 143–45; "Less Than One," 101–2, 115–16, 119–20, 130, 132–33, 146–47; "New Year at the Kanatchikova Dacha" ["Novyi god na Kanatchikovoi dache"], 111–15, 118, 122, 137, 140; "The North crumples metal..." ["Sever kroshit metal..."], 137; "A Part of Speech" ["Chast' rechi"], 19–20, 102, 104, 129, 133–47; "A series of remarks..." ["Eto-riad nabliudenii..."], 138–39; "There is always the option..." ["V segda ostaetsia vozmozhnost'..."], 141–42; "You know it's winter..." ["Potomu chto kabluk..."], 139–41
Brown, Julie V., 30
Bruckner, Anton, 215

Bukovskii, Vladimir: and depathologization of dissent, 6, 15, 19, 63, 66–67, 82, 85, 89–94, 96–97, 217; and dialogue or dialogism, 84, 91, 94, 96–97; hospitalizations of, 39–40, 68, 83, 181; and literary discourse or tradition, 19, 63, 88–92, 97–99; "Manual on Psychiatry for Differently Thinking People" ["Posobie po psikhiatrii dlia inakomysliashchikh"], 62, 65, 88–92, 94, 97–99, 193, 203, 217; on pathologization of dissent, 5, 65, 83, 89, 217; and pathologization of state or society, 6, 19, 25–26, 66–67, 91, 217; and psychiatric discourse, 19, 25, 62, 67, 82–84, 88–92, 203; psychiatric evaluations of, 39–40, 83, 219; and Socialist Realism, 25–26; *And the Wind Returns . . .* [*I vozvrashchaetsia veter . . .*], 5–6, 15, 25, 63, 66–67, 83, 92, 186

Bulgakov, Mikhail: *The Master and Margarita* [*Master i Margarita*], 10

Burry, Alexander, 198, 212

Butyrka (prison), 100

Byron, Lord, 203

Cantor, Georg, 74–75

Catherine II, 30

Central Committee, 25, 67

Chaadaev, Petr, 30, 98–99

Chagall, Marc, 158

Chaikovskaia, Ol'ga, 109

Chekhov, Anton, 63; "Ward No. 6" ["Palata No. 6"], 3–4, 6, 8, 114–16, 137, 193, 197–98, 228n11

Civil Code, Russian, 46

Civil War, 31

Clark, Katerina, 51

Conceptualism, Moscow, 54–55

consciousness and existence. *See under* Brodsky, Joseph; psychiatry, Soviet; Siniavskii, Andrei

Criminal Code, Russian, 46, 68

d'Anthès, Georges, 212

Daniel', Iulii, 39, 67–68, 83, 88, 148–49, 152, 181–82, 184

de-Stalinization, 10–13, 17, 50, 218

defamiliarization, 20, 103, 151–52. *See also* Brodsky, Joseph: defamiliarization; Shklovskii, Viktor; Siniavskii, Andrei: defamiliarization

deontology, 221

Derrida, Jacques, 194–95

Diagnostic and Statistical Manual of Mental Disorders, 35

dissent: and antipsychiatry, 64–66, 218; and awareness, 5, 8–10, 14–15, 21–22; definition of, 4–5, 227n4; depathologization of, 5–6, 9–15, 19, 22, 60–67, 92–93, 99, 217, 223; and dialogue or dialogism, 17–18, 93–94, 99, 103, 117; and literary discourse or tradition, 3–11, 18–22, 59–63, 116, 193, 218, 223; pathologization of, 3–6, 18, 24–28, 32, 37–43, 48–51, 59–64, 176–77, 217–18, 223; and pathologization of state or society, 6, 10, 14–15, 59–67, 93–94, 99, 124, 217–218, 222; and psychiatric discourse, 6, 12, 15, 18–19, 60–64, 92–93, 217–218, 222–23. *See also* Brodsky, Joseph; Bukovskii, Vladimir; Erofeev, Venedikt; Gluzman, Semen; Siniavskii, Andrei; Vol'pin, Aleksandr

dissidence, 4–5. *See also* dissent

dissimulation, 18, 43, 55–57, 186, 202. *See also under* Erofeev, Venedikt

Djilas, Milovan, 83

Dobrovol'skii, Aleksandr, 68, 83

Dostoevsky, Fyodor, 153, 158, 198; *The Double* [*Dvoinik*], 7–8

Dovzhenko, Aleksandr, 194

Duvakin, Viktor, 182–83

Eikhenbaum, Boris, 157

Engels, Friedrich, 170

Engelstein, Laura, 13

Epstein, Mikhail, 187–89

Eremin, Dmitrii, 179–80

Erofeev, Venedikt: and alcohol, 20, 188, 190–97, 200–201, 204, 208, 214; and awareness, 20–21, 187–88, 195–96, 214–16; and dissimulation, 186–91, 196, 199, 202, 205, 212, 216; hospitalizations

of, 20–21, 185, 188–89, 193, 196–97, 216; and "implied authorial persona," 20, 187–93, 195–97, 200, 204, 211–16; and literary tradition, 189–90, 193, 197–200; on pathologization of dissent, 192–93, 202, 216; and pathologization of state or society, 21, 187–92, 198, 201–206, 209–11, 216, 222; and performativity, 195–215; and psychiatric discourse, 189–93, 203–206; and simulation, 20, 186–207, 210–216, 222
Erofeev, Venedikt, works of: *The Dissidents* [*Dissidenty*] 200–201; *Moscow-Petushki* [*Moskva-Petushki*], 185, 188, 191–93, 196–98, 204, 209, 213, 215; *Notes of a Psychopath* [*Zapiski psikhopata*], 185, 189–91, 213, 215; *Walpurgis Night* [*Val'purgieva noch'*], 20–21, 186–89, 193, 195–216, 256n54
Erofeeva, Galina, 195
Esenin, Sergei, 67, 74–75

Fadeev, Aleksandr, 168
Fainberg, Viktor, 48, 61, 219, 222
Felman, Shoshana, 9, 11, 228n22
Formalism, 20–21, 103, 151, 157, 180, 187
Forman, Miloš: *One Flew Over the Cuckoo's Nest*, 256n54
Foucault, Michel: and dissent, 12–14, 65–66, 93, 99; *Madness and Civilization*, 12–13, 64–65, 93; psychiatrists' views on, 64–65
Freidkin, Mark, 193
Freud, Sigmund, 31, 116, 119–20, 127, 129

Galanskov, Iurii, 68, 83, 95–96
Garshin, Vsevolod: "The Red Flower" ["Krasnyi tsvetok"], 8
Genis, Aleksandr, 189, 198
Ginzburg, Aleksandr, 68, 83
Glazov, Yuri, 63–64
Gluzman, Semen: and depathologization of dissent, 19, 85–92, 94, 96–98, 217; and dialogue or dialogism, 91, 94, 96; "In Absentia Forensic Psychiatric Report on the Case of Petro Grigor'evich Grigorenko" ["Psikhiatricheskaia zaochnaia ekspertiza po delu P. G. Grigorenko"], 84–88, 94; and literary discourse or tradition, 19, 88–92, 98–99; "Manual on Psychiatry for Differently Thinking People" ["Posobie po psikhiatrii dlia inakomysliashchikh"], 62, 65, 88–92, 94, 97–99, 193, 203, 217; on pathologization of dissent, 65–66, 83, 85, 89, 217–218; and pathologization of state or society, 19, 91, 98, 217; and psychiatric discourse, 19, 83, 62, 83, 85–92
Goethe, Johann Wolfgang von: *Faust*, 198
Goffman, Erving, 64
Gogol, Nikolai, 63, 198; "Notes of a Madman" ["Zapiski sumasshedshego"], 7–8, 137, 177, 189
Golyshev, Viktor, 101
Gor'kii Institute of World Literature, 148
Gor'kii, Maksim, 9–10, 192
Gorbachev, Mikhail, 222
Gorbanevskaia, Natal'ia: and dialogue or dialogism, 94–97; "Free Medical Assistance," ["Besplatnaia meditsinskaia pomoshch'"], 94–97; "Locked inside the madhouse..." ["V sumasshedshem dome..."], 95–96; psychiatric evaluations of, 35–38, 40, 49, 235n68
Goya, Francisco, 158
Grigorenko, Petro: and dialogue or dialogism, 97–98; Gluzman's evaluations of, 84–88, 90–91; hospitalizations of, 25, 41, 84–86, 99–100; and own accounts of psychiatric evaluation, 25, 97–98; and pathologization of state or society, 11–12; psychiatric evaluations of, 40–42, 49, 192–93

Hašek, Jaroslav, 63
Hitler, Adolf, 72
Hoffman, E.T.A., 158
holy foolishness, 6–7, 29–30, 175, 188, 198, 200

Iakhimovich, Ivan, 56–57, 238n151
inakomyslie, 4–5, 24, 60, 217. *See also* dissent

incompetency, 46, 181
Independent Psychiatric Association of Russia, 65
Initiative Group for the Defense of Human Rights in the USSR, 5
Instructions on the Urgent Hospitalization of the Socially Dangerous Mentally Ill, 47
Ivan IV, 201
Ivan the Fool, 7
Izvestiia, 179, 219

Jakobson, Roman, 21
Jewishness, 18, 127, 131, 165, 197, 209–10
Joravsky, David, 33

Kalashnik, Iakov, 36–38, 45–46, 108
Kaplan, Fanny, 200
Kedrina, Zoia, 149–50, 179–80
Kerbikov, Oleg, 40–41
Kheraskov, Mikhail, 204
Khlebnikov, Velimir, 8–9
Khodorovich, Tat'iana, 93–94, 223
Kholodkovskaia, Elizaveta, 46
Khrushchev, Nikita, 10–11, 13, 17, 67, 70, 75, 176–77
Khurgin, Ia. I., 45
Kibal'chich, Nikolai, 192
Kline, George L., 135
Kogan, Ernest, 182–83
Konetko, I., 180–81
Kontinent, 197
Korsakov Journal (*S. S. Korsakov Journal of Neuropathology and Psychiatry*), 23–24, 33, 42, 45, 64, 66, 220–22
Korsakov, Sergei, 43, 46, 48
Kosterin, Aleksei, 11–12
Kraepelin, Emil, 32, 35, 43
Kruchenykh, Aleksei, 8–9
Kuperman, Victor, 202
Kutuzov, Mikhail, 72

Laing, R. D., 64, 66
Landau, Iakov, 48
Lashkova, Vera, 68, 83
Leiderman, Naum, 198

Lenin, Vladimir, 11, 31, 151–52, 155, 162, 173–74, 200
Leningrad Writers' Union, 108
Lermontov, Mikhail, 72, 212
Lerner, Iakov, 106–7
Lipovetsky, Mark, 198
Literaturnaia gazeta, 24, 29, 149, 179, 196, 220
Liubchikova, Lidiia, 189
Loseff, Lev, 106, 110, 116–17, 134, 143
Loyola, Ignatius of, 76–77
Lubianka (prison), 148
Lunts, Daniil, 24–25, 35–37, 42, 46–48, 56, 80, 98, 152, 178
Lupandin, Vladimir, 108

Magnan, Valentin, 43–44
Mahler, Gustav, 215
Maiakovskii, Vladimir, 158
Malaia Bronnaia, Theater on, 197
Martynov, Leonid, 212
Martynov, Nikolai, 212
Marx, Karl, 19–20, 31, 79, 101–5, 119–20, 130–31, 145, 151
Marxism-Leninism, 31–32, 46, 102, 139, 151–52, 218, 221
Medical Humanities, 16
Medvedev, Roy, 3–4, 13, 96–97
Medvedev, Zhores: and dialogue or dialogism, 96–97; hospitalization of, 3–4, 96; and literary discourse or tradition, 3–4, 96–97; *Who Is Mad? [Kto sumasshedshii?]*, 3–4, 13, 96–97
Mikheev, Rudol'f, 219–20
Ministry of Health, 47, 222
Ministry of Internal Affairs, 47, 85
modernism, 8–9, 21, 51, 53, 156–57, 166
Morkovkin, Valentin, 49, 51–56
Morozov, Georgii, 48–49, 51–56
Moscow City Committee, 68
Moscow State University, Student Theater of, 197
Murav, Harriet, 150–51, 181
Murav'ev, Vladimir, 189–90, 215–16

Nadzharov, Ruben, 38–39, 48, 219

INDEX   281

Napoleon, 72
Nathans, Benjamin, 69
Nekipelov, Viktor, 14, 26, 100, 186–87, 195
Nepomnyashchy, Catherine Theimer, 150, 181
Nicholas I, 30, 98
Nikiforova, P. G., 45
Nobel Prize in Literature, 156
nonimputability, 78, 80, 86, 189; definition of, 20, 46, 61; simulation of, 58, 149, 180–81, 189; theories of, 46–47, 152–53, 219. *See also under* Siniavskii, Andrei

Oath of the Physician of the USSR, 221
Ogonek, 67
Orlov, Iurii, 93

Pasternak, Boris, 156–57, 160, 164, 168
Pavlov Session for psychiatry (1951), 32–33, 50, 152
Pavlov, Ivan, 33, 152
Pelipas, V. E., 56–58
perestroika, 23, 219, 221–22
performativity, 47, 194–95, 206–7, 256n46. *See also under* Erofeev, Venedikt; psychiatry, Soviet; simulation
Perm-35 (camp), 84, 88
Peter I, 30, 192
Petrov, T., 181–82
Plato, 7, 140
Platonov, Andrei, 98–99, 243–44n135
Pliushch, Leonid, 5, 61–62, 93–94, 98, 219, 223
Podrabinek, Aleksandr, 61–63, 66, 94, 100
Politburo, 25
Polukhina, Valentina, 118
Popkin, Cathy, 31
Pot'ma, 96
Pravda, 177, 181–82
Presidium of the Supreme Soviet, 221
Proffer, Carl R., 116–17, 123, 134
psychiatric categories: alcoholism, 74, 173–74, 193–97, 253n2; delusional ideas, 26, 39–41, 57, 86, 193; paranoia, 38–42, 53–56, 69, 86, 238n151;

paranoiac development of personality, 40–42, 56, 86, 238n151; psychopathy, 5, 37–41, 53, 86, 106–9, 178, 235n68; schizophrenia, diagnoses of, 37–40, 53, 67–69, 74, 96, 108; schizophrenia, dissenters' use of term, 5–6, 63–64, 69–73, 77, 82; schizophrenia, theories of, 24–26, 32–35, 38–39, 42, 50–53, 56
psychiatric institutions: Dnepropetrovsk Special Psychiatric Hospital, 93; Gannushkin Hospital (Psychiatric Hospital No. 4, Moscow), 67; Institute of Psychiatry (Moscow), 65; Kaluga Psychiatric Hospital, 3; Kashchenko Hospital (Kanatchikova Dacha; Psychiatric Hospital No. 1, Moscow), 37, 69, 94–95, 106, 109–11, 114, 118, 122, 137, 140, 186, 188–90, 193, 196–97; Leningrad Special Psychiatric Hospital, 39–41, 48, 61, 67, 77, 86; Mental Health Research Center (Moscow), 193; Priazhka Hospital (Psychiatric Hospital No. 2, Leningrad), 106, 129, 247n83; Serbskii Institute (V. P. Serbskii Institute for Forensic Psychiatry, Moscow), 14, 25–26, 37–43, 48–49, 56–57, 69, 80, 83, 86–87, 97, 149, 152, 178, 183, 187, 229n34; St. Elizabeths Hospital (Washington, DC), 220; Stolbovaia Hospital (Psychiatric Hospital No. 5, Moscow), 69; types of, 47
psychiatry, Soviet: and antipsychiatry, 64–65, 218–19; and "art of diagnosis," 18, 22, 27–29, 33, 36, 40–50, 54–59, 62, 218; and composition of reports, 27–28, 31, 36–51, 57, 85–87, 106–7; and consciousness and existence, 31–32, 102, 151–2; and doctor-patient dialogue, 28, 43–45, 49; history of, 29–32, 221–22; and monologue or monologism, 12, 17, 28, 43–50, 84, 91, 93; Moscow school of, 32–35, 42–43, 47, 50–55; and nosology, 32–35, 58, 202; and patients' art, 49–55, 58, 107, 218, 237n128; performativity of, 47–49,

51, 55, 194–95, 203–7; reform of, 23–24, 218–22; and Socialist Realism, 17–18, 29, 49–56, 107; subjectivity or objectivity of, 18, 25–32, 43–49, 59, 107, 218–22
psychoanalysis. *See* Freud, Sigmund
Pushkin, Aleksandr, 72, 105, 115, 166, 212; "God grant that I not lose my mind . . ." ["Ne dai mne bog soiti s uma . . ."], 7–8, 99; *The Stone Guest* [*Kamennyi gost'*], 198–99

reflection theory, 31, 151–52, 170, 177–78, 183–84. *See also under* Siniavskii, Andrei
reflex theory, 152
Revolution, Russian (1917), 23, 31, 77, 156, 174
Rosenshield, Gary, 7
Rudenko, Roman, 109
Rumiantsev, Valerii, 88

Sakharov, Andrei, 84–85
samizdat, 3, 5, 11, 24, 60, 64, 81, 92–94, 223
Savenko, Iurii, 65–66
Scherr, Barry, 135
Sedakova, Ol'ga, 187–89, 191–92
Semichastnyi, Vladimir, 67–68
Serbskii Institute. *See under* psychiatric institutions
Serbskii, Vladimir, 229n34
Seredniak, Liuba, 84
Shakespeare, William, 153, 206; *Hamlet*, 189, 198–200
Shakhmatov, Oleg, 108–9
Shklovskii, Viktor, 20, 103, 151–53, 156, 158, 184, 244–45n9
Shmel'kova, Natal'ia, 195–96
Sholokhov, Mikhail, 168
shriekers, 29–30
Shternberg, Erikh, 218–19
Shumakov, V. M., 42–43
simulation: definition of, 14, 55, 186, 202–3; methods of, 29–30, 56, 58, 186–87; performativity of, 14, 55–58, 187, 194–95, 199–216; psychiatrists' views on, 18, 56–59, 186. *See also under* Erofeev, Venedikt; nonimputability; Siniavskii, Andrei

Siniavskii, Andrei: and Abram Terts, 149–50, 153–54, 165, 175–84, 187; and awareness, 20–21, 149–76, 180, 183–84, 195, 222; and consciousness and existence, 20, 145, 152–64, 167–73, 178, 184; and defamiliarization, 20, 151–84; and Fantastic Realism, 153, 155, 158, 180; and irony, 150, 157, 165–66, 169, 175–76, 182; and legal discourse, 150, 176, 181; and literary discourse, 149–50, 176, 179–81; and nonimputability, 20, 149, 178–82; on pathologization of dissent, 148–54, 158–59, 164–65, 175–80; and pathologization of state or society, 10, 20, 145, 149–55, 158–59, 162, 176, 183–84, 208, 222; and psychiatric discourse, 150, 176–81; psychiatric evaluation of, 149, 152, 176–78, 183; and reflection theory, 151–84; and self-elimination, 156–57, 160, 164–69, 174–76, 180–82; and simulation, 149–51, 159, 164, 175, 180–84; and *skaz*, 157, 164, 170, 175–76, 182; and Socialist Realism, 10, 149–58, 165–66, 179; trial of, 20, 39, 67–68, 83, 148–50, 153, 176–84

Siniavskii, Andrei, works of: "Dissidence as a Personal Experience" ["Dissidentstvo kak lichnyi opyt"], 150, 153–54; "Graphomaniacs" ["Grafomany"], 165–70, 173–74, 176–77, 182–83; "The Literary Process in Russia" ["Literaturnyi protsess v Rossii"], 148, 153–56; *Liubimov* [*Liubimov*], 170–76, 179, 182, 222; "A Point of Departure" ["Tochka otscheta"], 155, 162; "In Praise of Emigration" ["Pokhvala emigratsii"], 184; "The Space of Prose" ["Prostranstvo prozy"], 158; "Stalin: Hero and Artist of the Stalin Era" ["Stalin–geroi i khudozhnik stalinskoi epokhi"], 10, 155; "Thoughts Unawares" ["Mysli vrasplokh"], 157; *The Trial Begins* [*Sud idet*], 158–65, 167–68, 170, 172–76; "What Is Socialist

Realism" ["Chto takoe sotsialisticheskii realizm"], 10, 154–55, 157–58
Sirotkina, Irina, 16, 30–31
Sklifosovskii, Nikolai, 193, 255n30
Smoktunovskii, Innokentii, 193, 255n30
Smulevich, Anatolii, 49, 51–56
Snezhnevskii, Andrei: diagnoses by, 39–40, 108; diagnostic practices of, 27–28, 36, 43–46, 152; legacy of, 23–24, 32–33, 49, 193, 222; and literary discourse, 29, 51; theories of, 24, 32–36, 38–39, 42, 51, 220
Socialist Realism, 9–10, 17, 50–51, 55, 151. *See also under* Bukovskii, Vladimir; psychiatry, Soviet; Siniavskii, Andrei
Solzhenitsyn, Aleksandr, 82, 99
Sots-Art, 54–55
Sovetskaia Rossiia, 180
Stalin, Joseph, 4, 145, 159; and aestheticization of reality, 10, 149, 155, 162, 176, 184; authoritarianism of, 11, 24, 77, 93, 98–99, 217–18
Stoglavyi Sobor, 30
Szasz, Thomas, 64, 66

Tal'tse, Margarita, 48, 56
tamizdat, 5, 24, 60, 64, 67, 70, 88, 148, 223
Tarsis, Valerii: *Ward No. 7 [Palata No. 7]*, 193
Terts, Abram. *See* Siniavskii, Andrei
thinking differently. *See inakomyslie*
Timiriazev, Kliment, 27
Timofeev, Nikolai, 221
Tolstaia, Tat'iana, 158
Tolstoy, Leo, 153, 166, 174
Tomashevskii, Boris, 21, 187
Trial of the Four, 68
Twentieth Party Congress, 10–11

Umanskii, Aleksandr, 108–9
Union of Soviet Writers, 9, 50, 151, 174, 176–77, 179

Vail', Petr, 189, 198
Vainman, Fima, 84
Venclova, Tomas, 104
Vigdorova, Frida, 109
Vinogradova, Liubov', 65–66
Vishnevskaia, Iuliia, 68
Vol'pin, Aleksandr: and depathologization of dissent, 19, 70, 78–82, 89, 92–96; and dialogue or dialogism, 94–96, 98–100; and legal discourse, 19, 62, 69–70, 78–83, 89; and literary discourse, 19, 62, 70–80; and own accounts of psychiatric evaluations, 70–73, 80–81, 93–94; and pathologization of state or society, 19, 79–81; and psychiatric discourse, 19, 62, 69–73, 78–83, 92; psychiatric evaluations of, 67–69, 181
Vol'pin, Aleksandr, works of: "A Free Philosophical Treatise" ["Svobodnyi filosofskii traktat"], 70, 78; "Fronde" ["Fronda"], 76–78; "Juridical Instructions for People Facing Interrogation" ["Iuridicheskaia pamiatka dlia tekh, komu predstoiat doprosy"], 69, 82, 89; *A Leaf of Spring [Vesennii list]*, 67, 70–80; "Schizophrenia" ["Shizofreniia"], 70–73, 77; "Whether I'm indeed my father's son ..." ["Ot otsa rodnogo li rozhden ..."], 73–76
Vol'pin, Nadezhda, 67, 74
Vol'pina, Viktoriia, 82

Working Commission to Investigate the Use of Psychiatry for Political Purposes, 94
World Psychiatric Association, 64, 219–21
World War I, 31
World War II, 40, 58, 67, 72

Zagal'skii, Leonid, 24–25
Zislin, Josef, 202–3

www.ingramcontent.com/pod-product-compliance
Lightning Source LLC
Chambersburg PA
CBHW020111010526
44115CB00008B/779